AROUND THE
SACRED FIRE

AROUND THE SACRED FIRE

Native Religious Activism in the Red Power Era

A Narrative Map of the Indian Ecumenical Conference

JAMES TREAT

First published in 2003 by PALGRAVE MACMILLAN™
175 Fifth Avenue, New York, N.Y. 10010 and
Houndmills, Basingstoke, Hampshire, England RG21 6XS.
Companies and representatives throughout the world.

PALGRAVE MACMILLAN is the global academic imprint of the Palgrave
Macmillan division of St. Martin's Press, LLC and of Palgrave Macmillan Ltd.
Macmillan® is a registered trademark in the United States, United Kingdom
and other countries. Palgrave is a registered trademark in the European Union
and other countries.

ISBN 1-4039-6103-4 hardback

Library of Congress Cataloging-in-Publication Data
is available from the Library of Congress.

Design by Letra Libre, Inc.

First edition: January 2003

10 9 8 7 6 5 4 3 2 1

Printed in the United States of America.

As with any generation
the oral tradition depends upon each person
listening and remembering a portion
and it is together—
all of us remembering what we have heard together—
that creates the whole story
the long story of the people.

Leslie Marmon Silko, *Storyteller*

If an arrow is well made, it will have tooth marks upon it. That is how
you know.

N. Scott Momaday, *The Way to Rainy Mountain*

I have not cared to pile up more dry bones, but to clothe them with flesh
and blood. So much as has been written by strangers of our ancient faith
and worship treats it chiefly as matter of curiosity. I should like to empha-
size its universal quality, its personal appeal!

Charles Alexander Eastman, *The Soul of the Indian*

Every day is a reenactment of the creation story. We emerge from dense
unspeakable material, through the shimmering power of dreaming stuff.

This is the first world, and the last.

Joy Harjo, *The Woman Who Fell from the Sky*

CONTENTS

Consequences

Sharing, the great Indian tradition, can be the basis of a new thrust in religious development. Religion is not synonymous with a large organizational structure in Indian eyes. Spontaneous communal activity is more important. Thus any religious movement of the future would be wise to model itself on existing Indian behavioral patterns. This would mean returning religion to the Indian people.

Vine Deloria, Jr., *Custer Died for Your Sins*

We should have started something like this a long time ago. We have almost let all this religious squabbling smother our spiritual power and destroy us as a strong people.

Andrew Dreadfulwater, Indian Ecumenical Conference

"ALL THIS RELIGIOUS SQUABBLING"

I HAD COLD FEET. MY BOOTS HAD BEEN WET ALL DAY, soaked through by the dew still heavy in a thick carpet of summer grass. Morning sun had given way to overcast and the smell of rain; a light breeze tumbled down the eastern slope of the Rockies, filling the Bow River valley with the exhalation of glaciers. Waiting for dinner to be served, I stood next to the open door of my rent-a-car organizing my things and my thoughts. Fog covered the Kananaskis Country to the west and shadows moved across the clearing as thunderclouds jockeyed for position above my small, leaky tent.

We were nearing the end of the second day of the Indian Ecumenical Conference, an intertribal gathering being held once again in 1992 after a hiatus of several years. Stoney Indian Park in western Alberta had been the home of the religious encampment for over two decades, since the second annual meeting convened there in 1971. The Stoney Reserve at Morley is an idyllic setting in late July, full of natural drama. Traces of the forest, of weeds and wildflowers, of scattered campfires hung in the air as I jotted down some notes on events of the day. A herd of bison grazed in the meadow at the lower end of the valley. Mosquitoes scouted my neck and a streamliner sounded a crossing in the distance, every noise muffled by the moist atmosphere. Children played among the evergreens and white poplars that enclose the camping area, a plateau overlooking the river with room enough for a circle of tipis surrounded by other transient accommodations—canvas cabins, nylon A-frames, pickup truck campers. I could practically taste the fresh buffalo steak being grilled in the cookhouse nearby.

Glancing up from my meditations, I noticed someone walking toward my campsite: late twenties, about six feet tall with a long, braided ponytail of black hair, wearing glasses. I recognized him from Conference sessions under the brush arbor. We exchanged greetings as he approached from the other side of my car, then struck up a conversation across the roof of the rental as the skies began to drizzle. His name was Darin. Formerly a journalist, he had gone back to school to finish his bachelor's degree and was studying social work at the University of Calgary fifty miles to the east. I told him a little about myself: an American graduate student from Berkeley, finishing up a doctoral program in religious studies, concerned about the relationship between tribal and Christian traditions in native communities. He was surprised to hear how far I had traveled to participate in this event. I explained that I had been interested in the Conference since learning about it several years earlier. It was a popular and influential movement during the seventies, which made it a useful case study in interreligious relations, and it had never been documented in any systematic fashion, which made it a good dissertation topic. I had heard about the planned revival earlier in the year, while researching the history of the Conference, and managed to scrape together enough money for airfare. Drizzle turned to rain, so Darin and I took shelter in the automobile and continued our conversation.

The Indian Ecumenical Conference began during the fall of 1969 as an experiment in grassroots organizing among native spiritual leaders. Conference founders believed the survival of native communities would hinge on transcending the antagonisms between tribal and Christian traditions—a problem as old as the European colonization of the Americas—and they hoped to cultivate religious self-determination among native people by facilitating dialogue, understanding, and cooperation between diverse tribal nations and spiritual persuasions. The first Conference was held in August 1970 on the Crow Reservation in southeastern Montana. Respected elders, ceremonial leaders, medicine people, and ordained clergy met for four days to discuss the religious conflicts ravaging their communities throughout Canada and the U.S. They also joined in daily sunrise ceremonies, traded stories over shared meals, and socialized during the evenings. By the end of the gathering Conference delegates had discovered a new sense of unity and purpose. They formed an inclusive fellowship of native leaders committed to religious revival through toleration and respect, and they agreed to meet again the following year.

The movement grew by leaps and bounds and soon took on a life of its own, attracting scores of urban youth eager to spend time around elderly mentors. By the mid-seventies thousands of people were crowding into

Stoney Indian Park for annual weeklong encampments. The Conference played a pivotal role in stimulating spiritual revitalization among native people on both sides of the Canada-U.S. border, yet is rarely mentioned in written accounts of the period. Most historical studies of Indian country in the seventies highlight the American Indian Movement and other outspoken groups, organizations known more for their militant rhetoric and flamboyant style than for their success at achieving specific goals. The grassroots spiritual leaders who gave life to the Indian Ecumenical Conference strategized for social change in ways that differed from their youthful counterparts. The open-ended deliberations Darin and I had witnessed around the sacred fire were the living legacy of this movement, an important but overlooked dimension of native activism during the Red Power era.

Darin seemed interested in learning about the history of the Conference, and I appreciated his company. Discussing the day's proceedings, we discovered a shared fascination with the comments made by various participants, especially one young man who had recounted his personal visionary insights as cosmic prophecy. Other speakers were more humble, describing their own spiritual struggles and offering encouragement to those of us facing similar difficulties. The Conference was already a memorable experience, and we both were glad for the chance to make new friends across cultural, spiritual, and geographic distances. The ebb and flow of the rainstorm punctuated our dialogue as Darin and I got better acquainted.

Darin Keewatin is Plains Cree. His surname refers to the north wind and is drawn from oral tradition, invoking a story about the last storm before spring, sent as a reminder of winter's power. Darin was raised in southern Alberta not far from the U.S. border. The Keewatins were the only native family in a Mormon settlement that seemed more American than Canadian, and they were also among the few Catholics in town. Darin served as an altar boy until he was sixteen, when he and his folks finally lost interest in the formalities of bureaucratic religion and withdrew from church involvement. The following year he moved to northeastern Alberta to stay with his maternal grandparents on the Kehewin Reserve. Life on the reserve was a dramatic change from the dominant culture he had been immersed in since childhood, and these new surroundings also provided him with his first opportunity to participate regularly in tribal ceremonies. After a long period of watching and learning, he eventually made a conscious effort to practice Plains Cree spiritual traditions, and several years later he was presented with a pipe. During his early twenties he worked as a reporter and then editor for a native newspaper based in Hobbema. He went back to college when it became clear he wanted to be a social worker, following in his grandmother's footsteps. In 1992 he was juggling course work with the responsibilities of a single parent; his three-year-old son Russell napped in their tent while we visited.

I am mixed, with immigrant and indigenous ancestors on both sides of the family. Creeks and Cherokees populate the maternal line; we are enrolled with the Muscogee (Creek) Nation in eastern Oklahoma. I was born in the western part of the state, where my father served as the missionary pastor of three country churches among the Wichitas, Kiowas, and Apaches. We left Anadarko when I was two and lived in off-reservation communities in Kansas and South Dakota. I grew up as a typical Baptist preacher's kid, active in all aspects of church life whether I liked it or not. During my college years I explored several possible career paths before graduating with a degree in engineering. I also found myself drawn into religious leadership, a curious development in light of my adolescent aversion to my father's vocational legacy. I even became a full-time activist for a while, volunteering with several church-related organizations. But I eventually grew disillusioned with conservative Christianity, frustrated by its theological excesses and moral failings, and enrolled in graduate school to sort myself out. I took courses in religion and ethnic studies for several years while holding down technical jobs to pay the bills. In 1992 I was working as a teaching assistant and trying to focus on my writing.

I hoped to produce a manuscript addressing the problem of religious conflict in the contemporary period. Scholarly interest in developing nonsectarian approaches to interreligious dialogue is a fairly recent phenomenon, a product of postwar ecumenism among Protestants in Europe and North America, Catholic reforms initiated at the Second Vatican Council, and various postcolonial opportunities in Latin America, Africa, Southeast Asia, and the Indian subcontinent. Unfortunately, most of this academic literature focuses on relationships among the so-called world religions; scholars have practically ignored the dialogical significance of the religious traditions maintained by tribal communities. I thought a multidisciplinary interpretation of the Indian Ecumenical Conference might speak to this burgeoning—though still parochial—discourse on the theory and practice of interreligious relations. Religious contention is a root cause of many current political disputes, and even religious differences that stop short of provoking political division can frustrate community life. Is peaceful coexistence possible in a world of divergent truth claims and fierce competition over material resources? I wondered.

We paused as the downpour modulated, rain turning to hail. Frozen exclamation points bounced off the hood and impaled the grass around us. For a moment Darin and I reveled in this natural display of power and punctuation, though the weather seemed to be overacting just a bit. There was, after all, nothing particularly remarkable about our conversation: two young men interested in religion discussing religious traditions at a conference on religion. I have since come to realize, however, that if our meeting was unexceptional it was nonetheless unique, as singular an event as Darin and I are individuals. A year later he would fly to the Bay Area for my graduation ceremony, and a couple of months after that I would travel to the Kehewin Reserve for his wedding. Other transnational visits would follow along with the occasional letter, telephone call, or e-mail sharing news and good humor. Our collegial interaction at Stoney Indian Park inaugurated a friendship, a durable connection closing the gap between disparate worlds. It was the kind of experience that had always been at the heart of the Indian Ecumenical Conference.

"We talked about the Conference speeches," I wrote in my notebook later that evening. "He seems like a very intelligent, interesting person and we had a good talk." This terse account of our meeting strikes me now as a rather feeble gesture, especially in light of the relationship that ensued. Who can really explain the meaning of a human encounter, much less predict its subsequent significance? It has been hard enough to reconstruct the events of that summer day in 1992, even though I can rely on the luxury of memory along with my daily journal and interview notes, promotional materials and other documentary fragments, and hours of unedited videotape footage produced by a professional crew. I cannot help wondering now—as I did ten years ago—how I should narrate the history of a movement that was so important to so many people. Only the most callous scholar could fail to perceive the epistemological and ethical pitfalls of such a project. The obvious dilemma: How to appreciate and convey the subtle, complex, visceral qualities of religious experience, ineffable realities that elude description and defy analysis.

In 1992 I already knew that an analytical rendering of the Conference would not do it justice. The rationalist performances favored among academic audiences might serve the interests of social science, but they have little power to effect the kind of social change envisioned by Conference founders. Worse yet, the native people who appear as characters in such objectivist dramas often do not recognize themselves in these textual productions. I pondered methodological issues for years before settling on a discursive approach compatible with the subject matter—and practicable, given my own mortal limitations. My historical research on the movement and my experience at the 1992 gathering had shaken my faith in the authority of linear logic and argumentative discourse; whatever I might end up saying about the Indian Ecumenical Conference, it was going to be informed by personalist ideals and expressed in a narrative mode. I have tried to write a book that is relational, dialogical, and reflexive, that situates the movement in space and time, that illuminates the intersections of religion, culture, and politics in a diverse and conflicted world. At the very least, I hope to encourage the kinds of conversations that Darin and I heard under the arbor ten years ago, and that we ourselves enjoyed while passing time during a late-afternoon shower.

The storm subsided to a light sprinkle. From our vantage point in the car we could see people beginning to gather at the cookhouse, huddling under the eaves and feasting on buffalo and trimmings. My academic musings on the turmoil of tribal and Christian traditions evaporated in the moment—intellectual morsels are no match for a hearty meal among friends. The clouds were starting to clear and a small patch of blue sky appeared overhead, liberating a ray of light. Its sharp angle suggested the sun would drop behind the mountains before long; I shivered in my boots, then realized my toes had begun to warm slightly. I still had cold feet, but I also felt a little more optimistic about how this project might turn out. Leaving my notebook on the backseat, I walked with Darin to the dinner line.

One of the more provocative religious titles published during the fall of 1969 was *Custer Died for Your Sins* by Vine Deloria, Jr. Subtitled *An Indian Manifesto*, this influential best-seller brought national attention to the young Yankton Sioux author and secured his reputation as a leading commentator on Indian affairs. He was uniquely qualified for the role: seminary graduate, law student, and former director of the National Congress of American Indians, the nation's foremost intertribal organization. The title phrase originated as a theological gibe at American Christianity, suggesting an analogy between the biblical dialectic of covenant and atonement and the frontier pattern of treaty making and warfare. *Custer Died for Your Sins* appeared at a pivotal moment in native history, documenting changes already under way and anticipating transformations that would unfold very soon. The book was a prophetic intervention, both as social critique rooted in religious values and as accurate prediction of a "tribal regrouping" comparable to the Hebrew exodus from Egypt after four centuries of oppression.[1]

Deloria covered a wide range of contemporary issues in eleven topical chapters, with the Christian churches making an appearance in every one. He described his family background of religious leadership and cross-cultural mediation in an autobiographical afterword, where he also disclosed his goals in writing the book. He wanted to "raise some issues for younger Indians which they have not been raising for themselves," and to "give some idea to white people of the unspoken but often felt antagonisms I have detected in Indian people toward them, and the reasons for such antagonism." Deloria's revealing account of the "unrealities" facing native people in American society maps the divide between indigenous and immigrant lives. The European colonization of the Americas interposed many new values and behaviors, including some that menace spiritual sensibilities. "The largest difference I can see between Indian religion and Christian religions is in inter-personal relationships," Deloria wrote. "Indian religion taught that sharing one's goods with another human being was the highest form of behavior. The Indian people have tenaciously held to this tradition of sharing their goods with other people in spite of all attempts by churches, government agencies, and schools to break them of the custom."[2]

Among the most impassioned parts of the book, reflecting Deloria's personal background and his enduring interest in religion, is a chapter titled "Missionaries and the Religious Vacuum." Here he surveyed the history of interreligious relations in the U.S., highlighting the symbiotic relationship between proselytism and dispossession and offering an assessment of the missionary enterprise and its aftermath. "While the thrust of Christian missions was to save the individual Indian, its result was to shatter Indian societies and destroy the cohesiveness of Indian communities," he observed. "The creedal rhetoric of Christianity filled the vacuum it had created by its redefinition of religion as a commodity to be controlled." Legal proscriptions and assimilation programs have also taken their toll on tribal traditions, leaving native communities fraught with "religious competition, which fractures present tribal life." Noting that theological obsolescence and institutional racism have eroded interest in reservation parishes, Deloria halfheartedly challenged the denominations to create "a national Indian Christian Church" that would "incorporate all existing missions and programs into one national church to be wholly in the hands of Indian people." He believed that "an Indian version of Christianity could do much for our society."[3]

If Deloria was skeptical about the willingness of the nation's churchly bureaucracies to take such a leap of faith, he was considerably more optimistic about "the coming religious revival that many tribes expect in the next decade." Suggesting that "the impotence and irrelevancy of the Christian message has meant a return to traditional religion by Indian people," he pointed out that "more and more they are returning to Indian dances and celebrations for their religious expressions." Brief comments predicting a "national Indian awakening" during the seventies appear throughout *Custer Died for Your Sins;* an atmosphere of imminent revival is one of the most powerful themes animating the book. Native people throughout the land were engaged in self-examination and redefinition, "reordering their priorities" in a way that "threatens to make this decade the most decisive in history for Indian people."

Deloria called this period "the modern era of Indian emergence," anticipating "the coming Indian movement" when "the new Indian nationalism" would lead to "total Indian renaissance." He concluded that "tribalism is the strongest force at work in the world today. And Indian people are the most tribal of all groups in America. They are also in the most advantageous position of any tribal people in the world," so "an understanding of the forces and ideas brought forward by Indian people to solve particular problems during the next decade should prove to be useful information for solving similar problems elsewhere in the world."[4]

Nevertheless, Deloria's optimism regarding the revival of tribal traditions was tempered by pragmatic concerns about impediments to intertribal solidarity. "Unity for unity's sake is not yet a concept that has been accepted by the tribes," he explained. "If there is one single cause which has importance today for Indian people, it is tribalism," and "any cooperative movement must come to terms with tribalism in the Indian context." Deloria devoted an entire chapter to "The Problem of Indian Leadership," examining the impact of the reservation system on tribal political and social institutions and surveying historic attempts at forging intertribal alliances. "To understand Indians," he advised, "one must look at unity through Indian eyes. Unity is strictly a social function of the tribes. Indians prefer to meet and have a good time; conventions are when you have a chance to get together and renew old friendships and learn to trust one another," laying the foundation for intertribal cooperation. "What, after all, is unity but the fellowship of people?" Acknowledging the inherent limitations of a group such as the National Congress of American Indians, Deloria offered a more compelling vision of the future. "As Indians we will never have the efficient organization that gains great concessions from society in the marketplace. We will never have a powerful lobby or be a smashing political force. But we will have the intangible unity which has carried us through four centuries of persecution and we will survive. We will survive because we are a people unified by our humanity," he announced. "Above all, and this is our strongest affirmation, we SHALL ENDURE as a people."[5]

In November 1969, just one month after Deloria's prophetic manifesto appeared on bookstore shelves, a small group of native leaders gathered in Winnipeg to discuss the religious confusion, fragmentation, and conflict immobilizing tribal life throughout Canada and the U.S. Present at the three-day meeting were a dozen people representing native communities from the four directions: Creek and Cherokee, Apache and Sioux, Kwakiutl and Cowichan, Odawa and Cree. These religious elders and lay activists practiced a variety of tribal and Christian spiritual traditions, and they quickly reached a consensus that a similar gathering on a much larger scale would be the best way to begin the healing process. They resolved to hold an Indian Ecumenical Conference during the summer of 1970 and organized themselves into a Steering Committee to plan the event. They hoped this transnational gathering might lead to ecumenical meetings at the regional and local levels, sparking a general movement of interreligious cooperation among native people. Committee members met again several months later and reiterated their commitment to ecumenical activism. "We should have started something like this a long time ago," Cherokee leader Andrew Dreadfulwater remarked. "We have almost let all this religious squabbling smother our spiritual power and destroy us as a strong people." Deloria had anticipated these events in his perceptive juxtaposition of tribal values and Christian individualism: "Sharing, the great Indian tradition, can be the basis of a new thrust in religious development. Religion is not synonymous with a large organizational structure in Indian eyes. Spontaneous communal activity is more important. Thus any religious movement of the future would be wise to model itself on existing Indian behavioral patterns. This would mean returning religion to the Indian people."[6]

The fall of 1969 was a bountiful season in Indian country, producing a harvest of controversy and hope. The Winnipeg meeting coincided with another dramatic turn of events: An intertribal group of urban radicals ventured into the San Francisco Bay and seized Alcatraz Island, just as Akwesasne Mohawk activists a year earlier had blockaded an international bridge that crosses the St. Lawrence River at Cornwall Island. These and other militant occupations captivated the national media in Canada and the U.S. and stirred the imaginations of native people from coast to coast. Deloria's prophecies were bearing fruit in other ways as well: a grassroots movement among tribal traditionalists that Deloria considered to be one of the most potent forces for change; the ecumenical activism of Deloria's friend Bob Thomas, a Cherokee anthropologist and tireless intertribal organizer; an encouraging ecclesiastical reformation unfolding in Canada within the Anglican communion of Deloria's youth; and a native-run educational venture headed by an Odawa activist whom Deloria would later describe as a leading native spokesman. These four distinct developments were critical *contexts* for the Indian Ecumenical Conference, historical tributaries that converged in the fall of 1969. The following summer native spiritual leaders would initiate a series of free-flowing *conversations* when they gathered at Crow Agency, near an infamous battlefield on the Little Big Horn River and midway between the celebrated standoffs at Cornwall and Alcatraz. Over the coming years the unanticipated *consequences* of their venture would surface, carving new channels of thought and action through Indian country and beyond. This ecumenical movement is a fertile watershed that can and should be charted.[7]

CONTEXTS

Most so-called serious historians have seen a different Sixties than did many of the participants. Rejecting the counterculture and the hippies as a clownish sideshow, and the drug scene as an embarrassment, they have zeroed in on what appears in hindsight to have been really important, the political side of the decade's experience: the dramatic free speech, civil rights, antiwar, black power, and other protest and revolutionary movements.

Robert S. Ellwood, *The Sixties Spiritual Awakening*

Every time I come up here it seems like I've been in hell all my life and I'm coming into some sort of utopia. . . . This convention might not mean we'll have more food on the table, but it does mean spiritual revival for Indians. Man can't survive on bread alone.

Clifton Hill, Creek Centralization Committee

CHAPTER ONE

"SPIRITUAL REVIVAL FOR INDIANS"

OLD CARS AND PICKUP TRUCKS HAD BEEN PULLING into the camping grounds at Beeman Logan's place all day. Weary conveyances bearing battered license plates from the four directions—Washington, Oklahoma, Massachusetts, Ontario, and points beyond—were converging on the Tonawanda Seneca Reservation in western New York, every vehicle full of people eager to participate in this "Western Hemisphere meeting of Indians." It was the middle of August 1969, and after months of planning and preparation the "Indian unity convention" was finally coming to life. Respected elders and spiritual leaders, medicine men and women, tribal youth and small children unloaded themselves and set up tents and tipis, anticipating the momentous proceedings about to begin.[1]

The next morning Logan opened the convention by welcoming the assembled delegates to Tonawanda Seneca territory. The U.S. military establishment had landed its Eagle near the Sea of Tranquillity less than a month earlier, and an army of baby boomers massed at Woodstock were engaged in their own variety of high-altitude exploration as Logan made his opening remarks. "The first step is to unite Indians and then bring them to understand each other," he explained, in a more down-to-earth vein. "We don't understand each other any more. Many of us are enemies. And it is because of the white man. He has separated us so we cannot communicate." But "once the Indian begins to understand himself and other Indians, the problems they thought existed between them will disappear." Logan was also intent on stimulating the revival of tribal traditions and later that day led a thanksgiving ceremony, part of the ancient Iroquois ceremonial cycle. He instructed convention delegates to join hands, making them "one heart and mind," and to form a large circle around a central fire. Logan stood near the fire as he spoke, prayed, and made an offering of tobacco, and afterward everyone shared an evening meal provided by the local community. One aged Oneida leader later described the event as a milestone in Iroquois religious history.[2]

The unity convention met for four days "in an atmosphere of a large family gathering," as one local reporter described it. Only native people were allowed to attend formal sessions each morning, though the public was invited to participate in dancing and other social activities during the afternoons and evenings. Initial discussions made it clear that almost every tribal community represented at the convention was embroiled in some type of conflict involving land rights or cultural freedoms, and many delegates were quick to point out the importance of both for the survival of native religious traditions. Some speakers also expressed concern over the colonial policies of the U.S. Department of the Interior and its Bureau of Indian Affairs. The most controversial item on the agenda, however, was the growing influence of the Red Power movement, a new presence on the political landscape. Three native activists from New York City made impassioned speeches describing their newly formed "Pipe-Tomahawk Clan," an intertribal organization modeled after the Black Panthers. They pledged loyalty to the ideals of peace and unity but also declared their willingness to fight for the preservation of tribal traditions.[3]

Most convention participants were rural folk who showed little interest in the militant tactics advocated by these young urban radicals. "I suppose if we had our backs put to the wall, we could be militant," remarked one elder. "But violence is against the Indian religion." Expounding on their Great Law of Peace, Iroquois leaders encouraged all people to pursue nonviolent strategies in protecting the earth and its inhabitants. "My religion and upbringing would not allow me to fight as a militant," confessed Tom Porter, a Mohawk delegate. Addressing Canada's refusal to honor treaty-guaranteed rights of free passage across its southern border, he proposed an intertribal demonstration spanning the continent, a collective act of civil disobedience capable of shaming the Canadian government into responsible behavior toward native people. "There are custom houses from the Atlantic to the Pacific, and there are Indians on both sides of the border," he reminded those present. "What we should do is agree to unity of action. We should pick one day during which Indians would take carloads of groceries and challenge every Canadian custom house along the border. What we would do is get arrested." If these tribal citizens were pacifist, they were not passive.[4]

They also rejected colonial dependency as a solution to their problems. Wallace Mad Bear Anderson, a Tuscarora activist, told convention delegates "not to run to Washington and Ottawa" for help. "Those days are long gone. Those governments are crumbling," he said. "Let us go back to our own values and government. We are not trying to look for equality among the white men. We are looking for our own way of life." The recovery of tribal self-determination would require a comprehensive strategy embracing political, cultural, and spiritual concerns. Several hundred people representing some forty-five tribal nations were gathered at Tonawanda by the time they broke camp on August 20, when the unity convention caravanned across upstate New York to the Onondaga Reservation for another four-day meeting.[5]

Vine Deloria, Jr., had been following the developments that culminated in the 1969 unity convention, and he recognized that something important was happening in Indian country. "The awakening of the tribes is just beginning," he had written in *Custer Died for Your Sins*. "Traditionalists see the movement as fulfillment of ancient Hopi and Iroquois religious predictions of the end of white domination of the continent." Intertribal organizing among these traditionalists held "great potential for the future," and Deloria anticipated "a strong nationalistic push on the reservations" as a result of this movement. "Indian religion appears to many of us as the only ultimate salvation for the Indian people. Religion formerly held an important place in Indian tribal life," and "many Indians believe that the Indian gods will return when the Indian people throw out the white man's religion and return to the ways of their fathers." Native communities "now wait only for a religious leader to rise from among the people and lead them to total religious independence," someone who will "find a way to integrate religion with tribalism as it exists today." The tribal people who gathered at Beeman Logan's place in August 1969 were among those waiting.[6]

TRADITIONAL MOVEMENT

Iroquois leadership in promoting intertribal solidarity, cultural revival, and political autonomy actually began decades before they hosted the unity convention. In 1926 Tuscarora chief Clinton Rickard led a group of Iroquois men and women in founding the Indian Defense League of America, hoping to protect native political interests on both sides of the Canada-U.S. border.

Rickard was a devoted Christian who also believed in the integrity of tribal values, and his organization involved both church members and followers of the longhouse religion. During the early twenties he had come under the influence of Deskaheh, the great Cayuga leader from the Six Nations Reserve in southern Ontario, who stayed in the Rickard home while suffering from an illness contracted during one of his public speaking tours. Rickard made several trips across the border to retrieve medicine men who could treat Deskaheh, but in June 1925 the U.S. government began enforcing new immigration regulations that prevented Deskaheh's family and friends from visiting him on the Tuscarora Reservation. He died several days after receiving news that his doctors would not be able to return. "I was now more determined than ever to carry on the border fight," Rickard later recalled, "to obtain justice for our Indian people."[7]

The Indian Defense League initially focused on securing legislation that would exempt tribal citizens from U.S. immigration policy. Rickard vigorously opposed efforts by some to gain a legal exemption only for the Iroquois, and his organization was open to all sober, dues-paying native people. Senator Charles Curtis of Kansas, a Kaw and Osage tribal descendant, was among those in Washington who supported Rickard's cause, and the desired bill was signed into law in 1928. Rickard marked the victory by organizing a Border Crossing Celebration at Niagara Falls several months later. It became an annual commemoration, calling attention to sovereign rights documented in the Jay Treaty of 1794 and other international agreements. During the thirties the Indian Defense League lobbied against the Indian Reorganization Act and other assimilationist schemes hatched in Washington and Ottawa. In 1940 Rickard opposed the enforcement of the military draft in tribal communities and encouraged those who wanted to volunteer their services during the Second World War to enlist as alien nonresidents. He had volunteered four decades earlier, serving in the Philippines during the Spanish-American War, but fought the 1924 Indian Citizenship Act on the grounds that U.S. citizenship "was just another way of absorbing us and destroying our customs and our government. How could these Europeans come over here and tell us we were citizens in our own country? We had our own citizenship," and "our citizenship was in our own nations."[8]

In 1948 an Indian Defense League delegation visited the United Nations headquarters in New York City, where they reported on treaty violations and requested assistance in their struggles with Canadian and American authorities. The downstate pilgrimage became an annual event, and two years later the *New York Times* covered their visit, though reporters were more impressed by the delegates' feathered headdresses and beaded buckskin jackets than by their petition for membership in the international body. Rickard had observed that "for many years it had not been the custom to dress in Indian fashion" at Tuscarora, so he took the lead in reviving the tradition for ceremonial events and at his many public speaking engagements. He was harshly criticized by assimilationist detractors, who objected to his cultural nationalism and failed to understand his activist strategy: Rickard was using popular stereotypes to gain political leverage. Wearing tribal vestments was "another tactic" in his effort to "publicize our cause" among tourists at Niagara Falls, who were lectured on native rights and asked "to write to their congressmen when they returned home. In this way we were able to gain new friends and also put more pressure on the government to secure our rights." The accomplishments of the Indian Defense League figure prominently in Rickard's autobiography, *Fighting Tuscarora*, which concludes with an emphasis on the need for intertribal solidarity: "The one message I wish to leave with all my people everywhere is to work for unity. If we do not all work together, if we are divided, then eventually we face the danger of being destroyed." Rickard wanted "to see Indians help themselves, carry on their own affairs, and be independent. This we can do if we all pull together."[9]

The postwar period also saw the emergence of an activist faction among the Hopis in the desert Southwest. In 1941 Hotevilla clan leaders Dan Katchongva and James Pongonyuma traveled to Phoenix, where they testified on behalf of six Hopi men who had refused to register for the military draft. Ancient Hopi prophecies predicted a global conflict, they explained, and also warned the Hopis against taking sides in the fighting. Offering material evidence for their testimony, Katchongva and Pongonyuma displayed two stones bearing pictorial inscriptions of these prophecies. One stone "says that there will come a time when there will be great trouble involving many nations. The Hopi are to show their bows and arrows to no one at that time." Hopi teachings also predicted the arrival of a "white brother," a messianic figure "who will be able to read the things on the stone. When he comes we will know him and he will enable the Hopi and all other people to share equally in the wealth that is given to us who are living." In the meantime, the Hopis were "never to forsake that tradition and belief that is found within this stone," but to "live up to everything in our religion. For the tribe to go forward, it must stick to the religion." One of the young interpreters who accompanied Katchongva and Pongonyuma on their journey was Thomas Jenkins. Born into a churchgoing family at Moenkopi, he was one of the first Hopis to attend college and later worked in the Bureau of Indian Affairs for a few years. He grew disillusioned with the American way of life, however, and attached himself to Katchongva, replacing his Anglo surname with an initiation name used in one of the kachina societies. He called himself Thomas Banyacya.[10]

In 1946 clan leaders gathered for a kiva meeting at Shungopavi village. Discussing an ancient prophecy concerning a "gourd full of ashes," they concluded it had been fulfilled by the dropping of atomic bombs on Hiroshima and Nagasaki a year earlier. Several interpreted this development as a sign that the end of the present world is near and that they should begin sharing their religious teachings with non-Hopis. More meetings and discussions followed, and in 1948 Shungopavi hosted an important four-day gathering of village chiefs and clan leaders. They discussed strategies for revitalizing Hopi ceremonial traditions and also laid plans for disseminating their apocalyptic message to the outside world, appointing four interpreter-spokesmen including Banyacya. Hopi leaders met again at Shungopavi on four days in March 1949. Together they drafted a letter to President Truman from the Hopi Indian Empire, enumerating their concerns regarding Hopi sovereignty and American policy in an era of globalization and Cold War. "What we say is from our hearts. We speak truths that are based on our own tradition and religion," they wrote. "We know it is time for us to speak and act." Hopi society, these leaders asserted, is structured by a "divine plan of life" that "cannot be changed." Indeed, every society has "certain traditional and religious principles" its people are responsible for. "Now we ask you, American people, what has become of your religion and your tradition?" Warning the U.S. leader about a coming "judgment day" in this, "the most critical time in the history of mankind," they asked both the American people and "our own people, American Indians," to "give these words of ours your most serious consideration. Let us all reexamine ourselves and see where we stand today."[11]

During the next several years these Hopi activists sent additional letters to various government officials protesting U.S. policy, asserting Hopi autonomy, and threatening to take their complaints to the United Nations. Banyacya, meanwhile, toured the country as a missionary of Hopi prophetic apocalypticism. In 1953 Andrew Hermequaftewa recorded their version of Hopi history in a short narrative that was translated by Banyacya and published under the title *The Hopi Way of Life Is the Way of Peace*. Hermequaftewa recounted the struggles of Hopi ancestors in previous worlds and described the covenant relationship binding his people to the Creator of this present world. He also depicted the coming of "Bohanna, the white man," as a threat to Hopi existence. The last part of Hermequaftewa's narrative is a plea for tolerance and peaceful coexistence: "Hopi and Bohanna must respect each other. Respect and understanding can come best through conference where each speaks in his own way," as "there is too much good in all people for it to be lost." Inviting "the leaders of the Bohanna in Washington" to meet with them, the Hopi activists proposed a postcolonial relationship grounded in mutuality and cooperation. "'Hopi' means 'peaceful.' That is our religion," and "we believe that through an understanding, if you come and sit with us in council, we may save the Hopi way of life. We may help save others from destruction by sharing our way of peace. We know certain things will take place if we do not." Hermequaftewa's manifesto circulated widely and was reprinted several times by the Hopi Friendship Association, a group of non-native supporters based in Santa Fe.[12]

In the thirties the U.S. government used the Indian Reorganization Act to establish a federally recognized Hopi tribal council, though this alien form of governance proved to be ineffective and was disbanded in 1944. It was revived in 1951 to help the U.S. dispense with Hopi land claims through the machinations of the Indian Claims Commission; this colonial stratagem provoked increasing opposition from the Hopi activists and intensified the factionalization of Hopi communities. In 1955 Dan Katchongva and Thomas Banyacya led a delegation of Hopi leaders to Washington, where they paid a visit to the commissioner of Indian Affairs and persuaded him to convene hearings on Hopi grievances. The hearings were held at Keams Canyon during the last two weeks of July. The activists made their case, but Hopis representing other political and religious persuasions also participated in the proceedings, and no consensus emerged. Unable to supplant these other Hopi voices or to dislodge the tribal council, Katchongva and his colleagues instead sought out like-minded leaders in other native communities.[13]

The Hopi activists adopted an intertribal orientation in 1956 by hosting two gatherings at Hotevilla: the Meeting of Indian Brothers brought together leaders from other tribal communities, while the Meeting of Religious People welcomed both native and non-native participants. Andrew Hermequaftewa, Dan Katchongva, and others delivered lengthy speeches describing Hopi origins and prophecies. The Great Spirit "marked out the boundaries" of each tribal homeland and gave each group its "life plan with certain religious beliefs," Katchongva explained in one of his orations. "Our common life together is based on the life plan our Great Spirit has given to us. It is a life plan with strong instructions and serious warning that we must never lose faith—no matter how difficult that may be. *We must never lose faith*, for if we do, we will also lose our Great Spirit and we will once again destroy both life and land as was done before." Warning his listeners to be prepared for the coming day

of "purification," he argued that "it is up to the Hopi and other religious organizations not to participate in war." Katchongva closed by expressing his
confidence that "all other Indian people on this land know these same teachings." In the years to come, these Hopi activists would be among the most
vocal opponents of various development projects—such as the infamous strip-
mining operation at Black Mesa—approved by the Hopi tribal council.[14]

Many Americans remember the fifties as a decade of expansive prosperity,
but few also recall the intense exploitation of natural resources that facilitated
consumer extravagance. Like the Hopis, Iroquois communities endured repeated assaults on their lands and sovereign powers during this period. The
most severe violations were the massive hydroelectric projects imposed on the
Allegany Seneca and Tuscarora reservations and the Saint Lawrence Seaway
project that stripped land from the Mohawk reserves at Akwesasne and
Caughnawaga. Although the Iroquois ultimately lost each of these battles,
their spirited resistance caught the attention of the news media and inspired
native people elsewhere. The dramatic protests that began in 1958 over the
construction of a reservoir at Tuscarora were led by Clinton Rickard's son
William along with John Hewitt and Mad Bear Anderson, though Anderson
quickly preempted the other leaders and dominated media accounts of the
nonviolent "stand-ins."[15]

Miccosukee leaders threatened by similar development pressures in the
Everglades were among those who heard about the Tuscarora conflict. Later
that year they invited Anderson to meet with them and other southeastern
tribal leaders, and together they resolved to form an intertribal alliance of native people in the Americas. Native activists in the Far West also became more
outspoken during this period, coordinating efforts with their eastern counterparts through Rickard's Indian Defense League and through the League of
North American Indians, an intertribal organization led by Cherokee Frank
Tom-Pee-Saw. The Hopi activists hosted another Meeting of Religious People in 1958 as well. Dan Katchongva was unable to attend the event, which
was held in Albuquerque, but he did send a message from Hotevilla restating
his concerns and goals. "Who among you does not love your land, life or religion?" he asked. "Great Spirit has planted you to be of different tribe or race.
Let us all work so that that plant is preserved and not allowed to die." He also
announced plans to carry his message to Washington and to the United Nations, fulfilling another Hopi prophetic teaching.[16]

The year 1959 witnessed a number of important events in the rise of tribal
activism and intertribal cooperation. In March Iroquois activists occupied the
band council headquarters on the Six Nations Reserve for a week, until they
were evicted by Canadian Mounties. One week later an intertribal delegation

of more than one hundred people traveled to Washington, where they delivered a petition protesting Canadian and American policies and demanded the removal of the commissioner of Indian Affairs. Thirty-six of these men and women then met with the Miccosukees in the Everglades and laid plans for organizing a United Indian Republic that would eventually apply for membership in the United Nations. In May a delegation of Hopis including Dan Katchongva and Thomas Banyacya went to New York City, where their request to address the United Nations assembly was denied; instead, they met with Iroquois leaders at Onondaga before returning home. In July Pit River leader Ray Johnson died in Washington while picketing the Bureau of Indian Affairs over his people's land claim, so Mad Bear Anderson organized an intertribal caravan and carried Johnson's body home to northeastern California in a rented trailer. The League of North American Indians continued to enlist grassroots activists throughout the country and published a periodical titled *Indian Views* to disseminate their critique of Indian affairs.[17]

By 1960 activists from Iroquois, Hopi, and other tribal communities had established an intertribal network spanning the continent and had laid the political and religious foundations for the broad native activism that would follow over the next decade. Intertribal contacts among these activists intensified during the early sixties. Clinton Rickard, by then in his eighties, enjoyed a reputation as an elder statesman of intertribal organizing and was visited at his home by tribal contingents from near and far. His son William, who had experienced a spiritual awakening during a two-week stay with the Hopis, developed a close friendship with Thomas Banyacya. In 1961 William Rickard was invited to serve on the steering committee for the American Indian Chicago Conference and emerged as that historic event's most forceful voice of nationalist dissent. William's sister Karen also attended the Chicago Conference and several months later was one of the founding members of the National Indian Youth Council.[18]

Hotevilla village hosted several more gatherings of Indian Brothers and Religious People during this period and welcomed both groups at a combined meeting in 1963. The League of North American Indians convened a Grand Spiritual and Temporal Council in June of that year, and about five hundred people from thirty-five tribal nations attended. The Committee for the Great Council Fire, led by Ojibwa Francis Le Quier, issued a statement to "chiefs and Spiritual Leaders of the Indians of the North and South American Continents," declaring: "This is the day when all tribes shall come together and be one nation. This is the day when all the nations shall come together and be one world." Like the Hopi activists, Le Quier believed that "this is the day of the Great Justice." In Los Angeles a group called the Native American Movement proclaimed itself the "spiritual descendant" of earlier intertribal alliances—such as those led by Popé, Tecumseh, and Wovoka—and announced the "reawakening" and "revival" of native cultural traditions.[19]

By the mid-sixties these and other activist initiatives had coalesced into the traditional movement, an amorphous network of native groups and individuals who considered themselves to be traditionalists in contradistinction to the progressives controlling most federally recognized tribal councils. Native people in the Americas—like all human communities—have always recognized the cultural continuities that mark collective experience, those conspicuous beliefs and practices identifiable as tradition. Of course, any living cultural tradition is also a dynamic process, an indeterminate body of knowledge whose specific content is ever evolving in accordance with environmental and social circumstances. Even the very notion of a traditionalist orientation has emerged, in the aftermath of European imperialism, as a common native tradition, a convenient strategy for tagging the factionalism provoked by assimilationist aggression. Intertribal traditionalism was born in colonial-era experiments in military alliance, retreated underground during the repressions of republican expansionism, and has flourished in the postwar period as a distinctly postcolonial phenomenon. Developing in the context of nation-state policies aimed at extinguishing tribal land claims, terminating tribal governments, and relocating tribal people to urban environments, the traditional movement was intertribal and transnational, nationalist and populist, intergenerational and prophetic. As the growing consciousness that would soon be labeled Red Power gathered momentum, native activists formed a multitude of organizations that built on these pioneering efforts.[20]

UNITY CONVENTION

William Rickard had been a central figure in the Tuscarora resistance since 1957 and within several years had become one of the most influential young leaders in Indian country. His untimely death in 1964 was a major loss both for his own people and for the expanding intertribal network of traditionalists, and native periodicals as far away as the Pacific Northwest published his obituary. During the early sixties Rickard had served as president of the League of North American Indians. After his death Alfred Gagne, an old friend of the Rickard family, assumed leadership of the organization and broadened its scope, renaming it the League of Nations, Pan-American Indians. Gagne worked to protect native political rights, sponsoring meetings and lobbying the U.S. Congress. He also supported the growing interest in intertribal solidarity by cooperating with various traditionalist leaders, especially Tonawanda Seneca chief Beeman Logan.[21]

As the traditional movement grew stronger, political protests over fishing rights by tribal communities in the Pacific Northwest generated a new round of media attention to native issues. The involvement of the National Indian Youth Council in these "fish-ins" beginning in 1964 signaled a militant turn for that organization and reflected the increasingly varied forces that could be brought to bear on local conflicts. Logan and Gagne, meanwhile, began strategizing ways to bring together their many traditionalist colleagues in hopes of presenting a united front against territorial and cultural intrusions. Inspired by the intertribal religious gatherings first held at Hotevilla a decade earlier, they and other Iroquois leaders eventually settled on the idea of hosting a "unity convention" at the end of the summer of 1967. Logan and other Tonawanda Seneca chiefs volunteered their longhouse as a site for the gathering. Traditionalist leaders throughout North America soon received letters and telephone calls inviting them to participate, and local organizers prepared to host a large and diverse group of people.[22]

Some 175 delegates from more than fifty tribal nations turned out for the gathering during the last week of August, where they socialized, shared tribal foods and dances, listened to mythic and prophetic teachings, and discussed strategies for surviving the continuing invasion of the Americas. Iroquois and Hopi leaders took the lead during the proceedings, with Hopi elders recounting their warnings about the impending destruction of the "Fourth World" and Iroquois chiefs offering their "Great Law of Peace" as a model for regenerating social and environmental relations. Iroquois tradition recounts the story of Deganawida, the Peacemaker, who was sent by the Creator at a time when the people were at war among themselves. He was soon joined by the prophet Hiawatha, and together they reasoned with the leaders of the Mohawks, Oneidas, Onondagas, Cayugas, and Senecas, persuading all five nations to lay down their weapons and confederate. At their first council they planted a tree of peace after Deganawida outlined the legal system that would govern the Iroquois confederacy. The Great Law of Peace is an elaborate code of organization and conduct, maintained in oral tradition and practiced in daily life, which served as a model for the U.S. Constitution. The Iroquois hosts of the 1967 unity convention raised the possibility that the work begun by Deganawida and Hiawatha was not yet finished, expressing a desire to extend membership in the confederacy to other tribal nations across the continent.[23]

One delegate who took these teachings to heart was Clifton Hill, leader of the Creek Centralization Committee in eastern Oklahoma. Like most participants, he understood this gathering to be a fundamentally religious event. "Our movement was ignited," he later wrote, "by inspiration of the Great

Spirit." It pained Hill to know that he and his traditionalist colleagues were misunderstood by the U.S. government, by mainstream society, and even by many native people. "We Traditionalists have acted as a messenger from the Great Spirit to interpret the meaning of our Indian customs, languages, prophecies, and treaties," he contended. "The religious leaders of the Hopi and the Six Great Nations of the Iroquois only interpret faithfully their prophecies according to the Great Spirit. Every nation and tribe, band and clan should have a burning desire to unite our efforts again to rekindle the prophecies of our forebears." Intent on perpetuating tribal communities through both intertribal and transnational solidarities, these traditionalist men and women defied the cultural pressures and political powers that modern nation-states were exerting on them by collectively affirming the value and validity of their native religious traditions.[24]

Perhaps even more significant than the weeklong convention was the cross-country motorcade that followed. While most participants packed up and headed home after closing ceremonies, Beeman Logan, Alfred Gagne, and others—including Logan's assistant, Mad Bear Anderson, and Hopi spokesman Thomas Banyacya—arranged what they called the North American Indian Unity Caravan. On the second day of September five carloads left the Tonawanda Seneca Reservation for a pilgrimage across North America. Traveling through the Great Lakes region, the group was joined by a Canadian contingent at Whitefish Bay and continued westward, following the Canada-U.S. border. The caravan met with other traditionalists on the road and invited many to join them as they worked their way toward a large powwow on the Hoopa Valley Reservation on the West Coast. Returning home by way of the Southwest, caravan leaders planted sacred stones at key points on their circular path as they disseminated their message of apocalypse, natural law, and intertribal solidarity. Nearly two dozen tribal communities had hosted the unity caravan by the time it completed its transcontinental journey. Health problems prevented Clifton Hill from participating in the caravan, but he considered it to be a very important development in the traditional movement. "I rejoice when I think of the American Indian Caravan," he wrote. "The Almighty, the Great Spirit, watched and cared for them til they completed the circle. The world was shown that there are yet faithful Indians with a burning desire to stand and represent their people at whatever cost—their livelihood, their homes, loved ones. We should recognize these people gratefully for their contribution to unity." The caravan also inspired longtime Mohawk activist Ernest Benedict to found the North American Indian Travelling College, with the goal of providing cultural and educational resources to isolated tribal communities while promoting intertribal understanding and unity.[25]

The year 1967 was a watershed in modern American history. As protest strategies shifted from civil disobedience to power politics, a spirit of revolution intensified America's many social contradictions, from the summer of love among middle-class hippies to the long hot summer in urban ghettos. "Most so-called serious historians have seen a different Sixties than did many of the participants," writes Robert S. Ellwood in *The Sixties Spiritual Awakening*. "Rejecting the counterculture and the hippies as a clownish sideshow, and the drug scene as an embarrassment, they have zeroed in on what appears in hindsight to have been really important, the political side of the decade's experience: the dramatic free speech, civil rights, antiwar, black power, and other protest and revolutionary movements." Like sixties historiography in general, most historical accounts of intertribal activism during this period portray a decade very different from that remembered by many of its native participants, in part because "the long-term impacts of spiritual movements are less easily read in the morning headlines than those of political movements." While retrospective studies typically emphasize secular activity and rhetoric, firsthand reports on grassroots organizing often suggest that "what was really going on was not political but religious or spiritual revolution."[26]

In a study subtitled *American Religion Moving from Modern to Postmodern*, Ellwood argues that "the modern age in America died, and the new postmodern era was born, in July 1967," a month before tribal traditionalists gathered at Tonawanda. Sixties spirituality emphasized nonconformity, freedom, relevance, and the natural world, which suggests that the decade "may have been not so much an aberration as a restoration" of a classically American tradition. "In a certain sense," he concludes, "the characteristic Sixties religious style was like a recovery of the more fluid, sentimental, charismatic, psychic, magical, communalistic, and righteous-prophetic style of the first decades of the Republic, perhaps especially the 1840s and 1850s, the 'sentimental years' and the heyday of the covered-wagon Western migration."[27]

While many observers have styled modern tribal communities as exotic subcultures or denizens of the counterculture, a more historically informed perspective would recognize the priority of native tradition—if it must be labeled, call it anteculture. "The new Indian is a religious man," wrote journalist Stan Steiner in his noteworthy 1968 book, *The New Indians*. "Land is the measure of life. In his view of the land the tribal Indian denies the values placed on it by the white society. His own values are to him more eternal and essential to the human spirit, having existed before the advent of the barbed wire and commercial fence." As the traditional movement found expression in the institution of the unity convention and caravan, traditionalist leaders measured the land according to spiritual values and forged a communal refuge from the barbs of commerce. They pursued a vision of earthly existence that negates colonial borders and transcends tribal boundaries—the precarious fusion of old and new, of stability and disruption, that is named by a paradoxical juxtaposition: traditional movement.[28]

INTERTRIBAL SOLIDARITY

Inspired by his experiences at the convention and by the rousing mission of the caravan, Clifton Hill returned to his Creek Nation home and worked to spread the gospel of intertribal unity. He was well suited for the task, a Baptist minister fluent in the Creek language and active in grassroots political organizing. Born and raised in the small town of Okemah, he had worked as a field hand and also earned some money in the boxing ring as a heavyweight prizefighter. Hill eventually followed his father's footsteps into the ministry and settled in Okmulgee, the Creek Nation capital, where he and his wife, Betty, raised three sons. For many years he served the Baptist church there and in the surrounding Creek communities as preacher, teacher, and itinerant evangelist, establishing a reputation as a prophetic leader devoted to the spiritual and material welfare of his people. He also traveled to Washington to testify in congressional hearings on behalf of Creek land claims.[29]

Late in May 1965 Hill and other traditionalists formed the Creek Centralization Committee to advocate for tribal self-determination. The constitutional government of the Creek Nation had been forcibly dissolved by an act of the U.S. Congress in 1906, and since that time the office of principal chief had been filled by puppet leaders appointed by the U.S. president. Meeting in Okmulgee, "we raised our hand toward God to organize," Hill later recalled; the committee drafted a new constitution with bylaws and elected Hill as their leader. "All the Creek Centralization Committee desires is a voice in their own affairs and a working, representative government," he explained shortly after the meeting. "We have been fifty-eight years without representation and we do not want a drugstore Indian for a chief. We want a free election, a free voice, just like any other tribe." Hill was especially annoyed by appointed officials who took credit for federally funded projects that provided little relief to poverty-stricken traditionalists: "Why in the SAM HILL do we say we want to help the Indians but we want so much of the Indians' money to programize and so much money for tourists attraction. So much for this and so much for that. Then give the Indians a tiny drop of their own money. This is what some people call helping them. BIG DEAL." Hill also accused various bureaucratic personnel of trying to sabotage the committee's work by threatening support- ers with the loss of tribal services.[30]

In January 1967 the Creek Centralization Committee launched two weekly radio programs in the Creek language, broadcast at midday over KOKL in Okmulgee, with Hill serving as programmer and host. A thirty- minute program on Sundays featured announcements, music, and a "non- sectarian" sermon, and a fifteen-minute program on Wednesdays covered news affecting Hill's Creek and Seminole listeners. Hill's reputation and influ- ence as a traditionalist leader continued to grow, and later that year he was vis- ited by Stan Steiner, who was busy gathering information for his book on contemporary native activism. Hill struck Steiner as a prophet, perhaps even a messiah, who drew on tribal traditions and biblical narratives in fashioning a "dirt-farm, grass-roots, backwoods movement" that might just lead his people into a new age of prosperity.[31]

Hill likened his effort to that of the biblical David and the legendary Robin Hood, doing battle with a bureaucratic Goliath in order to redistribute economic resources. "I always tell my people we are like little David in the Bible," he explained. "Poor, but stands for justice." Like the Israelites, "lots of these Indians, they were looking for a man with great intelligency, vast amounts of money, a very educated man. They were always looking for some- one like that. That's why I tell my people the story of little David." He contin- ued: "I see myself as a Robin Hood. I take from the rich. And give it to the poor. That's what we need, a Robin Hood type. That's how I see myself." Hill envisioned a day when traditionalists would no longer be dominated by colo- nial authorities or by "mixed-bloods and educated Indians" and would have control over their own destinies. "Love is what combined our organization, not money or intelligency, but love of the poor. I am proud of being poor," and "the day of the poor will come. Long as there's breath flows through my veins, long as I am alive, I am going to try to spearhead that. I don't know how in the world I will. But I will."[32]

Hill and his supporters in the Creek Centralization Committee were not the only eastern Oklahoma activists organizing during the sixties. In June 1967 they joined with traditionalists in the Cherokee Nation to protest the opening of Cherokee Village, a tourist attraction built by the tribal govern- ment as the first phase of a Cherokee Cultural Center. Promoted as an accu- rate reconstruction of a typical eighteenth-century Cherokee settlement, the marketable caricature featured actors wearing yarn wigs and vinyl buckskin costumes living in crude mud huts; anthropologists disputed this primitivist portrayal of "red cave men," and Cherokee traditionalists dubbed it "the zoo." Politicians and developers promised menial jobs for unemployed Cherokees, though local motel and restaurant owners seemed to be the project's most enthusiastic supporters. The National Indian Youth Council also participated in what was billed as the first picket line in Cherokee history, financing leaflets that explained to visitors why the village was opposed by traditionalists, who "teach our children of the days when our prosperous nation had a constitutional government, fine schools, and financial solidity. Can you imagine how it pains us to be presented to you as unlettered savages?" The three groups sponsoring the protest joined forces "to denounce this 'Cherokee Village' as an indignity and a cruel misuse of our living heritage."[33]

In August Clifton Hill and other Creek and Cherokee traditionalists traveled to the Tonawanda Seneca Reservation for the 1967 unity convention and also met the caravan when it passed through eastern Oklahoma several weeks later. Encouraged by the new sense of intertribal solidarity generated by these events, Hill and Cherokee leader Andrew Dreadfulwater offered to host another intertribal gathering the following summer. Hill's Creek Centralization Committee and Dreadfulwater's Original Cherokee Community Organization agreed to cosponsor the National Aboriginal Traditional Convention and scheduled the meeting for the first week in June 1968. Hill's ailing mother offered her forty-acre allotment near Okemah as a gathering site, which she envisioned as "a central meeting place of traditional Indians in the United States and Canada and Mexico, where they could come and exchange their views, prophecies, and medicine and be helpful one to another as the Great Spirit dictates." Hill published an open invitation to the convention in the widely read periodical *Indian Voices* and offered for sale two booklets, titled "A Portion of Indian History, Part I: American Traditional Movement" and "The Whiteman's Climaxing and Crumbling Power Structure." Proceeds from the sale of both were earmarked for building arbors and bathrooms and providing meals at the convention. In April Hill and Thomas Banyacya made presentations at an international congress on education in Chicago, where Hill endorsed a policy of cultural pluralism and self-determination: "We must recognize each other's common and basic spiritual nature, taking into account all of our variety and sameness. Each people thus can contribute to one another's spiritual and material well-being."[34]

Delegates from sixty-five tribal nations throughout North America attended the 1968 unity convention on the Hill family allotment, some of them arriving in vehicles bearing bumper stickers that read "I Support the North American Indian Unity Caravan." During the weeklong gathering they discussed religious traditions and debated political strategies while enjoying the hospitality of their Creek and Cherokee hosts. In the end, they joined hands in a ceremonial embrace and then went their separate ways, looking forward to another opportunity for fellowship with their traditionalist kin.[35]

SPIRITUAL REVOLUTION

Iroquois traditionalists who attended the eastern Oklahoma gathering returned home to a season of transition and turmoil. In October word spread that Tadodaho had died. People throughout the confederacy mourned the loss of their leader and quietly speculated on the selection of his successor. It was a time of rising conflict with colonial powers and many traditionalists hoped their new "chief of chiefs" would be both wise and strong, able to defend their land against unrelenting encroachments. Long-standing tradition required that a confederacy council of hereditary chiefs—who governed under the watchful eyes of the clan mothers—select a new leader from among the Onondagas, the keepers of the fire. The waiting ended on December 7 when the council chiefs announced that fifty-three-year-old Leon Shenandoah had been installed as Tadodaho of the confederacy. Known as a humble man who supported his large family by working as a custodian at nearby Syracuse University, Shenandoah inaugurated his tenure by promising to be true to his tribal name, which can be translated as "Unfinished Business."[36]

Only eleven days later, Mohawk activists blockaded the international bridge at Cornwall Island to protest Canada's aggressive violations of the 1794 Jay Treaty, which guaranteed native people free movement and trade across the Canada-U.S. border. The influential Mohawk periodical *Akwesasne Notes* was born in the midst of this struggle, and the highly publicized—and ultimately successful—blockade generated a heightened sense of political consciousness in other Iroquois communities and among native people across North America. Unlike his predecessor, who had preferred the religious aspects of Tadodaho's leadership responsibilities, Shenandoah did not shy away from such conflicts and quickly distinguished himself as one who recognized the need to assert both the spiritual prerogative and the political authority of his office.[37]

A number of Iroquois leaders had been urging the council chiefs to endorse the movement for intertribal solidarity by sponsoring another unity convention, where they could discuss common concerns with other traditionalists. The Cornwall Island controversy brought the need for such a meeting into sharp relief, and on January 5, in one of his first official acts as Tadodaho, Shenandoah announced that the confederacy would host the hemispheric "super-council" during the summer of 1969. "We'll be discussing the warning signs of disaster and ways to prepare ahead," he explained to local reporters. "We don't know definitely what we'll talk about. That is why we will gather." A headline in the *Syracuse Post-Standard* called the Iroquois "disturbed" and their planned gathering a "pow-wow," but Shenandoah objected to these demeaning characterizations. "We're not calling it a powwow. It's a meeting," he insisted in an interview several weeks later, "to discuss plans for uniting all our people for action. We have to plan ahead for our future." He even suggested that the council chiefs might invite other native communities to join the confederacy, which could expand to include as many as one hundred tribal nations spanning the continent. "They are interested. There has been preliminary discussion. They may come into the confederacy."[38]

Initial plans called for a four-day meeting on the Tonawanda Seneca Reservation beginning August 16, an automobile caravan across upstate New York, and another four-day meeting on the Onondaga Reservation ending August 24. A joint Seneca-Onondaga planning committee formed, and invitations were mailed to more than a hundred tribal communities throughout North America, Central America, and South America. *Akwesasne Notes* published a handwritten advertisement in its March issue, encouraging "Native Aboriginals of the Americas" to attend the "Unity Convention" and billing it as "one of the largest Indian meetings of our times." Shenandoah anticipated that hundreds of delegates would attend the gathering. "It could be one thousand," he predicted. "We're just beginning our plans for uniting all of our people for action."[39]

Another *Akwesasne Notes* advertisement four months later reflected growing interest in the convention. Traditionalist men and women from a number of tribal communities—Algonquin, Cheyenne, Chipewyan, Cree, Creek, Hopi, Nisqually, Salish, Seminole, Shoshone—had already committed to attend, and the schedule had been extended to include meetings farther north on the Akwesasne Mohawk Reservation and the Maniwaki Algonquin Reserve. The political situation was little changed; although the Cornwall Island blockade had succeeded in forcing Canada to recognize native rights to free passage and trade across the Canada-U.S. border, Shenandoah and other Iroquois leaders still faced ongoing disputes involving their lands, schools, and sacred wampum belts. Convention organizers hoped to address these and other political issues but were even more concerned to foster the cultural survival of native people. Activities planned for the gathering included tribal feasts, social dancing, discussion of prophecies, and handicraft trading. Local leaders in the four host communities kept busy organizing the free food, firewood, and camping space that would be provided to delegates.[40]

The 1969 unity convention opened on August 16 when Beeman Logan welcomed old and new friends to Tonawanda territory. For four days they shared in various ceremonies, feasts, meetings, and social activities, then cara-vanned to the Onondaga Reservation for more of the same. Leon Shenandoah greeted his traditionalist colleagues at the Iroquois capital, encouraging them to consider the possibility of joining an expanded confederacy under his lead-ership. Picking up their discussion of political relations with the U.S., dele-gates issued a statement on August 22 calling for the immediate removal from office of Interior Secretary Walter Hickel and urging tribal leaders to resist any and all government initiatives until he was gone. A former governor of Alaska, Hickel "destroyed the faith of all Indians toward the U.S. Department of the Interior by his high-handed, inconsiderate and illegal theft" of Alaska native "tribal lands, rivers, hunting and fishing rights, timber, oil, gas and min-eral resources," and "has declared that he is against Indian people returning to their reservations once they have left them, thereby making the native Ameri-can a vagrant in his own country." Calling Hickel "one of the most dangerous men to have jurisdiction over the lands, waters, air and natural resources" of the U.S., the resolution warned Americans that "he will destroy the sources of life not only for you, but, even more important, the sources of life of your chil-dren and grandchildren." Hickel "will destroy the very air you breathe in the name of progress," because "his policies are flagrant violations of the natural laws of our creator, the giver of life."[41]

The next day convention delegates issued another statement, this one condemning the death sentence given by a South Dakota judge to Thomas White Hawk, a Rosebud Sioux university student convicted of killing an el-derly non-native businessman. The White Hawk case had "become a symbol to all American Indians of the widespread discriminatory treatment of Indians in the legal systems of most states. Without reference to guilt or innocence, we protest this flagrant injustice, all too typical of the double standard of jus-tice, one for whites and one for Indians, in local courts."[42]

As the Onondaga gathering drew to a close, Leon Shenandoah announced that the unity convention was "coming along well" and that Maniwaki Algo-nquin traditionalists had expressed interest in joining the Iroquois confederacy. On August 25 convention participants formed another caravan and moved north to the Akwesasne Mohawk Reservation at St. Regis, site of the Cornwall Island bridge blockade eight months earlier. Unhappy with media coverage of the convention and concerned about the intrusive presence of reporters at their meetings, delegates decided to bar the non-native press and issue regular news releases summarizing their deliberations. Animated sessions in the longhouse ensued, debating treaty rights and tribal sovereignty, social problems and natural law, cultural traditions and spiritual revival. At the end of the first day of the Akwesasne gathering, delegates issued a statement addressing the border-crossing dispute: "The imposed border that has been recently and illegally created by the United States and Canada has caused grave hardship and has divided our families and has always disrupted our spiritual, traditional way of life. This denies us our religious freedom." The statement also pledged support for Iroquois efforts to negotiate a peaceful resolution with Canadian and American authorities.[43]

In response to requests from the media, convention leaders agreed to hold a press conference. "Society has become sick," spokesman Mad Bear Anderson told reporters. "Democracy has failed and Communism will fail too. The only sanity left in the world is the unspoiled spiritual nature of the Indians," who will one day "reign supreme again on this continent. We will not always be squashed and Indians are already showing their strength. It's happening so fast, it's hard to keep up with." As one of the Akwesasne hosts, Tom Porter also served as a spokesman and consented to an interview with a Canadian television station, which quizzed him on the goals of the unity convention. Another Mohawk, delegate Mike Mitchell, tried to assure bewildered reporters that the intertribal gathering of traditionalists was "both spiritual and political." Clifton Hill seemed to be enjoying the hospitality of his Akwesasne hosts, though local newspapers used his offhand remarks to portray their reservation neighbors as prosperous compared to other tribal communities, a timeworn strategy for displacing colonial guilt. "Every time I come up here it seems like I've been in hell all my life and I'm coming into some sort of utopia," Hill was quoted as saying. "St. Regis Indians are wealthy people compared to us." Tribal communities in eastern Oklahoma are "the most poverty-stricken in the United States and it's getting worse. There are hundreds of Indians suffering from acute malnutrition. We hear others talk of poverty, but they haven't had a taste of what we have."[44]

Local media outlets clearly were interested in convention proceedings and eagerly excerpted comments made by designated spokesmen and other male participants, but reporters were not very adept at rendering a demographically accurate portrait of the event. Although a large photo in one local paper featured Glenna Shilling, a twenty-two-year-old photography student from the Rama Chippewa Reserve, the "many Indian women" described in the caption as being present were otherwise ignored in newspaper accounts of the unity convention. Such obvious gender bias, a familiar failing of the documentary record, certainly frustrates any historiographical effort that aspires to a balanced representation of personalities and voices.[45]

The three-day council ended on August 28 with a "Joining of the Hands" ceremony. Many considered the Akwesasne gathering to have been the best part of the convention yet, with new tribal delegations joining the group and momentum continuing to grow. As participants prepared for one more caravan, to the Maniwaki Algonquin Reserve north of the Canada-U.S. border, comments made by Tom Porter and Clifton Hill served to sum up the proceedings. "Our spiritual leaders have given us tranquillity," Porter said. "Indians are not an aggressive people. We believe in equality and brotherhood and peace." Hill agreed: "This convention might not mean we will have more food on the table, but it does mean spiritual revival for Indians. Man can't survive on bread alone."[46]

Canadian border agents quickly realized they were outmatched when a lengthy intertribal motorcade rolled across the Cornwall Island bridge on the morning of August 29, refusing to pay the toll. The caravan arrived at Maniwaki later that day and set up camp for a three-day gathering over the Labor Day weekend, the last stop of the convention. Hundreds of people representing more than seventy-five tribal nations were now present, and meetings were moved from the longhouse to a mammoth tent to accommodate the growing throng. Open discussions addressed the suffering caused by boarding schools, unemployment, and alcoholism, and a lively debate over police brutality and militant activism focused on the problem of violence. "The violence is already here!" cried Rose Ojek, an Ojibway from Upper Slave Lake. "There are young Indians in Alberta who are going to burn the schools and the churches. They're not criminals in their hearts, but one of them says he's going to get a huge Caterpillar tractor and go to High Prairie and bulldoze the liquor store, pretend he's drunk. The police arrest them when they get drunk; a girl was arrested for that, and when her brother tried to touch her hand, that she was reaching out of the police car, they arrested him, too, and he got six months! I can't stand it when I hear of talking peace!" Although they disavowed violence, traditionalist leaders did pledge their support for Kahn-Tineta Horn, a young Mohawk woman facing trial on charges related to the Cornwall Island bridge blockade. Delegates also expressed concern over the Canadian government's recent "White Paper" proposing terminationist and assimilationist policies toward native communities. They invited Prime Minister Pierre Trudeau to join them for a tribal feast of corn soup and roast beaver with beans baked in sand, but he kept busy vacationing in Europe instead.[47]

The 1969 unity convention drew to a close in formal ceremonies on the first day of September. Convention delegates and other participants had spent over two weeks together, covering some five hundred miles as they caravanned through a pair of colonial nation-states in order to visit four welcoming reservation communities. From the four directions they had come—Algonquin, Penobscot, and Narragansett; Seminole, Creek, and Cherokee; Carib and Nahuatl; Apache, Navajo, Hopi, and Zuni; Shoshone, Washo, and Chumash; Nisqually, Walla Walla, Salish, Blackfeet, and Cheyenne; Chipewyan and Cree; Ojibwa, Winnebago, Potawatomi, and Ottawa; Seneca, Cayuga, Onondaga, Oneida, Mohawk, and Tuscarora—hundreds of men, women, and children united in an intertribal circle of politics, prophecy, and peace.[48]

Iroquois activists, inspired by the 1969 unity convention, soon organized a communications collective called White Roots of Peace to promote the cause of intertribal solidarity on a year-round basis. In September a dozen traditionalist apostles led by Tom Porter left Akwesasne for a two-month tour of the West Coast, visiting reservation communities, urban centers, college campuses, churches, and prisons. Their public programs typically included tribal music and dancing, thanksgiving prayers, teachings on the Great Law of Peace, and a film documenting the Cornwall Island bridge blockade, titled *You Are on Indian Land*. *Akwesasne Notes* reported that the itinerant troupe interacted with more than ten thousand people, native and non-native, and was especially active in the San Francisco Bay Area, appearing at the Indian centers in San Francisco and Oakland and meeting with native students at nearby universities. Porter and company stayed with Richard Oakes, an Akwesasne Mohawk attending San Francisco State, for two weeks; they made a powerful impression on him and other young activists when they spoke to newly formed ethnic studies classes there and at the University of California in Berkeley. The group eventually left the Bay Area for other engagements, but not before it had stimulated a heightened sense of cultural pride and political power among a number of these energetic urban leaders, who organized themselves as Indians of All Tribes and began plotting a takeover of the abandoned prison on Alcatraz Island. White Roots of Peace was on the way home to Akwesasne by the first weekend in November; only one week later Indians of All Tribes laid claim to Alcatraz. "The Rock" was occupied again on November 20 and would remain under native jurisdiction for nineteen months.[49]

The surprising and highly publicized occupation marked the beginning of a new era in native activism. Over the next decade many other urban organizations and reservation communities initiated their own occupations and protests, exploiting the media's appetite for confrontational drama, though these radical actions were often trivialized by a consuming audience more interested in images than issues. The traditional movement had demonstrated the unqualified compatibility between traditionalism and activism, between religious commitment and political praxis, articulating community as a seamless experience of spiritual and social existence. These traditionalists also had developed a distinctive approach to intertribal organizing at the grassroots level, a paradigmatic model that soon would be emulated by other native groups including the Indian Ecumenical Conference. Through ceremonial participation, egalitarian dialogue, and interpersonal engagement, the traditional movement helped promote "spiritual revival for Indians," though it did so in a manner that sometimes allowed oppositional politics to overshadow religious freedoms.[50]

The objective of black ecumenism, unlike that of white ecumenical movements, is neither structural unity nor doctrinal consensus; rather, it is the bringing together of the manifold resources of the Black Church to address the circumstances of African Americans as an oppressed people. It is mission-oriented, emphasizing black development and liberation; it is directed toward securing a position of strength and self-sufficiency.

Mary R. Sawyer, *Black Ecumenism*

I could see that if we let things continue as they were going then every tribe would finally get tore to pieces by disharmony and religious feuds. I could see that all the tribes were in the same boat whether we like it or not. And I could see that if we didn't get together and do something to remedy this situation that we would all wash down the drain one by one.

Bob Thomas, Wayne State University

CHAPTER TWO

"DISHARMONY AND RELIGIOUS FEUDS"

FEELINGS OF DISAPPOINTMENT AND FRUSTRATION troubled Bob Thomas as he crossed the Canada-U.S. border on his way to Toronto. Driving gave him time to think. Approaching Lake Ontario, the Cherokee anthropologist reflected on his work, events of the summer now drawing to a close, and an upcoming meeting with a good friend.[1]

Thomas had been active in Indian affairs at the national level for over a decade. After some initial enthusiasm for the reformist social programs conjured up among liberal intellectuals and bureaucrats, by the mid-sixties he was convinced that such efforts usually fail because government agencies and other secular institutions "lack religious sanction" in tribal communities. "Indian elders, particularly Indian elders who held religious positions, needed to become more involved in Indian affairs," he later recalled, "not so much for their sake but for our sake, that is, people younger than them." Thomas saw in these grassroots leaders "the religious prestige, and also the analytic ability," necessary for effective organizing. "It takes a long time for a human being to become wise and to think about things with some balance and judgment." He understood that such wisdom is likely the only resource capable of restoring harmony to tribal communities, which have been fragmented by a colonial phalanx of depopulation, dispossession, missionization, proscription, education, commodification, and industrialization.[2]

"At that point in time," Thomas later explained to a friend, "I could see that if we let things continue as they were going then every tribe would finally get tore to pieces by disharmony and religious feuds. I could see that all the tribes were in the same boat whether we like it or not. And I could see that if we didn't get together and do something to remedy this situation that we would all wash down the drain one by one." Already a familiar figure in a number of native communities as a result of his various anthropological research projects, Thomas eagerly supported grassroots initiatives in community development and intertribal cooperation. He was involved in the traditional movement from its inception, joining other traditionalists from eastern Oklahoma for the first unity convention on the Tonawanda Seneca Reservation in 1967. He also worked closely with Clifton Hill and Andrew Dreadfulwater in organizing the 1968 gathering held on the Hill family allotment near Okemah.[3]

The elders and religious leaders who joined the traditional movement in its early days made a powerful impression on Bob Thomas, and "at the second Convention, in 1968, I thought we had it made. The crowd was small but most of the delegates were real 'grass-roots' country leaders. Clifton, Andrew, myself, and others thought that if we built the Convention to attract solid country leaders, whether Christian or traditional, then we might be able to accomplish something." But the 1968 gathering also surfaced differences between certain tribal delegations over the scope and meaning of traditionalism. Thomas later conceded that they had "hit a snag."[4]

Eastern Oklahoma is home to a large number of tribal communities, and "many of those communities have a native Christianity. And many of the Baptist deacons, for instance, in Cherokee communities that are Christian, are also medicine men. And so they came to this meeting, and some of the Iroquois and Hopi delegates were not very friendly to Christianity and began to take a decided anti–Christian-Indian stance." By the end of the second unity convention "many of these people from native Christian communities had flown the coop," and at the 1969 gathering back in Iroquois country the interreligious alliance dissolved in favor of a less inclusive, more ideological approach to traditionalist activism. The movement "tore up," in Thomas's view, as a number of outspoken individuals "started to beat the anti-Christian drum. Delegates from strong tribes like the Choctaws, who are old-time Indians but committed Christians, pulled out and I knew that we would never see most of the Christian leaders again." The annual unity conventions were increasingly "taken over by men who wanted to be big shots among Indians and by young Indian militant types," leaving little room for the grassroots interreligious dialogue Thomas and others had hoped for. More than a few reservation-based elders and tribal delegations withdrew from the traditional movement over this difference in vision.[5]

The rattletrap car clattered over the hard pavement of the freeway as it carried Thomas northward, tracking the contour of Lake Ontario's Canadian shore. The outskirts of the Toronto metropolitan area gradually crept into view while he pondered the possibilities for restoring harmony and balance to tribal communities. The summer of 1969 was coming to an end; he had left the unity convention when it seemed clear that the traditional movement was headed in the wrong direction. Although anti-Christian rhetoric might facilitate certain kinds of cultural revival and political protest, such essentialist intolerance could only intensify the religious conflicts already fracturing native peoples' lives. "So after all our work and struggle," he concluded, "we had to start all over again." Eager to find a new approach to intertribal organizing, Thomas arrived in Toronto anticipating his rendezvous with a valued colleague.[6]

CHEROKEE PROPHECY

Southern imperialists intent on expanding plantation slavery finally succeeded in forcing the Cherokees from their homeland during the 1830s. Some families escaped to the Appalachian backcountry where they hid from the greedy invaders, while many more were rounded up by U.S. troops for removal west of the Mississippi. The Cherokee citizens who survived the trauma of their Trail of Tears settled in the wooded hill country at the western end of the Ozarks, where they quickly rebuilt homes and communities. They also worked to reestablish their constitutional government, though an uncivil War Between the States two decades later spilled over into the Cherokee Nation, exacerbating political factions that had crystallized during the removal era. By the end of the nineteenth century, the bluffs and hollows surrounding the nation's capitol in Tahlequah were dotted with small settlements of people related by kinship and united around ceremonial grounds and churches. But the Oklahoma land rush of 1889 initiated a period of massive—and illegal—immigration by non-native squatters from neighboring states. The social dislocations caused by their presence only intensified after the turn of the century, as land allotment and the forcible dissolution of the Cherokee government paved the way for Oklahoma statehood in 1907. Unrestrained fraud and graft ensued, led by the new state's founding fathers, and by the 1930s only a small fraction of the tribal territory remained in Cherokee hands.[7]

A century after forced removal from their ancient dominion, many rural Cherokees were landless and disenfranchised, living in grinding poverty. Some left in search of better opportunities elsewhere, especially during the 1930s, when several decades of agricultural exploitation caught up with shortsighted Sooners and turned much of Oklahoma into a dust bowl. Other Cherokee families stayed, supported by the sons and daughters they sent to urban areas where wage employment was more readily available. Robert Knox Thomas was born in eastern Kentucky in 1925 to parents of Cherokee descent, Florence and Robert Lee Thomas. He spent his childhood there and in northeastern Oklahoma, where he was raised in a rural log cabin by his maternal grandparents and by other relatives scattered through nearby hills and valleys. He enjoyed the close-knit sense of community they maintained through constant cooperation and socializing; he once described his childhood as a sustained experience of "the familiar and the loved." Cherokee men could sometimes find part-time or temporary jobs working as laborers, but what little cash income they generated was spent at country stores on clothing and other staples. "We made most of our living from the land," Thomas recalled; his grandmother supervised a large vegetable garden each summer to supplement their year-round diet of wild game and the seasonal availability of berries, nuts, and other wild plants. In 1936 the U.S. government addressed these Depression-era conditions by implementing the Oklahoma Indian Welfare Act, a policy initiative patterned after the Indian Reorganization Act of 1934, which had specifically excluded Oklahoma tribal communities from key provisions. This New Deal legislation established additional legal protections for native-owned real estate and acknowledged certain rights to self-government by tribal people.[8]

As a child Thomas was nurtured by the healing traditions of his grandmother and aunt, who were herbalists and midwives, and by the stories and teachings of his male elders. He enjoyed tagging along with his grandfather, who taught him history and geography as they rode through the countryside, and he often "dropped off to sleep hearing discussions of wise, old men seated around the kitchen table or the fireplace." The family attended periodic stomp dances at nearby ceremonial grounds, and as he grew older Thomas was "trained to be an Indian priest," educated in Cherokee theology and ethics by tribal religious leaders. They taught him "God's rule," a comprehensive account of natural law guiding Cherokee thought and action. He was thereby initiated into a native worldview emphasizing stewardship of the land, simplicity of lifestyle, fulfillment of ceremonial obligations, and respect for all living things. "We have to understand the Rule that God gave us for living on this Island," Thomas later wrote. "That's just essential. God didn't give us that Law to throw away or to neglect. That Law is part of the agreement that He has with us, we are to follow it to have a good life. It's our responsibility to keep that Rule up and care for this Island."[9]

Thomas's family "followed the old Cherokee religion" rather than the Baptist faith practiced in many Cherokee communities. "My family never attended church," he once explained to a friend, "not because we had anything against Christianity but because we didn't feel the need for any 'extra help,' as they put it in the Cherokee language." They did, however, participate in periodic hymn-singing conventions held at local country churches, where a century of spiritual ferment had produced a distinctly indigenous Christian tradition, the focal point for what Thomas described as "a very rich religious life" in Cherokee settlements. "The services were all in the Cherokee language. The minister was a local Cherokee. The hymn books and the New Testament were in the Cherokee language. The ministers and the deacons of these churches were the elders of the settlement. Many of them were Indian doctors and all were the keepers of Cherokee traditional knowledge." The hymn-singing conventions represented opportunities for renewing friendships and strengthening tribal relations through conversation, shared meals, and religious exchange in an ecumenical setting. "One of the leading Cherokee Baptist preachers was a good friend of my grandfather's and he used to visit us often," Thomas recalled. "He was a famous Indian doctor and he and my grandfather sat up many a night talking together. They were 'seeking knowledge,' as they say in Cherokee. They would talk about our sacred wampum belts, the New Testament in the Cherokee language, our creation stories, the origin of our medicine, our prophecies, and so on. That friend of my grandfather's didn't speak a word of English nor had he been a day in school, but I think he must have been the smartest man I ever heard talk."[10]

One of Thomas's most memorable childhood experiences in the outside world was a trip to St. Louis with his grandfather, whose part-time employment as a town constable gave him mobility few rural Cherokees of the day enjoyed. As they walked along a downtown street, the young boy spotted a group of men in an alleyway behind a hotel who were eating discarded food retrieved from garbage cans. He waited until returning home to inquire about the confusing spectacle: abject desperation in the midst of capitalist extravagance. "Why couldn't they have asked those men to come in there and they could feed them?" Thomas asked. "Or at least have given them the leftovers before they throwed it in the garbage cans?"[11]

His grandfather used the situation as an opportunity to explicate the ideology of European imperialism: Like the Cherokees, Europeans were originally given divine guidance on how to live in the world, and when they strayed from this path they were given a second chance through the life and teachings of Jesus, the son of God. In medieval Europe they lived under monarchies as a political mechanism for enforcing the social precepts outlined in the Christian scriptures. But when they sailed west and encountered native people, who helped them adjust to their new environment, "the whites started looking around at this country. And they just went crazy. This land was so rich they just went wild." Rejecting their monarchs and the religious restraint they represented, these uncivilized settlers "made a new rule for North America and called it freedom," though their rendition of freedom was little more than a secular idolatry that fetishized private property. "The new rule was that you could keep as much as you could get a hold of any way you could get a hold of it." Once most tribal land had been taken, they turned their attention to "money-making machines," launching an industrial revolution in keeping with "the White Man's Rule." Thomas's grandfather warned him that future generations of Cherokees would be left with "hardly enough land to be buried in," because "the White Man will do anything to keep that rule going."[12]

During his adolescence Bob Thomas also came under the influence of George Smith, a respected Cherokee ceremonial leader and friend of the family. Smith was "a pretty wise old man" who had accumulated an abundance of valuable insights about human behavior and the natural world. "I'm going to tell you some things that you're going to see come to pass in your lifetime," he told Thomas on more than one occasion. Smith's prophetic teaching enumerated four enigmatic developments: slick roads running everywhere, a lot of deaf and blind people on the street, people who get too smart, and a fourth event too disturbing to describe but that would "follow from those first three things. When you see that fourth thing," he warned, "that's the time you'll want your children close to you." Thomas carried this ominous prophecy with him as he entered adulthood and left home, though he would not fully understand its significance until he reached middle age.[13]

Thomas experienced a very different kind of educational process when he attended "the white man's schools," where xenophobic bureaucrats punished tribal languages and denigrated tribal traditions. He earned his high school diploma in time to enlist in the Marine Corps and saw action at Guadalcanal, the first major Allied offensive of World War II, in the fall of 1942. As a boy Thomas had known people from neighboring Oklahoma tribal communities—Creeks, Osages, Quapaws, and others—but his worldly adventures at school and in the service helped him cultivate a broadminded intertribal consciousness. Life in the military gave him "a real new perspective on the world," he recalled years later. "Young Indians met a lot of Indians from different tribes in the service and we found out we weren't the only tribe that had these kinds of problems and thought these kinds of ways. We developed a feeling of kinship with the rest of the Indian tribes. We saw each other's common problems. We became more sophisticated." When his unit withdrew from Guadalcanal for leave in New Zealand, he and a Navajo friend "got out of that rest camp and went carousing around." They spent several weeks in a Maori settlement, where they discovered that "those Maoris danced and sung and had their tribal customs just like the Indians in the States. And the Whites in New Zealand didn't think that there was anything bad about that."[14]

The war was still raging when Thomas mustered out of the service. During the summer of 1944 he found himself working as a horse wrangler on an

Ojibwa reservation in the Great Lakes area, where he befriended a young man from southern Manitoba who was "obviously an Indian physically" but described himself as "a Red River halfbreed." It was Thomas's first encounter with the Métis, an ethnically distinct people descended from the mixed marriages that were common during Canada's fur trade era, and curiosity about Métis cultural history led to his first substantive contact with native communities north of the forty-ninth parallel. The perplexing intersections of race, ethnicity, and religion had been a source of confusion for the self-described "light-skinned" Cherokee traditionalist since his days in boarding school; he reflected on his rural childhood and his worldly travels while grooming saddle horses at the Ojibwa lodge. As a child he had witnessed the power of interreligious harmony within small communities, and as a young man he had developed a similar appreciation for intertribal solidarity on a global scale. In just two decades he had moved from his Cherokee homeland to the South Pacific to modern America. Thomas carried with him the wisdom of tribal elders as he remembered the pleasures of family life, teachings on natural law and private property, and a prophetic warning about challenges yet to come.[15]

ACTION ANTHROPOLOGY

It was not long before Bob Thomas relocated to Tucson, where he enrolled in classes at the University of Arizona despite his apprehensions about the American educational system. As a boy he had developed a healthy aversion to the bureaucratic machinations of the dominant culture; it was not unusual for various powerful officials "wearing suits and white shirts, carrying papers and fountain pens," to appear in tribal communities. "When those kind of people came to the house we used to hide and act like nobody was home," he later recalled. "We knew that when those kind of white men talked to the Indians something happened to us. You might lose your land or get hauled into court for something or have your kids taken off to boarding school or something unpleasant. Every time the Indian got tangled up in the white man's maze we lost out some way." But Thomas had also learned that "the weapon they used against us was that paper with the English writing on it. That was the white man's power." And so he became a college student, hoping "to learn the secret of the white man's power, to learn how to use those papers in that way. I didn't want to be like a clay pigeon at a skeet shoot any more of my life."[16]

Always working to cultivate relationships with other native people, Thomas took an interest in the tribal communities of southern Arizona. He was pleasantly surprised to discover that the Catholicism practiced by many Papagos existed alongside their tribal ceremonies. "Among the Papagos," he once explained to a group of denominational leaders, "a native medicine man may very well advise a patient to have a dance for his saint in order to cure a specific illness." The Christian faith had been brought to the Papagos by lay Catholics from Mexico rather than by ordained missionaries, and "up until 1950, Catholic priests in the Papago country functioned as ritual specialists who performed special ceremonies and sometimes conferred with Papago lay religious leaders about distinctly Papago Christian ceremonies. Other Papago Catholic ceremonies and organizations were completely in the hands of lay people." Recalling an analogous situation among the Cherokee Baptist churches of his childhood, Thomas was quick to recognize the significance of this distinctly indigenous Christianity: Papago Catholicism functioned as an integrative force in the tribal community that did not "fragment life for the people," as a mission church usually does.[17]

Thomas came to respect the Papagos as "a very old and wise people," and he eventually married into the community and started a family. "Since I was married to a Papago woman and living among them I felt I should take part in their religion so I danced in the old time ceremonies and at Catholic feasts, contributed to feast committees, helped in all night curing sings, helped make sand paintings, and had my children baptized both by a Catholic priest and the Papago medicine man." He also assisted the tribal council in land-claims research, interviewing his in-laws and other local elders about historic settlements and fields. Working with scholars trained in anthropology and history, Thomas produced ethnohistorical documentation that was used in support of the Papagos' case before the Indian Claims Commission, which had been established in 1946. American political leaders hoped to consolidate the national domain by adjudicating hundreds of territorial disputes and compensating the tribal communities involved, though many would argue that the claims process—which did not permit the return of stolen lands, only their dramatically discounted purchase—was little more than a nonviolent chapter in the ongoing conquest of the Americas. One positive side effect of these convoluted proceedings was the rise of ethnohistory as a research methodology, an approach to historical scholarship that attempts to account for cultural values and perceptions, as anthropologists and historians collaborated in applying their expertise to the practical legal problems facing specific tribal communities.[18]

An eager student, Thomas carried a full course load and spent a good deal of time in the library doing homework while pursuing his own reading interests as well. "That college library is the door to a lot of different worlds," he believed. "But you can't sit around waiting for some professor to spoon-feed you some knowledge you are interested in. You've got to stir around yourself and do a lot on your own. A person has to educate their own self." He also belonged to "The Yeibitchai Chowder and Marching Society," an informal group of anthropology students who gathered on moonlit nights to drink beer and sing. Thomas went by the nickname "K.Y.," a reference to his Kentucky roots, and he acquired something of a reputation for his extensive repertoire of hillbilly song and dance. His musical abilities eventually came to the attention of a faculty member, who persuaded him and one of his buddies to record some of their songs for the university's folklore archives. In April 1949 they performed fifteen songs in a single recording session: ballads, nonnarrative pieces, and gospel numbers. Most were songs that had been commercially released, though Thomas's distinctive renditions reflected the oral circulation by which he had learned them. Two of the ballads he recorded were unique musical texts; one tells the story of a young Cherokee man from Tennessee who was killed during a labor dispute in a Detroit factory, while the other recounts the lament of a coal miner struggling with poverty and black lung disease. Though he focused his attention on native communities throughout his adult life, "K.Y." Thomas clearly appreciated the affinities between the Appalachian folk and Cherokee tribal communities of his childhood.[19]

The 1949 recording session also generated Thomas's first autobiographical texts, fragmentary details that emerged as he described the source for each song he and his partner were performing. Over the next forty years he would produce an assortment of autobiographical narratives, some of them published under pseudonyms such as Anderson Dirthrower, Stand Middlestriker, and G. P. Horsefly, and others that were never published. The Cherokee boyhood portrayed in these various accounts is a complex synthesis of personal experience and oral tradition, a creative fusion of reminiscence and imagination, just as any biography is a selective composition mingling evidence and speculation. Thomas was the consummate storyteller and his narrative skills were often displayed in first-person renditions of third-person realities, not unlike the ballads he enjoyed singing. Friends and colleagues who were wise to his style regarded him as a trickster or shape-shifter; any factual deficits in his stories were overshadowed by his charismatic, magnetic personality. In the mid-forties he befriended an elderly Natchez woman during a visit to eastern Oklahoma. She taught him the importance of collective memory, and he concluded that "it was the remembrance of her childhood within the Natchez community that sustained her." Whatever the actual particulars of his first twenty-five years—which are largely inaccessible to subsequent biographers, save through Thomas's own textual performances—it is clear that his sense of personal and professional vocation was rooted in the emergent recollections of a diasporic survivor.[20]

Bob Thomas majored in geography at the University of Arizona, building on the spatial intelligence he had developed as a child while riding horseback across the Cherokee countryside with his grandfather, whose stories made the landscape come "alive with meaning and history." Years later his remarkable facility with maps would impress both students and colleagues, who marveled at his ability to explain the relationship between natural environment and cultural adaptation using elaborate cartographic representations drawn from memory. As an undergraduate he also came under the mentorship of anthropologist Edward Spicer, who introduced him to the principles of applied anthropology and encouraged him to practice field research. Thomas had worked in a variety of blue-collar industries— mining, manufacturing, construction, ranching, railroads, logging—and had served in the military, and by the time he finished his bachelor's degree in 1950 he thought he "knew a lot about the white man's way." It was a time when influential liberals and a few outspoken tribal leaders were advocating education as the answer for native people; although he rejected their underlying assumptions about the assimilation process, Thomas had come to share their enthusiasm for formal schooling.[21]

Thomas stayed in southern Arizona to pursue a master's degree in anthropology, and for the rest of his life he would pride himself on his professional stature as a university-trained social scientist. His master's thesis examined the revitalization of the Ketoowah Nighthawks under ceremonial leader Redbird Smith, an influential social movement among Cherokee traditionalists in the years before and after Oklahoma statehood. Thomas visited northeastern Oklahoma periodically during his college years and in 1951 conducted formal fieldwork on what he termed "the Redbird Smith movement." He attended as many community events as possible during the four-month period and worked closely with John and George Smith, sons of the movement's leader.[22]

Thomas understood Cherokee cultural history in terms of continuity and persistence, emphasizing the "differential acculturation" and other factors that resulted in the 1859 founding of the Ketoowah Society as "organized factionalism." In 1896 the Redbird Smith movement began among these Cherokee traditionalists as an effort to reaffirm their commitment to "God's Rule," emphasizing the importance of nonviolent resistance as signified by "the White Path," a vital philosophical motif analogous to Iroquois teachings on the White Roots of Peace. The movement began in a remote border region of the Illinois District of the Cherokee Nation where it unfolded in a rich intertribal context, and many of the Ketoowah leaders at this time were also Cherokee Baptist preachers. Redbird Smith's lifelong mentor was a tribal elder of mixed descent named Creek Sam who was well versed in Cherokee, Creek, Seminole, and Natchez traditions. Creek, Seminole, and Natchez traditionalists played central roles in the Cherokee cultural revival and "each of these ethnic groups contributed to the formation of this new culture," which was "a recombination of these older elements in a new pattern."[23]

This project was a significant personal experience for Thomas, allowing him to reconnect with the community of his childhood. He already knew John and George Smith as family friends, and in the process of interviewing them he recovered native fluency in the Cherokee language. In the thesis manuscript, however, he was careful to position himself as ethnographic outsider, downplaying his personal connection to the topic and describing himself as being "of Cherokee descent." Pursuing a conventional career path, in 1953 he enrolled at the University of Chicago intent on earning a doctorate in anthropology. He studied under Sol Tax, the originator of an applied research methodology called "action anthropology," which advocates the use of social scientific expertise to support reformist development projects in poor communities.[24]

As a doctoral student Thomas conducted fieldwork in various Plains tribal communities and helped compile a detailed map of tribal populations in Canada and the U.S. He also was an active member of the Chicago Indian Center, one of the many intertribal organizations established in metropolitan areas in the years following World War II. The urban migration accelerated during the fifties as the U.S. government intensified its assimilation efforts: the relocation program enticed native people with offers of vocational training and employment in urban areas, while the termination policy disestablished more than one hundred tribal governments whose citizenry bureaucrats had deemed ready for integration into the dominant society. While living in Chicago Thomas also helped organize and lead the Workshop on American Indian Affairs, a six-week summer program for native university students from around the country. Beginning in 1957 and held annually for over a decade, the Workshop influenced a generation of tribal leaders by offering hundreds of young people the opportunity to study native history, social scientific analysis, and contemporary legal issues in an intensive seminar environment.[25]

In 1957 Bob Thomas was hired as a research associate by the Cross-Cultural Laboratory of the Institute for Research in Social Science at the University of North Carolina in Chapel Hill. The Cross-Cultural Laboratory had been established to conduct an extensive ethnographic study of the Cherokee Reservation in western North Carolina, home to a small enclave whose ancestors had avoided the nineteenth-century removal. Thomas spent the 1957–58 academic year in the Great Smoky Mountains conducting research; eight other fieldworkers also studied contemporary Eastern Cherokee life during various phases of the three-year project. This was not an effort in action anthropology—the project's director studiously disowned any practical application of their findings—but it was hardly in Thomas's character to stay aloof from tribal affairs, much less when distant relatives were involved. The university had hired him for his personal background and language skills, after all.[26]

Working as both professional anthropologist and native informant, he produced five manuscripts outlining Cherokee philosophy, social organization, and cultural history. These writings demonstrate a sophisticated understanding of the relationship between current academic debates over theory and the practical dimensions of the Eastern Cherokee "problem." Thomas offered probing analyses of the cultural and political circumstances affecting this minority population and assessed their prospects for community development. In the end, however, he found himself bumping up against the limits of social scientific discourse; one colleague later eulogized him as "a premature postmodernist" skilled at deconstructing conventional categories and concepts while remaining "indubitably present" in his writings and lectures as "a reflexive and empathetic observer." After nearly a decade of enthusiasm, Thomas had begun to question the usefulness of the anthropological project. His final manuscript on the Eastern Cherokees, "Cherokee Values and World View," concludes with a provocative self-critical turn: "What really bothers me methodologically is that Cherokees sound so much like other American Indians," he wrote. "We haven't the terms to really describe this behavior and thus differentiate, except at a gross level." What are the objects of ethnography? "Are we seeing 'tribal' societies? Or are we just seeing the European in negative?"[27]

After finishing his work on the Eastern Cherokee project, Thomas moved to the University of South Dakota for the 1958–59 academic year. He served as assistant director of the Institute for Indian Studies and spent the year exploring Sioux country, expanding his repertoire of tribal traditions and his network of intertribal contacts. In 1959 he was recruited to join the social science faculty of Wayne State University's Monteith College, an experimental venture in undergraduate education targeting working-class students in urban Detroit. As a founding member of the faculty, Thomas helped fashion an integrated social science curriculum and played a key role in developing what came to be known as the Monteith "relational" theory. This interdisciplinary approach to cultural interpretation emphasizes the dynamic qualities of social existence; meaning emerges as the product of lived experience and interpersonal relationship. "The person trying to understand social behavior," one of Thomas's Monteith colleagues later wrote, "needed to be able to identify the actual experiences of the people involved, the relational system in which these experiences occurred, and the meanings that the people involved derived from this interrelation of experience and relation." With its focus on social interactions and their consequences, the relational theory is especially useful in understanding the differential power relations that arise in colonial contexts, an obvious characteristic of the tribal communities in which Thomas spent much of his free time.[28]

Thomas would serve on the faculty at Wayne State University for the next two decades, though his association with Sol Tax and the University of Chicago remained active through the sixties. In 1961 he helped Tax organize the American Indian Chicago Conference, a major gathering of tribal representatives and other native leaders, where he met Tuscarora traditionalist William Rickard. This watershed event "provided a valuable opportunity for Indians to meet, learn and work in seven days of intense interaction," recalled Shirley Hill Witt, a Mohawk delegate who later cofounded the National Indian Youth Council. "At the outset, each tribe was prepared to do battle for its own personal aims; by meeting's end, virtually all were working as Indians first and tribal members second." Some 460 delegates spent the week drafting a detailed "Declaration of Indian Purpose" opposing the U.S. government's assimilationist policies and practices. The Chicago Conference also generated a new intertribal periodical, the *AICC Newsletter*, which evolved out of informal "coordinator's reports" that had circulated during the months leading up to the June event. Sol Tax had encouraged native leaders to share their ideas and suggestions with him and other conference organizers as they prepared for the gathering, then included their letters in his intermittent reports. As correspondence increased and the distribution list grew, these periodic mailings became an important vehicle for intertribal communication, promoting both political empowerment and literacy development.[29]

Although he never completed his doctoral dissertation, Thomas's decision to pursue higher education in the dominant culture had been fruitful. In the fifteen years since first enrolling in college courses he had acquired professional skills in research and teaching while establishing himself as a key figure in Indian affairs at the national level. He was actively involved in many of the challenging issues facing native people in the postwar period: land claims, the termination policy, educational reform, the urban migration. Stimulated by these expanding involvements and the relationships they engendered, Thomas's boyhood appreciation for interreligious cooperation and youthful attraction to intertribal camaraderie had matured into an abiding commitment to ecumenical, progressive activism. Though he was beginning to recognize the limitations of the social scientific project, Thomas remained enthusiastic about the potential for social change through institutionalized education. He still had a few things to learn about Cherokee prophecy, action anthropology, and the challenge of tribal survival in the modern world.[30]

CROSS-CULTURAL EDUCATION

In the months following the American Indian Chicago Conference, Sol Tax secured funding from the Carnegie Corporation for a major research project on cross-cultural education. The Chicago Conference had demonstrated the value of intertribal organizing and the need for English literacy development in native communities; Tax hoped to capitalize on the momentum—and mailing lists—the event had generated. He soon hired Bob Thomas to be codirector of the project, and they decided to continue publishing the *AICC Newsletter* as an independent clearinghouse for tribal leaders while focusing their action anthropology efforts on literacy education among the Oklahoma Cherokees. Thomas took responsibility for editing the newsletter and after several issues he renamed it in keeping with its purpose: *Indian Voices*. In September 1963 the "Carnegie Cross-Cultural Education Project" moved to northeastern Oklahoma, where Thomas served as field director for the next four years. It was an auspicious homecoming for the Cherokee anthropologist but one that would entail considerable adversity, both professional and personal: his wife died that same year, leaving him as a single parent responsible for five children.[31]

Thomas set up offices at Northeastern State College in Tahlequah and hired several assistants to carry out research. The Carnegie Project made its presence felt very quickly, launching a Cherokee-language newsletter aimed at rural communities and sponsoring a Cherokee-language radio program that began several months later. Under the terms of the original grant proposal, Thomas was responsible for developing courses and materials to test the viability of programmed-instruction techniques in a cross-cultural literacy program, but he had other goals in mind as well. "I could only hope that our literacy research," he later admitted, "would help be a catalyst for or 'spark off' more general Cherokee community development and social action." The isolated settlements where many Cherokees lived in 1963 were among the most impoverished and disenfranchised tribal communities in the U.S. Their needs and desires were routinely ignored by the federally recognized tribal government, which was administered by marginal bureaucrats appointed by the U.S. government.[32]

The Carnegie Project encountered opposition from the political establishment almost immediately and was the target of a smear campaign for the duration of its four-year effort. At their first meeting with the principal chief and his henchmen in 1964, Thomas and his associates were interrogated by the tribal attorney, an anti-Communist zealot intent on unmasking their experiments in cross-cultural literacy education as a subversive plot linked to the vast conspiracy supposedly imperiling capitalist civilization. "From the moment of Thomas's arrival in Oklahoma," recalled Al Wahrhaftig, the project assistant responsible for ethnographic research, "they pulled out all the stops to derail the Carnegie Project—using tactics that ranged from having confederates go from community to community to label Carnegie Project personnel as communists and warn Cherokees to have no traffic with them, to persuading government agencies to tap Carnegie Project phones, to coaxing a Cherokee protégé to secure employment with the project and steal 'Professor Thomas's' briefcase in order to examine its contents. Initially they succeeded in scaring a lot of Cherokees."[33]

Although this systematic program of sabotage took its toll on their efforts, the Carnegie Project forged ahead under Thomas's leadership. His staff made progress in ethnographic, linguistic, and demographic research and began developing literacy materials and courses in cooperation with local community leaders. Thomas continued to publish *Indian Voices* on a more-or-less monthly basis, reprinting news items from other periodicals and commenting on current issues in Indian affairs in a regular editorial column, which always began with his trademark greeting "Howdy Folks!" His editorial in the September 1964 issue, for example, highlighted several recent skirmishes in the continuing struggle for cultural freedoms; he was "glad to see that Americans as a whole are becoming concerned" about the conformist pressures exerted by mass society. "I guess this is my main message to you," he concluded: "I want to congratulate American Indians for winning the battle against conformity and for keeping something alive which is very dear to Indians and which in future years could be a real contribution to a society concerned with conformity, with feelings of rootlessness, and with a loss of warm and genuine community life." The reactionary leaders of the nonelected tribal government had failed to drive the Carnegie Project out of northeastern Oklahoma, and Thomas continued to voice optimism about the fate of native communities.[34]

His faith in formal education and social scientific research, however, had been shaken by the end of his second year in Tahlequah. In addition to unrelenting harassment by local authorities, he had to contend with U.S. government officials representing the Office of Economic Opportunity, which was fighting the War on Poverty by funding misguided social programs designed by bureaucrats whose ineptitude became increasingly apparent. At the same time, Thomas's growing involvement with rural Cherokee communities led to a sophisticated understanding of their problems and a deep appreciation for their—increasingly, his—cultural traditions. After two decades away from home learning "the White Man's Rule," he found himself immersed again in the world of his childhood. Tiring of the grim spirit of social scientific analysis, in August 1965 he inaugurated a new feature in *Indian Voices*, a section devoted to satire and other amusements. "They tell me humor is a powerful weapon," he explained. "The old time Indians used to have the ability to laugh not only at situations but to laugh at themselves as well. Maybe we need to take a lesson from the old people in that regard."[35]

At the age of forty he also finally understood the meaning of the prophetic teachings George Smith had imparted to him years earlier; Bob Thomas had lived to see all four predictions come to pass. "Slick roads running everywhere" described paved highways and the destructive machines they carry, and the fast-paced lifestyle that has resulted from excessive mobility and industrialization. "A lot of deaf and blind people on the street" was a metaphorical reference to a society full of people who "had lost their kinship to one another" and were "cut off from everybody else and everything else," living "inside themselves, sewed up in their skins," utterly deprived of relational intimacy. "People who get too smart" alluded to the widespread faith in rationality, the notion that "thinking was the way to get through the world," a lifestyle that seduced many into "throwing away their traditions and religions, thinking they knew more than God." Based on these three observations, Thomas concluded that the "fourth event too disturbing to describe" predicted a day "when neither love nor human wisdom would have any value, and at that time people, even some Indians, would put their old people away" in rest homes "because they don't need them anymore." The degreed anthropologist had returned to his Cherokee homeland to direct a program in cross-cultural education, but he soon experienced a cultural cross-education of his own; the homecoming proved to be more than geographic. "Those old Cherokees told me that when I saw those four things come to pass I would want my children close around me," and Thomas found this to be true. "I sure want my children close around me in these days. I don't want them to catch that bad disease."[36]

As Thomas's personal allegiances shifted, he began to experience "grave doubts" about the liberal social programs that had consumed his energy for over a decade. The fifties had been an era of "great optimism in many sectors of American society about the possibility of reform, particularly by 'grass-roots' action and by protest," and he "did not see at the time that this view was based on little scientific evidence and was primarily a statement of faith in the general American society, in the American ideals, if you will." By the mid-sixties, he later admitted, "I was beginning to suspect that the 'system' was much more rigid and power much more centralized and self-protective than I had thought," and he "began to feel a strong sense of having been hoodwinked and betrayed." Thomas increasingly fixed his professional attention on the dominant culture, transforming himself from trained informant to reverse anthropologist.[37]

He authored several scholarly articles during this period, among his earliest published writings, and they reflect his gradual reconversion to Cherokee values. In the July 1965 installment of "Howdy Folks!" Thomas reported on his children's enthusiasm for powwow dancing and their recent excursions to area powwows; as an intertribal periodical, *Indian Voices* itself was an "integral part of a general American Indian social movement now underway." He offered a tentative assessment of these developments in an article titled "Pan-Indianism," published in the fall of 1965. Basing his interpretation on both formal fieldwork and "impressionistic contacts" with a variety of tribal communities and intertribal groups, Thomas identified pan-Indianism as "the expression of a new identity" with its associated "institutions and symbols," an "attempt to create a new ethnic group, the American Indian." Acculturation theory predicted that marginal individuals and families leaving tribal communities would move directly into mainstream society, but the intertribal organizations springing up in urban areas seemed to offer native emigrants an intermediate option: "partial incorporation while retaining the solidarity of the social group." He theorized that tribal people adapted in this way because the modern industrial nation-state, unlike earlier imperial civilizations that were agriculturally based, "demands not only the incorporation of tribal peoples but immediate incorporation and individual assimilation. Industrial civilization individuates and attacks the solidarity of the social group," and "the first reaction of tribes under this kind of stress is the banding together of tribal groups and a widening and bolstering of this new identity, in self-defense."[38]

In "Indians, Hillbillies, and the 'Education Problem,'" written a year later, Bob Thomas and coauthor Al Wahrhaftig compared the educational histories of "folk-Whites" and rural Cherokees. "Research on the small community as it engages in the process of dealing with a national environment is reflexive," they argued. "If our studies teach us nothing about our national social system, then we are learning nothing about the community, its educational processes, or its scholastic problems." Articulating a sharp critique of urban society and its assimilative power, they analyzed northeastern Oklahoma as a microcosm of the so-called education problem in the U.S.: "a 'problem' population low in income, education, and social rank dealt with by an administrative elite attempting to solve problems by acquiring power and money with which to amplify and strengthen educational and social institutions." Thomas and Wahrhaftig insisted that "the problem is not in the fit of people to their schools and institutions, as has been suggested by so many modern academic critics of the American educational system." Rather, "the problem lies in who does the fitting and why." They concluded that "innovative educational techniques"—such as those being employed by the Carnegie Project—were not enough to remedy situations in which "educational problems reflected more general difficulties of communities in a structural and experiential dilemma."[39]

If these two articles demonstrated Thomas's increasing attention to the political context of social phenomena, a pair of short but important essays published in the winter of 1966–67 signaled his full commitment to activist scholarship. "Colonialism: Classic and Internal" and "Powerless Politics" appeared in *New University Thought,* a self-consciously radical academic journal based at Wayne State University. In contrast to the "classic" model of colonialism, which is readily apparent and evident most recently in Africa and Asia, Thomas identified internal or domestic colonialism as a "hidden" model that "is less observable, but has to a large degree the same kind of effects." Both models compel administrative dependency by replacing native institutions with imposed bureaucracies, generating "a very high degree of social isolation" from other communities and from the physical environment. Cultural change is a normal response to collective experience, but "change really doesn't take place under such conditions, except in the form of internal decay," because "you have to make decisions in order to have experience." People who are prevented from controlling their own lives will soon find themselves alienated from the world around them and engulfed in a crisis of meaning. "A community doesn't change very much unless its people are experiencing themselves through their fellows and their environment. This is how a human being changes as he moves through life. Man is an experiencing being."[40]

Earlier in his career Thomas had developed a theoretical model of tribal society as an ideal type; now he proposed a similar approach to internal colonialism: "The control and administration of a people's affairs and destiny by outsiders from another culture is the prime characteristic of a colonial model and American Indian reservations are an ideal type of this model," he wrote. "The reservation is the most complete system of colonialism I know." He illustrated his argument by briefly analyzing the "total system of relationships" on the Pine Ridge Reservation, where racism and assimilationism had exacerbated the breakdown of social institutions during the twentieth century. "More and more of America," Thomas warned, "is coming to resemble an American Indian reservation in terms of social problems and the relationship of the local community to the federal government," which is "taking over the responsibility of integrating deviant communities into the general society, on middle-class terms, and appointing federal bureaucracies to do that job." He went on to suggest that "this trend is a symptom of a more general process in the American social system—the centralization of economic and political power in our society; the closing up and bounding of the 'system'; the exclusion of deviant minorities except for limited entry into the system by individuals."[41]

These influential writings notwithstanding, Thomas's most original contribution as field director of the Carnegie Project may well have been the "long hours of casual, rambling, even profane talk" he and his associates engaged in.

"What I best recall," wrote Al Wahrhaftig decades later, "is him sitting around and talking hour after hour—in his office, over coffee, at lunch, in his home in the evening, on weekends, with me, with Hiner Doublehead, Finis Smith, or Andrew Dreadfulwater, with anyone who would listen, Cherokee or white, in any conceivable permutation." Wahrhaftig insisted that these hours of talking "weren't just talk. They were the presentation and reiteration of a gestalt, a vision, something akin to a prophecy, compounded from his close study of Cherokee history, his extensive research into Native American demography, the lore he received from his grandparents, the enlightenment he received through his fieldwork on the Redbird Smith movement, all fused with an anthropologist's perspective on cultural process and Bob's structuralist thinking about internal colonialism." Thomas's charismatic presence provided a center of gravity for the Carnegie Project, which continued implementing various literacy education programs. He also played a key role in fomenting a grassroots social movement among the Cherokee traditionalists these programs served.[42]

Rural community leaders began meeting in the fall of 1965 to discuss infringements on their culturally indispensable—and treaty-guaranteed—fishing and hunting rights by state authorities. In a series of lively gatherings, at least one of which was held in Thomas's home, participants raised a number of other pressing issues as well: fraudulent land sales, disputes over taxation, discrimination in health care and social services, administrative neglect. What emerged from these discussions was a loosely knit confederation of traditionalist settlements headed by Finis Smith, a Ketoowah ceremonial leader and grandson of Redbird Smith, who served as an interpreter for the Carnegie Project and hosted its weekly radio program. In January 1966 the group decided to call itself the Five County Northeastern Oklahoma Cherokee Organization and selected officers, several of whom also worked for the Carnegie Project including Al Wahrhaftig, who was appointed English-language secretary.[43]

Later that month a Cherokee man by the name of John Chewey was arrested for hunting out of season; he decided to fight the charges and Smith's organization rallied to his defense, enlisting the help of the American Civil Liberties Union in hopes of establishing a legal precedent for Cherokee hunting rights. Thomas and Wahrhaftig were among the witnesses called, and the June trial provoked a regional controversy over the emergence of native activism. The Five County Cherokees issued a "Declaration" outlining their concerns. "We meet in a time of darkness to seek the path to the light. We come together, just as our fathers have always done," it read. "We stand united in the sight of God, our creator. We are joined by love and concern for each other and for all men," and "we offer ourselves as the voice of the Cherokee people." Enumerating a series of changes necessary to ensure political self-determination and cultural survival, the manifesto concluded: "In the vision of our creator, we declare ourselves ready to stand proudly among the nationalities of these United States of America." After several years in the U.S. court system, the Chewey case was eventually dismissed without a definitive ruling on Cherokee hunting rights.[44]

During the summer of 1966 the movement faltered under the pressure of external opposition and internal conflict. Finis Smith gradually withdrew as chairman and in January 1967 he was officially replaced by Andrew Dreadfulwater, the organization's Cherokee-language secretary. Dreadfulwater was a respected Ketoowah ceremonial leader and a devoted Baptist layman as well, and he quickly revitalized the Five County Cherokees. He assumed responsibility for the Carnegie Project's Cherokee-language newsletter and radio program, while Bob Thomas worked behind the scenes to procure a foundation grant allowing the organization to hire an attorney. In June Dreadfulwater's organization joined forces with the Creek Centralization Committee and the National Indian Youth Council to protest the opening of "Cherokee Village," the tribal government's misguided venture in economic development. A lawyer was finally hired in July and the Five County Cherokees reorganized as the Original Cherokee Community Organization. Dreadfulwater continued as president for over a year, but when the organization adopted a more formal structure—written bylaws, a board of directors—to satisfy its attorney and the funding agencies supporting him, this marked the beginning of the end for the grassroots movement.[45]

The summer of 1967 was a time of transition for the Cherokee traditionalists and action anthropologists gathered around Tahlequah. The Original Cherokee Community Organization achieved a degree of financial stability just as the Carnegie Cross-Cultural Education Project was coming to an end, having exhausted its research funding. Thomas packed his things for the long journey to Detroit, where he would return to his teaching post at Wayne State University. Mixed feelings accompanied the move: a sense of professional accomplishment, the vague anxiety of anticipation, growing skepticism toward liberal social programs. He had enjoyed living near family and friends in northeastern Oklahoma—leaving home was never easy—but this was not the first time he had ventured out to foreign lands, and the experiences of the past four years had produced in him an enduring personal maturity. He knew that he would see the Cherokee hills again someday soon.[46]

ECUMENICAL PERSONALITY

Bob Thomas arrived in the Great Lakes area in time to attend the first unity convention at the Tonawanda Seneca longhouse. He had begun to withdraw from the bureaucratic activism carried out through official channels, turning his attention instead to grassroots organizing among tribal traditionalists. "I had decided at that point in time," he later recalled, "that we needed to strengthen our social cohesion internally and 'preserve' our languages and cultures; and that working with the 'system' was not only useless, but perhaps socially destructive." He was impressed by the many elders and religious leaders who participated in the 1967 convention and he helped organize the 1968 gathering in eastern Oklahoma, returning home several times during the year. The traditional movement grew quickly, but it also came to be dominated by leaders who defined themselves by negation, their traditionalist reputations predicated on anti-Christian rhetoric. Thomas's first encounter with such behavior had taken place two decades earlier when he visited Hopi villages in northern Arizona and discovered "there were some Indians as bigoted as many whites are on religious matters." He found "plenty of Indian bigots up there, Christian and traditional both." As he got to know the Hopi traditionalists, it became apparent that "they were obsessed with resisting and countering Christian influence. Many were more concerned with countering Christianity than they were with living in harmony with their relatives. And some were slowly changing their religion from a set of laws which regulated all relationships in the universe, as do most Indian religions, into a rigid set of beliefs to which you have to swear allegiance."[47]

He attended the unity convention again when it returned to Iroquois country in August 1969, but left when he became convinced that the traditional movement was only fanning the flames of religious conflict in native communities. Pondering this turn of events, he followed the open road north to Toronto and his friend Ian MacKenzie. "Most Indian religions teach that you have to respect what spiritual road a man feels he must travel," Thomas later wrote, "and to give him a lot of room because you have no way of telling what kind of instructions or prohibitions he may have received in a dream, a vision, or the like. More than that, any bad feeling between people works to nullify the aim of our ceremonies and weakens our medicine. Harmony is essential to our religion."[48]

This Cherokee ethic of harmony is evident in the long history of ecumenical toleration among the ceremonial grounds and Baptist churches scattered through Cherokee territory since the early nineteenth century. The Cherokees' first sustained contact with Protestant missionaries occurred at a time when local communities were still strong enough to control the process of religious adaptation, and the result was a distinctly Cherokee variation on Christianity that did not provoke factionalism. The ceremonial grounds experienced gradual decline until the turn of the century, when they were revived through the Redbird Smith movement; many of the movement's traditionalist leaders were also Baptist preachers. Several decades later, Thomas witnessed Cherokee ecumenism firsthand when he attended hymn-singing conventions with his grandparents or stayed up late listening to philosophical discussions among Cherokee elders, some Baptist and some not. He had encountered this inclusive spirit again in recent years through his involvement with the Five County Cherokees movement, which brought together traditionalists and Christians for cooperative ventures in community development.[49]

Bob Thomas was an "ecumenical personality" in the terminology of Mary R. Sawyer, who surveys the history of ecumenical movements among African American Christians in her book *Black Ecumenism: Implementing the Demands of Justice.* Detailing the accomplishments of various twentieth-century organizations, Sawyer ably demonstrates how interreligious cooperation can facilitate both social activism and cultural survival: "The objective of black ecumenism, unlike that of white ecumenical movements, is neither structural unity nor doctrinal consensus; rather, it is the bringing together of the manifold resources of the Black Church to address the circumstances of African Americans as an oppressed people. It is mission-oriented, emphasizing black development and liberation; it is directed toward securing a position of strength and self-sufficiency."[50]

The Southern Christian Leadership Conference, the most widely known black ecumenical group, was organized in a series of meetings in 1957, the same year that Thomas moved south to conduct research among the Eastern Cherokees. A decade later he was wrapping up his work in Tahlequah and helping tribal traditionalists plan the first unity convention as SCLC leader Martin Luther King, Jr.—entering the final year of his life—began calling for "a radical revolution of values" in American society to conquer "the giant triplets of racism, materialism, and militarism." The SCLC "gave to the black religious community the insight that the full power of the Black Church is not to be realized in separate denomination or convention units but in interdenominational organizations that affirm the transcendent bonds of ethnicity and serve the agenda of equity and freedom," pursuing "both spiritual sustenance and political liberation." The SCLC and other black ecumenical organizations "have been tied together by a body of 'ecumenical personalities,' that is, individuals who have been or are active participants in three or four different movements and who provide an ongoing exchange of ideas, of lessons learned, and of goals aspired to." Sawyer's book mentions at least one group that included Black Muslim members, but the tradition of "black ecumenism" she recounts has nearly always been limited to Christian communities. The ecumenical organizing to which Bob Thomas devoted his time and energy was considerably more inclusive.[51]

Coaxing his weary sedan down the highway, Thomas reflected on his past and rehearsed stories for future audiences who might share his passion for tribal survival. He had first met Ian MacKenzie, a progressive Anglican priest, in 1966 at the Canadian Indian Youth Workshop held in Winnipeg. MacKenzie was one of the original organizers of the event, which was patterned after the Workshop on American Indian Affairs that Thomas had helped lead for years. After hearing praise for Thomas's work with native university students in the U.S., MacKenzie invited him to serve as the primary instructor for the Canadian version, which was held regularly through the early seventies. Based on his experience teaching at the 1966 Workshop, Thomas suggested several changes that reflected his involvement in the traditional movement, including recommendations that organizers move the program to a more natural environment and involve tribal elders as teaching staff. He also worked with MacKenzie during this period in leading a series of cross-cultural workshops offering non-native clergy and government officials a crash course in Indian affairs.[52]

Thomas was relieved to pass a road sign marking the city limits of Ontario's provincial capital. He headed straight for an office in central Toronto, where he and MacKenzie renewed their friendship and spent several days in conversation about religious conflict in tribal communities. "Many tribes are polarized with orthodox Christians at one polar extreme and the orthodox native religionists at the other," they concluded. "We decided to do something about it," MacKenzie later wrote, and together they outlined plans for an ecumenical gathering that might address the problem of religious factionalism. Thomas "could see that we needed a broader base than simply the non-Christian Indian leadership," and he and MacKenzie "thought it might be possible to bring Indian religious leaders together, of whatever stance—non-Christian, Catholic, Protestant, whatever—particularly if we could get Christian ministers, Indian Christian ministers, that were grassroots Christian ministers." Their timely collaboration would prove to be an important turning point in the rise of contemporary intertribal ecumenism.[53]

In the end, it was not the degree of success, or lack of it, that made the clerical activists noteworthy; nor was it their numbers, which were small; nor their influence, which was limited. What made these individuals important in both religious and historical terms was their very act of witness, their willingness and determination to back up their religious convictions with action.

Michael B. Friedland, *Lift Up Your Voice Like a Trumpet*

The churches must listen to Indians. But will we hear them? For hearing them demands that we examine certain fundamental questions about the nature of Christianity. . . . The churches must decide where they stand. We either support Indian organizations and enter into a partnership with them on their terms or we will end up fighting them.

Ian MacKenzie, Anglican Church of Canada

CHAPTER THREE

"THE CHURCHES MUST LISTEN"

A ROOMFUL OF DEVOUT CHRISTIANS had come under conviction. "I suggest to you that you pursue conversion," Dave Courchene told his well-dressed audience of Anglican clergy and lay leaders: "Conversion of the church from passive observers of the plight of the underprivileged to active participants in the fight for social progress." The energetic president of the Manitoba Indian Brotherhood, a prominent native political organization, was speaking to delegates assembled for the twenty-fourth General Synod of the Anglican Church of Canada. It was August 20, 1969, the third day of their periodic national gathering, which was being held this year in Sudbury, Ontario. General Synod organizers had planned an agenda for the day focusing on "The Changing World" and invited Courchene to give the keynote address, asking him to comment on "how an Indian looks at the future." He was pleased by the opportunity to present his views, hoping that "through better communication we will create an atmosphere of better understanding."[1]

Courchene began his remarks by suggesting the designated theme had taken on new meaning in light of the first lunar landing and moon walk one month earlier. Pointing out the obvious discrepancy between these "astonishing achievements in space" and the persistence of human suffering on earth, he found it hard to understand why "a world that has progressed from the ox-cart to the moon within the short span of one century still has not learned how to deal with the pressing social problems that have plagued Canada for a century." Native people viewed these developments "with utter dismay" and wondered "when, if ever, they will play a role in and share the benefits of such advancement. A century as Canada's forgotten people has left deep scars that will not soon be erased." Nevertheless, Courchene observed, many native people were "awakening" to the possibilities for change. "Throughout Canada the Indian today is developing a new ability and enthusiasm to cope with his problems. This new climate also reflects a restless resentment of past injustices and increasing impatience with bureaucratic and political impediments to change. Indians will no longer accept empty words and worthless promises; we will not settle for political pronouncements and isolated planning; we will not endure continued civil service paternalism; and we will not tolerate acceptance by condescension by our fellow Canadians."[2]

Courchene devoted most of his allotted time to a critique of the Canadian government's recent statement on Indian policy. Released in June 1969, the infamous "White Paper" proposed terminating all political rights and dismissing all land claims in order to assimilate native people into mainstream society as quickly as possible. This radical scheme provoked frustration and bitterness throughout Indian country and was universally condemned by native leaders in the weeks leading up to General Synod. Courchene announced his intention to challenge the government's position through legal action, in cooperation with other established native groups, but he also predicted the emergence of "young, and possibly not-so-young, volatile militants," a small but growing movement with "little patience" and capable of "violent reaction." He called on the government to "cool the fires of anger and resentment" by retracting the proposed changes and forming a committee of native leaders and government officials empowered to negotiate a new policy statement.[3]

"What of the obligations and responsibilities of society as a whole?" Courchene asked General Synod delegates. "Can the Canadian public really delegate their responsibilities to government, can they really park their social conscience in the corner in the hope or belief that the government, by itself, can effect social change?" Reminding his Anglican audience that the nation of Canada is predicated on "the Christian ethic," he questioned whether they would "rise up in righteous indignation" to protect the rights of oppressed minorities. "Where does the church stand on current issues affecting social change and particularly as such change applies to Indian people?" he asked. "The church represents a potential force for change. The church possesses the capacity to influence change as does no other agency in our society. It is literally invulnerable to external pressure. It can take a position and stand up and be counted on the issues of the day. It can make its voice heard." Courchene challenged the Anglican Church of Canada to "embark on a crusade of enlightenment" in every Anglo congregation, to "speak out now" in opposition to the government's Indian policy, and to help solve "the problems of social and economic inequality" by redirecting mission funds to native organizations.[4]

The assembled delegates responded to Courchene's forceful presentation with enthusiastic applause. He was followed on the program by Ernie Willie, a young Kwakiutl priest from the Diocese of New Westminster, who had been chosen to introduce a major report on "the work of the Anglican Church of Canada with Canada's native peoples." Titled *Beyond Traplines*, the report's subtitle asked *Does the Church Really Care?* and this question echoed in Willie's remarks. He commended the report to his audience and admitted it gave him "a glimmer of hope that you might become able to rise above your confusion and misconceptions," as it clearly documented the history of "Euro-Canadians who have deliberately and systematically denied our right to a future." Adopting a conciliatory tone, he told his fellow Anglicans that "more than ever before" native people "need a friend."[5]

Willie continued: "Now my people are beginning to realize our sad state of affairs and we, with your support, will begin to rebuild. Through effective dialogue, we can both learn to overstep the failures of the past and we can both grow in the true humanity of God our creator. Dialogue can lead to love, for dialogue can restore and revitalize relationships." He acknowledged the temptation to fall into "arguing about the past" but preached against such conflict, for "if we are to emerge from the wreckage of the past we must do it together, with the fullest cooperation on both sides. Only then can we live side by side in true harmony." Most General Synod delegates were already familiar with *Beyond Traplines* and its sweeping proposals for mission philosophy and policy. This book-length study had been published several months earlier and was featured in the May issue of the denominational monthly *Canadian Churchman*, stimulating debate among Anglicans from coast to coast. The detailed report enumerated a series of assumptions, realities, implications, strategies, and recommendations, asserting that "the church must listen to the native peoples" and give top priority to "changes in basic attitude" in order to "find effective ways of respecting and releasing the resources of indigenous leadership."[6]

The General Synod next heard from Alanis Obomsawin, an Abenaki musician and educator from Montreal, who performed two tribal songs and an original composition in English, her third language. She introduced her first number by commenting on the impact of missionization in tribal communities, offering a subtle comparison between native and Christian musical traditions. "I have nothing against hymns," she confessed, "I think they are most beautiful, but I would like you to think when I sing this song: What did you have against our own prayer and our own singing that we have loved so much?" She also described impoverished elders on her home reserve who still sing for creation and ask the Creator to "help the people—the Indian people—to show their light to the white man." These musical gestures "brought

tears to the eyes of some three hundred people" including an Anglican journalist covering the event, who was captivated by the youthful performer: "She
speaks softly and deliberately and wears a magic smile. She loves trees and animals and birds and small children and her singing is as beautiful as her face."
Obomsawin told the journalist that non-natives "have got to come around and
let people be what they are." Like Courchene and Willie, she was optimistic
about the future: "Things have to go better now, because all Indians are so
aware. They'll never be fooled anymore."[7]

Dave Courchene, Ernie Willie, and Alanis Obomsawin heralded the beginning of a new era in Anglican mission history, if not the end of an old one:
General Synod had heard from the chief, the convert, and the maiden, a veritable pageant of savage archetypes embodying the colonial experience, and
now these earnest Christian liberals were poised to debate their own capacity
for change. "Whenever an Indian or Eskimo rose to speak," observed a reporter from the *Toronto Globe and Mail*, "the delegates hung on to his every
word, beamed and applauded as if he were a precocious child or a puppy performing a trick." If an institutional revolution was being born this day, it
would be an easy delivery but a long and painful adolescence.[8]

ANGLICAN MISSIONS

The Society for the Propagation of the Gospel in Foreign Parts was founded by
the Church of England in 1701. Charged with the responsibility of managing
pastoral and evangelistic work in the British Empire's overseas colonies, the new
organization enjoyed the patronage of both church and Crown. In North America the SPG aspired to convert free natives and enslaved Africans while countering the influence of sectarian dissenters who were competing with the
established church. Yet none of the more than three hundred SPG missionaries
who served on the Atlantic coast during the eighteenth century actually lived in
a tribal community; most quickly retreated to parish work in colonial settlements, and only the Mohawk mission at Fort Hunter produced lasting results.
French Catholic missionaries had been working in Mohawk territory for several
decades when four Mohawk leaders traveled to London in 1710 to fortify their
alliance with the British government. They also met with Queen Anne, who ordered that a chapel be built for them at Fort Hunter. The new Mohawk church
opened in 1712 when an Anglican missionary arrived from England. Mohawk
loyalists who fled across the northern border during the American Revolution
carried with them silver communion vessels and other liturgical objects the
queen had presented to their forebears in London seventy years earlier.[9]

Other tribal communities in present-day Canada also encountered SPG missionaries during the second half of the eighteenth century, especially after Protestant England prevailed over Catholic France in the Seven Years' War, which ended in 1763. These early Anglican efforts were relatively ineffective compared to the accomplishments of the Jesuits and other celibate proselytizers, who had been active in the region since 1611; this situation eventually changed as a result of the evangelical revival that transformed the religious landscape in England during the eighteenth century. British evangelicals, led by the emerging Methodist movement, expressed their newfound enthusiasm by organizing voluntary societies to undertake humanitarian, educational, and evangelistic projects. The evangelical revival found expression within the Anglican communion through the founding of the Church Missionary Society in 1799. The goals of the new organization were similar to those of the SPG, but CMS personnel approached their task with considerably more devotion and fervor.[10]

The first CMS venture in British North America began in 1820, when John West was commissioned as chaplain for the Hudson's Bay Company colony on the Red River, near present-day Winnipeg. Native people in this area already possessed extensive knowledge of European attitudes and behaviors; generations of experience as key participants in the international fur trade had drawn many tribal communities into an increasingly global economic system. In addition to organizing a mission church and fulfilling his duties as parish priest, West established a school for native children that also enrolled local English and Métis students. He envisioned an aggressive program of religious and cultural conversion and soon gathered fifteen boys and fifteen girls from tribal communities throughout the region. A decade later one of West's successors, CMS missionary William Cockran, turned his attention to adult education by founding an agricultural settlement for native converts a few miles downriver from the colony. After several years of determined labor he was able to take pride in his accomplishment: a farming community he described as "twenty-three little white-washed cottages shining though the trees, each with its column of smoke curling up into the skies, and each with its stacks of wheat and barley." French Catholics during this period also planted a mission on the Red River, and the Methodists were not far behind; the Red River colony served as the gateway to northwest Canada, an arena for intense missionary competition throughout the nineteenth century.[11]

Neither of these Anglican educational experiments survived the transition from fur trade economy to European settlement on the Canadian prairies. Both were significant, however, as early expressions of emerging colonial policies regarding native people, and of church involvement in the administration of those policies. William Cockran's settlement was a precursor of the reserve system, which was designed to achieve conquest through assimilation, segregating native people on model farms where they could be trained in the rudiments of European agrarian and religious traditions. John West's school was the first Anglican contribution to the residential school system, which augmented the reserve system, targeting tribal children as the weak links in native resistance to cultural genocide. It was this alliance of church and state that smoothed the path to Anglo dominance in Canada, a cooperative but compromising relationship that many Canadian Anglicans would eventually regret.[12]

Several Catholic orders and various Protestant denominations joined the Anglican church in opening dozens of "Indian Residential Schools" during the nineteenth and twentieth centuries. These peculiar institutions became central to evangelistic strategy; each school was a focal point for mission resources and a tangible expression of sectarian competition. Funding for the operation of early Anglican residential schools came from CMS benefactors in England, with government support limited to construction expenses and food rations for students. Civil involvement in native education increased in the years after Canada's confederation in 1867, and by the 1880s the Canadian government was providing most of the funding necessary to maintain the denominational schools.[13]

The General Synod of the Church of England in Canada was established in 1893 and convened for the first time in Toronto, and in 1902 church leaders organized the Missionary Society of the Canadian Church. Noting the rise of autonomous Anglican institutions in Canada, the CMS announced its intention to transfer responsibility for the residential schools. The MSCC responded by forming a committee, which in 1905 produced the first in an interminable series of bureaucratic studies reporting on mission work in native communities. The committee surveyed government officials, Anglican hierarchs, and the leadership of other denominations—and very few native people—in order to "devise a plan that will put the money and energy expended on Indian work to the best possible use, produce the best results in the interests of the Indians themselves, and satisfy both the Government and the Churches." One of their first actions was to petition the Canadian government to compel attendance at residential schools by withholding rations "from such parents as refuse to send their children to school," a policy the government quickly adopted and practiced for many years. The Anglican church also actively supported government efforts during this period to criminalize tribal ceremonies. In 1919 the Indian Residential Schools Commission of the MSCC assumed administrative control over the schools; in 1923 the Anglicans were running twenty such institutions strewn from the Great Lakes to the Yukon.[14]

Every denomination relied on native converts to help propagate the faith in the era of missionary expansion. The residential schools played an indispensable role in this process, and the Anglicans were especially adept at cultivating native catechists and priests. During the nineteenth century it was CMS policy to make use of "native helpers under European supervision," and the MSCC maintained this tradition during the twentieth century; in 1916, for example, the Church of England in Canada employed ninety-two European and seventy-five native missionaries. This cadre of subordinate missioners proved to be a cost-effective means of covering more territory, supplementing the limited number of Anglo personnel available for evangelizing far-flung tribal communities. Christian ordination was also one of the few expressions of native leadership the dominant culture would permit in the context of Canadian colonization. Among John West's students at the Red River school were two Cree boys who had been baptized with the names Henry Budd and James Settee. They went on to become the first native Anglican priests, ordained in 1852 and 1853 respectively, and both were instrumental in the spread of Anglicanism to native communities. Budd founded and led a mission based at The Pas, an old French trading post, while Settee opted for an itinerant ministry among the Plains Cree. Like many other native missionaries in Christian history, Budd and Settee survived on stipends that were considerably lower than those afforded their non-native colleagues. Today Henry Budd's pioneering work is commemorated on April 2 in the lectionary calendar of the Anglican Church of Canada.[15]

One of the leading native Anglican priests of the twentieth century was Edward Ahenakew, a Cree from northern Saskatchewan. He was born in 1885 on the reserve at Sandy Lake that had been founded nine years earlier by Ahtahkakohp, his paternal grandfather's brother. The family name Ahenakew was the personal name of Edward's grandfather until he became the reserve's first convert and received the Christian name David. Edward's forebears included other Cree leaders and commoners, at least one French voyageur, and a Stoney poundmaker, a man supernaturally endowed with the ability to build enclosures used to trap buffalo.[16]

As a young boy Edward Ahenakew attended the local mission school, where one of his uncles was the teacher. At the age of eleven his family took him to the Anglican residential school in Prince Albert so he might continue his education. This traumatic separation left him "much depressed," but he was soon greeted by two cousins already enrolled at the school and "in a short time," he later recalled, "I forgot my troubles. Gradually I fell into the ordinary round of school life, winning a few minor honours both on the playgrounds and in the class room." Nevertheless, his residential school experience led Ahenakew to reflect on the poor fit between the plodding discipline of an English education and the Plains Cree love of freedom, which he remembered as "an intoxication of spirit, almost inhuman" in character. "Life in the open prairie" produced in his people "a daring and reckless temperament," since daily survival required "a quick application of all human powers, a superhuman effort, followed by total relaxation." In 1903 Ahenakew graduated from the Prince Albert school and returned to Sandy Lake, where he worked with his father and taught school on a nearby reserve. He would be a lifelong advocate for educating native children in local day schools rather than sending them away to residential schools.[17]

Ahenakew eventually decided to pursue a vocation in Christian ministry and enrolled at Wycliffe College in Toronto, transferring to Emmanuel College in Saskatoon when it reopened in 1909. He was ordained deacon in 1910 and priest two years later upon completion of his degree in theology, then was posted to the Anglican mission at Onion Lake, a Cree reserve on the Saskatchewan-Alberta border. He served this community with distinction, but the suffering caused by the flu epidemic of 1918 prompted him to leave parish work and study medicine in Edmonton. During this period he also took a leadership role in a new intertribal political organization, the League of Indians of Canada, which was founded in 1919 by a Mohawk war veteran. Ahenakew was appointed president of the League for Saskatchewan and Alberta and spent his free time traveling to reserves to discuss community concerns and recruit new members. During one such visit to Little Pine, a Cree reserve southeast of Onion Lake, he discovered that their local school had been closed by the Canadian government. Ahenakew took the lead in getting the school reopened and later claimed "it was a success from the beginning," developing into "a model Indian day school" that other reserves sought to imitate.[18]

The rigors of university courses, community organizing, and a spartan diet took a toll on his health, and after three years of study Ahenakew was forced to withdraw from medical school. Unable to work and deeply discouraged, he was taken in by the Anglican missionaries on Thunderchild's Reserve, a Cree community near Little Pine, for an extended convalescence. One of his church mentors suggested he occupy his time by recording the stories of local Cree elders, a project Ahenakew eventually embraced. He made arrangements to meet with Thunderchild and for several months listened to the aging leader's mythic and autobiographical narratives. Other listeners and narrators began attending the storytelling sessions, which evolved into regular gatherings where community members could share tribal humor and voice their frustrations over the constraints of reserve life.[19]

Ahenakew filled his journal with notes and produced three important English-language manuscripts. "Cree Trickster Tales" was published in *The*

Journal of American Folklore in 1929; these stories recounted the exploits of Wesakaychak in an epic cycle of twenty-six narratives. "The Stories of Chief Thunderchild" and "Old Keyam" were published posthumously in 1973 as *Voices of the Plains Cree*, edited by a family friend. The first was Thunderchild's life history in twenty brief chapters, autobiographical vignettes recalling life before the advent of the reserve system. Ahenakew believed the time had come when "that which has been like a sealed book to the masses of our Canadian compatriots" should be made known. "We have our own view of the life that has been imposed upon us, and these pages are written that others may glimpse what we feel and experience." He concluded the manuscript with Thunderchild's plea for social justice and religious tolerance: "I do not want to fight the white man's religion. I believe in freedom of worship, and though I am not a Christian, I have never forgotten God. What is it that has helped me and will help my grandchildren but belief in God? He looks upon the wrong that is done on earth, and knows what would correct it. But we ourselves must find the way and do it."[20]

The second part of *Voices of the Plains Cree* was Ahenakew's most compelling literary accomplishment. Having documented narrative fragments of his people's mythic tradition and cultural history, he created a discursive persona that would allow him to address the circumstances of native life in the 1920s and beyond. He imagined "Old Keyam" as a "representative character," a first-generation immigrant to the reserve system now lost in the abyss of colonial transformation, this tension evident even in his hybrid English and Cree name. Ahenakew called his alter ego "Old" as the storytelling successor to tribal elders who formerly exercised great influence in community life, and "Keyam" because "that word in Cree means 'What does it matter?' or simply 'I do not care!' and so expresses the attitude of many Indians who stand bewildered in the maze of things, not knowing exactly what to do, and hiding their keen sense of defeat under the assumed demeanour of 'keyam!'—while in fact they do care greatly." Ahenakew wanted native people to "face the challenge of our day," putting these words in the mouth of his autobiographical narrator: "When I talk to you, it is to make you know yourselves and your people; and sometimes I hope that my words may reach out to others in this country." At least one passage in the manuscript was taken directly from a speech Ahenakew made prior to living on Thunderchild's Reserve.[21]

The Old Keyam manuscript addressed intertribal conflicts, cultural change, religious traditions, colonization, gender relations, political activism, educational policy, and strategies for survival. Ahenakew's portrayal of Cree religious traditions was sympathetic if also parochial, occasionally referring to tribal spirituality as "superstition." He was a conversionist, but one who preached that conversion should be a voluntary process. "Like most of you," Old Keyam told his listeners—and Ahenakew his readers—"I was brought up under Christian teaching and I have had little to do with any religious matters apart from that faith. Yet I believe that I am free of prejudice against any sincere form of belief that may be in the heart of my fellow man. I would never come between him and what he holds to be his God, except with kindly advice, carefully and prayerfully considered." After recovering his health, Ahenakew went back to work for the church, supervising a number of western reserves as traveling missionary. He also edited a Cree-language monthly periodical, translated various church publications into Cree, and helped produce a Cree-English dictionary. In 1935 he took charge of the Anglican mission at Fort à la Corne, which had been established in 1857 by Henry Budd, the pioneering native priest. Ahenakew regularly served as a delegate to diocesan, provincial, and general synods, and his contributions to the work of the church were recognized in 1947 when he was awarded an honorary doctorate by Emmanuel College. One Anglican historian later remarked that Ahenakew "might well have been our first Indian bishop if only more imagination had been shown."[22]

Ahenakew retired in 1955 and lived with his brother at Sandy Lake until passing away six years later. His life was memorialized in 1962 with the construction of a new church at Sandy Lake, where his nephew Andrew Ahenakew was parish priest. Some have remembered Edward Ahenakew as little more than a textbook example of the convert-turned-missionary, a company man driven by his single-minded devotion to the institutional church. He certainly fulfilled this role in the eyes of his many Anglican admirers; the retired archbishop of Quebec, for example, eulogized him in 1963 as one who "may stand for the great band of Indian clergy and lay readers who have sustained the fabric which was built by the first missionaries."[23]

Yet Ahenakew's careful documenting of Plains Cree traditions was hardly an evangelistic gesture, at least not in the conventional direction, as the closing scene of the "Old Keyam" manuscript made clear. After his final discourse to the community, Old Keyam is commended by the chief, who praises his wise counsel and articulate voice. Old Keyam is surprised and lowers his head "to hide his emotion," then makes a startling revelation. His hands fumble at his belt, untying a leather bundle. "There is something here," he says, "something that I have wanted to show you." He produces an elaborately decorated pipestem, an ancient and sacred object given to him many years earlier by its previous keeper, "one who spoke to us of courage and of mercy, of love for our fellow men and reverence towards God." Old Keyam recounts how he was charged with the responsibility for these traditions, explaining his attempts to be faithful and admitting his mistakes along the way. "These teachings are the heritage of our past," the respected elder announces, now sure of his mission. "They are for all time; they belong to all ages, to all people." It was a graceful reminder that the terms of cross-cultural conversion are sometimes lost in translation.[24]

INDIAN WORK

Edward Ahenakew and other native advocates who labored during the first half of the twentieth century were voices crying in the wilderness of church bureaucracy. By the turn of the century native people had become an unglamorous backwater of the pagan world; interest in so-called home missions declined as native communities atrophied under the constraints of the reserve system. Evangelicals in Canada and elsewhere turned their attention to more exotic outposts in Africa and Asia, while on the domestic front church leaders focused on serving the religious needs of the growing numbers of European immigrants. The last of the eleven numbered treaties, which facilitated nonnative settlement by extinguishing native land claims covering much of the Canadian national territory, was signed in 1921. That same year the Anglican Church of Canada formed the Committee on Indian and Eskimo Work, an executive-level body responsible for coordinating the denomination's various native programs.[25]

Internal reports and publications documented the consolidation of Anglican policy toward native people during the twenties and thirties. In 1931 the Indian Residential Schools Commission reported to General Synod on the status and goals of the residential schools, which sought to "gradually lead to the Indians' release from their present position of wardship" by "assimilating them with the general population" and enabling them "to take their place as members of the Christian Church and citizens of the State." These regimented institutions taught farming and ranching, homemaking skills, health and hygiene, personal finances, acquisitiveness, progressive individualism, the English language, and the Anglican version of Christianity.[26]

National church leaders considered this to be the best strategy for helping native communities, but missionaries working at the local level were sometimes critical of their approach. "I am convinced the present residential school system is a failure," wrote an Anglican teacher in an editorial letter published by the *Canadian Churchman* in 1936. "The time has come when our policy should be overhauled. Give the men and women who are teaching the day schools a chance to state their case." One Anglican priest went so far as to defend native cultural traditions in his critique of the residential schools: "The children are taken away to school when they are about six years old, are instructed with more or less success in the white man's books, and miss all the irreplaceable treasures of traditional knowledge and tribal custom that are their right" and that they needed to survive. "The Indian mission situation is very bad," he wrote. "Can we not get away from sentimental admiration of these ancient mistakes and boldly formulate new policies?" The voices of dissent were not yet loud enough to change church policy, however, and in the late thirties the IRSC reiterated its position that "of all the helps, whether provided by the Church or the State, for the betterment of these indigenous races," the residential school system "is more beneficial than any other."[27]

Canada's declaration of war against Germany in September 1939, over two years before the U.S. officially entered the conflict, postponed substantive debate over Anglican policy toward native people. The national war effort did, however, take its toll on the residential schools. Staffing shortages and government funding restrictions, combined with higher commodity prices and growing enrollments, created operational and financial problems that strained the ability of school administrators to provide for the needs of their students. Concerned about rising deficits and also impressed by native enlistees who volunteered for military service, the Anglican church protested the Canadian government's inattention to native people during the war. In 1945 Anglican leaders organized a National Commission on Indian Work to evaluate their native programs and joined other influential observers in lobbying the government to undertake a similar effort. In 1946 the Canadian Parliament responded by convening a Joint Committee of the Senate and the House of Commons, which worked for two years and laid the groundwork for the revised Indian Act of 1951.[28]

Postwar stability and prosperity stimulated a renewed debate over Anglican involvement with native people, which was evident in 1946 when the sixteenth General Synod convened in Winnipeg. The IRSC affirmed the denomination's assimilationist and collaborationist heritage, asserting that "our native Canadians must receive education in order to fit them for full Canadian citizenship" and defending the symbiotic relationship between church and state. "By leaving schools in the care of the Churches, the Government obtains the services of a number of consecrated men and women," the IRSC report stated. "On the other hand, the Church derives great benefit by reason of the fact that splendid buildings are being constructed with public funds and their maintenance largely provided," enabling the Anglican church "to carry on her evangelistic and educational program among the natives at a very modest cost."[29]

The National Commission on Indian Work also submitted a favorable report to General Synod, claiming that "the alliance between the Government and the Church in education has been most happy and beneficial for the Indian." The NCIW, however, expressed greater concern about the efficiency of the residential school system, suggesting the central office be relocated closer to government agencies in Ottawa and calling for "a complete change in the basis of financial support which would supply the co-operating Churches with their actual costs in maintaining the required standards in Indian schools." More significant, if less successful, were the report's fairly radical proposals regarding school administration and curriculum: "The evidence makes it perfectly clear that there is urgent need of drastic changes in regard to diet, health, sanitation, hours of work, housing, social life, recreation, dress and so forth. New ideas and modern standards must be introduced." The NCIW recommended teaching students "the geography of their own regions, the history of their own people," and their own tribal "folklore" and "handicrafts." In 1947 Anglican leaders raised these and other points when they appeared before the Joint Committee of the Senate and the House of Commons, which heard similar criticisms from tribal leaders. It was the first time in Canadian history that native people were allowed to testify before Parliament.[30]

The revised Indian Act of 1951 initiated an era of philosophical and structural change in Indian affairs. The new law allowed for a greater degree of native self-determination and repealed prohibitions on tribal ceremonies, political organizing, and land claims advocacy that had oppressed reserve communities for decades. During the fifties the Canadian government asserted a more active role in native education, taking charge of teacher recruitment and mandating a full-day academic curriculum. The government also began promoting the educational advantages of local day schools and in 1958 assumed responsibility for the entire cost of operating the residential schools. At the end of the decade Anglican leaders found themselves in a confusing predicament, distressed by the decline of their control over education and their influence with the government, by the reemergence of native nationalism and tribal ceremonies, and by the rise of sectarian competition from aggressive Pentecostal and Fundamentalist missionaries. During the twentieth General Synod in 1959 the Anglican Church of Canada turned its attention to the problems facing native people in urban areas, directing its Council for Social Service to study the situation and determine how the church might "help Canadians of other origins to appreciate Indian culture and to receive Canadians of Indian origin into the fuller life of Canadian communities where they can make their unique contribution and also share in the rich cultural heritage of Canadians as a whole."[31]

The CSS had been founded in 1915, an Anglican expression of the Social Gospel reform movement that flourished among liberal Protestants in the

U.S. between 1880 and the First World War. During the first four decades of its existence the CSS focused on social problems among poor and working-class citizens who were casualties of industrial development in Canada. By the late fifties the Anglican church was more concerned about human suffering on a global scale, and it established the Primate's World Relief Fund in 1959. The following year a group of liberal activists formed the Indian-Eskimo Association of Canada, an independent organization devoted to advocacy on behalf of native people. This new voice in Canadian politics argued for a community development approach in Indian affairs, whereby outside agencies are supportive but not directive, allowing tribal leaders to grapple with "the problems of communities that they regard as their own" and to experience "the social-psychological consequences" that follow from autonomy and accomplishment. "This is the supreme advantage of 'community development' on the reserves," they explained before Parliament in 1960: "that it is *educational*, that by promoting change in activities and in the degree of local responsibility for them it can produce a change in general outlook, in self-reliance and initiative." The Indian-Eskimo Association also publicly challenged denominational mission policy, and many Anglican leaders were now wise enough to admit the accuracy of these criticisms. In 1961 the CSS and the Executive Council of the Anglican church issued a joint statement acknowledging "an awakening concern in many areas of Canada on the part of the general public concerning the situations faced by Canada's native peoples" and commending, without qualification, "the work of the Indian-Eskimo Association to clergy and laity who are concerned with the Church's ministry in Indian and Eskimo communities."[32]

The combined efforts of various native organizations and the Indian-Eskimo Association influenced the policies of both church and state in the early sixties. The transformation of Anglican involvement with tribal communities during this period was reflected in the pages of the *Canadian Churchman*, which typically included news from the home mission field every month or so, brief articles reporting on noteworthy personalities or events. This journalistic tradition changed in 1964 when the May issue featured a cover story on the Eskimos of Ungava Bay, who were caught in the middle of a political struggle between English Canada and French Quebec. Native leaders had made it clear they did not want to be placed under provincial jurisdiction, but politicians on both sides of the debate in Ottawa were ignoring their concerns. "Just how much does a minority group have to put up with before Christians stand up and cry 'Stop!'" asked the sympathetic Anglican reporter who was following the story. Another lengthy article in the same issue offered a critical analysis of the conflict, outlining the linguistic, ethnic, racial, and religious subplots of this political drama. Only five months earlier, Anglican leaders had pledged full cooperation with the proposed administrative changes. "Eskimos Have Rights," the lead editorial in the church's national paper now declared. "In this age of political enlightenment, self-determination is a fundamental right, and a misguided paternalism is no more acceptable when it is practised by the Governments of Canada and Quebec than it is by the Governments of Great Britain or the United States." Substantive follow-up articles in the *Canadian Churchman* allowed readers to track further developments in the Ungava Eskimo situation for years to come.[33]

The sixties were also an era of ecumenical cooperation on social issues in Canada. In 1965 the CSS organized the first Inter-Church Consultation on Indian Affairs, which brought together leaders from nine major communions to discuss cooperative ventures. Later that year delegates to the twenty-second General Synod passed resolutions directing the Anglican church to reform its mission policy—in consultation with native people—and authorizing church leaders to fund pilot projects in support of native community development. In January 1966 Ted Scott was installed as Bishop of Kootenay in western Canada. Scott was one of several clerical activists who rose to positions of power within the Anglican hierarchy during this period. He had been actively involved in Indian affairs as Associate General Secretary of the CSS, visiting native communities regularly and training non-native seminarians in cross-cultural ministry. Less than four months into his tenure as bishop, Scott circulated a position paper in which he argued that Canadian society "has changed so drastically in recent years that it is now necessary for the Anglican Church to re-think its approach to Indian work and that this re-thinking must relate to goals, methods of work, and general attitudes." He outlined a four-point program by which they might begin the process: first, "make possible the development of creative Indian leadership in the widest sense of the term and not be concerned with mere institutional membership or 'in Church' leaders"; second, "rejoice in the developing independent and direct action of Indian people and encourage and support it in every way possible"; third, "help our total Church membership to become conscious of the vital part which their attitudes play in influencing the attitudes of Indian people both to white culture and to the Church"; and fourth, "enter into close cooperation with other churches, and both community and government agencies."[34]

Later in 1966 Scott agreed to write the preface for an important study of Indian affairs by John Melling, the first Executive Director of the Indian-Eskimo Association. *Right to a Future: The Native Peoples of Canada* was published jointly by the Anglican church and the United Church of Canada on behalf of nine other denominations and ecumenical agencies. Scott's preface restated his belief that "a combination of factors has both drastically altered the situation of Canada's native peoples and also brought it from a peripheral to a more central place on the Canadian scene," and expressed his hope that this volume would "help stimulate much thought and action as we seek to develop more creative attitudes, relationships and policies in this area of our country's life."[35]

Melling's book was "written with a commitment," applying Christian values and social scientific methods to the project of reconceptualizing "Indian work." He perceived a "need for action" and argued for church involvement in the political process, articulating a mild version of the liberationist theological discourse that was emerging in other parts of Christendom as well: "Being occupied by the grand objectives of individual and social existence, the Church is the natural agency for formulating the purposes that liberate human life and the conditions that support that liberation." The first part of the book presented "some historical roots of today's problems," highlighting the ways in which the colonization of Canada affected native community life, a kind of "development-in-reverse." The second part of the book surveyed contemporary issues in native communities, especially the new challenges posed by the postwar urban migration. Melling concluded that both church and state should support a comprehensive strategy of community development with regard to native people, "helping them to help themselves." He also recognized the tactical difficulties involved in effecting social justice in the midst of gross inequities of power. "To the extent that our ideals and the practical aspects of our ideals lead us to try to help our native peoples, the first condition for success is that we must become ancillary to their ideas, plans and programmes," he wrote. "The second condition for success is perhaps more difficult. We have to help them, and this implies an engagement to them and with them. Yet the sort of engagement we have in mind is also a sort of disengagement, of intervening while holding back." Melling's challenge to his Christian readers was predicated as much on theological idealism as on historical and social realism: "If any group can ensure this helping and caring for others with complete respect for the liberty of others, it is the Church—for the very centre of its belief concerns human freedom."[36]

Right to a Future was "written in the belief that Canadians should pause in the midst of their centennial pride and consider their fellow-citizens of native background." A century had passed since Canadian confederation, and 1967 proved to be a year of historical reflection and social change throughout the dominion. The most conspicuous expression of the national anniversary was Expo 67, an immense world's fair hosted by the city of Montreal. This six-month exposition attracted fifty million visitors to its nearly one hundred pavilions, of which the Christian pavilion and the Indians of Canada pavilion turned out to be among the most controversial. The Christian pavilion featured graphic depictions of military violence and human suffering, a postmodern vision of chaos and apocalypse that many churchgoers found offensive, though teenagers and other skeptics were impressed by the exhibit's brutal realism. The Indians of Canada pavilion, which was bankrolled by the Canadian government but designed by native leaders, eschewed nostalgic exoticism in favor of a direct confrontation with the Canadian public. Visual and verbal texts presented the contemporary realities of native life and challenged non-native people to acknowledge their heritage of betrayal and paternalism; indeed, one local Iroquois community had lost part of their reserve to the construction of Expo 67. "Give us the right," read the last exhibit panel, "to manage our own affairs."[37]

The twenty-third General Synod of the Anglican Church of Canada convened that summer in the nation's capital. Reports were dutifully filed by various church bodies including the Joint Interdepartmental Committee on Indian/Eskimo Affairs, which fulfilled its bureaucratic responsibility by preparing "A Centennial Profile of Indian and Eskimo Canadians." This report outlined six important social problems experienced by native people: rapid population growth, educational deficiencies, unemployment and poverty, inadequate housing, destructive behavior, and a high mortality rate. "We, as Christians, must plead forgiveness for our participation in the perpetuation of injustices to Indians," the committee confessed, noting the incongruity of repentance and centennial pride. They repeated the call for policy reform and encouraged the church to support native leaders, organizations, and protest strategies, "what might be termed 'Indian power,'" in keeping with the philosophy of community development. The report also contained a reflexive critique, noting that the church, like the government, "has often failed to include Indians in making decisions about policies which will affect them" and implicating the committee itself, which "has no Indian or Eskimo representation at present. It is absurd that we should continue to make decisions at any level about Indians and not include those affected by these decisions in the decision-making process." Delegates responded by approving resolutions directing church leaders to "become actively involved in projects enabling Indians to discuss their own proposals for self-determination" and to "prepare a report to the next General Synod of the needs, concerns, and recommendations expressed in such projects." Many hoped this next report would lead to substantive institutional change.[38]

HENDRY REPORT

The trilateral dependency binding native communities, the Anglican church, and the government of Canada had weathered a complex evolution in the quarter-millennium since the arrival of SPG missionaries. The pace of change quickened in the years after the Second World War and by 1967 an emergent native renascence, Canada's most troublesome expression of the postcolonial consciousness flourishing around the globe, had left both church and state noticeably confused. Increasingly critical of government policy toward native people and of its own complicity in the colonization process, the Anglican Church of Canada embarked on a program of collective repentance, organizational reform, political action, and community development. General Synod delegates committed themselves to listening sympathetically and speaking prophetically, though few anticipated how difficult it would be to communicate across the colonial divide of civilization and savagism, where every conversation ricochets off hardened stereotypes, every relationship tracing an unpredictable trajectory. These earnest Christian liberals were ready for the beginning of a new era in Anglican mission history, if not the end of an old one: civilization had yet to exorcise the agent, the evangelist, and the pedagogue, a veritable trinity of colonial archetypes that would haunt their struggle for institutional redemption.[39]

In the months following General Synod, church leaders intensified their effort to educate Anglicans about the issues affecting native people. The December 1967 issue of the *Canadian Churchman* featured a lead story and nine more articles dealing with Indian affairs, an unprecedented level of coverage by the denominational newspaper. Associate editor Bill Portman had spent several months conducting research that only confirmed the conclusions of the "Centennial Profile." Marking the end of Canada's centennial year, he pointed out the "irony" invoked by native participation in the national celebration: "They dutifully donned buckskin to be displayed in Dominion Day parades and pageants—and then headed back to the ghettos created for them by the treaties they signed with representatives of the 'great white mother.'" Portman detailed the suffering caused by "benevolent despotism" but ended his lead article with an optimistic turn, noting that "educated, articulate, often bitter leaders and spokesmen have arisen from among the Indians themselves, demanding recognition of the needs and hopes of their people. There are indications that the whites in authority are listening." Additional articles by Portman and others explained the unique legal status of native people in Canada and described the "winds of change" blowing through the Department of Indian Affairs. In January 1968 the Anglican church joined six other denominations in supporting the publication of an Indian-Eskimo Association report, "Community Development Services for Canadian Indian and Métis Communities."[40]

Canadian society was passing through a period of rapid transformation but the Anglican bureaucracy took only cautious, deliberate steps toward

change. Denominational executives exchanged memos and attended committee meetings on what they informally termed the "Indian dialogue project,"
envisioning a comprehensive program of policy review, analysis, and reform;
they wanted the benefit of social scientific research before committing themselves to specific pilot projects in native community development. During the
summer of 1968 the newly formed Social Action Unit administered a survey of
Anglican clergy and lay ministers working among native people. They were
asked to answer a series of questions about their work and to identify "the
most pressing needs in Indian/Eskimo mission today." Fifty-one fieldworkers
responded to the inquiry, offering up a wide range of ethnographic facts and
opinions.[41]

In September church officials contacted Charles Hendry, director of the
School of Social Work at the University of Toronto, for advice on researchers
they might hire to study Anglican involvement with native people. He asked
for an extension of the deadline and then promptly accepted the project himself. Hendry was an ideal candidate for the task: a graduate of Union Theological Seminary in New York, an active member of the United Church of
Canada, and an internationally known expert in social work education with recent experience in field studies of community development projects in Latin
America. He had attended an interdenominational conference on poverty several months earlier, where he talked with a number of native leaders and "became acutely aware that the native people of Canada are in serious trouble."
Church officials presented him with their ministry surveys and other internal
documents, and he later told the *Canadian Churchman* he was "impressed with
the candor and forthrightness of the church's observations in the material provided for us. There was a minimum of defensiveness and a genuine awareness
that all is not well." He soon hired three research assistants and began work on
what came to be known simply as "the Hendry report."[42]

Hendry and his associates labored over the project for five months. They
completed a draft of the manuscript in early 1969 and submitted their findings to the executive task force overseeing the effort, who then hired a consultant to get feedback on the study from "a variety of concerned groups"
including Anglican clergy, government officials, and native leaders. "Indians
do not appear to want only the kind of help the church has offered in the
past," the task force later reported. "While some have welcomed the understanding of their attitude toward Church and State shown in the Hendry Report, because of history they are suspicious and reluctant to make
commitments until they are sure where the church stands in relation to their
immediate concerns such as their representations to the provincial and federal governments." Task force members concluded that "if the church really

means to get involved in a dialogue with the Indian people it will have to work with the issues which are important to Indians, not those which the church thinks are important for them."[43]

Hoping to stimulate wider debate over Hendry's findings and recommendations, Anglican church leaders also decided to release a paperback edition of the lengthy study. The *Canadian Churchman* devoted its May 1969 issue to the Hendry report, which was published in June under the title *Beyond Traplines: Does the Church Really Care?* A dozen articles, editorials, and excerpts introduced the book to Anglicans nationwide, preparing the way for its formal consideration at the twenty-fourth General Synod in August. Editor Hugh McCullum outlined the "hard-hitting" report in an extensive lead story, describing *Beyond Traplines* as a "carefully researched" study offering a "realistic and brutally honest" critique of both church and state. He also penned an editorial challenging the church to "get into the world as its founder did," fulfilling its role as "servant of the world" in pursuit of justice. Reminding his non-native readers of their historic "burden of guilt" and citing native statistics comprising "an arithmetic of shame," McCullum called for "political and social action at all levels on behalf of the oppressed natives of Canada." Ottawa-based correspondent Maurice Western, the newspaper's political commentator, offered a more cautious perspective on Hendry's "interesting" report. Claiming that the historic attitude of the Anglican church toward native people has been "essentially protective," Western wondered what a "program of political pressure" might entail. He urged church leaders to avoid "fashionable generalizations" and argued that "the Church should be very sure it has something specific and worthwhile to say" before meddling in the political process. Western found Hendry's view of power relations "unduly cynical," his approach to social change idealistic, and his social scientific jargon "depressing." Subsequent letters from *Canadian Churchman* readers furthered the debate over the Hendry report, which was also discussed in the mainstream press and on radio and television during the months leading up to General Synod.[44]

Beyond Traplines bore many similarities to John Melling's *Right to a Future* published a couple of years earlier, though Hendry's report was more narrowly focused on the Anglican church and more radical in its conclusions. Both books were titled to reflect their authors' progressive orientation, and both employed social scientific methods to uncover practical strategies for political involvement and community development, what Hendry termed an "action-oriented analysis." Like Melling's book, the first half of *Beyond Traplines* offered an overview of the situation by placing it in historical and political context. Hendry recognized that "within the church there has been a surge of

interest in intercultural problems," but he found that the bureaucratic response "suffered from two main defects: (1) a lack of clarity in the setting of
goals, which in turn leads to lack of clarity in talking about methods, and leads,
in fact, to a large amount of what the man-in-the-street might term blather
and doubletalk, and (2) a tendency to talk in generalities and to avoid specific
proposals for action." Hendry's study of community development had already
convinced him that "small piecemeal social-welfare programs are not enough
to make significant changes" in the problems experienced by native people.
"Only large-scale coordinated socio-economic planning and clearly-aimed,
vigorous action can succeed," and then only when the whole process is
"shaped by consensus in a back-and-forth dialogue of experts and people."[45]

The two books were marked by some important differences as well.
Where Melling had relied on official authorities and statistical data to generate his portrait of the native experience, Hendry made a conscious effort to incorporate the voices of local missionaries and native leaders in his narrative.
He was more aware of the limits of quantitative analysis in cross-cultural contexts, surmising that the native predicament "is of a type that escapes representation through numbers." Facts and figures on poverty, health, and
education often "succeed better in hiding the truth than in facilitating its
grasp" because they are based on ethnocentric assumptions about social existence; scientific inquiry is always a subjective project. "The truth of the matter
is that the present situation of our native people cannot be assessed simply by
quoting statistics or by using our own yardsticks. There are psychological and
cultural factors that cannot be measured. There are realities that we can grasp
only with the greatest effort of sympathetic imagination. To discuss the present situation simply in terms of social, economic or political indicators is an
artificial exercise in false categories." Hendry believed the native "situation"
was caused, first and foremost, by a conflict of "diametrically opposing value
systems." He predicted things would change only if non-native Canadians became conscious of the problem and abandoned their assimilationist heritage,
committing themselves to "perceiving, honouring and preserving the real life
values in any and every culture" in a genuinely pluralistic society. The "creative attitudes, relationships and policies" that Ted Scott had envisioned in his
preface to Melling's manuscript were more clearly delineated in Hendry's
probing, reflexive study.[46]

The second half of *Beyond Traplines* enumerated Hendry's ideas for Anglican activism on behalf of native people, a series of lists outlining a plan of action consistent with the principles of participatory democracy and the
philosophy of community development. His proposals were detailed, repeti-
tious, and mildly confusing at points, serving to undermine his own insistence

on clarity in institutional planning. Fortunately, Hendry's key points were not obscured, and two lists in particular proved to be influential in subsequent debates. Six "implications" for the Anglican church asserted that "the Church must listen to the native peoples," which means "developing a relationship of mutual respect, understanding, trust and helpfulness." Church leaders then must clarify goals, redefine roles, redeploy resources, revitalize ministry training, and commit themselves generally to "basic innovation." Nine final recommendations offered more specific proposals for institutional reform, though Hendry realized that "top priority must be directed to changes in basic attitudes, especially attitudes toward native peoples." He concluded that "the most fundamental need in this realignment of attitudes, which calls for an explicit reformulation of goals, is to find effective ways of respecting and releasing the resources of indigenous leadership."[47]

Anglican leaders formally approved the Hendry report for consideration at General Synod in August 1969, hoping it would persuade delegates to vote for new initiatives in native community development. Recent actions by the Canadian government had given even greater urgency to the need for reforming church policy. In March the Anglican church relinquished control over a dozen of its residential schools and promised to surrender its three remaining residential schools a year later. In June government officials released their belligerent "White Paper" proposing a policy designed to assimilate native individuals into mainstream society as rapidly as possible. The General Synod delegates from across Canada who gathered in Sudbury were aware of these and other controversies, and many were concerned about their institutional relationship to native communities. In the quarter-century since the Second World War, a complex transformation of values and behaviors—political, social, cultural, religious—had produced a dramatic, if incomplete, metamorphosis of the Anglican orientation toward native people.[48]

Among those who assembled on August 18 for the opening session of the gathering were eight native delegates, seven more than had been elected to participate in 1967; the native contingent included Mohawk delegate Ernest Benedict and his North American Indian Travelling College, which had been inspired by the 1967 unity convention and caravan. The third day of General Synod began with presentations by Dave Courchene, Ernie Willie, and Alanis Obomsawin, who challenged, coaxed, entertained, and otherwise moved their Anglican audience toward some type of favorable response. After lunch Adam Cuthand, a Cree priest from Winnipeg, rose to introduce a resolution concerning the Hendry report. He had been born and raised on the Little Pine Reserve and was one of the first students at the day school reopened by Edward Ahenakew; it was hard to miss the symbolic significance in Cuthand's presence at the national meeting. "This is the first time in the history of General Synod that native people have been allowed to express their own views," he told his fellow delegates. "You are in a position to help us improve our situation in God's changing world." The resolution gave "general approval to the recommendations of the Hendry Report" and directed church officials "to establish, in consultation with Native peoples, a program of development on the national level." This motion was seconded by Redfern Loutitt, a Cree priest from Moose Factory, and parliamentary debate yielded an amendment making the resolution even more emphatic, committing the Anglican church to "give due recognition" of native cultural traditions, to "speak clearly and directly at all times to all levels of government" on native issues, and to initiate native community development projects at the grassroots level "as soon as possible." The amended resolution passed by unanimous vote.[49]

The next item on the agenda was a resolution committing the church to ecumenical cooperation on global poverty and authorizing a national fundraising effort to support these and other projects in community development. After some debate over budgetary constraints and administrative responsibilities, it was eventually approved. Delegates then had their newfound enthusiasm for social change put to the test by an unscheduled resolution, which was moved by Ted Scott and seconded by Andrew Ahenakew. This resolution pledged support for the National Indian Brotherhood in its fight against the government's proposed policy changes, and for native treaty rights and land claims in general, and it directed the Anglican primate to communicate this position to the Canadian prime minister and other government officials. The resolution passed without amendment, and before the afternoon session ended General Synod had also considered resolutions addressing world hunger and industrial pollution.[50]

It had been a memorable day, possibly even a turning point in the history of the Anglican Church of Canada. Parallel developments were already under way within the Episcopal church, the Anglican communion in the U.S., which had resulted in the founding of a National Committee on Indian Work and a funding initiative called the General Convention Special Program. In Sudbury, native delegates and friends celebrated their accomplishments and quietly discussed their hopes and dreams as they shared an evening meal.[51]

CLERICAL ACTIVISTS

Many native leaders knew that one of their closest friends in the Anglican church was Ian MacKenzie, an energetic priest, educator, and organizer. He had studied psychology as an undergraduate at Dalhousie and earned his divinity degree at King's College, both universities in Halifax, Nova Scotia. In 1960 he moved down the Atlantic seaboard to New York City and enrolled at Union Theological Seminary. The influential Protestant institution occupies a city block in the Morningside Heights neighborhood of Manhattan, an imposing stone fortress situated between Columbia University to the south and Harlem to the north. Union had long been a bastion of liberal theology, ecumenical cooperation, and progressive politics, and during the fifties the seminary community had grown increasingly concerned about the abyss separating academic elites from the ghettoized underclass. Many had watched the Montgomery bus boycott from afar, but beginning in 1960 northern clerical activists were among those who traveled to the South to participate in nonviolent actions—sit-ins, freedom rides, marches, voter-registration drives—organized by the Southern Christian Leadership Conference, the Student Nonviolent Coordinating Committee, and the Congress of Racial Equality. The civil rights movement coincided with postwar ecumenical initiatives among mainline Protestants and Catholics; clergy already involved in these ventures appreciated the inclusive spirit of the movement. Martin Luther King, Jr., and other civil rights leaders welcomed the participation of the clerical activists, in part because their presence at demonstrations attracted media attention to these events.[52]

MacKenzie arrived at Union just as it was becoming a nerve center for northern Christian involvement in the African American struggle. During his four years at the seminary he worked with local organizations in Harlem and soaked up the redemptive ethos of the civil rights movement. He also studied theology, philosophy, and history, completing all requirements for the doctorate except the dissertation. In 1964 he recrossed the Canada-U.S. border to teach courses in race relations and conflict resolution at Trinity College in the University of Toronto. After a couple of months, he later recalled, he "realized there was something strange, something missing." Like Union, the Anglican seminary at Trinity had been producing liberal, progressive clergy since the early forties. It was still, however, a school that represented "the epitome of Anglo-Saxon traditions," and MacKenzie concluded that he felt out of place because he had been "acculturated" to the human diversity of the civil rights movement, leaving him "culturally deprived" at Trinity. Casting about for some organization that might provide him with a community of interest and an outlet for his activist energies, he eventually discovered the Indian-Eskimo Association of Canada.[53]

By his own admission, MacKenzie knew virtually nothing about native issues at the time; indeed, he had met only one native person in the first three decades of his life. He soon found himself appointed to a planning committee that established the Association's Ontario Division, and the months that followed were a crash course in Indian affairs. The Association was already heavily involved in supporting native legal rights and political self-determination. In 1965 MacKenzie attended its annual meeting in Kenora, where he joined other native and non-native activists in investigating the racial discrimination practiced by local businesses, prompting a landmark nonviolent protest march by four hundred native residents several days later. In 1966 he served as faculty advisor for the Trinity College Conference on the Canadian Indian, which brought together more than fifty native leaders from across Canada and allowed them to control the conference proceedings. In 1968 he invited Bob Thomas to be the keynote speaker for the Ontario Division's annual meeting, at which MacKenzie was elected president on a ticket with two native leaders. He had become a prolific advocate for native issues, speaking and writing to non-native audiences on a regular basis.[54]

In January 1969, for example, the Association published a short essay by MacKenzie on the relationship between native people and non-native religion in the context of "the Red Power issue." Disputing claims by some progressives that native people had rejected Christianity, he argued that they "seem to make a very clear distinction between the essence of that religion designated as Christianity and the institutional church." The churches "continue to function as colonial powers" in native communities, especially in remote northern outposts. "It is the institutional church, with its failure to practice its own teachings, which the Indians reject, not the basis of the teachings themselves, which for the most part Indians live despite the institutional churches." Could it be that native people were "the only true Christians?" MacKenzie asked. He joined a rising chorus of native voices by challenging the churches to "recognize the demonic elements of their own institutional life," to become "prophetic critics of the culture in which they live," and to "begin to learn something about how to live their own religion from Indians."[55]

Several weeks later Charles Hendry submitted his report to the Anglican church on its relationship with native people. In March church executives retained Ian MacKenzie's services as a consultant in community development, asking him to "test the points raised by Dr. Hendry's Report" before they presented it to General Synod in August. MacKenzie proceeded to organize some twenty consultations with various constituencies across Canada, soliciting their feedback on the draft manuscript. He summarized his findings and offered his own assessment of the situation in an article published by the *Canadian Churchman* as part of its May 1969 issue devoted to the Hendry report.[56]

Though many Anglicans could appreciate the need for structural changes in the relationship between native communities and non-native institutions, few were as perceptive as MacKenzie in recognizing the more basic challenges that characterize cross-cultural engagement. "The Canadian church should welcome the report," he began, because it details the dominant culture's failure to understand "the underlying modes of thought, styles of life, and values of native communities. Recognition of these differences is essential for any significant change in Indian–non-Indian relations." He then zeroed in on this point, explaining how cultural difference manifests itself in colonial contexts. "Dr. Hendry urges that the churches must listen to Indians. But will we hear them? For hearing them demands that we examine certain fundamental questions about the nature of Christianity." MacKenzie considered this to be "a time of crisis for the Indian people" and issued a bracing ultimatum: "The churches must decide where they stand. We either support Indian organizations and enter into a partnership with them on their terms or we will end up fighting them. For Indians have now organized themselves and they see the challenges and the problems. They will break the control of all white institutions on their own people eventually." Picking up on themes he had been sounding as a spokesman for the Indian-Eskimo Association, he invited his Anglican readers to work for "a change in our perspective and role" and to envision a future "radically altered for Indians and for our understanding of ourselves" as well. "We can go on as before, or we can respond to the challenges of the Hendry report and to the wishes of the native peoples."[57]

Ian MacKenzie, Ted Scott, and other clerical activists within the Anglican church represented a Canadian expression of the broad trend that Michael B. Friedland documents in *Lift Up Your Voice Like a Trumpet: White Clergy and the Civil Rights and Antiwar Movements, 1954–1973.* The title phrase is from the biblical book of Isaiah, invoking a passage in which the Hebrew prophet rebukes his own people for making pietistic sacrifices while ignoring social inequities. "In the day of your fast you seek your own pleasure, and oppress all your workers," the narrator announces, when it should be Israel's desire "to loose the bonds of wickedness, to undo the thongs of the yoke, to let the oppressed go free, and to break every yoke," not "to hide yourself from your own flesh."[58]

As Friedland suggests, this kind of reflexive critique is easier for clergy who are not directly involved in parish ministry. "Those who were able to devote much of their energies to social activism" during the sixties and seventies "tended to come from positions where they were not subject to pressure from the laity and had more freedom (and job security): bishops or other members of the denominational hierarchy, administrators, seminarians or the faculty of divinity schools, and campus chaplains." Like the biblical prophets of old, northern clerical activists who cast their lot with the direct-action protests that began in 1960 did so as individuals. Religious bodies in the U.S. occasionally passed resolutions endorsing nonviolent struggle but did not become actively involved in the civil rights movement until 1963, when Protestants, Catholics, and Jews joined forces at the National Conference on Religion and Race, a historic gathering held in Chicago on the centennial of the Emancipation Proclamation. "In the end," Friedland concludes, "it was not the degree of success, or lack of it, that made the clerical activists noteworthy; nor was it their numbers, which were small; nor their influence, which was limited. What made these individuals important in both religious and historical terms was their very act of witness, their willingness and determination to back up their religious convictions with action."[59]

Ian MacKenzie helped Anglican leaders choreograph the program for the 1969 General Synod, and he was on hand in August when delegates approved resolutions calling for sweeping changes in government and church policies toward native people and allocating major funding to support native self-determination. Encouraged by these remarkable developments, he returned to Toronto and his office at the Institute for Indian Studies on the seventeenth floor of Rochdale College. He was soon joined by his friend Bob Thomas and they "spent a number of days together," MacKenzie later recalled. "We spent most of our time discussing issues posed by religious divisions in Native communities, divisions between Christians and divisions between Christians and traditional Native religion." Hoping to capitalize on the Anglican church's newfound commitment to native community development, they began drafting a proposal for an ecumenical gathering of tribal religious leaders. The Institute for Indian Studies, a "secular non-religious organization" housed in North America's most notorious free university, would serve as the administrative center for their project, another curious circumstance of this new venture in ecumenical intertribal organizing.[60]

In the nineteenth century tens of thousands of Americans took a negative view of what they saw around them: an evil world. Then they took a positive step in response to its evils. They left traditional society and set out for a colony in an isolated area where they hoped to insulate themselves from its corrupt values. Even today countless people look for that same road, and as we know from stories that sometimes make headlines, some still travel down it.

Seymour R. Kesten, *Utopian Episodes*

Literacy has done more damage in the world than the people who functioned without literacy, and certainly along with literacy we have something called "civilization," which is to me a very bad word. I think that some things have to go if we're going to do anything about saving the world, and I think that literacy has to go. That's definitely my feeling.

Wilf Pelletier, Institute for Indian Studies

CHAPTER FOUR

"ABOUT SAVING THE WORLD"

DISSONANT RHYTHMS OF FOLK GUITAR, ACID ROCK, and the occasional burst of tribal drumming echoed through the halls and down the stairwells of Toronto's newest high-rise. Paying residents and their guests intermingled with transient bodies in the commotion of the first-floor lobby, a kinetic response to the psychedelic murals covering the walls. University students, young couples with small children, middle-aged eccentrics, and a few elderly pensioners milled around the elevators, reading the latest graffiti and waiting for a vertical trip home. The doors finally opened with a rush of air, disgorging passengers and the smell of human habitation. Quickly filled to capacity, the car began its ascent back up the unlit shaft, bearing its colorful load and more than a hint of exotic homegrown and other combustible herbs.[1]

Like most common areas in the building, the seventeenth-floor lounge of this high-density residence was a hodgepodge of humanity, an inharmonic convergence of sorts. Tribal people dressed like hippies, and a few hippies costumed as Hollywood Indians, passed the time and enjoyed their bird's-eye view of the metropolis below. Rochdale College was nothing if not a tribal community, so many believed, and nowhere more so than here on the seventeenth floor, sovereign territory of the Institute for Indian Studies. It was late in August 1969; the Institute had been founded less than two years earlier as an intertribal collective devoted to educational activism, and a couple dozen young people also called these new premises home. The world looked a little less threatening, and perhaps a little easier to save, from this lofty perch in the sky. Utopian and messianic pretensions notwithstanding, it was as good a place as any for civilization's discontents to plot the demise of the secular city.[2]

Bob Thomas and Ian MacKenzie were hunkered down in the Institute's cramped office, the converted living room of a one-bedroom apartment. MacKenzie had just returned home from General Synod, Thomas had driven up from the U.S., and now they and a few local native leaders were discussing various community development projects they might pitch to public and private funding agencies. "Since the Anglican Church of Canada had just committed itself to new directions," MacKenzie later recalled, "we figured we might as well ask it to finance our proposal to hold a major meeting of Native religious leaders." The idea for such a gathering had emerged from MacKenzie's consultations on the Hendry report, and Thomas was happy to endorse an alternative to the traditional movement. He took the lead in drafting a proposal: "Religious strife and turmoil is rampant in Indian communities," it read. "The need for an Indian 'ecumenical' conference is uppermost in the minds of many Indian leaders. Native Indian religionists, of all Christian and aboriginal sects, must assemble and begin the painful process of conceptually sewing together their fragmented sacred world, so Indians can once again take steps to act for their own future welfare."[3]

"A tribe is not just a collection of individuals," Thomas wrote, belying Rochdale's nonconformist ethos. "It is a wholistic, mutually agreed on system of consistent values. When it is fragmented by religious strife it becomes inoperative and the community must attend only to the problem of fragmentation." He and MacKenzie were asking the Anglican church to address "this difficult and urgent dilemma," a situation it had helped create, by enabling them to initiate a process of healing in tribal communities. They challenged Canada's Anglicans to demonstrate their newfound compassion for native people by freeing up financial resources, and to do so on native terms. Seated at the built-in desk of the Institute's "Aphrodite" suite—other Rochdale residential units were named for Zeus, Franz Kafka, the Gnostics, and India's ashrams—they explained why tribal self-determination "must proceed from the sacred. For the Indian there is no distinction between the sacred and the secular, the religious and the political. Secular activity is simply an activity from which an essential ingredient is missing—the sacred." A stray dog barked in the corridor.[4]

"For obvious political reasons," Bob Thomas and Ian MacKenzie argued, "no religious organization can sponsor such a conference. It must be done by a secular nonreligious organization such as the Institute for Indian Studies." Still, Rochdale College was a rather strange place from which to administer an intertribal gathering of grassroots spiritual dignitaries. This urban monolith next to the University of Toronto was the epitome of adolescent excess, with its thick shag hallway carpet and orange striped drapery, its bright trim painted orange and yellow and green, its green and purple elevator doors, its public washrooms labeled "Chicks" and "Cats." The interior walls were originally covered by an off-white color named "elephant tusk," an ironic hue that served only as canvas for this educational experiment that envisioned itself an anti–ivory tower. Many Rochdalians championed the apparent compatibility between their counterculture and tribal communities, especially when forced to surrender control over the property to government authorities several years later, but the identification was tenuous at best. "Literacy has done more damage in the world than the people who functioned without literacy," Institute director Wilf Pelletier remarked in an interview, "and certainly along with literacy we have something called 'civilization,' which is to me a very bad word. I think that some things have to go if we're going to do anything about saving the world, and I think that literacy has to go. That's definitely my feeling." It was a curious comment for an educational administrator to make, underscoring the cultural complexities of social transformation.[5]

ROCHDALE COLLEGE

The first housing cooperative at the University of Toronto was organized in the late 1930s when a divinity student persuaded several friends to pool their resources and found Campus Co-operative Residences. Their collectivist venture proved to be an economical alternative to university-owned facilities, and two decades later the organization had a hundred members living in five ramshackle buildings scattered around campus. By the late fifties it was clear that the shortage of affordable housing in Toronto would soon be exacerbated by a surge in student enrollment as the baby-boom generation reached college age. Led by Howard Adelman, an energetic nineteen-year-old entrepreneur, the Cooperative addressed this impending crisis by embarking on an ambitious program of modernization and expansion. Army surplus bedding was replaced by spring mattresses, ice boxes gave way to refrigerators, and the Cooperative's accumulated equity served as collateral for the acquisition of additional properties.[6]

Several years later the Cooperative owned seventeen houses and leased six others, with more than two hundred voting members on the rolls. This new generation of students constituted a demographic shift in more ways than one; besides their numerical strength, they brought with them new expectations for the university experience. By the mid-sixties Toronto student activists were meeting on a regular basis to discuss the educational system, which they found to be largely irrelevant in an era of rapid social change.

Participants in this informal "education seminar," many of whom were also Co-op members, wondered if it might be possible to add an educational dimension to residential life as a way of compensating for the university's failings. Co-op leaders were simultaneously plotting their first attempt at new construction, a high-rise apartment building on the northern edge of campus. These separate developments soon merged into a vision for an alternative educational institution; both groups recognized the potential for extending the cooperative model to the educational process itself, and plans for a "free university" quickly took shape. Rochdale College was born.[7]

These utopian rebels took their name—and no small measure of inspiration—from the Rochdale Society of Equitable Pioneers, a cooperative commissary organized in 1844 by textile workers in Rochdale, Lancashire. It was one of the first cooperatives in the British Isles and a successful one at that, able to provide its members with affordable staples as well as educational opportunities, cultural diversions, and other valuable services. The Rochdalians of Toronto elected their first governing council in April 1966, and several months later participants in the education seminar circulated their proposal for a "Rochdale College Education Project." They envisioned a "democratic and community oriented" school where "individuals and groups of people can create their own educational experiences" relevant to those involved and to society: "It will not be an ivory tower, but will be intimately involved with its larger community." As an unstructured "centre of intellectual activity," the College "will not offer a curriculum but will provide resources—staff, physical facilities and residence space—so that people who want to study or develop programs that cannot be undertaken elsewhere," especially those of an "experimental or unrecognized nature," can "find an intellectual base in Rochdale." The College would be staffed by individuals with "recognized critical intellectual abilities" and the capacity to "work with students in a free manner," scholars who "consider themselves as much students with questions to answer as teachers with knowledge to impart." Educational activities would include individualized exploration as well as "common interest groupings: seminars, study groups, research projects, study-research-action projects and workshops," with special attention to the educational experience itself, "not only as an object of study, but as a subject of day-to-day concern." Co-op members who chose to participate in the education project would elect an education council, which would work in tandem with the College's governing council.[8]

Interest in the fledgling institution and its experimental agenda increased with the opening of the 1966–67 academic year, especially after construction crews broke ground on the new building later that fall. The first edition of the *Rochdale College Bulletin* appeared in December 1966, offering itself as a vehicle for criticism of "the existing higher education system" and as a forum for discussion of "visionary alternatives to that system." The lead editorial admitted the venture faced some daunting logistical challenges: an eighteen-story residence housing 850 people in the middle of Toronto "could well become an unmitigated disaster of a magnitude never before perpetuated upon students in this country," and "it is also possible that the unstructured approach to education could be a flop." The editors then offered their answer to the obvious question: "Why Rochdale? In this place and at this time?" The intersection of Bloor and Huron streets "is an ugly corner of an ugly city," but "we say it is futile to retreat into an isolated 'community of scholars' if people want to live freely in this society and change the society to suit their desires." Unlike most utopian episodes in North American history, the Rochdalians were not willing to "go off into the hills," believing "the best place to establish an educational institution that aims to be a place where people can rise above the depersonalized, atomized, super-efficient technological and largely meaningless society is right in the thick of the whole mess."[9]

By the spring of 1967, Rochdale College had taken on a life of its own and become a source of tension within the Cooperative, whose other projects and constituencies were increasingly overshadowed by this high-spirited upstart. In March Co-op leaders called a general meeting, where the membership voted to make Rochdale an independent organization. Several months later the provincial government issued a charter to the new college, and the federal government agreed to provide financial support for a trial year of its educational program. This sizeable grant from the Company of Young Canadians, a social service agency established in 1966 to fund community development projects led by volunteer youth, allowed Rochdale to hire two full-time "resource persons" for the 1967–68 academic year: Dennis Lee and Ian MacKenzie.[10]

Lee, an aspiring poet, had completed B.A. and M.A. degrees at the University of Toronto. It was in the midst of a graduate seminar that he experienced a strange epiphany, a "sense of utter estrangement as I wound my way through the realization that what they were saying had no purchase on me, that the experience of being in that seminar was without meaning for me, that doing graduate work had not become real, and that my entire undergraduate and high school education had been mainly a sham." He stayed on after graduation to teach English literature and "collaborated again and again" with the system during those three years, "mainly I guess from baffled timidity, but also from sheer disbelief." Shortly before leaving the cloistered pretense of Victoria College he cofounded House of Anansi Press and published his first collection of poems, *Kingdom of Absence*. MacKenzie came to the Rochdale experiment from Trinity College, where he had been a lecturer in race relations and conflict resolution for three years. He had also involved himself in the struggle for native rights since returning to Canada from New York City, providing leadership for the Indian-Eskimo Association, the Canadian Indian Youth Workshop, and the Trinity College Conference on the Canadian Indian. Lee and MacKenzie shared a sense of profound dissatisfaction with the university system, and both were active participants in the education seminar that gave birth to the idea for a free university in Toronto.[11]

Work progressed on the new building but it would not be finished for another year, so the College entered a trial phase by renting a few of the Cooperative's properties, which were dubbed "the Rochdale Houses." Lee and MacKenzie marked the opening of the 1967–68 academic year by issuing the inaugural *Rochdale College Calendar*, detailing the school's philosophy, organization, history, and "seminar proposals." Lee offered to facilitate groups in literature and creative writing, MacKenzie proposed several topics in religion and social change, and various part-time resource persons suggested other provocative subjects. Programmatic initiatives emerged from the grass roots as well. In the winter of 1967–68 a half-dozen Rochdale mothers organized a cooperative nursery to provide a "non-authoritarian, non-competitive, and individually creative" environment for socializing their preschoolers; Lee's wife, Donna, coordinated this "Garden of Children." Although several women were elected to the College's twelve-person governing council during the year, nearly all of the twenty-three academic staff listed in the *Calendar* were male. An in-house newsletter called *Anything but Son of Rochdale* also circulated during this period. "We have reopened almost every question, every assumption that underlies the going versions of education," Dennis Lee wrote in the spring of 1968, though it is not clear how many Rochdale coeds shared his exuberant myopia. "Every item of human knowledge is the result of a decision to ask a specific question, to ask it in a specific way, or to welcome and endure the pathless necessities which bear in on us, or recede from us, when we admit that we do not know what question to ask at all."[12]

By the end of the academic year more than 150 members had joined the College, half of whom were living in the Rochdale Houses. It had been a rough year for Lee and MacKenzie as each struggled through the transition from university lecturer to college resource person. Lee found himself "exhausted, confused, and stubbornly heartened" by the experience, surprised that "the dangerous and liberating attempt to claim our own freedom" turned out to be "a process which takes more time, more confusion, and more turmoil than I had known." He was also struck by "the disparity between the rhetoric of freedom and openness and the reality of several dozen people doing their halting, semi-competent best to find their ways ahead," observing that "the staying-power required to keep with it during the spells of drudgery, dryness, and anxiety or bitterness is an attribute that has relatively little to do with an understanding of many of the ideals which were bandied about loosely during our founding." He summarized his year in more succinct terms: "It has been hell; we haven't accomplished much; I don't want to be anywhere else."[13]

MacKenzie described it as "a very traumatic experience" that forced him to reformulate his "own goals, ambitions and desires in a new way." Quickly discovering he was "far more conditioned to respond in traditional ways" than he thought, he found that "coming to grips with life in a situation where all the external structures have been removed was a painful, and at times frightening, experience." He spent much of the year worrying about organizational structure and finances but was heartened by the opportunity to "examine fundamental problems of human existence" through interpersonal dialogue free from institutional constraints. "When a group of people get together and make only one commitment to each other, which is, to meet regularly at stated times to discuss whatever they feel like talking about at that time," then "things begin to happen which have a total effect upon one's life."[14]

In 1968 House of Anansi Press published *The University Game*, an anthology of essays addressing the degeneration of Western intellectual life. Editors Howard Adelman and Dennis Lee along with seven like-minded academics offered "post-rebellious" critiques of the "multiversity," as the bureaucratized manifestation of North American higher education had been labeled by a prominent university president in the U.S. The book might have heralded a new age of liberal education in the rise of the free university movement, but its publication coincided with a critical moment in the Rochdale experiment.[15]

A three-month labor strike had put the construction project considerably behind schedule, jeopardizing the planned opening of the new building for the 1968–69 academic year. The College could have remained in the Rochdale Houses for another year, but most of the leaders wanted to capitalize on the momentum of the education project and voted to stick to their original timetable. Convinced that the College's precarious financial situation doomed it to failure, Adelman resigned in the spring of 1968. That summer, Rochdale staff received several thousand applications for 850 vacancies in the high-rise. Only ten floors were even marginally habitable at the beginning of the fall term in September, when the governing council made the fateful decision to begin occupying the building immediately and to bring in additional residents as new space opened up. Many of the Toronto-area university students who had planned to live at Rochdale had by then found other accommodations, so the College began admitting non-students to fill vacant space and generate rental income. Among these new recruits were "hoopies" and other social outcasts from the nearby neighborhood of Yorkville, "Haight-Ashbury North," heart of the counterculture in late-sixties Toronto. Oxbridge met Nirvana as liberal intellectuals and bohemian dropouts found themselves living under the same roof. The life of the mind ran into altered states of consciousness, a head-on collision at the intersection of Bloor and Huron.[16]

The new Rochdale presented an enormous logistical dilemma. Moving their unconventional organization into a building still under construction while undergoing a tenfold increase in population, College leaders struggled to assimilate these motley boomers. "The kind of responsibility we ask of our members is awesome," began the *Rochdale College Catalogue* issued in September 1968: "plan your own courses, seek your own evaluations, keep your room clean, make college policy. If you are interested, read on." What followed was little more than a statement of faith, offered in the hope of fostering devotion in the hearts and minds of these new residents. "Education at Rochdale is directed towards the re-opening of fundamental questions: What is important to know? What is the best way of learning it? How does academic knowledge relate to other kinds of knowing? How can the search for knowledge be humanely and fruitfully carried on within an institution?" The *Catalogue* went on to list an expanded roster of resource persons, seminar proposals, extracurricular activities, and affiliated organizations available to College members. Rochdale initiates also were reminded that "the responsibility of members is not merely to plan what they wish to study with and how to go about it. They assume also the burden of the whole institution—residence and school. Members often find that utopian schemes are tempered by the necessity of dealing wisely and inventively with the repetitive problem of meat and potatoes." Foreshadowing tensions that would rack the organization in coming months, the *Catalogue* concluded with a distinctly Rochdalian admonition: "The secret of dealing with the confusion and uncertainty of Rochdale is to use 'we' in place of 'they' when referring to the operations of the College. For example, say 'what are we going to do with the 17th floor terrace' rather than 'what are they going to do,' etc. This simple trick clarifies many otherwise ambiguous problems and helps eliminate bureaucratic flatulence."[17]

The opening of the new building attracted press coverage during the fall of 1968; what had been a largely local phenomenon now drew the attention of national media outlets in Canada and the U.S. On the first Sunday in November the *New York Times* ran a story profiling Rochdale's "experiment in communal living and deliberately unorganized education." The newspaper's Toronto correspondent briefly described the academic program of this adolescent "anti-institution" but otherwise focused on the College's unconventional living arrangements, which fostered sexual "promiscuity," recreational drug use, and religious experimentation. "This business of putting girls and fellows together is not such a good idea," explained one resident, a nineteen-year-old judge's daughter studying secretarial science at another Toronto-area school. "So many kids are wild in this atmosphere," she complained, "and not interested in their appearance." Most of her neighbors "don't seem to be very ambitious," neglecting their studies in favor of "wild parties, everybody invited, lots of liquor." Another disgruntled tenant found the noisy environment distracting and observed that "a lot of kids seem high all the time."[18]

Later that month *Newsweek* published a similar account of this "intentionally mixed bag of radicals, revolutionaries, hippies, and fairly straight people." The newsmagazine was more sympathetic toward Rochdale as "a showplace for their utopian ideas about learning" and produced a more balanced portrait of life in the unorthodox high-rise, though an accompanying photograph offered a suggestive side view of a nude model in a Rochdale art class. *Newsweek* also found a more reputable detractor than did the *New York Times*, quoting "Toronto's most famous educator," communications theorist Marshall McLuhan. "Rochdale has all the makings of a utopian flop," he announced. "They're all hurrying backward into the past as fast as they can go." A feature article in the *Canadian Churchman* presented a more optimistic assessment of the College, praising this adventure in "living and learning" for its cooperative approach to every aspect of residential life and of the educational process.[19]

Many Rochdale members considered these and other sensationalisms to be so much journalistic flatulence. Moralists were quick to condemn the new building's atmosphere of sexual freedom, for example, ignoring the fact that Rochdale was also the only university residence hall in Toronto offering accommodations for married students. Social problems did surface shortly after the building opened but remained a minor annoyance, at least until news reports depicted Rochdale as a "hippie college." As one College president later put it, "the promotion of these conditions as being the norm at Rochdale served only to attract those who would perpetuate and increase these very problems." The underground press joined the mainstream media in hyping this high-rise commune as a sanctuary above the law. The College achieved special notoriety on the U.S. side of the border when the Toronto Anti-Draft Programme published its *Manual for Draft-Age Immigrants to Canada*, listing Rochdale as a good place for dodgers, deserters, and other peaceniks to wait out the Vietnam War.[20]

The first year of life in this anti–ivory tower proved to be a challenging experience for everyone involved. The practical demands of daily survival cast a long shadow over the utopian aspirations that had drawn many initial occupants of the concrete-and-glass skyscraper some called "The Rock." All residents had to cope with the noise and dust of an active construction site, an influx of transients who crashed wherever they found space, and a growing commerce in hard drugs managed by Toronto's leading motorcycle gangs. College leaders endured constant criticism from paying tenants over these and other problems while struggling to set up a functional administrative structure, reduce the high turnover rate in rental units, and meet their monthly mortgage payments. Internal conflict bred discord and insolvency; factionalism stalked the hallways and financial crisis lurked outside the lobby doors through the cold winter of 1968–69. After six months of turmoil the governing council was finally impeached, and Rochdale leadership took an authoritarian turn. The new administration managed to restore civil order and stave off foreclosure, but the year had taken a heavy toll on the intellectual life of the College.[21]

If there was one neighborhood of this vertical village that thrived amidst utopian chaos, it was the artistic community. Rochdale students who wanted to express their creative energies could choose from a variety of workshops in film, photography, design, fine art, writing, and publishing, and they could also join performance groups in theater and music. The College was "a fever of creative and artistic effort," as one observer put it, and much of this feverish output was offered for sale at the Rochdale boutique. Aside from the building itself, the most durable physical artifact of the Rochdale experience was a massive monument installed on the sidewalk plaza at the corner of Bloor and Huron. In April 1969 members of the sculpture workshop unveiled the result of their first major project, a collaborative effort titled "The Unknown Student." Designed by a draft dodger from Indiana, this semiabstract, bronze-colored statue depicted a solitary youth: faceless, neuter, and larger than life-size. The *Toronto Telegram* reported that "visitors have noted how the sculpture—a beefy humanoid body sitting yoga style with its head tucked down—characterizes Rochdale. It exudes innocence simultaneously with strength, is large and a trifle mysterious." Perhaps even more symbolic was the statue's orientation, having been positioned on its concrete pedestal with its back to the street, a striking artistic statement signifying Rochdale's attitude toward "straight" society.[22]

The memorable edifice has long been a cornerstone of North American colonization, a favored strategy among the continent's real estate developers, utopian and otherwise. The European prophets of nineteenth-century utopianism "captivated the movement with grandiose architectural visions. The basic social unit they saw in their imaginations consisted of a huge palace-like building," large enough to "house living quarters, industrial shops, schools, and cultural facilities, all under one roof." In this "carefully planned urban environment people would live, work, and enjoy themselves." Seymour R. Kesten considers the dreams and failures of this diffuse movement in *Utopian Episodes*. "In the nineteenth century tens of thousands of Americans took a negative view of what they saw around them: an evil world. Then they took a positive step in response to its evils. They left traditional society and set out for a colony in an isolated area where they hoped to insulate themselves from its corrupt values. Even today countless people look for that same road, and as we know from stories that sometimes make headlines, some still travel down it." The Rochdalians of Toronto fled up rather than out, though their architectural choices still expressed an ideological consensus, as had been the case among their utopian forebears. "The whole construction is, after all, nothing other than a citadel," Kesten writes. "The walls did three things: they separated the enclave from evil; they created a barrier that encouraged isolation; and they helped turn the members' focus inward to their utopian refuge, away from the 'outside world.'" The navel-gazing pose and backward position of "The Unknown Student" spoke volumes about these latter-day architects of North American utopianism.[23]

Kesten's book is a useful study despite his disregard for the imperial implications of westward migration; indeed, native people appear only twice in his colonialist narrative, as obstacle to utopian settlement and as object of utopian benevolence. Its subtitle, *Daily Life in Experimental Colonies Dedicated to Changing the World*, signals the two important contributions this book makes to the academic debate over utopian communities. Many scholars have been impressed by the longevity of certain groups, crediting their relative success to the religious homogeneity enforced within these communities: the Shakers, the Amana colonies, and other sects that have preached a gospel of personal sin and individual salvation. Kesten turns his attention to what he calls "the movement for social reorganization," a loose coalition of groups who shared the conviction that suffering and deliverance are social phenomena. "Religion played an important role in the colonies of social reorganization," he points out, "but with a key distinction." Judeo-Christian pluralism was normative in these settlements, and Kesten explores this inflection of the utopian impulse through a close reading of everyday life. "As we look into the religious life of the movement, a picture emerges of devout leaders, members, and sympathizers and of sacred observances and services in the colonies typical of their time and place." The leadership of nearly all these colonies included Protestant clergy, but ones who generally refrained from theocratic vanity. "Most of the colonies dedicated to social reorganization had guarantees of tolerance in their constitutions," and "with no established creed and no imposed ecclesiastical forms, members had the freedom to worship according to their own beliefs."[24]

If these utopian communities held a common belief in any human activity, it was education. "People in the movement placed all their faith in it" as the key to a better society, particularly Robert Owen, the British industrialist and social theorist who inspired the founding of the Rochdale Society of Equitable Pioneers. Nineteenth-century families were drawn to the colonies of social re-organization by the promise of tuition-free schools, just as young people a century later entered Rochdale College for the opportunity to learn in a bu-reaucracy-free environment. If the Rochdalians of Toronto would be no more successful at transforming society than their utopian predecessors had been, it was not for the lack of a compelling vision but of the maturity to translate this vision into the language of daily life. In the fall of 1968 Dennis Lee had pro-posed a reading seminar on "Free School Education," hoping to review the lit-erature on utopian communities, sociological theory, progressive politics, and the history of alternative education. "The free school experience elsewhere needs to be understood," he had warned after his first year as a resource per-son, "and taken very seriously in any new experiment such as Rochdale." Toronto's utopian college might have lasted longer if more of its students had enrolled in Lee's seminar.[25]

INDIAN STUDIES

The site of present-day Toronto has long been a meeting place for native people. Hurons, Mohawks, Mississaugas, and others appreciated the natural abundance of this area, which served as a focal point for settlement, exchange, and spiritual renewal, and early colonial documents attest to the region's im-portance in the expanding fur trade. One popular legend maintains that the city's name is a native-language expression that translates to "the meeting place," an appropriate designation even if it is based on flimsy linguistic evi-dence and map transcription errors. Urban growth displaced tribal communi-ties during the nineteenth century and native people were rendered a mythic presence in modern Toronto, appearing on the city's coat of arms but not on its streets.[26]

Native people began returning to the Toronto area during the first half of the twentieth century. Arriving as individuals and families in search of educa-tional and vocational opportunities, many found refuge during the twenties and thirties at the home of Minnie and George Jamieson, who were them-selves recent arrivals from the Six Nations Reserve on the Grand River. The Jamieson family welcomed tribal expatriates from near and far, engendering community in the midst of the bustling metropolis. This intertribal fellowship was formalized in 1950 with the founding of the Indian Friendship Club, which gathered in the home of Millie Redmond several times before moving its weekly socials to a meeting room at the downtown YMCA. The Club's first major service project involved visiting native people who were hospitalized in a nearby sanatorium. By the early sixties Club leaders recognized the need for a full-time agency to serve their growing urban community, and in 1963 the Canadian Indian Centre of Toronto opened its doors. It was one of the first such organizations in Canada, preceded only by the Native Friendship Centres established in Vancouver and Winnipeg several years earlier. The Toronto Centre made social service referrals, organized clothing drives for northern reserves, held fundraising events, arranged support groups, and offered "a homey atmosphere" to anyone who dropped by. Volunteers also taught Ojibway language classes and built floats for the Grey Cup parade, seemingly incongruous activities united by a desire to compensate for the failings of the dominant educational system.[27]

Presiding over the Centre's opening ceremonies in the spring of 1963 was Wilf Pelletier, an Odawa from Manitoulin Island and president of the Toronto Indian Club. He had been raised on and around the Wikwemikong Reserve at a time when this tribal community was experiencing the agonizing transition from subsistence economy to wage labor, from extended family to welfare state, from cooperation to competition. Pelletier's family moved around quite a bit and he managed to avoid the trauma of residential school, though the public and parochial institutions he did attend were bad enough.[28]

"School was a crazy experience for me," Pelletier later recalled. "The reserve school was not really a school at all, it was a correctional institution. Indians had to be turned into nice, obedient, English-speaking copies of white children before they could be taught anything." He and his reluctant classmates were "confronted with masses of departmentalized information *about* the world, about nature. You were trapped between the teacher and a wall of abstractions. Beyond that wall lay the real world, the material world, always waiting, beckoning to you, and there wasn't supposed to be any way of getting back to it except by working. You were supposed to attack the wall, subdue the information, master it by taking it all apart and putting it together again." Pelletier preferred listening to the stories told by his grandfather and other village elders; "the only thing I can remember that I really liked about school was when the teacher would read us a story." He eventually concluded "the object of that whole system is to bring about a displacement," and to do so in a way that varied according to the cultural background of the student: "For whites, school is the accepted passage from childhood to adult status. For Indians, it's a big detour that takes you out of reality, out of life." Pelletier played a lot of hooky and quit altogether after his family moved to Sault Ste. Marie during the war, convinced that "schools stand in the way of life and learning."[29]

The teenage dropout passed his time in pool halls and bowling alleys. He also tried his hand at various blue-collar professions including several stints as a hunting guide, "baby-sitting" primitivist clients hoping to get in touch with their inner warriors. He later managed and then owned several businesses, outwardly successful but inwardly confused as "an Indian trying to make it in the white man's world." His ambition and insecurity grew to the point that he changed the spelling of his family name, Peltier, adding two letters to give it a more Francophone ring, thinking "that's what I'll become: French." But Pelletier soon learned that this ethnic graft failed to resolve his existential dilemma. The Odawa businessman felt "split or torn, trying to be two people," living a "double life" that nearly killed him. He finally bailed out of the capitalist ship and went home to Manitoulin Island.[30]

After a two-year recuperation he moved his young family to Toronto, where he worked at odd jobs and resolved "to make it as Wilf Pelletier, Indian." He also joined the Toronto Indian Club and applied his entrepreneurial skills to "becoming an Indian. That's a pretty crazy trip," he later realized. "How can you become something or someone when that's what you are already? I didn't know I was doing that, but I had the idea that in order to be Indian you had to know all about Indians everywhere and you had to be able to do all the things that Indians do." He also began teaching classes in powwow dancing "because I thought Indians in the city should be occupied with Indian activities. I guess the people in that Indian club weren't becoming Indian fast enough to suit me. I really didn't know anything about Indian dancing, except I'd been to a couple of powwows, but I went ahead anyway. Well, it caught on and everyone was into making costumes and practicing dancing." These involvements brought Pelletier his first contact with liberal reformers, who persuaded him to focus his charismatic energies on social welfare programs addressing "the Indian problem."[31]

Thus began Pelletier's activist period. He became a "professional Indian helper," an "Indian do-gooder," and he "began joining organizations—I went on an organization orgy." He was elected to the presidency of the Toronto Indian Club and to leadership roles in the National Indian Council and the Indian-Eskimo Association, and he also allowed himself to be appointed as a token presence on several government advisory committees. He developed into a popular speaker and before long was a captain of the benevolent industry he would later refer to as "the Indian business—the business of making Indians acceptable to whites." The liberal reformers who had helped establish the Canadian Indian Centre of Toronto took control of the Centre's board and administration shortly after it opened, using the organization "to fill their own needs—the need of a cause to promote which would make them feel good." They also encouraged Pelletier in his attempts at community organizing, so long as he conformed to their assimilationist vision of social reform. "Try to help your people," they told him: "Try to bring them up to your level."[32]

But Pelletier ultimately realized that bureaucratic, hierarchical organizations did not serve the real needs of his intertribal community. "That's when it hit me. Boy, and it hit me solid," he later recalled. "Son of a bitch, I'd done it again! Denied my true identity, this time by trying to make an exception of myself. I was Indian, but I wasn't a problem. All those other Indians were problems—drunks, bums, ignorant—and I was going to help them. That's how I'd been seeing myself. That's what I'd been up to." Community organizing in the urban context could have little value to native people so long as it was guided by non-native values. "The Indian business! The problem business! It was like being back into that whole business life that I had left behind" in Sault Ste. Marie. "I'd learned that whites just can't seem to help taking over and running everything." They "always ended up in the driver's seat."[33]

For years native leaders in Canada had been discussing the possibility of establishing their own schools. Pelletier and some of his young colleagues on the National Indian Council had made it one of their goals in 1964, and the idea was championed several years later by Harold Cardinal, a Cree university student from the Sucker Creek Reserve in northern Alberta and president of the Canadian Indian Youth Council. Another key figure in this small network of activists was Ian MacKenzie, who had met Pelletier through the Indian-Eskimo Association. In the summer of 1967 MacKenzie, who had just been hired as one of the first two full-time resource persons at Rochdale College, drafted a proposal for an "Indian Institute" to be based at the College.[34]

"The basic problem with the education of Indian people in Canada," he began, "is that there are no Indian schools. The whole process of education of the Indians is directed towards the assimilation of the Indian people into our society, with no attention being paid to the cultural differences which exist between Indians and non-Indians." MacKenzie conceded that reversing this colonial policy would require a lengthy struggle; he proposed that the government's Company of Young Canadians provide funds for a beachhead, establishing the first native-run educational institution in modern Canada. This "Institute for Indian Studies" would provide a residential community for native high school and college students in the Toronto area, gather resource persons qualified to teach and write about native history and cultural traditions, encourage the preservation of tribal languages through research and training, promote community development projects on impoverished reserves, and serve as a clearinghouse for native organizations throughout the Americas. The Institute was organized during the 1967–68 academic year by a group of six activists: Wilf Pelletier, Ian MacKenzie, and University of Toronto professor Farrell Toombs, along with Jeannette Corbiere, Carol Wabegijig, and Edna Manitowabi, three native leaders involved with various Toronto organizations. These founding members envisioned a symbiotic relationship between the Institute and the College as each constituency explored the meanings of self-determination and community in a rapidly changing world.[35]

One of the initial projects of the Institute was the "Cross Cultural Workshop," first held in May 1968. Designed for employees of government and church agencies serving native people, the Workshop offered training in cross-cultural communication in an intensive, participatory format and from a native perspective. Ian MacKenzie invited Bob Thomas to be one of the leaders of the weeklong event, which was held in Toronto under the auspices of Rochdale College. More than two dozen men and women participated in the Workshop including Ted Poole, a freelance activist who described it as a "laboratory" in human relations, an opportunity to "share a personal and experiential knowing rather than an academic learnedness" and to "experience himself dynamically, as a human being in a network of human relations, rather than statically, as a function within a vertical complex of routine human functions." He concluded his lengthy evaluation of the Workshop with words that also captured the ethos of the Institute and that could have described the Rochdale philosophy as well: "Given the opportunity to explore, we may make some primal discoveries together, namely: that social problems are never other than wide-screen projections of personal problems; that solutions are implicit in people rather than programs; that even though our clamouring doubts and anxieties stimulate the belief that living is no more than a management problem, we must make our first investment of faith in the growingness of people rather than in engineering."[36]

Wilf Pelletier and Ted Poole joined Ian MacKenzie as full-time resource persons for the 1968–69 academic year at Rochdale. A new brochure described the Institute as "an educational-residential centre" for native people and "a centre for cross-cultural exploration and dialogue" for others, a microcosm of the Rochdale experiment in cooperative living and learning. Institute members watched and waited as the College moved into its new building during the fall of 1968; MacKenzie had wielded his influence as a Rochdale pioneer to negotiate a prime location for the Institute, reserving an entire wing of the seventeenth floor, which was one of the last parts of the building to be ready for habitation. The Institute finally occupied its new quarters in November and by the end of 1968 had established a residential community of some twenty people. Its roster of part-time resource persons continued to grow, and fundraising efforts attracted support from a local foundation, private donors, and the Anglican Church of Canada.[37]

Young Rochdale suffered from growing pains during the spring of 1969, but Institute members managed to rise above much of the turmoil. The Institute hosted regular Tuesday night gatherings "for anyone interested in Indians or the Indian way of life," and it quickly established itself as a meeting place for native people in the Toronto area. Institute leaders also intensified their efforts to build national and transnational networks of academic intellectuals and grassroots leaders committed to native community development. As the dust settled, many College residents noticed that "the members of the Institute have developed a decentralized decision-making structure which is becoming a model for the rest of the College. It is the seventeenth floor which has managed to have a real sense of community during the hectic opening months of the College." In January a journalist described Wilf Pelletier as "a twinkly-eyed Odawa Indian, probably the most popular person at Rochdale," a charismatic personality who also served on the Rochdale governing council. In March a progress report by the College registrar suggested that "the cross-cultural awareness which the members of the Institute want to foster has been particularly easy to highlight at Rochdale," and that "because many of the members of the Institute see the need for such an approach more clearly than others, they have taken a lead in other areas of the College" as well. "Members of the Institute are surprisingly prominent (to whites, probably) in the government of Rochdale." College founder Howard Adelman considered the Institute to be one of "the two most active and successful of the social involvement programs" at Rochdale.[38]

ECUMENICAL CONFERENCE

Native people occupied a prominent place—both spatially and politically—in the utopian episode known as Rochdale College, certainly more so than they had in other such experimental colonies. Wilf Pelletier and Ian MacKenzie grew increasingly involved in College governance during the second half of 1969, a period of financial crisis for the heavily mortgaged building. "They made a concerted effort to explain tribal horizontal government as well as the mystical power of Canada's autochthonous people," wrote one participant-observer, but "the power of the peace pipe and a trust in consensus was difficult for many to accept." MacKenzie served a brief term as Rochdale president, Pelletier was hired to be acting general manager for several months, and both participated in ongoing negotiations with various government and corporate officials. The Institute also enjoyed greater visibility in religious circles during this period, including an article in the July-August issue of the *Canadian Churchman*. Citing one of the recommendations of the Hendry report, this brief notice encouraged Anglicans to support the work of the Institute: collecting the tribal "stories, legends, and music of Indians and finding ways of sharing these collections with other Indians," and providing "a residential environment" where "Indians who migrate to cities" can "study about their own life styles in a technological society."[39]

The Institute held its third "Cross Cultural Workshop" in Regina that summer, a ten-day event beginning on August 6 and cosponsored by the anthropology department at the University of Saskatchewan. Bob Thomas lectured on racism in Canadian society, Wilf Pelletier addressed the topic of language and culture, and Ian MacKenzie participated as a resource person along with nine other academics and community leaders, all of them male. Afterward Thomas traveled to upstate New York for the 1969 unity conventions, while MacKenzie went to Sudbury to attend General Synod. Ten days later they rejoined Pelletier at Rochdale; the Anglican Church of Canada had just approved resolutions pledging support for native community development, and Thomas had just withdrawn from the traditional movement. Now they put their heads together and brainstormed the Institute's future.[40]

On August 28, just two days after General Synod ended, they tested the Anglican waters. That morning MacKenzie and Thomas walked down Bloor Street to Church House where they met with Trevor Jones, the Anglican church official responsible for implementing the recommendations of the Hendry report. They explained the Institute's goal of revitalizing tribal languages—a need clearly documented by Hendry and his associates—and discussed the possibility of organizing a national summit of Algonquin-speaking communities. Jones was receptive to their proposals, and later that day he sent a letter to Pelletier outlining the Anglican church's various translation and publication projects and offering advice on fundraising strategies. Thomas and MacKenzie were already back at Rochdale and working on funding proposals for other Institute ventures, including an intertribal gathering of grassroots native religious leaders they called the Indian Ecumenical Conference.[41]

Thomas had been ruminating on the problem of religious conflict among tribal people for some time. Several years earlier, when he was still living in northeastern Oklahoma, he had been invited to Anadarko for a National Council of Churches consultation on the relationship between Christian denominations and native communities. Thomas opened his address by pointing out that all societies must adapt to new circumstances, but that such transitions are more difficult for tribal people, and especially so under colonial domination. "Life in tribal societies is integrated and sacred," he said. "What we could call religious ritual and meaning sanctions all social usages and explains the meaning of life to the tribal person," whose self-perception is generated collectively. Like any society, tribal societies "tend to integrate and fuse new religious ideas with older conceptions," but "change in a tribal group is probably slower than among a more urban society because any change must be accounted for, integrated with, and made consistent with all aspects" of life. "Since religion is the 'cement' of that kind of society," religious institutions and values "must be flexible enough to integrate these changes."[42]

Native people might very well have chosen to incorporate Christian traditions into their religious world, Thomas speculated, but most tribal communities in North America have been denied the opportunity to control this natural process of integration. "In many Indian communities the church is like a huge crowbar crammed into a delicate machine," producing religious factionalism and social fragmentation. "Only the native people themselves can integrate a new religion and then use it to make life consistent for themselves. An outsider cannot do this and usually only succeeds in doing the opposite." Invoking both American democracy and Christian social ethics, Thomas challenged church leaders to respect and encourage native religious self-determination: "Indian communities *must* have control of their own churches with native leadership in the important institutional niches, so the church can in fact become a Kiowa or a Navajo institution, express this 'Kiowaness' or 'Navajoness,' be integrated into the life of the people, and be an integrative mechanism itself. The only people who can do this job are the people themselves. Outsiders cannot do this, nor can the institution."[43]

Bob Thomas and Ian MacKenzie began their proposal for the Indian Ecumenical Conference in a similar vein. "Christian churches are and have been one of the most active institutions in Indian life in both the United States and Canada," they wrote. "But strong evidence accumulated since the early 1950s indicates that something has gone wrong in the churches' relationship to Indian communities." Drawing on insights gained from the Hendry report consultations he had conducted for the Anglican church several months earlier, MacKenzie summarized the Canadian situation by identifying three typical attitudes among native people: a widely held view that the churches should "practice what they preach," accompanied by "a strong sense of betrayal" over their repeated failures; a desire by many to "retain their ancient religious patterns" as a more meaningful spiritual practice, especially among older people; and a younger generation that had "rejected the Church completely and were moving toward a completely secular political world or towards an ideological version of the aboriginal religious pattern." Thomas reported a similar situation in the U.S., with a couple of additional complications: "irresponsible competition between Christian sects among Indians which has resulted in 'confusion, conflict, and turmoil'" in native communities; and antagonism provoked by "adherents of the native Indian religion who are active in their opposition to Christianity and the Church."[44]

"Religious strife and turmoil is rampant in Indian communities," Thomas and MacKenzie concluded. "A conference of native Indian religious leaders, both aboriginal and Christian, is possibly the *only* vehicle" that could guide native communities and Christian denominations in their efforts to "begin to solve this difficult and urgent dilemma." Recapitulating Thomas's ideas on the importance of religious integration in tribal societies, they described the immobilizing effects of religious conflict. Tribal communities "will not take any action except in terms of the sacred, on the basis of unanimous sacred agreement, and when sanctioned by the sacred." Native people "cannot act in their own behalf in any direction in modern times because of this religious fragmentation. No one is more aware of this than Indians themselves. And the need for an Indian 'ecumenical' conference is uppermost in the minds of many Indian leaders." Advocating a new direction in Indian affairs, their proposal closed with an imperative: "Native Indian religionists, of all Christian and aboriginal sects, must assemble and start the painful process of conceptually sewing together their fragmented sacred world, so Indians can once again take steps to act for their own future welfare."[45]

Native people were never far from the minds of Anglican leaders during the fall of 1969. On September 4, Primate Howard Clark followed up on the resolutions passed at General Synod by sending a letter to Prime Minister Pierre Trudeau, with copies to Indian Affairs Minister Jean Chrétien, all 264 members of Parliament, and every provincial premier and legislative leader. "The members of Synod were deeply perturbed," Clark warned, "by the feelings of discontent with the new government Indian policy expressed by the elected leaders of treaty Indians forming the National Indian Brotherhood and its Provincial affiliates." He urged the Canadian government to reconsider its "White Paper" and to strive for "a fair and just settlement" of native legal claims. "You will note that the Anglican Church of Canada has officially adopted the position of supporting native Canadians in the pursuit of justice through the honouring of these ancient treaties made in good faith between equal parties." Six weeks later the *Canadian Churchman* reported that official response to the letter "has been generally cursory and non-committal." Mohawk activists at Cornwall Island considered the Anglican intervention newsworthy enough that they reprinted the *Canadian Churchman* articles in their fledgling periodical *Akwesasne Notes*.[46]

Institute leaders, meanwhile, continued their conversations with Anglican officials, who quickly agreed to provide funds for a meeting to organize the Indian Ecumenical Conference. In its proposal for this planning grant the Institute identified a Steering Committee composed of Wilf Pelletier and Bob Thomas along with several native religious leaders representing various tribal and Christian traditions on both sides of the Canada-U.S. border. Ian MacKenzie offered to work with the Committee as a resource person, and he served as an important link between the Conference and its primary funding source. The Institute had scheduled another cross-cultural workshop for early November at a resort lodge near Winnipeg; Pelletier, Thomas, and MacKenzie planned to participate, so they decided to convene the Steering Committee at one of the city's downtown hotels the following week. From their headquarters high above modern Toronto, they hoped this meeting would mark the beginning of a movement toward ecumenical cooperation in tribal communities across Canada and the U.S.[47]

BUCKSKIN CURTAIN

One of the more provocative political titles published during the fall of 1969 was *The Unjust Society* by Harold Cardinal. Subtitled *The Tragedy of Canada's Indians*, this influential best-seller brought national attention to the young Cree author, securing his reputation as a leading commentator on Indian affairs. He was uniquely qualified for the role: sociology student, cofounder of the Canadian Indian Youth Council, president of the Indian Association of Alberta, and board member of the National Indian Brotherhood, the nation's leading intertribal organization. The title phrase originated as a moral gibe at Canadian politics, suggesting a discrepancy between the prime minister's rhetoric of creating a "Just Society" and his simultaneous attempt at abrogating tribal legal rights. *The Unjust Society* appeared at a pivotal moment in native history, articulating a fierce response to the Canadian government's "White Paper" and proposing a more humane course of action. "I will challenge our fellow Canadians to help us," Cardinal announced; "I will warn them of the alternatives." The book was a prophetic intervention, both as social critique and as accurate prediction that native people had "reached the end of an era" and "will not be silenced again, left behind to be absorbed conveniently into the wretched fringes of a society that institutionalizes wretchedness. The Buckskin Curtain is coming down."[48]

Cardinal covered a wide range of contemporary issues in sixteen topical chapters, with government bureaucrats making an appearance in every one. He grounded his arguments in personal knowledge by beginning with an autobiographical introduction, where he also disclosed his goals in writing the book. He wanted to "open the eyes of the Canadian public to its shame," and to "point a path to radical change that will admit the Indian with restored pride to his rightful place." Cardinal's revealing account of "what it means to be an Indian in Canada" traced the convergence of indigenous and immigrant histories. "From the beginning, the Indian accepted the white man in Canada. We allowed him differences. We helped him overcome his weaknesses in trying to make his way in our environment. We taught him to know our world, to avoid the pitfalls and deadfalls, how to trap and hunt and fish, how to live in a strange environment. Is it too much to ask the white man to reciprocate?" This foundational hospitality has been forgotten by most non-native people, who have erected a "buckskin curtain" of indifference, ignorance, and bigotry that Cardinal intended to open. "As the stream needs the woods, as the flowers need the breeze, as the deer needs the grasses, so do peoples have need of each other, and so can peoples find good in each other." Native people "know that men of different cultures and races have much to offer one another. We offer our culture; we offer our heritage. We know it is different from yours. We are interested in your culture and your heritage; we want you to discover ours."[49]

Among the most impassioned parts of the book, reflecting Cardinal's personal experience at a church-run residential school, are two chapters detailing the impact of Christian missions, which "introduced two critically important institutions—religion and formal education." Here he surveyed the history of interreligious relations in Canada, highlighting the symbiotic relationship between assimilation and colonization and offering an assessment of the missionary enterprise and its aftermath. The missionary "came to preach his way and to convert, and he cared little even when he understood that his way disrupted" tribal communities. "The new religion focussed on abstractions; the old religion had been oriented toward people," and "when the missionary shoved the old medicine man aside he failed to fill all of the void left. He disrupted Indian society by removing from it the checks and balances that had been maintained under the old system." Legal proscriptions and vocational programs have also taken their toll on tribal traditions, leaving native communities fraught with the "divisiveness and bitterness" of religious competition. Noting that "today the church faces a generation of Indians who are, to say the very least, skeptical of the church's sincerity," Cardinal halfheartedly challenged the denominations to "fill the void they have created by returning to their original purpose—fulfilling the spiritual and moral needs of the people."

He also reminded them that "if there is still a place in modern-day Indian society for the church, that place must be found and designated by the Indian."[50]

If Cardinal was skeptical about the willingness of the nation's churchly bureaucracies to take such a leap of faith, he was considerably more optimistic about the prospects for "social rebuilding, psychological renewal, and cultural renaissance" in tribal communities. Suggesting that "the church is so discredited in native society that quite possibly its smartest move in the long run would be to cease all its activities on behalf of native peoples," he encouraged the church "to yield up its considerable influence upon our fate and to encourage the restoration of native beliefs and religions. Many Indians once again are looking toward the old as the hope of the future. Many Indian leaders believe a return to the old values, ethics and morals of native beliefs would strengthen the social institutions that govern the behavior patterns of Indian societies." *The Unjust Society* ends on a hopeful note, offering a vision of life in Canadian society "when the curtain comes down." Will the seventies be a decade of "cultural renaissance or civil disorder?" Tribal communities throughout the land should be engaged in self-examination and redefinition: "The Indian people of Canada must assume new confidence. There must be a rebirth of the Indian." Cardinal concluded that "the Indian people are not afraid of responsibility; in fact, they welcome the chance to play a new role in contemporary times." There is still a conviction "among our people that we were given this country to share with all peoples and to ensure that its natural resources are used for the good of mankind," and "our older people think that it is part of the responsibility of the Indian to help the white man" recover a greater "sense of humanity."[51]

Nevertheless, Cardinal's optimism regarding the revival of tribal traditions was tempered by pragmatic concerns about impediments to intertribal solidarity. "National Indian unity represents a dream long held by Indian leaders," but geographic and linguistic barriers have kept tribal communities "isolated not only from the mainstream of society but from one another" as well. "Conditions vary so widely from reserve to reserve that common needs, aspirations and goals that can be attributed to the entire Indian people are often difficult to determine." Differences in legal status among native people further complicate the situation, erecting an "inner Buckskin Curtain" that needs to be torn down. Cardinal devoted two chapters to "the long fight to organize," examining the impact of the reservation system on tribal political and social institutions and surveying historic attempts at forging intertribal alliances. "One of the most painful lessons that Indian peoples are learning is the need for organization through which they can articulate their needs and their alternatives to the Canadian society. If the situation of the Canadian Indian is to be altered, even alleviated," he argued, "the central issue is the degree of sophistication that we can develop in creating organizations which are Indian controlled and representative at the reserve level." These organizations must be committed to "restoring and revitalizing a sense of direction, a sense of purpose, and a sense of being" among native people, remedying "the psychological and spiritual crisis of the Indian." The new native leadership must "know and be able to relate positively to the traditions of the past, to the culture of our people, and at the same time be tuned into life in the twentieth and twenty-first centuries." Heartened by the recent founding of the National Indian Brotherhood, Cardinal looked to the future convinced that "we will survive the stupidities of bigotry, the indignities of condescension and the gushing of the do-gooders."[52]

In November 1969, a few weeks before Cardinal's manifesto appeared on bookstore shelves, a small group of native leaders gathered in Winnipeg to discuss the religious confusion, fragmentation, and conflict immobilizing native life throughout Canada and the U.S. They resolved to hold an Indian Ecumenical Conference during the summer of 1970 and organized themselves into a Steering Committee to plan the event. Cardinal had anticipated these developments in his perceptive juxtaposition of Christian individualism and tribal values: "The white man is a paradox," he wrote. "He believes in the concept of unity. He believes in a God and adheres to a monotheistic religion. Yet even in the area where he could offer most, in the one area where he could exemplify unity—in his religion—he is ridiculously fragmented." Alluding to discussions then under way among national church leaders concerning the possibilities for denominational merger, Cardinal asserted that "the Indian was the first member of the ecumenical movement. He was willing to accept the white missionary's message of love for his fellow men, because it came as a complement to rather than a contradiction of the Indian way of life." For many first-generation converts, "the switchover from indigenous beliefs to those of Christianity was relatively smooth," and this transition "was smooth for the Indians since none of their beliefs were stretched too far in the new direction. They dovetailed rather than clashed."[53]

Harold Cardinal's *The Unjust Society* itself dovetails nicely with a contemporaneous work, *Custer Died for Your Sins* by Vine Deloria, Jr. Both books are hard-hitting critiques by energetic young activists, the first major publications of two authors who would become the leading native political voices of their generation. Both books were provoked in part by government attempts to abrogate native legal rights—the "White Paper" in Canada, the "termination" policy in the U.S.—and both speak in a distinctly tribal idiom of righteous clarity and sarcastic humor. Both books offer remarkably similar assessments of life in grassroots tribal communities, based largely on the firsthand experiences and observations of their authors. The only significant thematic difference between the books lay in their authors' views of the relationship between material and spiritual considerations in the struggle for tribal survival: Cardinal stressed the need for political and social organizing, while Deloria underscored the importance of cultural and religious integrity. Yet even this difference in emphasis was little more than a reflection of their distinct personal backgrounds—Cardinal's father had been band chief of the Sucker Creek Reserve, while Deloria's father had been Episcopal priest on the Pine Ridge Reservation—and each clearly appreciated the value of a comprehensive strategy. Taken together, these two landmark books map Indian country as a continuous territory undivided by the forty-ninth parallel. That they were conceived and written independently and published simultaneously in the fall of 1969 testifies to the uniformity of Western colonialism, the resilience of tribal communities, and the fidelity of these particular literary representations.[54]

The fall of 1969 was a bountiful season in Indian country, producing a harvest of controversy and hope. Like Deloria, Cardinal had been following various developments that were beginning to bear fruit: he recognized the importance of grassroots mobilizing among tribal traditionalists as a force for social change; he appreciated the cross-cultural insights of Bob Thomas, whom he had first met through the Canadian Indian Youth Workshops; he had known Ian MacKenzie for several years and supported the advocacy work of this Anglican activist; and he served as a resource person with the Institute for Indian Studies, having played a key role in its early development. Convinced that native people in Canada could learn from the struggles of their global counterparts, Cardinal also kept an eye trained southward, crossing the border on several fact-finding trips and a dozen times mentioning the U.S. in *The Unjust Society*. It was a critical moment in the history of intertribal alliance. The traditional movement and the Institute for Indian Studies had demonstrated the viability of transnational organizing in both rural and urban settings, and the occupations at Cornwall and Alcatraz showed that even small islands can defy the effrontery of colonial nation-states. Now a small group of native leaders decided to cross the most troublesome frontiers in the land: the Indian Ecumenical Conference would transcend the boundaries of religious tradition by cultivating interpersonal relationships. It was an elegantly simple strategy, addressing our primal need for personal connection, a disposition with deep roots in the human psyche. Hallowed ideologies notwithstanding, there can be no humanity without humans.[55]

North American Indian Unity Caravan in downtown Henryetta, Oklahoma, October 1967. Holding the smaller sign, which reads "Official Car; League of Nations, Pan Am. Indians," are Thomas Banyacya, left, and Tom Porter. Standing directly behind Porter is Wallace Mad Bear Anderson. Local host Clifton Hill is at the far right, and the young boy next to Porter is Hill's middle son, Kirby. Photograph courtesy of Henryetta Daily Free Lance.

Akwesasne Mohawk protesters with one of the signs used at the Cornwall Island bridge blockade, December 1968: "Our Nation Has Been Here Always, Your Line Divides Us! RESTORE INDIAN RIGHTS AT BORDER! under 1794 Jay Treaty." Still image from video version of You Are on Indian Land.

Bob Thomas in Tahlequah, Oklahoma, during the summer of
1967, at the end of his tenure as codirector of the Carnegie
Cross-Cultural Education Project. He is smoking a pipe.
Photograph by Paul Friedman. Reprinted by permission of
Transaction Publishers. Copyright © 1969 by Transaction
Publishers.

Ian MacKenzie, consultant in community development with the Anglican Church of Canada, discussing the Hendry report during a radio interview in the spring of 1969. Photograph courtesy of General Synod Archives, Anglican Church of Canada.

Wilf Pelletier, director of the Institute for Indian Studies, at a meeting of Rochdale College's governing council during the 1969–70 academic year. Still image from video version of Dream Tower.

Aerial view of Crow Fair, August 1970, at Crow Agency, Montana, site of the first Indian Ecumenical Conference. Photograph by Dennis Sanders, courtesy of Hardin Photo Service.

Steering Committee of the Indian Ecumenical Conference at the end of the 1971 gathering in Stoney Indian Park. Front row, left to right: Aubrey Perley, Ernie Willie, Ernest Tootoosis, Bob Thomas, Andrew Dreadfulwater, Alex Bonaise. Back row: Albert Lightning, Joe Mackinaw, Chris Cromarty, Ian MacKenzie, Larry Thompson, Wilf Pelletier, Andrew Abenakew, Stewart Etsitty, Clifton Hill. Photograph courtesy of John A. (Ian) MacKenzie.

CONVERSATIONS

The Parliament, however noble its goals and aspirations, was tainted by the same parochialism, ethnocentrism, imperial pretensions, and hegemonic intentions as the entire Exposition. In philosophical terms, it failed because the premises for its universalistic agenda turned out to be particularistic. In crude theological terms, it failed because the God of the organizers of the Parliament turned out not to be quite the same as the Gods of the Asians.

Richard Hughes Seager, *The World's Parliament of Religions*

The most prominent feature of the Conference—which emerged clearly to nearly everyone's surprise and pleasure—was the unanimity of purpose and thought of the delegates. Everyone agreed that modern Indian religious life must be a furthering of the historic continuity of time-honoured Indian values and philosophical concern; that both modern Indian ceremonies and Indian Christianity must be part of that continuity; and that both native ceremonials and Indian Christianity can be mutually supportive or parallel and cooperative or integrated, according to the desire of the particular tribe involved.

The Indian Ecumenical Conference

CHAPTER FIVE

"MODERN INDIAN RELIGIOUS LIFE"

A STORM WAS BREWING OVER WINNIPEG. The cold north wind rolling off the Canadian shield whistled an eerie tune, erasing any doubts about the arrival of winter. Office workers scurried along sidewalks and ducked into entryways without lingering for Monday-morning gossip. This seasonal turn had convinced pedestrians to move at a quicker pace but it was having the opposite effect on mechanized transport; schedule delays were already being announced at the local airport, where a couple of native spiritual leaders were expected on flights from the south. Bob Thomas, Ian MacKenzie, and Wilf Pelletier watched and waited for the skies to clear, anxious to receive these last two delegates so they could begin their planned meeting. Someone in the welcoming party voiced his fear that this bad weather was the work of tribal conjurers, who might be using malevolent powers to thwart their effort at ecumenical organizing. Interreligious conversation can be a risky venture.[1]

Clifton Hill and Bernard Second finally arrived safely and joined their colleagues at a hotel in downtown Winnipeg. Hill was a Baptist minister and head of the Creek Centralization Committee, while Second was a Mescalero Apache ceremonial leader and vice president of the National Indian Youth Council; along with Thomas, they made up the U.S. contingent at this transnational gathering. Representing the Canadian side of the border were Pelletier and five other delegates: Ernest Tootoosis, a Cree sun dance chief and lay minister in the Church of Christ who also served as vice president of the Federation of Saskatchewan Indians; Andrew Ahenakew, a Cree Anglican priest in the Diocese of Saskatchewan; Joe Mackinaw, a Cree traditionalist from western Alberta; Elwood Modeste, a Cowichan elder and Shaker Church minister from Vancouver Island; and Ernie Willie, a young Kwakiutl Anglican priest in the Diocese of New Westminster. It was "a rather impressive group of men," Thomas later recalled, a handpicked committee of individuals chosen for their influence with certain critical constituencies. Representing a wide range of tribal communities and spiritual communions, these nine activist leaders had been brought together to discuss the problem of religious conflict among native people.[2]

The conversation began on Tuesday morning when one of the delegates offered a simple prayer. It was November 11, a national holiday on both sides of the border, a day for remembering the armistice of 1918 and the veterans of armed conflict—and celebrated in 1969 with protests and counterprotests over U.S. involvement in the Vietnam War. A second NASA lunar landing was only a week away, and a few days after that researchers at Harvard Medical School would announce the isolation of a single gene; Western science was claiming mastery over the astronomic and the microscopic, the infinite and the infinitesimal, but intermediate challenges at human scale were proving to be more intractable. The respected authorities gathered in a Winnipeg hotel meeting room spent several hours getting acquainted, each one introducing himself and describing the religious situation in his particular corner of Indian country. Some were more cautious than others, but these initial apprehensions quickly gave way to an atmosphere of empathy, trust, and cooperation. Wilf Pelletier chaired the meeting with a casual demeanor; this was not an occasion for parliamentary debate or other formal maneuvers. Much of the three-day gathering was occupied with storytelling as delegates took turns recounting religious experiences and sharing spiritual insights.[3]

When the time was right, Bob Thomas introduced his idea for an intertribal conference of grassroots native leadership focused on resolving the religious antagonisms in their communities. It would be a grander version of this small caucus, he explained, involving a much larger number of representatives from throughout Canada and the U.S. Thomas believed in the ability of tribal elders to make wise decisions, and he knew that native religious leaders could overcome their differences if they were freed from the interference of missionaries, anthropologists, and other colonial bureaucrats. He pointed to the success of this meeting in Winnipeg as a demonstration of what could be accomplished in an autonomous context. His colleagues were quick to agree with him on this point; they were encouraged by the easy rapport that characterized their discussions and excited to discover a sense of common purpose transcending religious, ethnic, and political distinctions. Thomas hoped their informal consultation might serve as prototype for "an Indian 'ecumenical' conference" the following summer.[4]

The meeting stretched into the evening hours and resumed the next morning after a good night's rest. Ian MacKenzie watched and listened intently, hopeful that Thomas's proposal would be affirmed. Several other observers were on hand as well: Ted Poole, a resource person at Rochdale College; Yvonne McCrae, Pelletier's sister and a board member of the Indian-Eskimo Association; and Mary Defender, a Standing Rock Sioux woman living in Winnipeg. At one point in the proceedings these four left the meeting room for a few hours, allowing the delegates to continue their deliberations in a more intimate setting. MacKenzie bundled up for a walk. His most memorable experience at the Winnipeg meeting was actually something that happened outside the hotel, when he ran across a newspaper rack with the latest issue of the *Winnipeg Free Press.* The cover story exposed a church-run residential school where native children were being chained to their beds. He was outraged and later reported his discovery to those assembled at the hotel, where he was startled again to find that these native leaders were not particularly surprised by the news. It was a dramatic illustration of the challenges they faced back home, where religious conflict was just one dimension of the trauma generated by colonial domination. There was a great deal at stake in this modest conversation among friends.[5]

Yet neither these sobering realities nor the harsh weather outside could dampen the spirit of optimism that had appeared in the heart of Winnipeg, perhaps the most geographically central city on the North American continent. This gathering had been a liberating experience for everyone involved and now they wanted native people from the four directions to share in this freedom. As their time together drew to a close, the delegates acknowledged a clear consensus emerging from their collaboration. "This group of leaders decided to go ahead with plans for a large Indian ecumenical conference in the summer of 1970," Bob Thomas and Ian MacKenzie wrote afterward, "and they formed themselves into a steering committee to plan and organize the meeting." Thomas later recalled two goals motivating this decision: "to get Indian religious leaders together to give each other emotional support and ideas and so forth," and "to deal with the problem of religious strife in Indian communities." Hoping to generate "a series of local and regional Indian ecumenical meetings and a general movement for ecumenicity among American Indians," the new Steering Committee "felt that there was urgent need to call an Indian Ecumenical Conference and they proceeded to lay the ground work for it."[6]

The Committee charged Wilf Pelletier and Bob Thomas with responsibility for organizing the Conference, using the Institute for Indian Studies as administrative headquarters, and asked Ian MacKenzie to participate as a resource person. Their first order of business would be to raise money for Conference expenses—and to do so as quickly as possible, in time for another planning meeting in February, when the Steering Committee would ratify their decision to host the Conference. Each member of the Committee agreed to help spread the word among his own tribal and religious colleagues, and Mary Defender was asked to help contact native leaders in Manitoba and to serve as liaison with the Roman Catholic Church. If sufficient funding could be secured by February, several fieldworkers would be commissioned to visit prospective delegates and recruit them for the Conference. A third planning meeting was tentatively scheduled for June, when the Committee would finalize arrangements for the August gathering.[7]

The Winnipeg meeting ended with another heartfelt prayer of gratitude and anticipation. A dozen ecumenical activists bid one another safe journeys and went their separate ways, now bearing a mutual commitment to interreligious organizing among native people in Canada and the U.S. Other camps were busy pursuing their own agendas for social change in Indian country. Rural traditionalists and urban radicals were attracting support for their nativist crusade, which raised the political stakes while advocating a narrower conception of cultural existence. Academic anthropologists were increasingly suspect yet still powerful arbiters, discursive authorities who shared the nativists' racial and ethnic determinism if not their political commitment. Denominational missionaries were dispirited by their historic failures, some conflicted and doubting the rhetoric of conversion, others discouraged but committed to finishing the job. Professional educators were mired in ideologies of progress, happy to assimilate diverse peoples and pedagogies though largely unwilling to question their own domineering epistemologies. Embracing an altogether different vision of native survival, members of the new Steering Committee headed for home. The Indian Ecumenical Conference would be an inclusive, autonomous, pragmatic alternative to the other positions being staked out in tribal communities, a postcolonial strategy based on the affirmation of "modern Indian religious life" in all its complexities and contradictions.[8]

STEERING COMMITTEE

Bob Thomas left the Winnipeg meeting heartened by the group's response to his idea for an ecumenical movement among native people. He and Ian MacKenzie promptly updated their funding proposal, detailing the formation of the Steering Committee and its endorsement of this venture. Then

Thomas, MacKenzie, and Wilf Pelletier launched an aggressive fundraising campaign. They needed just over fifty thousand dollars to cover the bottom line; their preliminary budget included two more Committee meetings, salary and travel for seven short-term fieldworkers, administrative overhead, and Conference expenses for 162 delegates. During the winter of 1969–70 they circulated the proposal to a number of denominations and foundations on both sides of the Canada-U.S. border. The United Church of Canada was one of the first organizations to endorse the Indian Ecumenical Conference, granting three thousand dollars in time to underwrite a second Committee meeting at the end of February. The women's group at Bloor Street United Church in Toronto donated twenty-five dollars.[9]

The Steering Committee met for three days at a hotel in St. Louis, another centrally located city. Present were all delegates from the first meeting except Bernard Second, along with three new Committee members: Andrew Dreadfulwater, Thomas's Cherokee friend from eastern Oklahoma; Wylie Butler, a Creek medicine maker who worked with Clifton Hill; and Albert Lightning, a Cree elder from the Ermineskin Reserve in central Alberta. As in Winnipeg, opening and closing prayer ceremonies framed their deliberations. Wilf Pelletier chaired the proceedings, which began with a financial report by Bob Thomas and Ian MacKenzie. The Steering Committee directed these three "coordinators" to continue their efforts and earmarked what was left of the United Church grant to pay for a fundraising trip to New York City and to support a couple of fieldworkers on the Canadian prairies and the American plains. This led to a lengthy discussion of the delegate selection process for the Conference in August. The Committee finally concluded that each member should be responsible for identifying nominees in a particular area, relaying these names to the coordinators in Toronto. They also reached agreement on selection guidelines: "Delegates must be persons who are indigenous religious leaders" and who were not employed by "Federal, Provincial or State government agencies." The minutes also noted these dozen men "decided that women delegates to the conference must be fifty-five to sixty years of age. This decision was taken in deference to the strong Indian religious tradition of recognizing Indian women as religious leaders only when they have reached maturity," though it is unfortunate that no tribal women had a direct voice in this determination. Several Committee members reported that "news of the conference was spreading rapidly among Indians and receiving an enthusiastic response. Many Indian families were planning to come and listen to those parts of the proceedings which would be open to them."[10]

Confident that adequate funding would be forthcoming, the Steering Committee scheduled another planning meeting for June and discussed logistical details of the August gathering. Ernie Willie agreed to serve as Conference administrator beginning in July, taking a leave of absence from his parish duties in Hatzic, British Columbia. Committee members expressed considerable concern over media representations of the Conference before, during, and after the event. They "decided to make no press announcement until after the June meeting," at which a spokesman would be appointed, and they encouraged the airing of radio spots "only where it was possible to use an Indian language." They also discussed the idea of publishing a collection of speeches delivered at the Conference and of starting "a newsletter for Indian religious leaders." Intent on making this a self-governing and self-propagating organization, they laid plans to reconstitute the Steering Committee at the August gathering and "decided that no structured agenda should be prepared" beforehand. Instead, the Committee resolved to develop "a series of recommendations" for Conference delegates' consideration. Their first two recommendations addressed the desecration of burial sites and the repatriation of sacred objects. Before leaving town the group crossed the Mississippi River to visit Cahokia Mounds, where they held a prayer ceremony and meditated on the challenges that lay before them.[11]

The St. Louis meeting ended with a surplus of optimism but not much money in the bank, and it would be two long months before the coordinators' fundraising efforts would yield their first major success. The winter of 1969–70 was a hectic time for the Anglican Church of Canada as well. Following the 1969 General Synod, denominational executives quickly erected bureaucratic "machinery" to implement the resolutions passed in support of political commitment and community development. They appointed one of their own—Trevor Jones, former head of the Missionary Society—to coordinate this effort and convened an advisory task force that included Carol Wabegijig from the Institute for Indian Studies along with Andrew Ahenakew and his Cree Anglican colleague Redfern Loutitt. Addressing a Hendry report recommendation that "the role of the church must be redefined," Jones believed that "the key to this redefinition lies in the theology and sociology of liberation." In October Anglican officials traveled to Ottawa and met with native political leaders from across Canada, posing a simple question: "What do Indian leaders ask of the Church now?" A number of issues were raised during the two-hour meeting, which produced a list of six points intended to guide institutional advocacy and benevolence. In November the Canadian Council of Churches and the Canadian Catholic Conference, the nation's leading Christian organizations, publicly expressed their concern over the Canadian government's "White Paper." That same month Anglican leaders renamed the Primate's World Relief Fund, their central philanthropic apparatus, to reflect these new priorities.[12]

The born-again Primate's World Relief and Development Fund received grant applications from dozens of native organizations but could not respond until after its annual fundraising campaign during the Lenten season of 1970. Meanwhile, the Anglican church's Social Action Unit distributed a couple of meaty pamphlets describing the native political struggle, their first such publications in fifty years of a series that had produced two hundred previous editions: *Bulletin 201* collected statements related to the resolutions passed by General Synod in 1969, while *Bulletin 202* offered excerpts from the Indian-Eskimo Association's landmark study of "Native Rights in Canada." In March the *Canadian Churchman* devoted its second *Horizons* supplement to an in-depth report on "Indians and the Church." A dozen feature articles and sidebars challenged popular stereotypes by allowing readers to "see what contemporary Indians are like and what they are saying. And we want to let people know," editor R. S. Fellows explained in mixed-gender metaphors, "what the church is up to as she seeks to stand beside and assist her native brothers." Rank-and-file Anglicans—women, mostly—responded generously to the Lenten appeal, and by the end of April denominational executives had approved a Conference grant in the amount of fifteen thousand dollars. They also pledged their support to several other native organizations including the National Indian Brotherhood, the Federation of Saskatchewan Indians, and the Institute for Indian Studies at Rochdale College.[13]

Rochdale had floundered through the 1969–70 academic term, its second year in the new building, and there was only so much the Institute could do to help sort out this utopian quandary. Wilf Pelletier and Ian MacKenzie took active roles in College governance but were unable to negotiate a truce between warring images of its mission: free university or rebellious commune. Little in the way of constructive education could be accomplished in this environment, and Institute leaders finally broke ranks and pulled out of Rochdale. They did manage to move forward on some of their own projects during the year, establishing an in-house press they named with the Cree-language term for the number four. In the fall of 1969 Neewin Publishing Company issued *Two Articles* by Pelletier, "a little brown book with yellow pages" in which he narrated his philosophy of educational leadership. "They say I am director of the Institute of Indian Studies. This is not true," he maintained. "Where I am everyone makes up their own minds in terms of what they want to do, and they do those things, and if I can be of assistance, then I assist. I've got my own thing that I hope to do." In the summer of 1970 the organization changed its name to the Nishnawbe Institute, using an Ojibwa-language word that translates to "the people."[14]

The Institute had proven to be adept at raising funds from Canadian denominations, but Conference coordinators found it harder to sell their proposal on the American side of the border. In March Ian MacKenzie pitched their plan at a meeting with the church executive responsible for Episcopal Indian affairs, then elaborated on the Conference proposal in a follow-up letter. Writing "with a sense of urgency," he identified "three pressing reasons for holding this conference" in addition to those spelled out in the proposal.[15]

First, "it is quite apparent that native communities in both the United States and Canada are in turmoil and crisis," evident in rising rates of crime, suicide, and mental illness and in "a total breakdown of race relations." It is imperative to "stop this process of deterioration, which we feel can only lead to destructiveness and violence." Second, "one of the things which is happening on the Indian scene is the recent and rapid growth of the Traditional Movement, a non-Christian Indian religious movement which is bringing together Indians from all tribes in both countries. If this movement continues to grow in the absence of an Indian ecumenical movement, there will be no possibility of a reconciliation between native religious movements and Indian Christians." Instead, these antagonisms will aggravate "the destructive tendencies so apparent now in Indian communities." Third, though nativist movements might lead to the recovery of cultural and spiritual traditions, they can also further isolate tribal communities, "which are more and more cut off from constructive participation in Western society." Because denominations "cut across the boundaries of race, culture and nationality, they provide the possibility for creative learning experiences" among native people. "The Church may be the only institution within which Indians have a chance to establish some kind of relationship with the rest of society." MacKenzie requested five thousand dollars from the Episcopal church and assistance in securing another fifteen thousand dollars from other American denominations "to fund the American Indian participation in this meeting."[16]

The Episcopal church official evaluated the Conference proposal and forwarded it to the Indian Ministries Strategy/Screening Task Force of the Joint Strategy and Action Committee, an interdenominational agency based in New York City. He also communicated his assessment to Ian MacKenzie; it was a bureaucratic critique, preoccupied with Conference delegates' national and denominational affiliations and mildly suspicious of the Steering Committee's ability to organize the gathering. MacKenzie, Wilf Pelletier, and Bob Thomas quickly met in Detroit to discuss these objections, and three days later they mailed a point-by-point response to the Episcopal evaluation. They began by restating the purpose of the Conference: "It is apparent to all who are close to the Indian scene that religious divisiveness among Indians is not only acute" but is also "the most sensitive and difficult area to deal with effectively." Members of the Committee had been able to overcome their differences only because each one "knew at least three other members of the committee and was a personal friend of at least one other member" beforehand, and "this kind of internal dynamic, predicated on personal relationships and mutual trust, is the key" to organizing a successful ecumenical gathering. "The Steering Committee considers this criterion to be of far greater importance than denominational or regional representation." They used the balance of the letter to explain how some criticisms were already being addressed and why others were misguided. The most important consideration was that every delegate selected be someone who was "ready" for ecumenical cooperation, regardless of religious affiliation. "The main work of the conference is to revitalize our own communities and we feel we understand the requirements of such an endeavor," they concluded. "If those requirements bring into question the validity of the conference to white institutions, that would be unfortunate, but we must deal with the facts of Indian life as it is lived in Indian communities."[17]

Conference coordinators also had trouble convincing the Catholic hierarchy of the value of this ecumenical venture. Ian MacKenzie requested fifteen thousand dollars from the missions office of the Canadian Catholic Conference; its "off the cuff" response affirmed the need for such a movement but identified a number of "apparent difficulties" that were similar to the objections raised by the Episcopal church, with a bit more emphasis on holding Conference delegates accountable to ecclesiastical authority. The Catholic church official expressed concern that "the assembly will be a gathering of friends who all think alike and relate to one another. While this would be a very meaningful personal experience for the delegates, it is unlikely that their views will be challenged sufficiently to create the climate needed for resolving disagreements, misunderstandings, strife and bitterness." He encouraged the Steering Committee "to allow at least another year of pre-Conference groundwork and planning" so the gathering might be made more acceptable to church authorities. "Since Indians are sharing the same human nature as the rest of us," the celibate cleric deduced, "it seems reasonable to expect that there will be the same human problems in their organizations as we have in ours."[18]

Both Wilf Pelletier and Bob Thomas felt compelled to answer this critique. "The only reasonable way to 'choose' delegates is to allow that process to happen in the communities themselves," Pelletier argued. "That may seem a rather haphazard approach to a society that has premised itself on impersonal structure and tight organization, but it must be remembered that other

societies have functioned in other ways for thousands of years." He also reiterated his hope that "the Conference will be a gathering of 'friends' who can 'relate to one another,' for that is the only spirit in which unity and agreement can
develop. Imposing alien concepts of authority and representation could only
tend to remove the meeting from the people who are and must be involved."
Pelletier aimed his strongest riposte at the good priest's denial of cultural par-
ticularity: "Indian communities differ in their concept of organization—and
perhaps of human problems—from Western society," he asserted. "Indian people have dealt with each other in their own terms for a long, long time, and can
draw on their experience in determining their organizational and procedural
needs. I think that is basic to our view of the Conference and its success."[19]

Thomas agreed with Pelletier "completely" but took a different approach,
offering his personal observations on interreligious relations among the
Creeks, the Papagos, and the Sioux. He then summarized his vision for the
Conference: "It seems to me that our most important job is to establish the
mood of ecumenism. Indian religious leaders, even if they are of an ecumenical bent, do not engage in dialogue or make institutional compromises. Life
for these men is not a poker game nor a ledger account book nor a series of
bureaucratic 'treaties.' A general harmony and good fellowship must be created among these religious leaders before they will start to draw upon what
things they have in common and what things they will mutually agree not to
mention." He hoped the Conference would "be the spark that will allow people on the local level to reverse the trend of disintegration and start the
painstaking and time consuming task of conceptual unity, which all of us agree
is the only way to revitalize Indian communities."[20]

In April Ian MacKenzie and Clifton Hill traveled to New York City for a
meeting of the Joint Strategy and Action Committee to discuss the Conference proposal with various denominational bureaucrats in charge of native
ministries in the U.S. Hill wore his tribal regalia and brought along some tobacco prepared by Wylie Butler, lighting up a corncob pipe as he and
MacKenzie made their presentation. The Creek medicine worked, and a
month later the Episcopal church's National Committee on Indian Work approved a grant in the amount of three thousand dollars. Bob Thomas was able
to secure five hundred dollars more from a couple of his Episcopal contacts in
Detroit. Other mainline denominations, however, were "in the process of getting their Indian work committees established" and were unwilling to review
grant applications for the time being. The Joint Strategy and Action Committee task force had canceled its June meeting and was "immobilized at the present time," the Episcopal church official reported, "so it appears there may be
no grants from the other member denominations of JSAC" in support of the

Conference. Fortunately, sympathetic constituencies within the Anglican Church of Canada were prepared to help cover the budget deficit. In the spring of 1970 Anglican Church Women indicated their desire to support some project in native community development with a grant of ten thousand dollars, and in early June church executives designated these funds for the Conference. Wilf Pelletier expressed his appreciation by stopping by Church House to pose for a photograph with the Anglican primate.[21]

Flush with working capital but still twenty thousand dollars short of its fundraising goal, the Steering Committee assembled in Henryetta, Oklahoma. The meeting was held during the third week of June to coincide with a traditionalist gathering hosted by Clifton Hill and his Creek colleagues. Bob Thomas opened the proceedings by introducing three new members he had invited to join the Committee: Stanley Smith, a local Creek spiritual leader; Keedah Johnson, a Navajo member of the Native American Church; and John Hascall, an Ojibwa Catholic priest from Michigan's upper peninsula. Then Ian MacKenzie presented the financial report. Grant applications were still pending with denominations on both sides of the border, but they had to face the possibility of ending up with "far less than the original estimate needed" to cover expenses for 162 delegates. The Steering Committee "decided to go ahead" with the Conference but "prepared to cut the number of delegates if necessary."[22]

Committee members had been working from a delegate budget drawn up at their first meeting in Winnipeg. The Canadian delegation of seventy-seven was apportioned evenly among the ten provinces while omitting the Yukon and Northwest Territories. The Committee believed that "the problem of religious strife was not yet acute in those areas and felt that to raise the issue for those tribes might simply bring about the very condition we are trying to deal with in the more southerly tribes. They hoped that if the more southern tribes solved the dilemma in their area, acute religious strife in the north could be avoided." The American delegation of eighty-five was concentrated in Oklahoma, the Northern Plains, and the Southwest, with only one or two delegates allotted for each of a dozen other states. The Steering Committee concluded that in certain parts of the U.S. native religious conflict "was either resolved or was unresolvable." Some tribal communities are "highly acculturated and have lost all traces of Indian religion, language, etc.," while "in the case of those tribes where Christian and non-Christian factionalism is extremely bitter, the committee felt significant delegate representation would result in the imposition of this bitterness on the conference as a whole. We felt that such tribes could be included in an Ecumenical movement at a later date when the movement had a more solid foundation."[23]

At the Henryetta meeting Committee members reported on their progress in identifying and screening potential delegates for the Conference, which was now less than two months away. Tabulating the invitation list was proving to be a huge task, requiring diligent networking and extensive leg-work—and a high degree of cultural sensitivity—to find suitable grassroots representatives scattered over a geographic area of some six million square miles. Every Committee member had to develop a basic understanding of the religious peculiarities within each tribal community for which he was respon-sible. The Navajo delegation, for example, needed to include a couple of singers, a peyote roadman, a Protestant minister, and a Mormon leader, each one amenable to ecumenical cooperation.[24]

The Steering Committee spent the last day of its meeting in Henryetta firming up logistics for the Conference. Bob Thomas had arranged for the event to take place on the Crow Reservation in southeastern Montana; his contact in the tribal government there had agreed to provide food and lodging for delegates and office space for the Committee. The Conference would be held in the middle of August to coincide with the annual Crow Fair, a renowned intertribal encampment often called the "teepee capital of the world." Thomas, Keedah Johnson, and Ernie Willie were charged with re-sponsibility for media relations in the weeks leading up to the Conference. Journalists would not be allowed at the gathering, though press releases would be issued by a publicity committee consisting of Bernard Second, Ernest Tootoosis, and Allan Campbell, an anthropology student at the University of Regina who worked with the Nishnawbe Institute. Determined to inaugurate a democratic movement, the Steering Committee decided that each day of the Conference should be chaired by a different person and appointed Wilf Pel-letier, Ernest Tootoosis, Andrew Ahenakew, and Stanley Smith for this duty.[25]

Wilf Pelletier, Ian MacKenzie, and Bob Thomas drove back to the Great Lakes as soon as the Henryetta meeting ended. MacKenzie and Thomas had a couple of weeks to tie up loose ends before leaving for a month of field re-search in the Northwest Territories. From his faculty office at Monteith Col-lege in Detroit, Thomas dashed off a few letters to tribal leaders around the U.S. reminding them of the Conference. "Let me tell you what the deal is," he wrote to Cheyenne elder Harvey Twins. "I am on the committee to arrange the meeting," he told Hopi traditionalist Thomas Banyacya. "There are four-teen of us—seven from the U.S. and seven from Canada. And all of them are Indian holy men or Indian ministers who respect our medicine." The Steering Committee was anticipating "about two hundred delegates," he disclosed to Onondaga chief Irving Powless, "religious leaders from all over the U.S. and Canada—medicine men, prophets, chiefs, Indian ministers, ceremonial leaders," and others. "Our main business is to make peace among ourselves," he explained to Mississippi Choctaw medicine man Cameron Wesley, "between tribe and tribe, between Christian and Native Religionists, between different factions, etc. We want to make our peace and thus make our medicine strong, instead of pulling the people this way and that way." Conference organizers were anticipating "quite a few delegates and it looks like that this will be the biggest meeting of its kind ever held in North America," he informed Mesquakie activist Don Wanatee. "Nearly any tribe of any size and importance is sending delegates" to the Conference. "Could you come up to our meeting or send someone to represent you?" he asked Yurok ceremonial leader Calvin Rube. "Preferably a man since there will be a lot of medicine making going on there. We can pay transportation up and back."[26]

Ernie Willie faced a daunting list of action items when he arrived at the Nishnawbe Institute to begin work as Conference administrator on July 6, the same day that Bob Thomas and Ian MacKenzie traveled to Yellowknife to launch an expedition down the Mackenzie River. They had been contracted by the Anglican Church of Canada to assess the condition of tribal communities in the western part of the Northwest Territories as part of the church's effort to implement the recommendations of the Hendry report. Employing a participant observation method, Thomas and MacKenzie traveled by boat from settlement to settlement, conducting interviews and studying social interactions. They discovered "a caste system as rigid as anything you might find in India," an "occupational hierarchy" corresponding to a cultural continuum "from very urban white to very tribal Indian," with "real social discrimination and racial prejudice on the part of the powerful whites." Although these settlements were not yet factionalized, most of them had sprung up as "collections of tribal families rather than real tribal villages with village institutions. This means that the Indians in these villages have no structure by which to guide their actions or through which to act. The situation is set up for social chaos when any type of strain comes upon the village." Thomas and MacKenzie recommended that "the churches sponsor community development programmes" aimed at creating "some type of native institutions," especially "a native Christian religious structure, religious organizations, and local Christian ceremonial forms." In the Yellowknife area they also noted "a strong upsurge of Indian nationalism expressed through a native religious revival," which could lead to "the creation of new institutions and relationships," depending on how the churches responded to this evolving movement.[27]

Meanwhile, back in Toronto, Ernie Willie was hard at work on final arrangements for the Conference. On July 7 he drafted a press release for distribution to native media outlets, describing the Conference as "a Grand

Council in the old Indian tradition, but on a scale never before seen. Indian religious leaders of all faiths will be in attendance" at this "history-making event." Conference delegates "are committed to healing the religious strife so prevalent in modern Indian tribes and rebuilding a general harmony and religious faith among all Indians. As one delegate put it, 'We have to create a feeling of fellowship and harmony once again among our people. We need to strengthen our religious faith if we are ever going to solve our more secular problems.'"[28]

Willie then quoted several members of the Steering Committee, substantiating this rationale for the gathering and demonstrating their inclusive approach to the problem. "This may be the last chance we will have to save our communities and revitalize them," Bernard Second warned. "We are, by nature, a people who look to our religious traditions to guide us." Some believed the Conference should also address "current issues of American and Canadian society." Ernest Tootoosis argued that "we are going to have to do more than just make our own medicine strong again. We may have to start teaching our white brothers how to live in our sacred land without polluting the whole continent and destroying themselves and us. When we had the responsibility of caring for this land, it was a Garden of Eden. Perhaps we will need to instruct the newcomers how to live in respect and spiritual harmony with our Mother Earth." Ernie Willie offered his own observations as well: "This is just the beginning of a more general religious movement among our people. I feel a religious mood growing, especially among the young. Of course, it has always been there among our older people. We are basically a very spiritual and religious people."[29]

Willie also mailed invitation letters to more than a hundred delegates and a handful of non-native observers. Writing "on behalf of the Steering Committee," he welcomed each one to the forthcoming event and recounted the genesis of the Conference in Winnipeg eight months earlier. "Our main business will be to make peace among ourselves as Indian people," overcoming tribal and religious antagonisms, "thus making our stand as a unified body. We must be united if we are going to rebuild and remould our future, no matter what that future may hold. We want to experience anew what our ancestors believed and what they fought so hard to maintain. We must not let them die for nothing but rather we must again experience a resurgence of our former qualities of life." This was a progressive vision of nativist praxis, paradoxically committed to constructive engagement with both past and future, a pragmatic strategy more intelligible in grassroots communities than in the urban diaspora. Willie also explained the open-ended format of the meeting and asked each delegate to "come prepared to participate" in religious discussions and ceremonies.[30]

Conference coordinators received one last grant at the end of July. It was "a token contribution" in the amount of three thousand dollars from the

Canadian Catholic Conference, whose missions office "decided that it could only offer this gesture of encouragement at the moment, for reasons already outlined" in their earlier response. Ian MacKenzie, Bob Thomas, and Wilf Pelletier had managed to raise nearly thirty-five thousand dollars to finance an ecumenical movement among native people, but in August 1970 they were still some fifteen thousand dollars short of their fundraising goal. This looming budget deficit forced them to scale back the number of delegates invited to the Conference and to rely on in-kind contributions from the Crow tribal government and other sympathetic organizations. They would economize wherever possible and trust that any monetary shortfall could be covered by the Nishnawbe Institute. Their cause was too important to turn back now.[31]

Years later Bob Thomas would interpret the birth of this movement as the fulfillment of a postcolonial prophecy he recalled from his youth. Around the turn of the century, amid the barbarities that accompanied Oklahoma statehood, a small group of Cherokee elders had sought a vision of the future. Their revelation came through an ordinary water bucket, which was found leaking and empty one evening but miraculously full the next morning; they determined this sign "meant that the Indian's bucket will have to become empty before it will ever become full again." By the 1960s many Cherokee traditionalists believed that "our bucket has now become plumb empty," and so "it's possible for it to start to fill again. We are now at the place where things are going to change. We've gone downhill as far as we can go." Thomas elaborated on this symbolic narrative: "When the pail is empty, the way that the Indians are going to come back up again, the way that the pail is going to fill again, is if just little bunches of Indians sit down together and think of things to do and start helping one another. That way the pail is going to start to fill." It was a prophetic blueprint for grassroots organizing, predicated on interpersonal relationships rather than bureaucratic programs. "I think this is what happened with the Indian Ecumenical Conference," Thomas wrote. "Just a few of us got together and we talked a little bit. And people in other sections, in little bunches here and there, got together and talked a little bit. Then we came together and decided what we wanted to do. And we did it all ourselves—just by sitting down together like the prophecy says." They could already hear the first drops hitting the bottom of the bucket.[32]

CROW AGENCY

Conference organizers headed for southeastern Montana in early August, intending to iron out a few last-minute details and then welcome delegates to the Crow Agency gathering. A postal strike in Canada had forced Ernie Willie to coordinate travel arrangements by telephone, which he found "many of the religious leaders to be contacted did not have," so he and other organizers were already contending with some logistical anxiety. They arrived on the Crow Reservation anticipating an abundance of tribal hospitality only to learn that Bob Thomas's contact had been defeated in tribal elections a couple of weeks earlier; the rest of the locals were preoccupied with hosting their own annual encampment and "behaved as if they didn't know anything about" the Indian Ecumenical Conference. A verbal pledge of food and lodging had fallen victim to the vagaries of majoritarian politics, leaving Thomas and his colleagues to arrange accommodations for a sizeable group of people in a rural area already inundated with Crow Fair participants and tourists. Anxiety had given way to crisis.[33]

After considerable negotiation, tribal authorities finally grasped the importance of this ecumenical gathering and offered the use of a large multipurpose building with attached kitchen. Delegates began pulling in on August 13, the first day of Crow Fair, and they socialized while Conference organizers scrambled to accommodate them. "A group of people was sitting under a big tree—it was the only shade they had and it was a hot day—so I went over to listen," remembered Stewart Etsitty, one of the founders of the Native American Church among the Navajos. He saw several people "running around and helping out" including Thomas, who "was very active, running around here and there. He was the camp crier, hollering at other people what to do next." Some of the delegates had brought along spouses, children, and extended family, and there were other observers on hand as well; "sensing an emergency situation," another eyewitness reported, "many of these people now came forward and offered to help." This all-volunteer work crew erected a large circus tent to provide relief from the summer sun. The multipurpose building could double as a dining hall by day and a dormitory by night. Conference organizers rented a truckload of bedding and arranged for daily deliveries of provisions. "Cooks appeared as if by magic, and waiters and waitresses along with dishwashers. Smoothly, efficiently and spontaneously all essential needs were taken care of. The conference began in an atmosphere of lighthearted goodwill and cooperation."[34]

Delegates continued to arrive over the next couple of days. Feeling that a quorum had been reached, the Steering Committee assembled on August 14 and called a general meeting of delegates later that afternoon, where they discussed the schedule and format of their gathering. The Conference would be in session for four days, an affirmation of the fact that four is a sacred number in many tribal traditions. Sunrise ceremonies would be held each morning in

Albert Lightning's tipi, "and all who cared to participate would be welcome." Several medicine men were asked to identify and bless a suitable location for the daily deliberations; they selected a grassy spot in the shade of a nearby cottonwood grove. "Everyone felt that the structure of the actual meetings should emerge as interest and consensus dictated," should have "no design save that of providing an opportunity for those who felt moved to do so, to speak." The Conference "would unfold and assume shape" according to the needs and desires of those present. Delegates spent the rest of the day making new friends or attending evening events at Crow Fair.[35]

The Conference formally began on August 15, a Saturday, with prayers and ritual gestures to accompany the rising of the sun. The weather was clear and warm but comfortable in the shade of the cottonwoods, where delegates sat or reclined in a large circle. Morning and afternoon sessions during the first two days were spent getting acquainted as people "introduced themselves and told others, from the 'floor,' of their own and their communities' concerns." One after another stood up "to express concern for the spirituality of Indian life and the safety of the sacred soil itself. That is, concern for the sacredness of the Indian community," which now included those gathered at this place. "The earth I stand on is our altar," said Clifton Hill, "the sky our canopy." Members of the Steering Committee took turns chairing the proceedings. An anonymous observer remarked that as "delegates arose and spoke to the assembly it became apparent that many of these people had been carrying a great burden on their hearts for a long time, and that some had long since concluded they would never be able to share their deepest concerns and feelings with anyone. Some had been living underground for so long they could only look around the gathering and, with tears in their eyes, shake their heads in non-belief. They had not known there were others like themselves." Bob Thomas was impressed with this "very august body" of spiritual leaders and confessed he "saw something that I never thought I would see in my lifetime. I saw Indians get up and talk about their religion. I saw a Chippewa medicine man pray to the fire with an audience there. That means that the older Indians have a tremendous concern. You have no idea what a revolution that is."[36]

Another who appreciated the novelty of this gathering was Sam Stanley, an anthropologist from the Smithsonian Institution, one of a handful of non-native observers invited to the Conference: "Many Indians from tribes in Canada and the United States met and exchanged information for the first time. They spoke of their own traditional, as well as contemporary, religious ways. In the process," he noted, "what I perceive as the basic Indian tolerance for others' religious experiences became the spirit of the meeting. Christian

Indians acknowledged that being Christian did not negate the older truths by which their ancestors had lived. Traditionalists could tolerate Christianity as an adjunct to their own religion. Peyote was seen as another form of spiritual medicine suitable for its Indian practitioners. In truth, an ecumenical spirit permeated the meeting." Various tribal ceremonies and Christian liturgies took place during the Conference, though the proximity of Crow Fair crowds sometimes made it difficult to conduct these events in public. In a press release Allan Campbell explained that "unity, the first objective, came easily with the emergence of basic agreement about the nature of the world and man's place in it. All life—all that which exists, in fact—is sacred because it manifests the Creator." Perhaps "the most productive part of the Conference" was the informal socializing that happened after formal sessions had ended. "In the cool of the evening, after a good meal, the old folks gathered in small groups on the steps of the administration building or around the little fire or seated on three or four beds pulled close together in the dormitory-dining hall. Often they talked and smoked into the wee hours of the morning. They had much to say and much to hear."[37]

This "continental meeting of Native peoples" was proving to be a memorable exercise in free speech; Canadian and American participants alike hailed from nation-states where they had been silenced in a number of ways. "At no time was any delegate blocked from saying what he wanted to say," Bob Thomas announced, "and genuine religious concerns, prophecies, and so forth pervaded the whole four days." Allan Campbell identified other issues raised in the formal sessions: secularization, consumerism, drug abuse, and a "sickness of the spirit" among native people, which delegates "saw as basic to many of today's problems." John Snow, a United Church minister and band chief from the Stoney Reserve, was struck by his colleagues' concern "about the future and the need to revive our native religion," and about the survival of tribal languages and cultural traditions, "which are essential to our religion." One observer discerned a pair of overriding themes emerging from this expansive conversation: "The first was concern for the people. Delegate after delegate spoke movingly, sometimes bitterly, always sorrowfully of the degradation of his people—physically, morally, psychologically." The second was concern "for the land. The deterioration of the quality of the environment. The shrinking reserves. The depleted resources. The vanishing wildlife. The polluted waters and atmosphere. From the manner in which they spoke of these things," it seemed clear that delegates were describing coextensive realities. "The people and the land where they lived were one."[38]

Having generated a sense of community among these native spiritual leaders, the conversation turned to more practical matters. Crow Fair had ended and life in Crow Agency was returning to normal as delegates got down to the Monday-morning business of ecumenical activism. The last two days of the Conference were devoted to organizational affairs; a program committee coordinated the various proposals submitted for consideration. By the end of the last session on August 18 delegates had discussed and unanimously approved eleven resolutions, with three more proposed but not considered because of time constraints. These written statements documented a consensus on critical religious issues and called for specific actions on the part of non-native authorities. Aimed at dominant governments, denominations, universities, and commercial interests, the Conference resolutions charted the path to a postcolonial society grounded in religious freedom, tolerance, and respect.[39]

The Steering Committee sponsored a resolution addressing concerns it had raised at its February meeting in St. Louis, across the Mississippi from Cahokia Mounds. The Committee proposed that the Conference "go on record as opposing the indiscriminate desecration of our historic and religious monuments, our burial grounds, our pictographs, etc.," by "outside institutions" such as universities and government agencies. "We would strongly recommend that the Indian religious leaders of the tribes involved be consulted before any excavations of these sacred places take place." Their resolution also urged that "the sacred relics which are now in museums and which were collected by quasi-legal and immoral methods be returned on request to the tribe involved. Moreover, those sacred relics acquired legitimately by museums should be on loan for such periods as they are needed by Indian tribes. Further, museums should hire Indians qualified to care for such sacred objects now in their possession."[40]

The defense of cultural property rights also found expression in two resolutions submitted by Conference delegates. David Clark, president of the Native American Church of Navajoland, authored a resolution "expressing the strongest disapproval of the perversion of Indian sacred dances for commercial purposes by unauthorized groups, the taking of the Peyote sacrament by non-Indians in a secular context, and all other undignified mockeries of our ancient traditions." Jimmy and Fred Erasmus, Dogrib leaders from Yellowknife, collaborated on a resolution "opposing all interference in the natural and sacred relation between the Indian people and the animals and birds which the Creator placed on this island for our physical and spiritual sustenance." They were particularly aggrieved by "such things as requiring Indians to have a permit to hunt eagles, disregarding of Indian hunting rights in Oklahoma, the encouragement of commercial hunting of caribou in the Northwest Territories, the promotion of sportsman hunting to the detriment of hunting for food by Indians, etc." Painfully aware of the connection between environmental stewardship and the political economy, the Erasmus brothers suggested that "Canada and the United States cannot address the problem of pollution and ecological balance by ignoring traditional Indian religious practices. Conservation offices should consult Indian religious leaders about conservation practices." One of the unconsidered resolutions condemned the "industrial pollution" caused by reservation development, singling out the controversial mining operation at Black Mesa among the Hopis and Navajos.[41]

Keedah Johnson proposed two resolutions defending the civil liberty of the peyote religion. The first one pointed out that "the states of Arizona, New Mexico, and Utah have failed to recognize the sacred character of the rites of the Native American Church," which "has caused severe hardship and is a violation of their constitutionally guaranteed freedom of religion." He asked these state governments "to cease harassing members of the Native American Church and to immediately grant formal recognition of the sacred character of their rites," noting that Conference delegates were "themselves members of many different Christian and traditional faiths." Johnson was joined by Bob Thomas in sponsoring a second resolution aimed at mainline Christian denominations, calling on each church "to take specific action to ensure that all of its members extend their respect and assistance to small Christian denominations such as the Native American Church. In view of the recent ecumenical movement, it is untenable that religious persecution of a Christian Indian group be allowed to continue. Their plight is the concern of all Christians and we urge all Christians to take up their cause." Another unconsidered resolution sought "official recognition of Native Religions as legitimate religious groups, even though they are without a formal dogma," by Christian churches and "government agencies such a tax bureaus, draft boards, etc."[42]

Andrew Ahenakew also made reference to postwar ecumenism among mainline Christians in his resolution on evangelistic policy and practice. "In view of the recent ecumenical movement among Christian denominations," he requested "that mission activity be better coordinated so as not to encourage excessive competition among sects in Indian communities, which results in confusion and heightens such social disintegration as psychological turmoil and religious strife. Further, we ask that missionaries always keep in mind that they are guests in our reservations and communities and that we are no longer a conquered, passive people to be exploited spiritually." John Hascall went a step further by proposing a resolution petitioning "denominational authorities" to grant church leaders in tribal communities "the freedom to use native languages, traditions, dances, legends, and their own ancient religions as instruments of expression of the Christian faith."[43]

Three resolutions asserted the relevance of tribal spiritual values to social and political institutions, demonstrating Conference delegates' concern for all aspects of native community life. Stanley Smith suggested that public health agencies be ordered "to work in cooperation with Indian medicine men and native Indian doctors," that government hospitals "be made aware of local Indian health and religious practices and be required to take them into account in hospital practice and procedure," and that "local Indian committees be formed to act as liaison between the hospitals and the community," providing information "about Indian religious practices such as these agencies have about other religious groups." Bob Thomas encouraged "the teaching of Indian culture and language in those schools not now having such programs," requesting "that those who teach Indian culture and history in schools be appointed after consultation with the Indian people involved and that non-essential educational standards be waived so that native religionists can be utilized in such school programs." David Clark forcefully reminded "the governments of the United States and Canada that our treaties with them are not secular contracts to us but sacred covenants, ordained and sanctioned by God, which guarantee our existence as peoples and which establish a sacred reciprocity among the Indian, God, the natural world, and our recent European brothers. Any disregard of our treaties is, in fact, a violation of our religion and Judeo-Christian ethics as well."[44]

Perhaps the most far-reaching resolution was submitted by Charles Red Corn, an Osage activist standing in for Leroy Logan, a tribal elder and peyote roadman who was unable to attend the Conference. Both were members of the Osage Nation Organization, a grassroots group pursuing democratic reforms within its own tribal government. Red Corn had driven up from Oklahoma City with his wife and two young children and bearing a resolution crafted by Logan. "This Convention supports the efforts toward American Indian self-determination," it read, "and attempts of all American Indian communities to create viable community organizations, both local community organizations and tribal organizations." Red Corn's wife Jeri already knew Bob Thomas, having attended one of the summer workshops in Boulder during her college days, and the Red Corns' son and daughter enjoyed playing with other children they ran into around the Conference grounds. But Red Corn himself initially felt out of place at this summit of spiritual leaders and wondered aloud whether political issues should be discussed at a religious gathering, until an acquaintance from eastern Oklahoma assured him of the assembly's comprehensive mission. Conference delegates made their intentions clear when they approved Logan's resolution by acclamation. One even circulated a petition addressing an imminent political crisis back home. Randy

Jacobs, a Presbyterian minister and the lone Choctaw representative at the Conference, made a passionate plea for help in resisting the U.S. policy of termination, which had targeted the Choctaw tribal government. His ecumenical colleagues were happy to sign his petition calling for "the passage of a bill before Congress repealing the Choctaw Termination Act."[45]

As the proceedings drew to a close, many delegates admitted to having attended the gathering "out of genuine interest but with some skepticism 'to look things over.'" By the end of the formal sessions "they were enthusiastic and 'ready to have a Conference,'" better acquainted with each other, more willing to share. Participation in the sunrise ceremonies had increased each day and on the last morning Albert Lightning's tipi was filled to overflowing. "More sat in a circle outside it than were inside it. Coincident with the daily growth in attendance was an increasing feeling of power and peace. Many spoke of this feeling and then the last morning it was almost tangible." Some even felt that the schedule had been too hectic and "not enough time was spent considering important theological matters." One delegate expressed his appreciation to the coordinators with these words: "I cannot tell you how grateful I am to have been invited here. It has been one of the greatest experiences of my life but I see now that when your invitation came to us back home, we did not understand what kind of a conference this was to be. Personally, I didn't even know what the word 'ecumenical' meant." A Conference organizer later wrote that the "joy and reassurance" these religious leaders "experienced in meeting allies and friends more than justified" the effort and resources required to bring them together.[46]

On the morning of August 19 delegates assembled one last time for an "unofficial" session to plan their collective future. "Unanimous in their desire to have another Conference next year," they reelected all members of the Steering Committee and commissioned them with the responsibility of planning and organizing a gathering in 1971. They also codified the name of their organization, agreeing that it should continue to be known as the Indian Ecumenical Conference. "Most felt also that they needed to talk with their co-elders in their home areas for a time and to 'let the pot simmer' for awhile. Nearly all were of the opinion that many more Indian religious leaders had to be in attendance at such a Conference before hard decisions" could be made. The Committee encouraged delegates to help spread the word by forming regional committees, hosting regional conferences, and establishing regional organizations that would advance the cause of intertribal ecumenism. The assembled delegates also approved the appointment of an official Conference "spiritual leader" who could "be contacted by any community in trouble to call for a day of fasting, prayer, and medicine-making on its behalf. All delegates would be notified of this day and would ask their communities to participate." A committee of medicine men headed by Albert Lightning was authorized to "choose this man by spiritual means."[47]

Crow Fair had provided a suitably intertribal backdrop for the Conference, but delegates generally agreed that convening a religious gathering adjacent to a noisy fair overrun with tourists "was not such a good idea," so they entertained suggestions for a new location the following year. Two individuals volunteered to host the 1971 Conference: Ed Loon, a Sioux leader from the Standing Rock Reservation several hours east of Crow Agency; and John Snow, who offered the use of the Stoneys' new tribal park in the foothills of the Canadian Rockies. Bob Thomas and other organizers had envisioned an annual encampment held in a different place each year and alternating between Canadian and American sites. The Stoney Reserve would be an idyllic setting on the appropriate side of the Canada-U.S. border, but Standing Rock is more centrally situated and would likely draw participation from a wider range of tribal communities. Delegates were unable to reach a consensus in choosing between these two alternatives so the decision was left to the Steering Committee, which would take up the question at its fall meeting. John Snow returned home "with a feeling of encouragement and realization that there were many Indian leaders who were concerned with the revival of our cultural, spiritual and religious heritage."[48]

Conference participants packed up and headed for home while Allan Campbell, the budding anthropologist, drafted a press release. It was a melodramatic impression of the event, situating this unprecedented gathering closer to the military headstones of Custer Battlefield National Monument than the tribal drums of Crow Fair, a tragic interpretation dwelling more on colonial guilt than postcolonial redemption. "European immigrants failed to learn from their Indian brothers the rules of North American citizenship, so we today continue to be strangers in what we now call our own land," Campbell lamented. "All of this was not news to the delegates assembled at this Indian Ecumenical meeting. They came from communities across two countries, scarred communities, still living, whose individual histories reveal the moody arrogance and casual cruelties of the European invaders."[49]

To his credit, Campbell did recognize the novelty of this intertribal meeting, a timely rendezvous of native religious leaders. "What is most encouraging," he admitted, "is a sense of renewed hope, rising from the act of communion and communal worship. One Apache ceremonial leader, feeling himself alone in his own community, gave thanks to the meeting for the support which, he said, he had found for the first time." Conference delegates "departed with renewed hope. Like the Apache leader, others—medicine men, ministers and doctors—have for the first time found a community of interest. Now there is the promise of a movement which will carry this commonality of interest beyond these transitory few days of meeting toward cooperative efforts to sew together the social fabrics of Indian communities." Contending that "despair has not been fully dispelled at the first Indian Ecumenical Conference," Campbell closed with a predictable measure of social-scientific skepticism: "What happens to this newly found unity of purpose will depend, of course, on the abilities of those who have created it to maintain it. Their friends will be expected to help. This help may be critical." His press release was distributed to non-native media outlets and published by at least one, appearing in the September issue of the *Canadian Churchman*.[50]

Bob Thomas also prepared a report on the Conference, though his account was less tragic and more informative than Allan Campbell's, emphasizing native agency at Crow Agency. Thomas's rendition was unabashedly optimistic as well—better suited for a native readership—and it was published by the National Indian Youth Council in the August issue of *Americans Before Columbus*. He opened by naming many of the forty-seven tribal communities represented among Conference delegates, most of whom "felt that there was a surprisingly large 'turnout' for such a new endeavour. And most interpreted this as a sign that such a Conference had struck a very responsive chord among Indians." He also highlighted the religious diversity of the gathering, noting that "most of the delegates were either Christian ministers or native Indian ceremonial leaders. Some delegates combined both roles in the same person." He then provided a concise overview of the organizational background, daily activities, and future plans of the Conference.[51]

Thomas determined that "the most prominent feature of the Conference—which emerged clearly to nearly everyone's surprise and pleasure—was the unanimity of purpose and thought of the delegates." Explaining how unifying sentiment can be translated into a praxis of solidarity, he elaborated on this emergent theory of interreligious relations among native people: "Everyone agreed that modern Indian religious life must be a furthering of the historic continuity of time-honoured Indian values and philosophical concern; that both modern Indian ceremonies and Indian Christianity must be part of that continuity; and that both native ceremonials and Indian Christianity can be mutually supportive or parallel and co-operative or integrated, according to the desire of the particular tribe involved." It was an ingenious vision of collective survival, at once venerable and contemporary, accommodating both local autonomy and global concern, informed by a healthy balance of tribal idealism and pragmatic candor. "Most felt that the work of future Conferences would be to evolve a way of implementing this process," Thomas concluded. "The delegates left for home full of enthusiasm and high hopes."[52]

Conference coordinators documented the event in other ways as well, producing a list of resolutions, a financial statement, and a roster of participants. The roster named fourteen Steering Committee members, seventy-nine delegates, twenty-nine "unofficial" delegates, and eight non-native observers who attended the gathering, though at least a hundred more native and non-native participants were present for some Conference activities. The Committee had made good on its commitment to organize a transnational meeting; fifty-six of the named native participants were living in Canada, sixty-six in the U.S. Most of the Canadian delegates had mailing addresses in the provinces of Ontario, Saskatchewan, Alberta, and British Columbia, with very few attending from the rest of the country. More than a third of the American delegates had mailing addresses in the state of Oklahoma, with smaller regional concentrations from the Southwest, the Northern Plains, and the Great Lakes along with a handful of individuals from various far-flung communities. Conference coordinators and fieldworkers had not achieved an even geographic distribution, though they had brought together native spiritual leaders from as far away as Quebec and Nova Scotia, Florida and Texas, California and Washington, Alaska and the Northwest Territories. The roster did not list religious affiliations—many delegates could claim more than one—but there were at least eight ordained Christian ministers among the named native participants. In his report Bob Thomas noted that "a substantial number of tribes sent both their principal ceremonial leader and their most prominent Christian functionary." The most conspicuous demographic discrepancy between the Conference and the tribal communities it hoped to represent lay in the fact that only thirteen of the named native participants were female, and at least four of these were related to male delegates already in attendance. Tribal women have always played a more active role in spiritual affairs than has been acknowledged outside their homes and communities.[53]

The most surprising demographic aspect of this intertribal gathering involved some participants who were not included on the official roster. "An unexpected but significant development was the large number of Indian young people who came to observe the Conference," Bob Thomas wrote. "For example, the Native Youth Summer Programme of Toronto sent twenty young people to observe the proceedings," and others drifted over from the Crow Fair grounds. Sunrise ceremonies were not the only Conference activities where attendance grew each day; as word spread that a large group of tribal elders and spiritual leaders were gathered nearby, curious onlookers gravitated to the cottonwood grove and listened in, and a few even spoke up. According to Thomas, "those numbers of young Indian people who participated in the Conference felt it was a sure sign that the religious aspects of their cultural communities are being continued." Allan Campbell also commented on the implications of an intergenerational dynamic, suggesting this encounter had "laid to rest that old myth of a vanishing society, tied tenuously to the lives of the 'old people.' Educated Indian youth, those who might be seen as de-tribalized, de-culturated," were ready to "ask their religious leaders for action. Coming from the cities and university, their statements underscore their awareness and the corrosive effect of secular society on their own communities. And this, they see, is a measure of the attack on their identities as Indian persons. At the conference they have found in ceremonial participation (some for the first time) a new commitment to serve their people." Campbell's observations would prove to be unwittingly prophetic; the unanticipated presence of these earnest native youth said more about the future of the movement than did delegates' careful deliberations over official resolutions, logistical arrangements, and media representations of the Conference.[54]

The Anglican Church of Canada had provided nearly three-fourths of the funding it took to hold the Crow Agency gathering, and afterward church officials asked each Anglican participant to evaluate the Conference. Five who responded were enthusiastic about the experience, and each one commended Anglican leaders for supporting this new venture. "I think and feel and I am proud to say that the Anglican Church is taking the bold and right step," declared Andrew Ahenakew. Gary Woolsey, a missionary pilot in northern Ontario, listed a number of beneficial outcomes including a village-wide ecumenical meeting he and the two native delegates from Big Trout Lake organized as soon as they returned home. "I was proud to be a member of the Anglican Church at this Conference," he concluded. "To know that the Anglican Church is leading the way in providing the means for Indian People to come together to discuss the very core of their life is indeed encouragement to all of us." Ernie Willie described the event as "a dream come true" that brought back memories of his childhood days in Kingcome Inlet and of the "wise, gentle, humble" elders who cared for him. "It has been good to get together and talk over our mutual difficulties and to realize that our task of rebuilding is going to take cooperation on all sides. There is no sense in putting blame on others and hoping that someone else is going to restore us as a race to our former selves." Native leaders "will have to roll up our sleeves and dig in. The challenge is great but if it can be surmounted it will be greatness restored to a people who have and are suffering."[55]

Vine Deloria, Jr., also weighed in on the significance of this movement in an ambitious but little-known survey of American political history. Jennings

Wise originally published *The Red Man in the New World Drama* in 1931, interpreting the colonization of the Americas as "part of a world drama of conflicting religions." The book was an ambitious effort at documenting "the fundamental differences in cultural outlook, in part inspired by different religious world views," between native and non-native people. Deloria admired Wise's work and updated it forty years later; in the last of the revised book's thirty-six chapters, he assessed "The Rise of Indian Activism" and its implications for the future.[56]

Predicting the failure of any intertribal coalition founded on purely political ambitions, Deloria asserted that "only in those rare moments when religious fervor enables a people to coalesce for action have any significant changes been made." The various activist groups would contribute to the survival of native people only insofar as they triggered a revival of interest in tribal traditions. "For by returning to Indian religions, by adopting the traditional customs by which tribal members related to one another, by forming useful and efficient alliances with forces in contemporary society, by these means alone could the red men ensure their survival. The beginnings of such a movement were clearly evident" in the Indian Ecumenical Conference, Deloria concluded. Originally organized by Bob Thomas and others "against the advice of supposedly knowledgeable Indian political leaders, the conference was an unqualified success. After a week's meeting in which ideas and evaluations of the contemporary scene were made, the rapid movement of Indian emotions toward the traditional values was evident to everyone." The "inherent strengths of the basic tribal beliefs" had surfaced and "were beginning to dominate every decision made by Indians." Echoing the prophetic overtones in Thomas's view of the Conference, Deloria cited earlier native spiritual leaders who had predicted these developments. "Even Wovoka had foreseen the day when the irresistible movement of Indians would reclaim the continent. The meeting at Crow had made clear that this time was approaching."[57]

Seventy-seven years earlier on the shores of Lake Michigan, a few miles from the University of Chicago where Bob Thomas would later pursue graduate studies in action anthropology, another ecumenical gathering had promised to inaugurate "a new era of religious peace and progress." Organizers of the World's Parliament of Religions, the most celebrated of two hundred auxiliary congresses held during the World's Columbian Exposition of 1893, dreamed of hosting an event that might "unite all Religion against all irreligion." Charles Carroll Bonney welcomed some sixty delegates and an enthusiastic crowd of onlookers to the Parliament's opening assembly on September 11: "We come together in mutual confidence and respect, without the least surrender or compromise of anything which we respectively believe to be truth or duty, with the hope that mutual acquaintance and a free and sincere interchange of views on the great questions of eternal life and human conduct will be mutually beneficial." For seventeen days Parliament participants listened to formal papers delivered by religious leaders and scholars representing Buddhism, Christianity, Confucianism, Hinduism, Islam, Jainism, Judaism, Shintoism, Taoism, and Zoroastrianism. These scripted performances were among the most popular attractions of the entire Exposition, which was staged to commemorate the four-hundredth anniversary of European colonization in the Americas. Political dignitaries had dedicated the Exposition on October 12, 1892, giving birth to a new national holiday—Columbus Day—and to other patriotic traditions such as the "Pledge of Allegiance to the Flag." As Richard Hughes Seager shows in his study of the Parliament, the Exposition was a millennial world's fair designed to promote American civil religion, a monument to "the Columbian myth of America."[58]

The Parliament "deserves a central place in a pluralistic account of American religious history," but it should not be mistaken for an inclusive assembly of the world's spiritual traditions. The agenda included three times as many major addresses by Christians as by representatives of the other nine religions put together. Tribal religious leaders were not even invited to participate in the Parliament, though at least one Asian delegate did comment publicly on their absence. Native people appeared only in ethnographic exhibits that were part of the Exposition midway, living dioramas arrayed in a pseudoscientific continuum from civilization to savagery and interspersed with commercial amusements. "The Parliament, however noble its goals and aspirations, was tainted by the same parochialism, ethnocentrism, imperial pretensions, and hegemonic intentions as the entire Exposition," Seager writes. "In philosophical terms, it failed because the premises for its universalistic agenda turned out to be particularistic. In crude theological terms, it failed because the God of the organizers of the Parliament turned out not to be quite the same as the Gods of the Asians." Though Seager acknowledges that there are other valid interpretive approaches to such a complex historical phenomenon, he focuses his analysis on "the East/West encounter." Seen from this particular angle, the great irony of the Parliament was that an event representing the culmination of Western imperialism could simultaneously signal its eventual demise. "Having failed as a liberal quest for religious unity, the Parliament unintentionally turned out to be a revelation of the plurality of forces on the American and world scenes. As a result," Seager concludes, "it was a harbinger of the rise of the idea of religious pluralism that is alternatively celebrated, studied, decried, and in various ways struggled over in many different quarters today."[59]

The Parliament may have been a memorable occasion for "East/West encounter," but it hardly marked "the dawn of religious pluralism" on the American landscape, as Seager contends in his collection of Parliament texts. The year 1893 witnessed not the dawn of religious pluralism but its midnight, the darkest chapter in our collective spiritual history, coinciding with the nadir of native population and of the tribal diversity represented therein. The Americas have yet to see the degree of religious pluralism that existed before the onset of European colonization, post-Parliament developments notwithstanding. It is unfortunate that tribal religious leaders were excluded from the Parliament, and that their spiritual traditions have been written out of the historical record by scholars preoccupied with an Orientalist binary bounded by East and West. Even more distressing is the fact that the varieties of native religious experience are still ignored by contemporary theorists of interfaith dialogue. Elite voices continue to formulate conversational rubrics amenable to the so-called world religions, which they favor on the basis of demographic strength or geopolitical influence rather than any measure of spiritual integrity. Few dominant religionists are prepared to admit that tribal people are an indispensable presence in the postcolonial interreligious encounter.[60]

From a native perspective, the Parliament failed because its organizers considered religious unity to be a theological problem rather than a relational challenge. In their minds, Judeo-Christian theism could serve as this gathering's central unifying principle and the philosophical foundation upon which to build a universal religious discourse. It turned out to be a self-serving criterion by which they would judge other religions. Many of the Asian delegates eschewed rationalistic debate, delivering Parliament addresses emphasizing ethical and mystical and other experiential bases for religious devotion, but even their most liberal Christian counterparts tended to refract these insights through a theological prism. "In the West you observe, watch, and act. In the East we contemplate, commune, and suffer ourselves to be carried away by the spirit of the universe," explained Hindu scholar P. C. Majumdar in an extemporaneous speech titled "The World's Religious Debt to Asia." Acknowledging that European colonialism had taken its toll on Asian dignity, he concluded that "in the midst of the sadness, the loneliness, the prostration of the present, it is some consolation to think that we still retain some of our spirituality, and to reflect upon the prophecy of Ezekiel, 'Behold, the glory of the Lord cometh from the way of the East.'" Material inequity can compromise any relationship, but the most challenging impediment to ecumenical solidarity is epistemological bias.[61]

The World's Parliament of Religions and the Indian Ecumenical Conference were pivotal moments in the history of interfaith cooperation. Both were animated by a vision of "religious peace and progress," intent on transcending various social boundaries in favor of a broader spiritual unity, though the obvious differences in their pursuit of this goal produced divergent outcomes. Even their chosen names foreshadowed this divergence. A parliament is a formal assembly of elite officials deliberating over matters of public concern; to parley is to negotiate with an adversary. A conference is a more relaxed gathering of people exchanging views on matters of common interest; to confer is to talk with an ally. Whereas the Parliament promulgated abstract truths contingent on a propositional theology, the Conference elaborated practical solutions grounded in a personalistic experience. The Parliament laid claim to a global constituency but fell prey to the provinciality that is nearly always the corollary of power, whereas the Conference aspired only to help tribal communities and ended up forging a model of conflict resolution useful in many other religious contexts.[62]

This paradigm for interreligious relations was grounded in the realities of contemporary life in Indian country. The success of the Conference was a product of its pragmatic orientation, and its credibility as an intertribal movement was contingent on its ability to address current issues in grassroots communities. Conference organizers and fieldworkers labored to identify delegates whose spiritual stature was acknowledged at the local level. Steering Committee meetings and the Conference itself were inclusive events, bringing together representative leaders who related to one another as equals and who collectively embodied the full range of religious traditions among native people. Delegates were encouraged to bring along family members and friends, whose presence at Crow Agency helped create a comfortable atmosphere for the gathering. The Conference schedule was relatively unstructured; morning and afternoon sessions were devoted to open discussion of religious issues, while mealtimes and evening breaks provided opportunities for informal conversation and socializing. Participants were asked to articulate concerns and insights drawn from their own personal experiences. They were also invited to demonstrate their ecumenical commitment through public prayers and other cooperative ceremonies, sharing spiritual expressions rather than theological dogmas. Relying on a consensus decision-making process, Conference delegates approved resolutions supporting religious freedom, cultural survival, and political sovereignty. Responsibility for fundraising and communication was assigned to the Nishnawbe Institute, a religiously neutral organization that handled administrative logistics on behalf of the Steering Committee but was not empowered to make policy. Bob Thomas and his colleagues envisioned annual transnational gatherings along with periodic regional and local meetings that together would stimulate "a general movement for ecumenicity" in tribal communities, laying the foundation for spiritual revival throughout Indian country and, ultimately, around the world.[63]

Thomas later summarized the consensus on how this "general movement" might proceed, identifying three key principles that bear repeating. "Everyone agreed," he wrote in his report on the Conference, "that modern Indian religious life must be a furthering of the historic continuity of time-honoured Indian values and philosophical concern; that both modern Indian ceremonies and Indian Christianity must be part of that continuity; and that both native ceremonials and Indian Christianity can be mutually supportive or parallel and cooperative or integrated, according to the desire of the particular tribe involved." Cultural history, contemporary diversity, and local autonomy are the inescapable contexts for ecumenical organizing among native people. Religious self-determination is reduced to little more than a slogan by any such movement that disregards these three principles. Spiritual revival is about the human desire for connection, for interpersonal revelation, for transcendence in the face of mortal boundaries. Interreligious dialogue is a reflexive—not didactic—vocation, bearing the potential for mutual transformation.[64]

INTERRELIGIOUS ORGANIZATION

One of the first challenges Conference coordinators tackled as they began planning a gathering for the summer of 1971 entailed dashing off a letter to the Anglican Church of Canada. Writing from the Nishnawbe Institute, Wilf Pelletier thanked church executives for their sizeable financial contributions in support of "Indian ecumenicity," enclosing several reports that documented the 1970 Conference. He also characterized this experiment in interreligious organizing as an unqualified success. "The enthusiasm of the delegates to the conference and the whole mood of ecumenism certainly bears out the correctness of the analysis in our first proposal to you," he explained. "At this juncture, it is evident that the conference both defined Indian ecumenism and turned feelings and mood into action. At present, the movement is 'snowballing.' Right now, delegates are promoting ecumenism in their own areas with considerable missionary zeal."[65]

The immediacy and urgency of Pelletier's account reflected the fact that this epistle was part reportage, part solicitation; he and his colleagues needed to raise more money. The Indian Ecumenical Conference had amassed a substantial budget deficit—which the Institute was covering for the time being—and organizers had already scheduled another Steering Committee meeting at a Vancouver hotel. Wilf Pelletier, Bob Thomas, and Ian MacKenzie were asking the Primate's World Relief and Development Fund for an early commitment of fifteen thousand dollars, seed money that might encourage other funding agencies to invest in the Conference. Denominational executives in the U.S. had been especially reluctant to support the 1970 gathering, in part because the Conference was being administered by a Canadian organization. "It is quite apparent that this conference and this new spirit of ecumenicity among Indians in North America owes a great deal to the Anglican Church of Canada and to other Canadian institutions," Pelletier wrote. "We hope to persuade American sources to be as socially responsible as some Canadian churches." The balance of the letter stressed the importance of continued Anglican support, financially as well as through the native Anglican clergy who were participating in the Conference. "Indian ecumenism is now part of the Indian scene and a force with which to be reckoned," but "it is very hard for many Indian religious leaders, Christian or otherwise, to temper the anti-church feelings of young Indians. If the churches 'leave the field' the movement will be pressured toward an anti-Christian complexion."[66]

The Steering Committee convened in Vancouver during the third weekend of November. Twelve months had passed since its initial meeting in Winnipeg, where Bob Thomas had outlined his vision for an intertribal gathering of grassroots native leadership focused on resolving the religious antagonisms in their communities. From Winnipeg to St. Louis to Henryetta to Crow Agency, the Committee had circled the heart of the continent and witnessed the birth of an ecumenical movement in Indian country, even as the dominant culture in North America was spawning an ever more volatile mix of technological prowess and human animosity. The year 1970 was a good time to begin the healing process.[67]

Most members of the Steering Committee were present at the Vancouver meeting, including two individuals who had been recruited at the Crow Agency gathering: Ed Loon, the Standing Rock Sioux leader; and Stewart Etsitty, representing the Native American Church of Navajoland. Their first session on Friday began with a pipe ceremony led by Albert Lightning, which took most of the morning. Public prayers were offered at other times during the weekend by Ed Loon, Stewart Etsitty, John Hascall, Andrew Ahenakew, and local Squamish leaders Simon Baker and Dominic Charlie, each drawing on the ritual tradition of his own religious community. Spiritual practice was a prominent theme of the meeting, evident both in these shared experiences and in the various issues raised for consideration. Committee members briefly discussed appointing a Conference "spiritual leader" who would be available for crisis intervention, an idea first proposed at Crow Agency, but again postponed their decision until more elders could be consulted. Bob Thomas informed his colleagues about an elected official in Virginia who had blocked the desecration of a burial mound in his city; they agreed to send a letter of commendation. Several Committee members expressed concern over the U.S. government's recent efforts to restrict recreational drug use, which had needlessly criminalized the peyote sacrament and further eroded the religious freedom of the Native American Church; the Committee resolved to send a letter of protest.[68]

One of the more engaging items on the agenda was a proposal that the Steering Committee establish a "National Indian Day of Prayer" and lobby various church and government authorities for official recognition. This course of action had been suggested at Crow Agency by delegate Browning Pipestem, an Otoe-Missouria lawyer who provided legal advice to the Conference. He thought a quiet campaign seeking support for such an annual observance might legitimate the Conference as "a real religious body" while helping Conference organizers reach out to new constituencies. "This would be a way of not only doing some good for ourselves spiritually," Pipestem believed, "but also giving a broader base to our efforts." After considerable discussion the Committee arrived at a consensus: "most of the members thought that June 21st, the day when the sun is longest in the sky, is probably the most sacred single day of the year to most tribes." They agreed to set aside the summer solstice as a time for spiritual devotion and directed the coordinators to start spreading the word. Bob Thomas saw this commemoration as a powerful opportunity to revitalize tribal communities: "Indian churches and ceremonial grounds could use that day to pray, or make medicine, or dance, or fast to ask for peace and harmony."[69]

The Steering Committee also dealt with political concerns pressed by some native youth who were sitting in on its deliberations. Even before the meeting began, Stanley Smith had encountered several local activists who were upset about a recent book that portrayed their home communities in an objectionable manner, and they were also irritated by their own band chiefs' unwillingness to protest its publication. The book was *How a People Die*, a fictionalized, tragic critique of social conditions among native people in British Columbia, written by a former Indian Affairs bureaucrat. Steering Committee members approved a couple of resolutions responding to this situation, one calling for a boycott of the book, another encouraging both native and non-native officials to take these spirited activists seriously. "The Committee felt that there must be a voice for young Indians in both the political and religious affairs of concern to Indians," the minutes reported. "One of the most significant events of this meeting was the involvement and interest of a large number of young Indians who attended all of our sessions." These outspoken observers also petitioned the Committee to pursue official recognition for tribal religious traditions, in part so that native men following pacifist teachings might have a legal basis for claiming conscientious objector status when drafted by the U.S. military. Committee members declined to take formal action on this matter, though "all agreed we needed some way to help the young men going into the service. Most of the Committee agree that even more important than some political act or semi-political act such as getting sanction for Indian religions would be actual spiritual help in some way for the young men going into the service and now in the service." This was a pragmatic approach to the problem, given the fact that most native men who served in the armed forces during the Vietnam War era were volunteers, not conscripts.[70]

Much of the Vancouver meeting was devoted to organizational business. Ian MacKenzie presented the financial report for the 1970 Conference, which showed a deficit of nearly sixty-six hundred dollars, generating a lengthy discussion of fundraising strategies. The Steering Committee directed the coordinators to continue pursuing church and foundation money and also considered the pros and cons of soliciting funds from native organizations and from grassroots communities. Most members of the Committee "felt that the amount of funds raised would not be large but that the social value of such a fund raising program would be great. Indian communities could take up collections at dances and have pie suppers to raise funds," which "would not only be some contribution to the general effort but would also give local people a feeling they had a hand in the movement itself." Several Committee members reported on regional ecumenical gatherings planned for southern Florida, the American Southwest, and the Great Lakes borderlands; these were autonomous ventures but the Committee agreed to "give any organizational help that they can." They also reached a consensus that the Conference would eventually need its own central office and administrative staff—and possibly several full-time fieldworkers as well—to relieve the Nishnawbe Institute of this burden. Bob Thomas initiated a conversation about the difficulties encountered by Conference delegates when crossing the Canada-U.S. border, where customs regulations made it "very possible that sacred objects might be confiscated or handled in a manner which might pollute the sacredness of the objects," and where "the laws on both sides of the line regarding eagle feathers, as well as herbs and other things," posed an additional threat. The Steering Committee asked the coordinators to contact customs officials in both countries and "get some kind of working situation set up." Addressing these and other logistical challenges, Committee members demonstrated a keen appreciation for the local, regional, and transnational forces at work in their ecumenical endeavor.[71]

The most contentious moments at this meeting involved the effort to choose a site for the 1971 Conference. Picking up where the delegates at Crow Agency had left off, on Friday evening the Steering Committee reviewed two earlier invitations to convene on the Stoney Reserve or the Standing Rock Reservation and also discussed three new possibilities: a Creek town in eastern Oklahoma, an Ojibway reserve on the Canada-U.S. border, and a Cree community in southern Saskatchewan. "There was a great deal of division and differences of opinion" among Committee members, so they "tabled that issue and adjourned" for the day. They revisited the question on Sunday afternoon but "after much discussion it became apparent again that there was no consensus on this matter and quite a bit of disagreement." Unable to resolve its most pressing logistical dilemma through a consensus decision-making process, the Committee resorted to majoritarian measures: it directed the coordinators to explore each alternative and then poll Committee members by mail-in ballot. The meeting adjourned with a prayer in the Anglican tradition and a handshaking ceremony in the Creek and Cherokee manner, and most Committee members also attended a Sunday evening event at a local church where Ernie Willie presented a program on Kwakiutl cultural history.[72]

Anglican church officials were continuing their effort to implement the recommendations of the Hendry report, making progress on several fronts during the fall of 1970. In September the *Canadian Churchman* reported on the resolutions that Conference delegates had approved at Crow Agency, which the Anglican church would be asked to endorse at its next General Synod. Hendry report coordinator Trevor Jones admitted to having had "grave doubts" when he agreed to oversee this work; he believed that many Anglicans "did not fully realize the implications that their approval to the report has," and he was "not yet convinced the church means the dramatic action it accepted last year." In December he spoke at the Provincial Synod of Rupert's Land, encouraging Anglican leaders to support native self-determination at the regional and local levels—and to welcome the collective metamorphosis this commitment might bring. "Perhaps a more important objective for all of us should be that we explore vigorously ways by which our Native peoples can make their own unique contribution to the life of the Church and the Nation. I have in mind," he remarked, "the Ecumenical Indian Religious Conference held in Montana, which may in fact be the most important single event organized by the Native peoples of North America to date. It is generally recognized that any people or any individual must be liberated from the structures that restrict them and permitted to rediscover their own identity and heritage before they can really be free to make their unique contribution to the global community." Reminding his audience of the liberatory potential of the Christian tradition, Jones offered a theological rationale in arguing that native people should be "free to express their own self-identity; free to make their maximum contribution to the world community; free to worship in their own way, or in ours, or in a combination of both."[73]

The twenty-fifth General Synod of the Anglican Church of Canada was held in January 1971, scheduled to coincide with the twenty-fourth General Council of the United Church of Canada. The two mainline denominations had been courting the possibility of institutional merger; both national gatherings took place at Niagara Falls, where church officials hoped for a honeymoon of sorts. Anglican leaders also anticipated further discussion of the Hendry report and of the ecumenical organizing they had facilitated in Indian country. Trevor Jones originally wanted Ernest Tootoosis to represent the Conference, pitching him in an internal memo as "a very wise and highly respected Indian leader, an articulate speaker in English and even more colourful than Alanis Obomsawin, with his feathers, necklace, bracelets, and beaded jacket of moose skin." Instead, the Steering Committee had designated Andrew Ahenakew as its liaison to Canadian churches. He attended General Synod and presented two motions on behalf of the Conference, one pledging action on the resolutions approved at Crow Agency, the other recognizing the National Indian Day of Prayer and directing "all dioceses to commend this day to parishes and congregations" across Canada. "In other days this would have been called pagan," Ahenakew said from the rostrum, sporting his clerical collar. "Today, the North American Indian asks the church to recognize their earlier worship to the one great creator whom we knew ten thousand years ago."[74]

Both motions carried with little debate, and the assembled clergy and lay leaders also reaffirmed their commitment to implementing the Hendry report recommendations over the next five years. The Conference garnered additional support at the United Church gathering, where General Council commissioners voted to recognize the National Indian Day of Prayer and "to make this action known to the people of the Church" through their Board of Home Missions. In March the Mohawk periodical *Akwesasne Notes* reprinted several articles describing these and other encouraging developments in the relationship between tribal communities and Christian churches.[75]

In May, Bob Thomas asked LaDonna Harris, a Comanche activist whose husband was a U.S. senator, to help the Conference drum up congressional support for the National Indian Day of Prayer. "We are hoping to designate this one day as a symbol of Indian religious unity," he wrote, "as a day that Indian Christians of all denominations as well as non-Christians could observe simultaneously but each in their own way. Of course, if whites want to share this day with us we are only too happy to receive their brotherhood." The

June issue of the *Canadian Churchman* featured a lead story on the National Indian Day of Prayer, reminding readers to "share in this day around the theme of thanksgiving for all of life" and suggesting they meditate, fast, or attend special liturgies centered on "the unity of man, God, and the world." Two related stories detailed the significance of the summer solstice among native people in northern Quebec and transcribed a model prayer contributed by John Hascall on behalf of the Steering Committee. "O Great Spirit, you speak to us and guide us through all that you have made. We come now to make our peace," it read. "Let us take only what we need and not anger you by wasting what you have given. Help us respect Earth and all the creation you have given so that we will continue to receive in abundance."[76]

This was also a busy time at the Nishnawbe Institute. Steering Committee member Keedah Johnson joined the staff in January 1971, hired on a two-month contract to coordinate a regional gathering in the American Southwest and to help organize the 1971 Conference, so that others could focus on fundraising. The Institute had spent the previous six months settling into life after Rochdale and was now facing financial difficulties of its own. The Conference budget deficit continued to grow, and Institute leaders were committed to other major projects as well: the cross-cultural workshops; the summer youth workshops previously administered by the Canadian Indian Youth Council; the Algonquian Project, a cultural preservation effort; and several more initiatives under development. In March Wilf Pelletier convinced Anglican executives to give the Institute another twelve thousand dollars, granting a short reprieve from financial crisis. Ian MacKenzie and Bob Thomas, meanwhile, devoted much of their time to pursuing Conference funding from various denominations and foundations, especially those on the American side of the border.[77]

In February MacKenzie mailed another proposal to the Joint Strategy and Action Committee in New York City, hoping he could persuade the large American denominations to join their smaller Canadian counterparts in funding the Conference. Reflecting developments since his first attempt a year earlier, he identified "three overriding concerns" animating the movement: the "divisive effects of religious strife" among native people and the need to "unite around the sacred" in mutual respect; the "internal breakdown" of tribal communities and the need to address social problems through spiritual revival; and the "alienation of young Indians from both urban society and their own communities," disclosing an urgent need for guidance from elders. Conference coordinators also had a clearer sense of direction and were now able to outline a five-year plan for administration and fundraising. They envisioned a decentralized movement of ecumenical organizing at the regional and local levels, supported by a central office and unified by an annual gathering that would be financially self-sufficient by 1976. These goals were interdependent: only nuts-and-bolts ecumenism really matters, and grassroots communities should be responsible for selecting and supporting their own delegates to the Conference.[78]

MacKenzie also began wrapping up his work as a consultant in community development for the Anglican Church of Canada. He had been retained in the wake of the Hendry report two years earlier, but in a few short months his contract would expire. In March he submitted a comprehensive report to church executives, enumerating explicit recommendations on how the Anglican church should structure its relationship with native people in order to support their struggle for self-determination. Probably the foremost liaison between Anglican and native leaders, MacKenzie was concerned that the process of institutional reform continue after his departure. He touched on most of the Institute's major projects in his nine recommendations, three of which specifically mentioned the Conference. "Many would say that this conference has been the most significant event in Indian life in a long time," he explained. "The Church will need to give ongoing support to those Indian priests involved in this movement. Some Indian priests may come under criticism from Bishops and white clergy because of their involvement." The Conference itself "will need continued funds from Church sources, as secular sources are unlikely to fund the movement" and "one can hardly expect the government to finance religious programs." Noting that social service agencies had failed to address "the critical problem of identity" among tribal people in urban contexts, he warned Anglican leaders that "young Indians are rapidly moving in the direction of frustrated, cynical, bitter advocates of anti-white positions. Since we have deprived them of their own background they become homeless and can only find their identity, ultimately, in a movement similar to the Black Power Movement." He closed with a personal testimony dramatizing the intimate connection between peace and justice: "I have now been assaulted three times," the non-native cleric confessed, in each case by young men whose "expectations of the Church had not been realized."[79]

An executive committee promptly voted to approve most of MacKenzie's recommendations and referred the rest to other administrative bodies within the Anglican church. Parliamentarian triumphs were easy to come by in this new climate of liberal reform, but MacKenzie worried about the plodding pace of bureaucratic response to the Hendry report, and he became increasingly outspoken as his official duties came to an end. "None of the recommendations have been implemented so far," he told a reporter from the English-language *Montreal Gazette*. "The success of the report can only be evaluated over a longer period of time. But there is a great, great danger that the implementation of Hendry could be just a flash in the pan." In April he reminded another denominational committee that "the Anglican Church has been consulting with Indian organizations for a year and a half" without acting on some of their most urgent proposals. A large task force of Anglican and native leaders did meet in June to formulate a five-year plan, though it was authorized only to pass more resolutions making more recommendations. The task force singled out "the Indian Ecumenical Conference as having a high priority in the continuing implementation of the Hendry report recommendations" alongside other concerns involving liaison staff, community development, religious freedom, political organizing, and cultural education.[80]

Perhaps the most sensitive matter Conference coordinators had to address as they organized the 1971 gathering involved deciding where to have it. In February they mailed a form letter to members of the Steering Committee asking each to rank the three invitations that were still on the table. A few weeks later organizers traveled to the Stoney Reserve in western Alberta and met with the tribal council, which agreed to host the Conference and to provide accommodations and meals for all delegates. This settled the issue and alleviated some of the financial pressure on Conference coordinators, though they could only trust that this offer would prove to be more durable than similar arrangements they had made with the Crow tribal government a year earlier.[81]

In April 1971 they issued a press release announcing the "Second Indian Ecumenical Conference," scheduled for the third week of July. "The Steering Committee once again most earnestly invites all American Indian religious leaders of all religious faiths to attend," it read. "A few tribes did not have religious representation" at the first Conference, "but we hope to have an even bigger turn out this year and to see every tribe in North America represented." Conference organizers had failed to persuade any American denominations to underwrite the 1971 gathering, so it appeared they would be unable to cover travel expenses for delegates from the U.S. Instead, they encouraged local communities to get involved by raising funds through "individual contributions, pie suppers, give-aways, raffles, etc. We are a poor people, but it seems like we can always dig up the money to do something we really want to do. And every North American Indian community has a right and a duty to be represented at this Conference." The Committee also invited "younger Indians" to attend the gathering, recalling that "young Indians' participation in our Conference last year in Montana made everybody, both young and old, feel good." As an added enticement, their Stoney hosts hoped to provide "wild meat for the delegates—buffalo, moose, etc." In the months leading up to the Conference, articles based on this press release appeared in the leading native periodicals in Canada and the U.S.[82]

By mid-July Conference coordinators had raised more than thirty-two thousand dollars from the two mainline denominations in Canada. Nearly half of this support came from the Anglican and United Church women's auxiliaries, which administered their own charitable programs. These funds were sufficient to erase the deficit from the 1970 Conference, to cover administrative expenses during the 1970–71 planning cycle, and to provide travel money for Canadian delegates at the 1971 Conference. The Canadian Catholic Conference and the Episcopal Church in the U.S. had withdrawn their financial support, though organizers did pick up a last-minute grant from the W. Clement Stone Foundation of Chicago: six thousand dollars earmarked for taping and transcribing the Conference proceedings. Wilf Pelletier and his colleagues were cautiously optimistic about the Conference as they coordinated final arrangements from the offices of the Nishnawbe Institute.[83]

They were also pleased with the publication of the Institute's first full-length book. In the summer of 1971 Neewin Publishing Company released a collection of essays "concerned with the quality of human relations between the red and white peoples of this continent." Titled *For Every North American Indian Who Begins to Disappear I Also Begin to Disappear*, the volume included pieces by Wilf Pelletier, Ian MacKenzie, Bob Thomas, and two other individuals affiliated with the Nishnawbe Institute, interspersed with nostalgic illustrations by Daphne Odjig, an Odawa artist from Manitoulin Island. Pelletier contributed the title essay, discussing the "profound physical and spiritual dislocation" native people have experienced under European colonization. Even well-intentioned outsiders do more harm than good in tribal communities when they underestimate the gravity of cross-cultural difference. "Our way of life is continuously being assaulted from every direction," Pelletier wrote. "Even if I as an individual Indian might be able to hold on to my identity, I am undermined by the collective fate of my people. For every North American Indian that begins to disappear, I also begin to disappear, because I cannot be an Indian, if that identity is taken away from all the rest of the people, my people."[84]

Ian MacKenzie explored this dilemma from the other side of the cultural frontier in his essay, "On the Demonic Nature of Institutions." Informed by his own experiences as a clerical activist in political, religious, and educational contexts, he had grown increasingly concerned about the assault on personal values and interpersonal relations in a bureaucratic society. "We have unconsciously identified the nature of life with the institutional framework in which we operate," he concluded. Western Christians, for example, "have made the Church into a secular institution like all other institutions, and like all other institutions, have made that institution God. It is this denial of the sacred which is the root cause of the demonic nature of institutions and, I think, one of the root causes of the continuing conflict which exists between whites in our society and native people." Secular idolatries have corrupted modern social institutions, making them "impassive and impersonal and dehumanizing," so that "men and women function with a view of the world which is more and more confined within the particular institutional framework in which they live. Their life is determined by the categories and rules of a framework to which they belong and there is little basis for questioning or challenging it." MacKenzie believed "the power of love can overcome the demonic element in institutions. One must accept all people as they are." He was articulating a social philosophy in harmony with the Indian Ecumenical Conference, which had succeeded in bringing together religious people from tribal communities throughout Canada and the U.S. "Somehow the demonic nature of institutions has become so deeply embedded in our nature that we have lost any feeling for men and women as people, which is the underlying and first reality. This includes accepting all of their being, not necessarily agreeing with it. To love must mean total acceptance." It is hard to imagine a better starting point for interreligious dialogue.[85]

1974 Indian Ecumenical Conference at Stoney Indian Park, looking west toward the Rocky Mountains. Camping grounds, powwow circle, and parking area are in the foreground; the arbor is off camera to the right.

Restrooms, cooksback, serving line, and dining tent at the 1974 Conference; the arbor is off camera to the left.

Conference participants waiting in line to eat at the 1974 gathering. Photograph by Karen Ibbitson.

Canvas, bark, and log tipis surrounding the powwow circle at the lower end of the camping grounds, 1974 Conference.

Tipis, tents, vans, and pickup trucks at the upper end of the camping grounds, 1974 Conference.

John Snow, chief of the Wesley Band of Stoney Indians, being interviewed by CBC personnel during the 1975 Conference. Still image from video version of People of the Sacred Circle.

Ernie Willie performing as cannibal dancer and as Anglican priest in 1970. The Kwakiutl ceremony was filmed on a Saturday evening in the community house at Alert Bay, British Columbia. The Anglican service was filmed the next morning in Christ Church; the stained glass window in the background depicts St. Uriel, the archangel of justice. Still images from video version of Kah-Sah-Las.

One of the younger participants at the 1974 gathering, wearing an Our Lady of Grace pendant and an I.E.C. button. Photograph by Karen Ibbitson.

CONSEQUENCES

As the highest and most dramatic features of the natural landscape, mountains have an extraordinary power to evoke the sacred. The ethereal rise of a ridge in mist, the glint of moonlight on an icy face, the flare of gold on a distant peak—such glimpses of transcendent beauty can reveal our world as a place of unimaginable mystery and splendor.

Edwin Bernbaum, *Sacred Mountains of the World*

It is a real inspiration and challenge to live the traditional life as we view these hills and mountains, these valleys and rivers: to be close to nature and to be reminded that the Great Spirit made all these things. It is good to return to the sacred land of our forefathers.

John Snow, Wesley Band of Stoney Indians

CHAPTER SIX

"THESE HILLS AND MOUNTAINS"

ALBERT LIGHTNING PAUSED BRIEFLY AT THE FRONT of his tipi, then stepped out into the hazy half-light of dawn. His compact body passed easily through an opening that forced some to stoop; he was not a tall man, but many native people looked up to him as one who understood the meaning and power of tribal traditions. This morning the air was calm and fresh but very cool, a chilling embrace for even the most seasoned spiritual leader, and his joints momentarily ached for a warmer obligation. Surveying the camp through metal-frame eyeglasses, Lightning snugged the collar of his sweater and headed for an open area nearby. He was carrying an old pipe bag almost as weathered as the hand clutching it. Others soon joined the amiable Cree elder and quietly arranged themselves in a circle. He began by lighting a braid of sweetgrass, syrupy smoke curling skyward as it purified the gathering. Then he assembled a hand-carved pipe and packed its bowl with tobacco, speaking a few words in English about how these gifts should be used "on behalf of the people." Running his thumb along the pipestem in an absentminded gesture, he explained the importance of faith and asked everyone there to pray for the past, present, and future of native communities. He removed his glasses; a few curious birds looked on from the treetops. Finally, and with a prayerful confidence, Lightning brought flame to the ceremonial herb.[1]

"The sun rises with a blood-red headdress of prairie clouds throwing fiery colours to the mountains," wrote one who participated in this solemn observance. "The mountains seem closer in the morning light, enclosing the whole valley in a great cathedral which the Great Spirit built for Himself and His people." Acknowledging the sacred mystery of creation, each person in turn offered Lightning's pipe to the four directions: to the east beyond the buffalo paddock, where a small herd now grazed after a century's absence; to the south past the icy waters of the Bow River; to the west over the foothills and jagged peaks of the Rockies; to the north toward the Kootenay Plains, Stoney territory from time immemorial, now claimed by the Canadian government. Lightning and his native colleagues savored the moment as the first crisp rays of daylight warmed the clearing in Stoney Indian Park. It felt good to wake up with a prayer.[2]

This sunrise ceremony opened the second day of the second Indian Ecumenical Conference, hosted in 1971 by the Stoney people on their main reserve at Morley. One of the larger reserves in all of Canada, the Stoney homeland is known far and wide for its natural beauty, a picturesque detour on the road from Calgary to Banff. In recent years even Hollywood producers have discovered its photogenic terrain: portions of the epic feature *Little Big Man* were filmed on the reserve during the fall of 1969, employing a couple hundred band members as extras. Their ability to portray nineteenth-century mounted warriors in the movie's battle scenes was not unrelated to the rugged topography of their reserve; the Canadian government's assimilationist schemes failed at least in part because the Morley reserve lands are forested and rocky and undulating, inhospitable to agrarian pursuits. In 1971 nearly all of the sixteen hundred Stoneys still spoke their native language, which is closely related to that of the Sioux people they played in Hollywood's comic reenactment of the Battle of the Little Bighorn.[3]

Humorless government agents dominated Stoney affairs from the 1880s to 1968, when the Department of Indian Affairs did an about-face and announced a new policy promoting local self-government. The Stoney people were among the first in Alberta scheduled for limited independence, and elections were held at year's end. In January 1969 John Snow took office as chief of the Wesley Band, one of three Stoney bands sharing the Morley reserve and two smaller reserves some distance away. "There was no shortage of challenges," Snow later recalled, as he and his fellow chiefs and councillors grappled with the sudden recovery of political responsibility. One of their first official acts was to commission a study of economic development opportunities, which led to the opening of Stoney Indian Park in July 1970. Tribal leaders hoped to capture a share of the steady tourist traffic passing through the area while also introducing their guests to Stoney history and cultural traditions. As Snow and Lightning and many other native people discovered a year later, the park was also a good place to conduct tribal ceremonies—and to hold an intertribal gathering of native spiritual leaders from the four directions.[4]

Albert Lightning had traveled to Morley from his home on the Ermineskin Reserve a couple hours drive to the northeast. He was a successful rancher known for his ability to communicate with horses, and humans generally held him in high regard as well; he could converse in Cree, Blackfoot, Stoney, and English. Now in his seventies, he focused his aging energies on meeting the demands of life as an itinerant medicine man, offering guidance and inspiration to native communities around the continent. He was something of a mystic—and an ecumenical one at that—whose visionary experiences included encounters with the "little people" of Cree tradition and the Jesus of Christian tradition. A buffalo spirit also visited him from time to time; Lightning's Cree name translates to "Buffalo Child," and many people knew him for his unusually large tipi decorated with bison around its base and a four-color rainbow framing the entrance. He was gratified by this opportunity to camp near the Stoneys' new buffalo paddock. As one of the most respected elders involved in the Conference, he appreciated the importance of spiritual traditions and had taken the lead in providing opportunities for ritual participation.[5]

The pipe ceremony drew to a close after each person had been given a chance to pray. Lightning smoked the last of the tobacco, then held the pipestem skyward and offered a final prayer in Cree. The sun climbed above the horizon as he disassembled the pipe and cleared its bowl of ashes and stowed everything in his weathered bag. The colorful cardigan he had worn to fend off the cold mountain air was already feeling a bit too snug, and he looked forward to more shared experiences that would warm both body and spirit. It was a new day; the gift of life itself was occasion enough for reverence and thanksgiving. Several observant birds took flight as Lightning and his colleagues shook hands and then ambled off to break their overnight fast.[6]

STONEY COUNTRY

"Long ago," wrote Stoney leader John Snow, "my ancestors used to go to the mountain tops to pray. They were a deeply religious, sincere, and tradition-oriented people" who followed the teachings of their forebears, "respected the creations of the Great Spirit, and lived in harmony with nature." The Stoneys occupied the foothills and prairies on the eastern side of the Rocky Mountains, from the Castle River north to the Brazeau. Nobody knows exactly how long they have been in the area, though it seems clear they had made it their home long before European visitors first documented their territorial presence in the eighteenth century. Oral traditions and linguistic affinities recall an ancient association with the Great Sioux Nation far to the southeast; fragmentary historical evidence suggests that these Nakoda-speaking people moved north and west to satisfy the demands of the fur trade and to escape the smallpox epidemics ravaging their compatriots.[7]

The Stoneys found themselves in an abundant land, surrounded by "the spirits of all living things," and they learned to communicate with "the rocks, the streams, the trees, the plants, the herbs, and all nature's creations. We called the animals our brothers. They understood our language; we, too, understood theirs." According to Snow, the most sacred Stoney vocation was the spiritual pilgrimage known in English as the vision quest. Preparations for this ritual involved the whole community, but the experience of "seeking wisdom and divine guidance" was a solitary oblation performed deep in the mountain wilderness. Fasting and prayer sometimes produced visionary revelation. "From these mountain-top experiences my fellow tribesmen and women were given unique tasks to perform to help the tribe prepare for things to come." The Rocky Mountains "are our temples, our sanctuaries, and our resting places. They are a place of hope, a place of vision, a place of refuge, a very special and holy place where the Great Spirit speaks with us." Snow foregrounded this fundamental relationship between the Stoneys and the Rockies by titling his tribal history *These Mountains Are Our Sacred Places: The Story of the Stoney Indians.*[8]

Stoney life, he recalled, "was one in which religion (and reverence for nature, which revealed religious truth) was woven throughout all parts of the social structure and observed in conjunction with every activity." The Stoneys relied on bison and other game animals for physical sustenance, so hunting was a ceremonial pursuit infused with spiritual power. Every part of the animal had some practical or sacrificial use; meat was often cooked in rawhide bowls by adding water and hot stones, a distinctive culinary technique that prompted Ojibwas and Frenchmen to call them the "Stone Sioux." The Stoneys followed the buffalo herds and occasionally came into conflict with their native neighbors, though they never strayed far from the Rockies. Tribal healers ventured into the mountains to collect and preserve certain plants, then prescribed these herbal remedies to people suffering from a variety of injuries and ailments. "The sacred waters of the mountains—the mineral hot springs—were also important to maintaining our health and curing illness," Snow added. "A person would journey to the sacred waters at the direction of a medicine man or woman and use them with suitable preparation and prayer." Stoney society was organized around extended family groups that came together on a regular basis to form loosely structured communities. Each was led by a patrilineal chief and council, with informal leadership provided by elders whose very survival demonstrated their wisdom. The various Stoney

bands united in times of crisis, but tribal governance was a function of cooperation and consensus, not bureaucratic coercion.[9]

English traders and missionaries first set up shop among the Stoneys in the
early nineteenth century. This commerce in skins and souls accelerated what
had been a more gradual process of adaptation, but Snow's people had little difficulty incorporating new gods and gadgets into their daily lives. "The freedom
of the woods and the plains and the mountains was still ours," he wrote, "and
still the most important part of our lives." Smallpox and whiskey were more
formidable challenges, however, and the suffering caused by these strange spirits made some Stoneys interested in novel approaches to spiritual power. The
members of a band led by Jacob Goodstoney proved to be particularly receptive
to the Christian teachings they heard from Methodist circuit riders. "If one un-
derstands the native religion of my people, it is not difficult to understand why
so many of us embraced the gospel of Christianity," John Snow mused. "There
was simply not that much difference between what we already believed and
what the missionaries preached to us." The Stoneys had concerns about this
new religion, but their familiarity with tribal religious diversity had already
convinced them there are many paths to spiritual truth. "We had been taught
not to question various forms or ways of worshipping the Creator. Who were
we to question? It was up to the Great Spirit and the tribe or the individual who
was given a vision on the mountain top or other sacred ground." After all, how
could any mere mortal claim absolute knowledge of ultimate reality? "And so
we listened to the missionaries and many converts were made."[10]

The first permanent mission in Stoney territory was established in 1873 by
George McDougall and his sons John and David. They had befriended Jacob
Goodstoney: "Child of the woods, a son of the mountains, coming out of a natural school, richly endowed with native graces," as John McDougall once described him, "a man to be loved and greatly admired, perfect in stature and
handsome in countenance and form, an athlete in constant training, a mighty
hunter and now, by the grace of God, a humble Christian." Goodstoney persuaded other Stoney leaders to let these Methodist missionaries settle on their
camping grounds in the Bow River valley, which is warmed during winter by
chinooks that blow down the eastern slope of the Rockies. The Stoney people
welcomed the McDougalls, guiding them to an appropriate site and helping
them erect several buildings. Two years later the missionaries opened a church
and a school; they called the settlement Morleyville, naming it for the preacher
who delivered the sermon at John McDougall's ordination.[11]

What the Stoneys did not know was that their new friends were already
consorting with government authorities to pave the way for non-native settlement—and to secure the best agricultural lands for themselves and their own

family members. John McDougall "told us to close our eyes and pray," Stoney elder Matthew Hunter later said, "and when we opened them our land was gone." The Stoneys trusted the McDougalls but would come to see these not-so-humble Christians as little more than "advance men" for a "new regime" intent on dispossessing tribal communities from coast to coast. "There is a common saying among Indians," John Snow wrote in his account of these events: "'Before the whiteman came we had the land, they had the Bible. Now, we Indians have the Bible, they have the land.' Sometimes I think the entire history of Indian–non-Indian relations on this continent is summed up in that statement."[12]

The North West Mounted Police appeared on the scene in 1874, the first tangible expression of colonial dominance in Stoney territory. The Mc-Dougalls told the Stoneys that the Mounties had been sent to combat bootleg-gers, squatters, and other frontier outlaws. Stoney leaders welcomed the presence of armed peacemakers, but there was more to this show of force than they realized at the time. Political developments far to the east were plotting a new course for Canadian history, one that would lead to dire straits for native people north of the forty-ninth parallel.[13]

The British North America Act of 1867 had confederated several eastern colonies as a self-governing Commonwealth nation. The Dominion of Canada was constituted with a strong central government, in part to facilitate territorial expansion into the northwest, and one of its first official acts in-volved buying Rupert's Land from the Hudson's Bay Company. Two centuries of relatively peaceful trade came to an end as Canada's new leaders embarked on an ambitious campaign to extinguish aboriginal land rights. Canadian im-perialism met with immediate resistance on the prairies, expressed most force-fully by Louis Riel, Jr., and the Red River Métis. Many native communities, however, were convinced of the futility of open conflict with their invaders and welcomed the opportunity for a diplomatic settlement. Beginning in 1871, federal agents and tribal leaders negotiated a series of "numbered treaties" by which the Canadian government claimed clear title to much of the North West Territory while native communities settled for small reserves, token cash payments, and annual annuities. The treaty-making process reached the western prairies several years later, targeting Stoney territory with the signing of Treaty 6 in 1876 and Treaty 7 a year later.[14]

By this time the Stoneys had organized themselves into three major bands: a group led by Jacob Goodstoney that wintered on the Kootenay Plains to the north, a group led by Chiniquay that wintered near Morleyville in the Bow River valley, and a group led by Bearspaw that wintered in the Highwood River valley to the south. Jacob's band occupied lands that fell within the geographic boundaries of Treaty 6, but they were not allowed to participate in that diplomatic convention. Instead, all three Stoney bands were invited to join the Blackfoot Confederacy—their historic rivals—as parties to Treaty 7.[15]

Linguistic ambiguity, cross-cultural misunderstanding, and colonial duplicity marked the negotiations at Blackfoot Crossing in September 1877. Tribal leaders were given the impression this was to be a treaty of "peace and good will" with "Her Most Gracious Majesty the Queen of Great Britain and Ireland," promulgated so that "her Indian people may know and feel assured of what allowance they are to count upon and receive from Her Majesty's bounty and benevolence." Canadian officials, however, produced an English-language document emphasizing territorial borders, land cessions, and the establishment of subsidized agrarian reserves. The various Blackfoot groups were assigned to separate parcels within their respective territories, but the written version of Treaty 7 contained no mention of Stoney lands on the Kootenay Plains or in the Highwood River valley; all three Stoney bands were to be concentrated on a single reserve next to the Methodist mission at Morleyville. John McDougall had played a key role in organizing the negotiations for both Treaty 6 and Treaty 7, and he acted as the Stoneys' advisor at Blackfoot Crossing, persuading the Stoney chiefs and councillors to make their marks on the dubious legal instrument. "We now know," one Stoney band chief later wrote, "that John McDougall had a personal interest in having one large reserve established at Morleyville; the church was there, his home and farm buildings were there, the hay fields were nearby, and a small area was under cultivation."[16]

"All this time we thought the missionaries were making the best possible deal for us," John Snow continued, "but in fact they were working to secure land for white settlers." The capitalist partnership of church and state paid handsome dividends at the treaty signing, and "today the descendants of Reverend McDougall still have the rich soil and best agricultural land just east of Morley," while the descendants of Goodstoney, Chiniquay, and Bearspaw "have the reserve, which is on rocky ground unsuitable for farming." The Dominion of Canada laid claim to its share of the spoils in 1879, when a government surveyor arrived to sketch boundaries for the Stoney Reserve. Lines of ink on a colonial map now contoured the territorial limits of Stoney life.[17]

Tribal leaders had explicitly reserved the right to hunt throughout the Treaty 7 domain; for a few years the three Stoney bands returned to their respective hunting grounds each summer, using the reserve only as a base camp, and several families even continued to winter on the Kootenay Plains and in the Highwood River valley. The Stoneys gradually settled near Morleyville, however, as their nomadic lifestyle became more difficult. The disappearance of the buffalo from the Canadian prairies in 1880 led to widespread famine, a crisis federal agents exploited by withholding treaty-guaranteed rations from native people who refused to stay on their reserves. The completion in 1885 of the Canadian Pacific Railway—which followed the Bow River valley through Morleyville, bisecting the Stoney Reserve—brought a horde of homesteaders to southern Alberta. In 1887 government officials established Rocky Mountain Park, appropriating a sizeable portion of the Stoneys' hunting grounds and further restricting their ability to support themselves. By 1890 the authorities were enforcing a pass system for native people who wanted to travel outside their home reserves, and local newspapers were demanding even more repressive measures in the name of civilization. In December of that year U.S. soldiers massacred more than three hundred of the Stoneys' Sioux relatives at a creek called Wounded Knee.[18]

Life on the reserve was better than imprisonment and starvation, but not by much. Government policies grew increasingly harsh and unforgiving; commissioned bureaucrats came to dominate all aspects of Stoney existence, even to the point of dictating who could serve as a tribal leader. John Snow called this period in Stoney history "the long rocky trail," when imperial Canada consolidated its power and imposed its authority over native lands and peoples. Chronic shortages of food, medicine, seed, equipment, and technical expertise exacerbated the cultural trauma induced by this sudden loss of freedom and self-sufficiency. Local agents were ordered to civilize on the cheap, to assimilate native people as quickly as possible and at the lowest possible cost to the Canadian government. New administrative edicts placed further restrictions on subsistence hunting, while civil servants and missionaries alike tried to stop the sun dance and other tribal religious ceremonies. Stoney children were confined at a residential school run by the Methodists and financed by Indian Affairs.[19]

The "seeds of discontent" had been sown by Treaty 7 and had taken root in the rocky soil of the Stoney Reserve. "Inequity flowered and the problem of land became very serious indeed" in the years that followed. This crisis reached a breaking point in 1892 when Peter Wesley, a renowned Stoney hunter, led a hundred members of Jacob's band back to the Kootenay Plains. "His courageous action was a joyous and happy occasion for my people," John Snow wrote. "With him they returned to their traditional life of freedom: to hunt, to fish, to roam, and to worship the Great Spirit." Under Canadian law these people were squatters in their own homeland, and government officials steadfastly denied their requests for a reserve along the North Saskatchewan River. But the Stoneys refused to leave, and in 1903 Wesley was chosen to be chief of Jacob's band, serving in that capacity for over thirty years. This group came to be known as the Wesley Band, commemorating their leader's vision of Stoney survival on the Kootenay Plains. During the winter of 1917–18 another group of Stoneys, members of the Bearspaw Band, left Morley for their ancestral lands. They moved south to the Highwood River valley, where they worked on area ranches while petitioning the Canadian government for a reserve of their own.[20]

Throughout the twentieth century, leaders of all three Stoney bands continued to assert their rights to the land. In addition to physically occupying the territories they had claimed at the Treaty 7 negotiations, Stoney leaders made their case in formal documents filed with Ottawa, often waiting months or even years for a response as various government agencies traded memoranda on the issue. Indian Affairs became the final resting place for a voluminous correspondence; the department's file cabinets now overflow with the archival remains of these and other native land-claims efforts. Following this tiresome paper trail meant "many a moccasin wore out," in John Snow's words, as the Stoneys weathered "government red tape, conflicting and contradicting government Indian policy, and false accusations from the newspapers." At times the only power sustaining them in this struggle was their love for the land, and "even today, hunting, fishing, trapping, gathering, and camping in forest woodlands are an integral part of our cultural values, religious belief, and economic base." Ironically, the Stoneys' most strident adversaries within the Canadian government were officials at the Forestry Branch of the Department of the Interior, whose rhetoric of resource management served as political cover for the commercial exploitation of public property. Even private conservation groups lobbied against tribal land claims in the Rocky Mountains, arguing that native people have no sense of stewardship, that their natural subsistence should be banned in favor of recreational diversions. "The problem was that the conservationist movement emerged from a money-oriented society which never learned our ways, our values, our traditions," Snow observed. "The sacred waters, the hot springs that we used for healing and cleansing, were to become tourist resorts; our sacred mountains were to become ski areas and parks where we no longer have the right to pursue our religious practice."[21]

Stoney grievances were finally addressed at the end of the Second World War, when Canadian leaders realized that the rationale behind federal Indian policy was embarrassingly similar to the ideology of their Axis enemies: racial superiority and imperial aggression. In 1945 Indian Affairs approved the acquisition of two large ranches east of Morley, expanding the reserve by about fifteen percent. The catch was that the Stoneys had to pay for the land themselves, accepting a half-million-dollar loan from the Canadian government and agreeing to make annual interest payments out of the fee income they received from a local utility, which had built three hydroelectric dams on the reserve. In 1946 government officials arranged the purchase of a small ranch for the Bearspaw Band families living along the Highwood River. They called it Eden Valley in recognition of the area's pristine beauty, though this new reserve was not large enough to allow the community to become economically self-sufficient. That same year Parliament convened a special joint committee of the Senate and the House of Commons to review federal Indian policy, which led to some small but important revisions to the Indian Act in 1951. The Canadian government retained decisive colonial power over native communities, but these changes gave the Stoneys more leeway to hold band elections, to manage their own resources, to pursue land claims, and to conduct giveaways and other tribal ceremonies.[22]

The long struggle for a permanent Stoney settlement on the Kootenay Plains proved to be more problematic. In 1930 the prairie provinces got control of Crown lands within their boundaries, making Alberta a party to any negotiations that might require the transfer of public property to reserve status. "Ottawa had gained a little wisdom over the years" and was willing to act on the Stoneys' behalf, John Snow remarked, but now Edmonton stood ready to block any native land claim on the eastern slope of the Rockies. In 1947 the secretary of the Indian Association of Alberta submitted a report to Indian Affairs, proposing the establishment of a small reserve for those members of the Wesley Band who were living along the North Saskatchewan River.[23]

After a protracted, secretive correspondence between federal and provincial officials, it was decided that these Stoneys would be assigned to a tract at the mouth of the Bighorn River, east of the Kootenay Plains. This was to be a "special" reserve intended for temporary occupancy; an administrative order stipulated that the Stoney people possessed "no claim to the land in question, having received grants of land consistent with the terms" of Treaty 7, and they did not receive title to the land or any subsurface mineral rights. Government representatives again misled the Stoneys when explaining the particulars of this arrangement, and Wesley Band leaders resumed their campaign for a Kootenay Plains homeland in the summer of 1948, several weeks before the new reserve had even been officially constituted. Snow later characterized Canada's land claims maneuvers as little more than charitable gestures that failed to address the basic legal issues at stake for the Stoneys. These three real estate deals may have helped mitigate colonial remorse, but they hardly satisfied the residents of the Morley, Eden Valley, and Bighorn reserves: "the first was very costly for the tribe, the second gave us only a small piece of land, and the third did not give us the reserve land we needed or believed we were entitled to."[24]

If postwar Canada could manage only incremental improvements in its treatment of native communities, this changing political climate did at least provide tribal leaders some encouragement in facing the formidable challenges that lay before them. The fifties and sixties were a period of transition for the Stoney people, bringing the demise of what little remained of their subsistence economy. Prevented from supplying their own basic needs, the Stoneys found themselves incorporated into the modern welfare state, a liberal face of colonialism bearing dependencies that are measured in domestic conveniences and social problems. By the late sixties most cabins on the three reserves had electricity—several new homes boasted indoor plumbing as well—but very few of their occupants had steady employment. It was in the midst of this nagging crisis that Indian Affairs finally decided to implement the self-government provisions of the 1951 Indian Act, pressuring the Stoneys to be one of the first native communities in Alberta granted these new responsibilities. Some tribal members suspected they were being set up for failure, while others feared success might spark a backlash against their aboriginal and treaty rights. "One protective force that helped us through the difficult years of adjustment and learning was the strength and wisdom of our elders. We were aware that the Great Spirit created us for a purpose and placed us on this Great Island. Our elders reminded us to have faith in the Creator," John Snow recalled, "and that everything would fall into place as though it were planned." In July 1968, shortly after government officials announced the new program, Snow was appointed minister of McDougall Indian Mission Church at Morley. After ten years away from home, he moved his young family back to the Stoney Reserve.[25]

ORDAINED CHIEF

Tom and Cora Snow welcomed their fifth child into the world on a cold winter night in January 1933. After several days they presented him to the community at a Wesley Band powwow, where his great-grandfather Jonas Goodstoney gave him the Nakoda name that translates to "Walking Seal." There would be six more children added to the Snow household before it was complete; all eleven were raised in a one-room cabin equipped with only one modern convenience: a wood-burning stove. Walking Seal and his siblings were weaned on Stoney oral history, taught to respect their elders and the traditions they represented. "My mother and father were good parents," he later wrote. "At meal times we all gathered around the table and prayed and ate together. We thanked the Great Spirit for what he had provided. When we shot game we thanked the Creator and, even though there was little money, we had dried meat, pemmican, wild meat, rabbits, grouse, and bannock to eat. Somehow, we always managed to get by." Walking Seal had little use for the English language or his own English name—John Snow—until the age of eight, when he was sent to the residential school at Morley.[26]

Snow's parents lived off the land and had very little formal schooling themselves, but they realized how important education would be in adapting to life under Canadian rule. Mindful of the sacrifices this would entail, they encouraged their children "to get as much as we could stand." The Morley school was staffed by United Church missionaries, some of whom were not even certified to teach, and they ran the institution with a Protestant vengeance. "It was very difficult," John Snow recalled. "Stoney culture was condemned," and "we were taught that the work and knowledge of our medicine men and women were of the Devil." Stoney children were expected to believe "that Christianity was the only true religion and that all others—including the faith of our fathers—were false." The residential school experience was one of "real indoctrination and some of the students dreaded going to church," though these compulsory sacraments did provide some relief from the monotony of schoolwork and manual labor. Administrators balanced their meager budgets by exploiting the school's captive workforce: girls handled domestic chores, boys toiled in the fields. These adolescent farmhands worked the Morley plantation from September to June, with just a few days off to visit their parents over the Christmas holiday. The two months of summer break were their only opportunity to immerse themselves in Stoney traditions, and Snow enjoyed attending religious ceremonies in the sacred lodge or taking family trips into the mountains to hunt and gather food. Most students left long before completing the curriculum; Snow was among the few Stoneys to finish all eight grades offered at the school. At the age of sixteen, having withstood eight years of psychological duress, he went home to live with his parents.[27]

John Snow helped support the family by taking odd jobs to supplement their income and by joining in the search for daily provisions. "My father taught me much about big-game hunting and trapping, wild life, the forests, and the rugged mountain country," he related. "I learned to identify the various edible plants and herbs, to read the weather, and to identify direction and landmarks so as to find my way home, even at night." His father also tutored him in "the traditional custom of sharing the hunter's kill" with other families, and of "leaving some small parts of the animal for the birds, our feathered brothers." Snow spent his spare time visiting elders on the reserve, learning more about Stoney philosophy and history from those who remembered life before Treaty 7. He particularly admired Walking Buffalo, a respected leader who stressed the importance of observing and understanding nature, appreciating its "harmony of variety," and of living "according to the plan of the Creator," which required a commitment to piety and service. "A man must choose to be governed by men who are governed by God," Walking Buffalo often said, and it was a threefold lesson in self-determination that Snow took to heart. These tribal apprenticeships generated a wealth of natural knowledge and cultural wisdom, though the practical skills he acquired in the process had little value in the postwar economic order. During this period he also sought to further his education in the dominant culture, attempting a high-school correspondence course and trying to enroll at a technical school in Calgary, but these efforts were frustrated by bureaucratic obstinacy.[28]

Snow also explored Christian traditions and teachings in his quest for a vocation, attending services at the church in Morley "quite regularly," he confessed. He enjoyed helping the local missionary conduct Bible studies and prayer meetings in various homes on the reserve and served as translator whenever the need arose. After years of careful introspection, in the spring of 1957 he "took a stand and accepted the Lord Jesus Christ as my personal saviour. By this time I had an idea of the true mission of the church and was hopeful that I could help my people in a real way through it." A year later he enrolled at Cook Christian Training School, a Presbyterian institution in Phoenix offering secondary and ministerial education aimed at native people. Snow worked his way through school as a janitor; he also met and married Alva Townsend, a Cook classmate from a nearby Pima community. In 1962, at the age of twenty-nine, he graduated and became the first Stoney to earn a high school diploma. The United Church of Canada then agreed to sponsor him for a year of seminary course work at St. Stephen's Theological College in Edmonton, and in May 1963 he was ordained to the Christian ministry alongside several non-native colleagues.[29]

Snow spent the next five years serving native and non-native parishes in Canada and the U.S. In late 1967 he and his young family were stationed at the eastern Alberta town of Ashmont—where he pastored the local church as well as two Cree congregations on the Goodfish Lake and Saddle Lake reserves—when they received word that Walking Buffalo had died the day after Christmas. Snow was asked to officiate at the funeral; he chose to recite a prayer his revered Stoney mentor had taught him. "Oh Great Spirit, whose voice I hear in the winds," it began, "let me rise again, let me rise to the mountain top!" Hundreds packed the community hall to mourn the passing of this ninety-six-year-old elder. A long procession to the graveyard marked the end of an era, but many Stoneys were already looking ahead to the new year and what it might bring. A few months later they were encouraged to learn that one of their own had been appointed minister of McDougall Indian Mission Church.[30]

The Snow family moved to Morley in July 1968 and found a reserve community struggling to adjust to the new political climate. After nearly a century of colonial administration, Indian Affairs wanted the Stoneys to assume responsibility for their own governance in conformity with the modern Canadian legal system—and to do so by the end of the year. "Psychologically," John Snow concluded, it was "the worst of times for my people." Just three of the sixteen hundred Stoneys were employed on the reserve, only one in an administrative capacity. "We had been brainwashed into believing that Indians were not capable of handling their own affairs," and "we knew that we lacked the training or preparation for the job." Ready or not, band elections were set for December, with the new government scheduled to take charge shortly thereafter.[31]

Snow was one of the few tribal members with academic credentials and professional experience in the outside world, and his father had been a tribal leader in the early fifties. Soon some Wesley Band elders asked him to run for the position of band chief. He initially declined, convinced that serving as ordained clergy was the best way for him to address the Stoneys' spiritual, social, and economic needs. He reconsidered after a disturbing experience at the local clinic, where native people were routinely turned away by callous, discriminatory medical personnel. When he approached government officials with his pastoral concerns, the input was brushed aside: "Keep to your preaching," they told him, "we listen only to the elected representatives on the reserve." After several such encounters, Snow came to believe that "unless I held elected office, I would never be heard and my concern for my people could only be a fruitless effort." He finally relented and was elected chief of the Wesley Band. In January 1969 he was sworn into office along with two chiefs for the Chiniquay and Bearspaw bands and twelve councillors representing the three bands spread over the Morley, Eden Valley, and Bighorn reserves.[32]

INDIAN PARK

There were plenty of challenges facing the new tribal council as it set out to effect "a better quality of life" for its Stoney constituents. Chronic deficiencies in health care, social services, education, vocational training, employment, economic development, and housing demanded immediate attention. As John Snow and his colleagues discussed their predicament, they began to sense "how deep rooted our problems were and how deep rooted the solutions had to be. The basic problem, we realized, was to rebuild the shattered Stoney tribal society." This would require facing "the harsh realities of the twentieth century" rather than agonizing over what might have been. They would need to contend with the institutions of the dominant culture, but they did not have to adopt their colonizers' values and behaviors. "In other words, we came to realize that it was not an either/or choice: acculturation to the dominant society or clinging to our old ways in a world where they could no longer offer us and our children a good life. We came to understand that there was a third way—the way of *biculturalism.*"[33]

Stoney leaders believed they could adjust on their own terms by "matching what we already have with the demands of today's world," hoping "to retain the best in the Stoney culture and to take the best in the dominant culture." They were on the right path, but it was going to be a long and difficult pilgrimage. "We would have to take an embittered, despondent, confused people and point them toward rediscovering, recapturing, and revitalizing our cultural philosophies and values, while adapting this traditional culture to modern times. And to give our people the hope to do this, we would have to discover or invent employment programs and opportunities whereby they could put bread on their tables without degradation." This bicultural vision took material form in the Stoneys' first major construction project, a unique administration building shaped like a tipi but furnished with modern amenities. "Having our own government offices and leaving behind forever the Indian agent's office, with all its bureaucratic, paternalistic, dictatorial, insulting, and degrading experiences of the past, marked a very important step on our journey toward regaining our traditional pride as a people."[34]

Among the tribal council's first official acts in 1969 was hiring a private firm to conduct a land-use study of the Morley reserve. These professional consultants quickly recognized the potential for developing commercial ventures that would take advantage of tourist traffic passing through the reserve, which is situated on the Trans-Canada Highway midway between the urban sprawl of Calgary and the mountain resorts in Banff. Later that year the Stoneys fenced a large meadow overlooking the Bow River and took delivery on twenty-five head of bison from Elk Island National Park near Edmonton. Some tribal members expressed concern about the cost of maintaining a captive herd of animals when so many humans on the reserve still lived in poverty, but most agreed they had a responsibility to provide for these "monarchs of the plains," on whom their ancestors had depended. "The return of the buffalo was a happy occasion," John Snow observed. "The elders performed religious ceremonies, smoked the sacred pipe, and thanked the Great Spirit that the buffalo had survived." These indigenous survivors came in handy during the fall of 1969, when film crews arrived to shoot scenes for the Hollywood epic *Little Big Man.* The buffalo paddock would also serve as the cornerstone of a new park catering to tourists; Stoney leaders hoped to provide employment opportunities for tribal members while cultivating cross-cultural understanding with their non-native visitors.[35]

The Canadian government was happy to repatriate a few of its zoological wards, but federal bureaucrats proved to be somewhat less enthusiastic about allowing native people to recover a measure of their former glory. Snow and his colleagues spent much of their first year in office embroiled in political controversies over the Kootenay Plains land claim, government Indian policy, and their local school system. As chief of the Wesley Band, Snow took the lead in opposing construction of a hydroelectric dam on the North Saskatchewan River that would flood the Kootenay Plains and destroy Stoney homes, traplines, graves, and religious sites. He first met with provincial officials in March 1969, explaining "why the Big Horn dam should not be built," and asking them to "have some feeling and thought for us Indian people" by canceling the project. They refused, the dam was eventually completed, and the dispute over Treaty 7 lands remained unresolved.[36]

Snow also played a key role in rebutting the "White Paper" released by Canadian officials in June. He joined the National Indian Brotherhood in an immediate challenge of this policy initiative and contributed to a detailed counterproposal published by the Indian Association of Alberta a year later. Formally titled *Citizens Plus*—a phrase useful for characterizing the political status of native people in Canada, according to a government study issued just three years earlier—this "Red Paper" was one of the most influential responses to Ottawa's radical proposals, which were subsequently withdrawn. A third major confrontation erupted in August, when Stoney leaders had to resort to a reserve-wide boycott of the Morley school before Indian Affairs officials agreed to let them participate in setting policy and hiring personnel. Calgary newspapers covered the story and editorialized on behalf of the Stoney people during their eight-day struggle. "Our victory went much further than the field of education. We began to get a feeling of what self-government was all about," Snow sensed. "We knew we had the right to control many of our own affairs, to publicly protest those policies we question, to present our own alternatives—and to win" some battles. "In that knowledge we could see a glimmer of hope and possibly the dawn of a new day."[37]

The Stoneys ventured into the private sector in July 1970 when they opened Stoney Indian Park, a recreational area designed for non-native tourists. Encompassing the ruins of an old British trading post and the buffalo paddock erected a year earlier, this tribal enterprise offered modern facilities for camping and picnicking in a backcountry setting. Visitors could explore a simulated tipi encampment, take guided nature tours by foot or on horseback, try their luck in nearby fishing holes, and buy locally made souvenirs at a handicraft shop. Long-range plans called for excavation of the trading post and its reconstruction as a museum to house and display the artifacts recovered. The park's biggest attraction was its scenic beauty: a string of meadows interspersed with thick stands of timber and perched on a bluff high above the river, with a panoramic view of prairies to the east and mountains to the west. The Stoneys developed and built their new "Indian Park" without the administrative oversight or financial assistance of the Canadian government. Stoney leaders saw this as an opportunity to combine economic development with public relations while demonstrating the ability to manage their own affairs.[38]

A month later John Snow traveled to Crow Agency for the first Indian Ecumenical Conference. As an elected band chief who had been trained in both tribal and Christian traditions, he was an obvious choice to be the Stoneys' lone delegate at this important gathering of spiritual leaders. Religious turmoil had been a problem on the Morley reserve since the early days of the McDougall mission; aggressive proselytizing by various Fundamentalist groups after the Second World War only exacerbated the situation, producing more conflicts than conversions. "As we look back over the past century, it has been like a long cold winter for my people," Snow commented. "The sacred fire of our religion has almost been put out by people from foreign lands, who do not understand our belief in the Great Spirit, the Creator." Like many Conference participants, he was grateful that "a few dedicated native religious leaders and medicine men and women from many reserves and communities have kept our sacred fire going. They have been in close touch with nature, the animal world, the birds of the air, and the spiritual world. They still retain the ancient truth" and have "kept the religious fire burning over the long century of indifference."[39]

The Crow Agency gathering was a heartwarming experience for the young Stoney leader. Through sunrise ceremonies in Albert Lightning's tipi, during morning and afternoon sessions under the cottonwoods, over shared meals at the makeshift dining hall, and amid the evening festivities of Crow Fair, Snow found a sense of community transcending his tribal and denominational loyalties. It was encouraging to meet native people from other parts of Canada and the U.S. who were concerned "about the future and the need to revive our native religion," and who shared his commitment to bicultural survival. The ecumenical spirit of the Conference seemed a natural complement to his own pragmatic vision of postcolonial tribal recovery. On their last day together the assembled delegates decided to meet again during the summer of

1971, but they also agreed on the importance of continuing their conversation in a more tranquil setting, away from the noisy crowds of Crow Fair. In a moment of inspiration, Snow realized that the Stoneys' new tourist attraction could double as the site for this intertribal encampment, so he "extended an invitation to the religious leaders, medicine men and women, clergymen, and chiefs" to hold the next Conference at Stoney Indian Park. Although it would take the Steering Committee over six months to accept Snow's invitation, he went home to Morley "with a feeling of encouragement and realization that there were many Indian leaders who were concerned with the revival of our cultural, spiritual and religious heritage."[40]

The first Conference had been a mountaintop experience for many of those who participated, and the second would take place in the shadow of some of the most majestic peaks in North America. John Snow considered it "a real inspiration and challenge to live the traditional life as we view these hills and mountains, these valleys and rivers: to be close to nature and to be reminded that the Great Spirit made all these things. It is good to return to the sacred land of our forefathers." Reflecting on the ecumenical gathering in his book *These Mountains Are Our Sacred Places*, he reiterated the point by quoting a pilgrim's song from the Hebrew scriptures: "I will lift up mine eyes unto the hills, from whence cometh my help." The peculiar relationship between humans and high places is a ubiquitous phenomenon, one that mountaineer and scholar Edwin Bernbaum explores in *Sacred Mountains of the World*. "People have traditionally revered mountains as places of sacred power and spiritual attainment" and as "natural objects of religious devotion," he writes. "As the highest and most dramatic features of the natural landscape, mountains have an extraordinary power to evoke the sacred. The ethereal rise of a ridge in mist, the glint of moonlight on an icy face, the flare of gold on a distant peak— such glimpses of transcendent beauty can reveal our world as a place of unimaginable mystery and splendor." While the Stoneys may be a unique people in the history of the world, their profound attachment to the mountainous territory they call home is a common human condition.[41]

Bernbaum's high-altitude adventures led him to graduate work in religious studies and to a comparative study of the "landscape of infinite grandeur." Drawing on the humanistic insights of theorists such as Rudolf Otto and Mircea Eliade, he describes the spiritual power of mountains as "an inscrutable mystery that attracts and repels us" with "feelings of wonder and fear." Some mountains "evoke impressions of a strange and alien universe," belonging to "a world utterly different from the one we know, inspiring in us the experience of the sacred as the wholly other," arousing "spontaneous feelings of reverence and awe." Bernbaum introduces his topic by generalizing over the mountaintop experiences reported by various individuals across space and time. "Despite the hardship and fear encountered on the heights, people return again and again, seeking something they cannot put into words," he says. "Religious pilgrims are drawn to a power or presence they sense in a peak; tourists come to gaze on splendid views; trekkers return to wander in a realm set apart from the everyday world. The fascination of mountains casts a particular spell on mountaineers," Bernbaum admits, though he is careful to downplay the metaphors of conquest favored by professional and recreational climbers alike. Around the world certain peaks are regarded as "places of revelation, centers of the universe, sources of life, pathways to heaven, abodes of the dead, temples of the gods, expressions of ultimate reality in its myriad manifestations."[42]

The bulk of his book is devoted to a geographic survey of the planet's sacred mountains organized according to topographic and political boundaries. "Because of their power to awaken an overwhelming sense of the sacred," Bernbaum observes, "mountains embody and reflect the highest and most central values of religions and cultures throughout the world," and his extensive discussion of Asian, European, and African peaks makes this point in a straightforward manner. Turning eventually to the Americas and Oceania, the lands most extensively colonized during the European diaspora, he encounters an ethnographic dilemma. The dominant population in North America, for example, consists of modern nomads whose immigrant sensibilities give them little appreciation for the spiritual qualities of this place. "Most people from mainstream American culture who seek a sense of the sacred in mountains do so in nontraditional ways, eschewing the aid of religious rituals," while "the intensity with which some Native Americans still revere certain of their peaks makes the sentiments of sublimity experienced by many white Americans seem pale in comparison." Bernbaum thus focuses on "the richness and diversity of indigenous cultures" in his overview of sacred mountains in Canada and the U.S. Juxtaposing native and non-native subjectivities—which he associates with "traditional religious" and "secular, modern" worldviews—allows him to mount a mild critique of Western colonialism. Unfortunately, he stops short of interrogating the profound sense of alienation implied in his own determination to conceptualize the sacred as wholly other.[43]

Bernbaum's study concludes with a few chapters of thematic synthesis, culminating in a personal reflection on "mountains, wilderness, and everyday life." After several hundred pages of detailed exegesis unearthing the sacred meanings of the world's more prominent peaks, he closes with a provocative insight: "The reality revealed by a mountain can be experienced anywhere. Mountains are no more sacred than any other feature of the landscape." This is a startling claim, undermining the encyclopedic ethnography that precedes it and illustrating a classic blunder of Western objectivist rationalism. Like the alpine adventurer who indulges in a mountain-top fantasy that he is master of all he surveys, any comparativist project can fall prey to the allure of ethnocentric abstraction. Academic speculation becomes hegemonic discourse when it fails to respect the integrity of local knowledge. The Stoneys, for example, "knew every trail and mountain pass " in their territory. "We had special ceremonial and religious areas in the mountains," John Snow explained, and it is this historic relationship with specific natural landmarks that makes the Rockies a source of inspiration for the Stoney people—and that prompted Snow to insist *"these mountains are our sacred places."* If Bernbaum oversteps his own perceptual limits in deducing that sacred mountains merely symbolize some transcendent reality, still many native people would agree with him that "the sacred by its very nature eludes all our attempts to define and grasp it," and that "just when we think we have grasped the nature of things as they are, some new aspect appears to confound our knowledge and understanding." The Indian Ecumenical Conference was one place where humans could experience this natural, sacred mystery.[44]

SACRED FIRE

The buffaloes were restless. Stoney Indian Park may have seemed peaceful by human standards, but these native animals had never been surrounded by so many people, at least not since taking up residence in the Bow River valley two years earlier. For several days vehicles from all over Canada and the U.S. had been pulling through the entrance gate and unloading in the campground, upwind from the buffalo paddock. By the morning of July 18 there were hundreds of men, women, and children in the area, some of whom now watched from the fenceline. A large bull moved slowly at the edge of the herd; he was solid as rock, with the profile of a mountain range, tufts of winter coat clinging like glaciers to his massive shoulders. Four-leggeds and two-leggeds alike sensed that something important was happening here.[45]

It was a midsummer Sunday, and the Steering Committee met at noon to finalize arrangements for this second Indian Ecumenical Conference. Conference leaders had originally planned to begin the 1971 gathering with religious observances earlier in the day, but a number of delegates were still making their way to Morley, so opening ceremonies were postponed until Monday morning. Instead the Committee invited everyone to a preliminary session on Sunday afternoon, where those present got better acquainted and voiced concerns that needed to be discussed. Afterward they shared a meal, and that evening some congregated for an interdenominational worship service coordinated by John Snow and led by native clergy representing the Anglican, Evangelical, Southern Baptist, and United Church traditions. The park's mountainous backdrop made this outdoor liturgy an expansive, memorable experience, a brief Christian prelude to the unmistakably tribal drama about to unfold in the shadow of the Rockies.[46]

Official proceedings got under way the next morning when a group of Navajo delegates performed an abbreviated version of the blessingway ceremony. Blessingway is a staple tradition in Navajo spiritual life, a fundamental but flexible rite that undergirds a complex ceremonial system. The mythic narrative behind blessingway includes the Navajos' most elaborate account of the creation of the present world; the ceremony itself is a reenactment of this primordial epoch in tribal history, aligning contemporary human existence with the holy people and the ordered universe they made. The first part of every blessingway involves consecrating the hogan where the rest of the ceremony will be performed, establishing an identification between the distinctive Navajo dwelling and its paradigmatic predecessor in the creation epic. As the most versatile Navajo ceremony, blessingway can be employed in a variety of situations to promote harmony and balance, happiness and well-being. One common use is to bless a new family home.[47]

Although the journey to Stoney Indian Park had taken them far beyond the sacred mountains that bound the Navajo homeland, Stewart Etsitty and his colleagues wanted to share this ceremonial tradition with their ecumenical relations. Conference leaders had designated a shady spot surrounded by white poplars as their meeting site, recalling the good feelings they experienced under the cottonwood trees of Crow Agency a year earlier. Etsitty hoped to evoke that same spirit as he moved around the clearing in a sunwise circle and marked the four directions with corn pollen brought from home. Then he retraced his steps in a reverse circuit while sprinkling cornmeal on the ground behind him. He called on the holy people by singing and praying with verbatim precision, careful to articulate the ancient formulas whose very words he knew to be spiritual beings created at the beginning of the world. Etsitty concluded with a short prayer of his own to cover any inadvertent omissions. The blessingway complete, this meeting site was now a microcosm of the Navajo world, a sacred place where native people could gather in peace and equanimity.[48]

Conference participants assembled on these blessed grounds over the next four days. Each morning and afternoon session opened and closed with prayers offered by delegates representing a variety of tribal communities and spiritual traditions. Albert Lightning conducted a sunrise ceremony on the second morning, using his pipe to cultivate religious solidarity at this ecumenical gathering. The pipestem he carried was a surrogate for the one found in the sacred pipestem bundle, which was given to Lightning's people in ancient times, along with instructions on how to make and use the holy object. The sacred pipe is a ubiquitous element of Plains Cree spiritual life. Bowl and stem are stored in a disassembled state; when unwrapped and joined they become a powerful instrument for communicating with the Creator and the spirit powers. An assembled pipe is packed with tobacco and smudged with sweetgrass, then lit and offered up. The first words intoned are addressed to the Creator, and then the pipe is extended to the spirit powers, who are invited to participate in the ceremony and to mediate on behalf of human concerns. Sharing the pipe precludes disagreement and conflict; tobacco is a sacrament of diplomacy and goodwill, and smoking it the surest path to peaceful coexistence. Lightning appreciated the Navajo blessing he had witnessed the day before, and the sunrise ceremony he led on Tuesday was his own Plains Cree contribution to the success of the Conference.[49]

On Wednesday morning Bob Thomas and several Cherokee, Creek, and Seminole delegates invoked yet another source of spiritual power by laying a sacred fire in the middle of the meeting site. Fire is an ancient blessing and an earthly manifestation of the sun. The eastern Oklahoma countryside is still dotted with ceremonial grounds where sacred fires are maintained, having been carried to Indian Territory during the removal era. Every ceremonial ground holds periodic stomp dances and a yearly green corn ceremony; each of these ritual gatherings comes to life around the sacred fire. The annual cycle climaxes with the celebration of green corn at midsummer, a tribal holiday bearing seasonal, political, and religious significance—in American terms, it is New Year's Day, Independence Day, and Thanksgiving Day combined in an elaborate four-day observance. On the morning of the third day, after cleaning and preparing the grounds, a new fire is kindled at the center of the dancing area. It is fed by four logs aligned with the cardinal directions, their ends meeting in flame. The sacred fire is kept burning until the close of the ceremony. The celebration of green corn is an occasion for socializing, making repairs, fasting and feasting, dancing and singing, taking medicine and scratching, offering prayers, conferring names, and playing ball. Above all, it is a time of purification and renewal through the power of the sacred fire, which serves as a link between physical and spiritual worlds. The green corn ceremony is an interval of jubilee, requiring that injuries be forgiven and conflicts be resolved; the sacred fire marks a spot where new beginnings are possible.[50]

Thomas and his colleagues had these and other meanings in mind when they stepped forward on the third morning of the Conference. Billy Osceola, a Seminole Baptist minister from the Florida Everglades, was moved by their actions: "We should thank God for what he has given us," including herbal medicine and tribal ceremonies. "Those logs that have to push together in the fire, that is love," he said. "We must keep the medicine and fire and love." Some traditions were reserved for use at the ceremonial grounds of eastern Oklahoma, but the sacred fire had found a home in western Alberta.[51]

Blessingway, pipe, and sacred fire symbolized the tribal diversity represented at the Conference and illustrated the ecumenical possibilities of such a gathering. They also demonstrated the vitality of native spiritual practices; these were living traditions drawn from three distinct religious communities, each rooted in an unbroken history of adaptation and survival on the North American continent. "We're all different tribes and different faiths. Still, we've got a lot of things in common," Bob Thomas told the assembled delegates on Monday afternoon. "We know that we're all natives of this island here, we know that God made us out of this soil here, we know there's a creator above—there are certain rules he gave us and certain relationships we're supposed to have with this land." The Conference was now more than a meeting of religious people; it had become a meeting of religions.[52]

Yet few Conference participants realized how effective these three ceremonial interventions had been, or just how powerful this particular place had become. Blessingway, pipe, and sacred fire are potent spiritual traditions; their presence signified important truths, but their ritual performance also enacted critical realities. The cumulative effect of this intertribal convergence was implied in two unforeseen outcomes of the 1971 gathering. First, Stewart Etsitty, Albert Lightning, and Bob Thomas had unwittingly inaugurated a situational tradition: future Conferences would begin with a series of tribal ceremonies intended to make the meeting site a safe space for interreligious dialogue. "On sacred ground we are all equal people," said Ojibway artist and activist Lloyd Caibaiosai, expressing a sentiment shared by many who witnessed the birth of this pluralistic rubric. Second, John Snow and his Stoney colleagues had unintentionally established a permanent home for the Conference; regional and local meetings would continue to promote ecumenical cooperation in other parts of Canada and the U.S., but the transnational gathering would return each year to Stoney Indian Park. "It is great to be alone with God in the wilderness," remarked Lazarus Wesley, the Stoney lay minister who had succeeded Snow at McDougall Indian Mission Church, and many delegates readily appreciated his attachment to the Morley reserve's rugged landscape. Conference leaders had envisioned a flexible, decentralized organization promoting "a general movement for ecumenicity among American Indians," but their new venture was already institutionalizing in ways that might compromise this original objective. Some delegates had become so enthusiastic they were "impatient to stabilize the Conference, to hold regional meetings and to deal as a body with their mutual concerns," the final report stated. "The only question that remains at this point is what forms it will take and what will its relation be to non-Indians and to the Churches as national institutions."[53]

Open sessions each morning and afternoon gave Conference participants an opportunity to introduce themselves, express their concerns, and pledge support for their new friends. One after another rose to speak; most of the issues they raised had been discussed during the 1970 gathering, though "it was apparent that many of the delegates had, because of last summer's experience at the Conference," found the courage to "take action" on the religious conflicts, social crises, and cultural dilemmas troubling their home communities. "Two large tribes notable for secrecy in religious matters openly talked about their religion from the floor or performed their religious rites," Conference coordinators reported. "Christian delegates spoke openly and honestly about their faith" and participated in interdenominational liturgies. "Moreover, people did not feel so hesitant about making public" their "religious differences," which many had been reluctant to do the year before. "Delegates generally showed enormous trust in each other." Some joined in tribal dancing at the powwow circle on Monday and Tuesday evenings, but after dinner on Wednesday they went back into official session as the end of the Conference drew near. By Thursday morning delegates had approved eighteen formal resolutions, including three originally proposed at Crow Agency.[54]

One resolution explicitly affirmed the resolutions passed in 1970, while several others addressed familiar concerns over the theft and plunder of tribal lands, the desecration of burial grounds and other sacred sites, and the restrictions on native religious freedom imposed by governmental and denominational authorities. Joe Mackinaw, a member of the Steering Committee, explained his recent decision to leave the Ermineskin Reserve and establish a settlement far from modern conveniences and afflictions. "We live in the mountains," he said through an interpreter. "I used to go in and out of the hospital but since I adopted the old way in the mountains, I am healthy again." Conference delegates responded with a resolution commending his effort—and that of Robert Smallboy, another traditionalist leader who had fled Western civilization—to "return to the proper way of life which was prescribed by the Creator to enable the Crees to be religiously whole and socially and physically healthy." Harry Daniels, a Métis leader from Lac La Biche in northeastern Alberta, asked the Conference to recognize "the half-breed nation," those who "have been rejected all our lives by white society" and today "live as native people" in Canada. "I was born an Indian, I'm going to die an Indian, whether I was covered by a treaty or not." Delegates endorsed a resolution acknowledging the Métis as native people and promising to include "representatives of their communities in future conferences." They also approved a resolution authorizing the Steering Committee to begin laying the groundwork for a "North American Indian Cultural and Religious Centre." Funded by public and private agencies, this would be an intertribal clearinghouse where the work of the Conference could be carried out on a year-round basis.[55]

At one point Bob Thomas took the floor to discuss the idea of declaring an "Indian Day of Prayer." The Steering Committee was recommending that June 21 "be set aside as a holy day, as a day of prayer and fasting to all Indians everywhere, a day when we could think about our place in this universe and what we're supposed to do to carry on what our old people told us." Tribal communities' "partnership with this land, and the whole spiritual world that's a part of it, we know how that's out of kilter now," Thomas said. A transnational commemoration might help them get things "back in balance again, the way it used to be."[56]

Several leaders spoke in support of this proposal, and on the broader question of how they should relate to the dominant culture. "I believe us Indians, as custodians of North America, will have a contribution to make to white society," Ernest Tootoosis told his colleagues. "We have to go back and take some very fine things about our culture, about our teaching and our way of praying to God, take these good things and try to find something good about the white man, the way they make a living now, and piece these two things together for survival." Wilf Pelletier warned that although they should "do those things that our old people can teach us," native people would still be "in danger because of the white man. They will annihilate themselves and take us with them. I don't feel sorry for Indian people, I feel sorry for the white people, they are the ones that are sick." He argued for an inclusive understanding of cultural stewardship: "As this movement grows bigger and bigger, I think it is our duty to give our knowledge to the people who are controlling this country or they will destroy it. We have to help them. When they first came here we helped them survive and again we are going to have to help them survive. They are people like us and we cannot exclude them or push them down just because they pushed us down." Conference delegates passed a resolution sanctioning the effort to promote "an annual Indian Day of Prayer all over the United States and Canada."[57]

The closing session on Thursday morning began with a short Anglican liturgy led by Andrew Ahenakew. Then delegates addressed a few remaining agenda items and offered words of gratitude to Conference organizers. Sidney Parrish, husband of the renowned Kashaya Pomo spiritual leader Essie Parrish, spoke for many when he thanked the Stoneys "for the kind and lovable hospitality that they have given to each of us." He encouraged everyone to "get out to the people and reach them" after returning home. "Reach out with the words, reach out with the spirit. This is the only way we're going to band together, and this is the only way we're going to become a strong nation of Indian people. We have to unite in all things." John Snow presented gifts to various delegates and expressed the Stoneys' appreciation for being allowed to host "so many speeches, so much wisdom from across the nations." He also explained the need to conduct one last ceremony: the buffalo herd had escaped from its paddock during the Wednesday evening session, and local elders believed this happened because the animals had not been properly welcomed to the Morley reserve two years earlier. A number of delegates joined in a "special blessing of the buffaloes," who reminded the Stoneys of "the time when we were independent, the time when we were strong as a tribe."[58]

People shook hands as the sacred fire was extinguished, marking the official end of the Conference, and some gathered up ashes to carry with them to their home communities. Though no one knew at the time, it was a scene that would be repeated at Stoney Indian Park for years to come. "I think most Indian people relate to that fire more than any other thing," observed Wilf Pelletier. "The fire is comfort, Indian style." John Snow was particularly impressed by this impromptu Conference tradition. "Often people would gather around the Sacred Fire for prayers, meditations, telling stories, sharing experiences, and encouraging one another in the journey of life," he wrote years later. "Many of us felt the presence of God the Creator, and were touched, and felt a deeper understanding of our faith as we sat around the fire." He also penned a short poem describing its power to kindle devotion, companionship, perseverance, and hope—and using the sacred fire as a metaphor for the movement itself. Intertribal and ecumenical unity was his theme in the third line: "Around the Sacred Fire we stood together as one people." Recalling more than a decade of annual meetings of the Indian Ecumenical Conference, the elected chief of the Wesley Band remarked that "the favourite place, the centre of the gathering, was around the Sacred Fire." It was a fitting complement to the sacred mountains standing watch over the Stoney homeland[59]

Baby boomers have found that they have to discover for themselves what gives their lives meaning, what values to live by. Not since the cataclysm of World War II have most of us been able simply to adopt the meanings and values handed down by our parents' religion, our ethnic heritage, our nationality. Rather, what really matters became a question of personal choice and experience.

Wade Clark Roof, *A Generation of Seekers*

Whereas there seems to be dissatisfaction evidenced by some Native American youth regarding the format of the Indian Ecumenical Conference, and whereas many youths have requested a seminar-type forum or small groups led by a Native traditionalist to ensure a more concentrated examination of various tribal beliefs and religious systems, therefore be it resolved that the Steering Committee consider this suggested change for further conferences.

Renee Tree, Little Big Horn High School

CHAPTER SEVEN

"DISSATISFACTION
EVIDENCED BY SOME"

PEOPLE HAD COME FROM FAR AND NEAR TO ATTEND the Indian Ecumenical Conference. A delegation of five Papagos drove to Stoney Indian Park from their homes in the Sonoran Desert of southern Arizona, and a busload of thirty—some representing communities above the Arctic Circle—made the long journey from the Northwest Territories. Others came from Nova Scotia's Cape Breton Island and from the Florida Everglades. Many more lived on reserves within a few hours of Morley. The total number of delegates was better than double that of the Crow Agency gathering, and hundreds of casual participants further multiplied the increase in overall attendance; Stoney officials estimated they served eight hundred people at each meal on Wednesday. "A substantial number of Indian observers were young people from all over the United States and Canada," the Conference report noted, "who came on their own initiative and resources."[1]

Two non-native observers also commented on the demographics of the 1971 Conference. "The sincerity of the people who attended was striking," wrote Smithsonian Institution anthropologist Sam Stanley. "There was a good mixture of young and old people. I would say older people predominated, but there were enough younger people to present the hope that this movement can extend beyond the lives of the people who were present. A number of people brought their families," including Stanley, who was accompanied by his teenage son. Harold Turner, a former missionary in Africa who now taught world religions at a Methodist seminary, enjoyed meeting delegates "spanning

the religious spectrum from traditional ceremonial leaders to Christian ministers of all denominations." He was impressed by their "shared depth of concern for the spiritual renewal of the Indian peoples as having priority over all
other approaches to the solution of their problems. Noteworthy also was the
number of educated young Indians who participated."[2]

Conference organizers took pride in the dramatic growth of the movement. They were gratified by the involvement of so many spiritual leaders and
elders, and they were encouraged by the interest of the younger generation as
well. "The Conference is having a tremendous impact on young Indians," they
reported, "and may become a more stabilizing force in their lives than all the
schools and social programs which purport to deal with their problems." The
presence of native youth was a surprising development at the Crow Agency
gathering, but a year later many Steering Committee members had expanded
their vision for the Conference to include an intergenerational component.
The 1971 Conference announcement specifically encouraged "younger Indians to attend our meeting."[3]

Among the many who responded to this invitation were two Toronto-
based organizations: the Native Youth Summer Programme of the Canadian
Indian Centre and the Canadian Indian Youth Workshop coordinated by the
Nishnawbe Institute. Both ventures had been patterned after the Workshop
on American Indian Affairs, providing tribal youth in the urban diaspora
with an opportunity for cultural immersion and intensive study. Both groups
convened in early July on the Sweetgrass Reserve in northwestern
Saskatchewan, then caravanned to Morley so that these young men and
women could participate in the Conference. Many of them had a hard time
understanding "what these elderly religious and traditional leaders were
talking about." Leaders of the Canadian Indian Youth Workshop observed
that "students were finding the transition from urban life to travelling and
camping, and direct contact with older reserve people, a kind of cultural
shock. Some were interested in pursuing the discussion of the older ways,
but others wanted to put that aside and spend time in the nearby cities."
John Snow was struck by the ethnic ambivalence of these city-bred youth
and announced his willingness to host a "summer program in religious education" on the Stoney Reserve in 1972.[4]

Many of those who spoke up during Conference sessions expressed concern for the younger generation. Some were grateful that educated native
youth could start "rewriting" the history texts, reforming "the education system," and providing leadership for their own people. "If you are sending your
youngsters out to the urban city for an education, welcome him back," Kwakiutl school counselor Jim White told his colleagues. "Make sure you can utilize

his education. That's what he went in and got educated for, and don't let him stand around and not do anything about it."[5]

Others were distressed by the loss of cultural knowledge among students who lived far from their tribal communities. "We believe in educating young Indians, but we do believe that we should live our first culture," explained Emma Delgarito, a Navajo delegate who worked at an off-reservation boarding school. Laura Cranmer, a Kwakiutl teenager whose grandmother was a Conference delegate, argued that "the young people will have to listen—there are no two ways about it—they will have to listen to the old people." Joe Bananish, an Ojibway Catholic lay leader, recounted his childhood experiences learning tribal traditions and encouraged native youth to sustain their cultural heritage: "We should preserve it—whatever we can—and preserve our own tribal languages and be proud of them." Young people were specifically mentioned in half of the eighteen formal resolutions approved during the Conference, including one submitted by representatives of the National Indian Youth Council. The delegation from the Northwest Territories sponsored a resolution urging tribal elders to "celebrate and honor not only traditional accomplishments of their children, but also modern accomplishments as well." Several other resolutions addressed the bicultural challenges facing native people born in the postwar period.[6]

Most baby-boom observers had been content to listen from a respectful distance during the 1970 Conference, but in 1971 many of them wanted to be part of the conversation. Native spiritual leaders who had come to Stoney Indian Park anticipating ecumenical dialogue in an intertribal setting found themselves deliberating how to accommodate a third major axis of difference. Even Conference organizers were divided over the issue. Wilf Pelletier made "a plea to the delegates on behalf of the youth that are here," asking that "the youth may have a voice. These young people can tell you the reasons why, and what is happening to them when they are sent away from their reserves." Ernie Willie seconded "the idea of opening up to the young people, because if you don't hear from them, then how do you think that we as a people are going to handle them or in any way try to give them assistance? I do sincerely invite the views of the young people." Bob Thomas was concerned about native youth as well but devoted his public comments to several initiatives that might help Conference participants "call on the things that we have in common." He hoped to keep this particular movement focused on its original goal of promoting religious solidarity and spiritual revival in tribal communities.[7]

An especially insightful commentary on this rising generation gap was offered by a middle-aged Cree leader. "I'm very concerned, too, about our young people," Chris Cromarty said, "and I'm wondering what it's going to cost us in terms of attitude, in terms of devotion, and in terms of effort." He went on to describe his own adolescence. He had earned a high school diploma and taken a government job in Toronto, where he joined the Indian Friendship Club. "We were like drugstore Indians," he recalled, "trying to find out what being an Indian is about." Cromarty made the rounds of the powwow and conference circuits before realizing he should "look to my own people, see what they're all about." He finally left the city and went home to Big Trout Lake, marrying back into the community and immersing himself in local affairs. "You can't know immediately what the old people know—it doesn't happen that way," he cautioned his youthful listeners. "It's something that the young people should understand, that these old people are not going to teach them all in a package neatly wrapped up—all the information that you will require in life. You have to learn it yourself, that's the only way you're going to understand it, you have to be a part of it." At the end of the Conference a group of delegates from eighteen remote communities in northwestern Ontario selected Cromarty to represent them on the Steering Committee.[8]

Native youth also met as a group to discuss their participation in the Conference. After some debate they "decided that they did not want to organize or behave in any way which would separate them as a generation from the rest of the Indian people. They, in effect, declared their peoplehood." Gerald Wilkinson, an Eastern Cherokee delegate and executive director of the National Indian Youth Council, conveyed this message to the rest of the gathering: "One of the things about the Indian people is that we are one. Just because we are a certain age doesn't mean that we identify solely with people of the same age. We may identify with our family, our friends, our community on the reservation—we are one. Oneness is the kind of thing I have felt here and this is the kind of thing that I am taking back with me." He closed by expressing his hope that "all the spiritual leaders will pray for Indian young people." They were happy to do so, though this was not the last time that intergenerational tensions would surface at the Conference.[9]

GROWING CONCERN

The gathering at Stoney Indian Park had been a success. Wilf Pelletier marveled that "after nearly five hundred years of persecution, the old-way-of-life religions were still very much alive." He knew the event had meant different things to different people, "but there was one thing about it that was very personal: I had the feeling that I had come full circle and had finally made it. It felt like at last I was back home." Sam Stanley considered the Indian Ecumenical Conference to be "one of the most promising movements for American Indians because it seeks to transcend a very deep problem which has beset them ever since the white man landed here," the problem of "religious divisiveness, that is, where you get factions based on religious beliefs. The Ecumenical Conference is an attempt to get these people to look at each other positively, rather than negatively." Harold Turner thought "the invaluable feature of this movement" was its "authentically Indian initiative and manner of operation." He commended Canadian church leaders for supporting the Conference and hoped that "others throughout North America will take the trouble to learn what has been set moving, will have the humility and imagination to see its potentiality, and the desire to participate in at least two ways—by encouraging some of their own Indian ministers to learn about it and share in it, and by contributing to its necessary support, without our usual white control procedures." Years later he would characterize the Conference as "a significant new independent religious movement."[10]

Concerned about the miserly behavior of American religious institutions, Steering Committee members from the U.S. side of the border had offered to withdraw from the Conference at the end of the 1971 gathering. "The Canadian Indian delegates refused to consider such a motion, which reflects not only a mutual trust and unity but also a recognition" that the movement needed to be a transnational effort. In September, after a brief respite from the rigors of nonprofit activism, Conference coordinators hit the fundraising trail. They revisited the Anglican Church of Canada, the United Church of Canada, and other previous donors while pursuing new commitments from the Canadian Council of Churches and various U.S. denominations. They insisted that "the rationale for the Indian Ecumenical Conference remains the same" and reiterated their desire to stabilize its financial condition "so that the real work of the Conference can continue" over the next five years. Wilf Pelletier and his colleagues were optimistic about the future, but they were getting tired of begging for money. They were especially frustrated with the unwillingness of American church leaders to commit monetary resources to the movement.[11]

This was also a busy time for the Anglican leaders assigned to implement the recommendations of the Hendry report. In October they formed yet another task force, this one charged with studying the 1970 Conference resolutions that General Synod delegates had endorsed in January 1971. A few conservative bishops had become concerned about "certain dangers" of ecumenical organizing among native people and were questioning whether Anglicans should be involved in the Conference at all, much less supporting it with large grants. On December 7 the task force met at Church House, where Andrew Ahenakew related the history of the movement and identified a number of positive effects it was having in native communities. He also commented on the difficulty of explaining the Conference to outsiders—and of justifying it to uninformed detractors—noting that "it is hard for the white man to understand Indian ways." Task force members then discussed the eleven resolutions, formulating a specific plan of action for each one. In the end, they concluded that "it was a good thing for the Conferences to have been held, and that they should go on being held as long as the Indian religious leaders want them, with no reservations from the Anglican Church." They also recommended "strong support" for future Conferences and asked church staff "to arrange financial resources accordingly." Conservative Anglicans stepped up their attack several months later, accusing Conference organizers of propagating "misdirected revivals" and of selecting delegates who were not held in high regard by the communities they supposedly represented.[12]

Conference leaders thought these allegations reflected a lack of trust, and even Church House executives were perceptive enough to discount such reactionary rhetoric. The movement would always be susceptible to criticism on the issue of representation. Organizers were trying to confederate hundreds of disparate and widely scattered communities, many of which were already marked by internal differences and divisions, and they readily admitted the difficulty of their project. Although overall attendance had increased dramatically at the 1971 gathering, some areas were still largely unrepresented, especially parts of eastern Canada and the western U.S. Conference coordinators blamed these disparities on inadequate funding, which prevented them from hiring fieldworkers and sponsoring regional meetings that could have remedied the problem. They did manage to broaden the makeup of the Steering Committee, expanding its membership to twenty-four men, many of them selected by delegates from their own regions. Women constituted a higher percentage of delegates in 1971 than they had a year earlier but still had no official voice in Conference governance.[13]

In March 1972 the Steering Committee met for four days at a Catholic seminary in suburban Toronto. The first and last days were devoted to Conference business, while the intervening weekend was reserved for a joint meeting with the Inter-Church Committee on Indian Work of the Canadian Council of Churches. Wilf Pelletier chaired the proceedings and most members of the Steering Committee were present, along with a handful of observers. They began on Friday morning with a prayer offered by Huron Miller, a preacher in the Iroquois longhouse religion and an advocate of intertribal exchange. The open discussion that followed touched on a number of topics. The most pressing issue at hand involved deciding how to allocate their limited financial resources. Should they convene another large Conference that summer, or focus on smaller regional gatherings instead? Ernest Tootoosis reported that he was coordinating a regional ecumenical meeting, to be held on the Onion Lake Reserve in northwestern Saskatchewan at the end of April, and he emphasized the importance of getting young people to attend. Other Committee members raised concerns about Conference publicity and the Indian Day of Prayer. A lengthy conversation focused on various manifestations of substance abuse: alcohol and drug addiction among native people, but also non-native misuse of sacraments such as peyote in the wake of Carlos Castaneda's invention of *The Teachings of Don Juan*. The Steering Committee also discussed strategy for its impending meeting with the Canadian Council of Churches. "The Council *must* be convinced," Sam Stanley reported in the minutes. "How to do this? With sincerity, with wisdom, with feeling." After dinner a representative from the W. Clement Stone Foundation explained how Conference organizers might pursue funding from nonchurch sources as well.[14]

Saturday morning they were joined by a dozen denominational leaders representing the Council's various affiliates. The meeting began with an intertribal pipe ceremony led by several members of the Steering Committee. After some brief introductions between the two groups, Council staffer Maurice Wilkinson explained that he and his colleagues were there to "learn more of the purposes, goals and objectives of the Indian Ecumenical Conference," inviting the native people present to "teach us." For the rest of the day and late into the night, a series of impassioned individuals stood at the center of the circle and described the struggles of their communities. Some highlighted the problem of religious competition and conflict and appealed for cooperation and solidarity across confessional boundaries. Others offered a historical perspective on the decline of tribal societies and emphasized the need for a devoted effort at cultural revival. A few admitted to wrestling with how they should relate to religious institutions that had collaborated in the colonization of native people—and that were still profiting from their dispossession. Many mentioned children in their remarks, voicing anxiety about the future of native community life. Winona Arriaga, an Ojibway homemaker raising a family in Detroit, told of the troubled son she had sent to Morley the previous summer; participating in the Conference changed his life, and now he was "reaching out and following the Indian way." Several more speakers testified to the power of prayer in the search for sustenance, inspiration, healing, and compassion.[15]

Most important, all who spoke on behalf of the Conference did so in an autobiographical manner, disclosing concerns by narrating personal experiences and insights. If their interdenominational audience had come to this meeting expecting a programmatic presentation, what these churchly bureaucrats encountered was something very different. Conference leaders avoided pitching their proposal as a linear plan of action backed up by statistical data and theoretical footnotes. Instead, they welcomed their guests to Indian country and initiated a relationship that was both social and sacramental in nature. "Let's get together on this thing," Ernest Tootoosis said as the day's first speaker, and later he wondered whether it was the "first time whites and Indians have sat together and talked about God as equals, man to man." After a number of native people had spoken, Conference organizers asked "the white holy men" to "respond in terms of their faith." Not all of these denominational representatives were able to grasp the tenor of this meeting, and not all of them were prepared to discuss the spiritual life in experiential, personalistic, relational terms. One of the first to respond was Doug Sanders, a lawyer representing the Quakers: "This meeting is a personal one," he observed. "Indians speak from their own experiences," while "whites tend to speak abstractly." He went on to relate his own experience growing up under the colonial ideology taught in public schools, and later he commented on the similarities between this meeting and a typical Friends gathering.[16]

On Sunday morning the two groups celebrated the Christian Sabbath with an ecumenical service led by individuals representing the Anglican, Baptist, Catholic, Mennonite, and United churches, the Salvation Army and the Society of Friends, the Indian Shaker Church and the Native American Church, and several tribal spiritual traditions. Conference coordinators described it as "a highlight of the four-day meeting," and afterward the two groups marked the end of their time together with a buffalo steak dinner at the local Indian center. Maurice Wilkinson characterized the whole event as "a very significant experience" for the Council representatives who participated. In his report on the joint meeting, he noted that the native people who had spoken "all paid tribute to the values of their Indian culture in having a strong family influence, building up respect for parents and the elders, militating against pollution and abuses of nature and natural resources." This was a perceptive synthesis of some memorable orations, reiterating the connection between intergenerational relations and environmental ethics—and acknowledging the centrality of both in native spiritual life. Wilkinson's observation also held true for the movement in general, betokening shifts in momentum that would be increasingly apparent. The Conference had originated as an experiment in interreligious dialogue, but both the logic of native traditions and the gravity of social realities were pointing in other directions. Engaging religious issues from an experiential, personalistic, relational perspective had inspired many Conference leaders toward a deeper commitment to intergenerational and environmental concerns. The challenges facing native youth in the postwar period, and those facing their planet in an era of ecological havoc and Cold War, bore an urgency that threatened to eclipse the movement's original agenda.[17]

The Steering Committee meeting ended on Monday morning with a contentious discussion of fundraising. Various individuals expressed their feelings about the distribution of Canadian and American wealth in the aftermath of European colonization, and together they debated what this meant for ecumenical organizing among native people. Their deliberations were difficult but cathartic and eventually generated a consensus: they would have another Conference during the summer of 1972, to be held at one of the five sites offered by local leaders who had expressed interest in hosting the intertribal gathering. Conference coordinators announced this decision several days later. The Steering Committee "reaffirmed that they share a growing concern for man's relationship with the Great Spirit and the welfare of their children," and they had been heartened by their interaction with denominational leaders as well. The press release also called for justice in the recent killings of two native individuals: Fred Quilt, a Chilcotin family man stomped to death by a couple of Canadian Mounties during a routine traffic stop in November 1971; and Raymond Yellow Thunder, an Oglala Sioux laborer who died at the hands of some Nebraska border town rednecks in February 1972. Both homicides had garnered national publicity after hundreds of people turned out for protest marches in Vancouver, where the Quilt case was investigated, and in Gordon, where Yellow Thunder had been murdered. The violent deaths of these two posthumous celebrities were sobering reminders of the sociopolitical backdrop for any native movement.[18]

Ernest Tootoosis convened his regional ecumenical meeting on the Onion Lake Reserve at the end of April. The three-day gathering mustered only a small number of delegates, but it did provide an opportunity to publicize the Conference and the National Indian Day of Prayer. Dene leader Georges Erasmus organized a regional assembly in Yellowknife for the people of the Northwest Territories, and another small ecumenical meeting was held in Vancouver for native communities on both sides of the British Columbia–Washington border. Conference coordinators were encouraged by these grassroots initiatives, and in May they finally announced that another annual gathering would take place in mid-August on the Stoney Reserve. Several other tentative invitations had fallen through, while a firm offer from Micmac chief Don Marshall was turned down because of the difficulty and expense of travel to Cape Breton Island. The Conference would return to Stoney Indian Park; native people throughout Canada and the U.S. were again invited to participate, though this time they were asked to bring their own bedding and told that meals would be provided only for "registered delegates."[19]

In June 1972 Ernie Willie was appointed to serve as consultant in human rights at Anglican church headquarters. He replaced the retiring Trevor Jones, who had been coordinating implementation of the Hendry report since its approval three years earlier, and Anglican executives were glad to have a native priest on the payroll. Ernie Willie was born at Kingcome Inlet, a remote Kwakiutl village on the northern coast of British Columbia. He grew up in an era when potlatching traditions were strong and at the age of eight was initiated into the elite society of cannibal dancers. They gave him a Kwakiutl name that translates to "The Path," a designation bearing the responsibility to "be in the forefront," to "try to find a way." Later he attended the Anglican residential school at Alert Bay, and he was one of the first villagers sent to Vancouver for high school.[20]

American writer Margaret Craven was impressed by Willie and his schoolmates when she visited the area while conducting research for her first novel. *I Heard the Owl Call My Name* was finally published in 1967 and became an international best-seller, introducing the people of Kingcome Inlet to millions of readers. Craven's parable follows the last days of a terminally ill priest posted to the village's Anglican mission. Although the story revolves around the protagonist's gradual assimilation by his Kwakiutl parishioners, an important subplot deals with the bicultural struggle of an ambitious student named Gordon, a character based largely on Willie. "Gordon was not interested in the past," the narrator remarks. "His mind reached only ahead with that urgent intensity which makes youth seem selfish, and is so necessary to difficult accomplishment." His progressive outlook is even more obvious during his first visit home only a few months after leaving: "Gone was the shy and eager boy in the fisherman's trousers and jacket, the dark hair a little long on the neck. How much he had changed and how fast—a handsome young man in his city suit, his white shirt and tie, and on his face the discipline that marked the size of the battle." Ernie Willie was one of many who praised the book, commenting that Margaret Craven had "written a masterpiece of our people." Six years later a Canadian production company released a feature film based on the novel.[21]

After high school Willie enrolled at a Vancouver vocational institute to learn carpentry. It was not long before he opted for a Christian vocation, continuing his studies at Emmanuel College in Saskatoon and pursuing ordination in the Anglican church. He was serving a parish in the Fraser Valley when he left in July 1970 to coordinate the first Conference, and after the Crow Agency gathering he took a job as a social worker serving native people in

North Vancouver. In October of that year he appeared on national television as the subject of a half-hour documentary produced by the Canadian Broadcasting Corporation for its popular series *Man Alive*, a weekly program covering religious affairs. *Kah-Sah-Las* was filmed at Alert Bay, where Willie had first encountered the outside world—and where many from Kingcome Inlet were now living.[22]

By 1970 the young professional had become deeply concerned about his people's struggle with the dominant culture, especially their battle against alcoholism. CBC producer Sig Gerber was fascinated by Willie's effort to reconcile two ostensibly incompatible callings: cannibal dancer and Anglican priest. The film stops short of drawing parallels between the dramatization of cannibalism in Kwakiutl ceremonial traditions and the ritual cannibalism symbolized by the Christian sacrament of communion, but it is an otherwise incisive profile of a sensitive personality.[23]

The opening sequence juxtaposes shots of Willie preaching in an Anglican church on Sunday morning and dancing in the new community house at Alert Bay the night before. He had come to appreciate the connection between cultural heritage and spiritual survival; he had outgrown the self-centered ambitions of his youth and was determined to help "replant the seed of life that will allow our people to stand erect, proud of themselves." Talking with three Kwakiutl boys on a deserted beach, he encourages them to "let the world know what it means to be you," to overcome ignorance and prejudice through interpersonal relationships, to "integrate with life itself." It is a scene that could have been filmed at Stoney Indian Park the following summer. Ernie Willie had been raised by tribal elders, and now he was starting to act like one himself. He understood the need for ecumenical dialogue in native communities, but he was also young enough to empathize with the existential dilemma facing members of the baby-boom generation; he hoped the movement could be all things to all people. Returning to the Stoney Reserve for the 1972 Conference, he encountered hundreds of other native people with similarly high expectations—and with voices that were varied and sometimes dissonant.[24]

CRASH COURSE

The encampment came to life on Wednesday, August 16. Dozens of conical dwellings were already situated around the edge of the meadow, and Albert Lightning had set up his renowned tipi at the center of the circle. That evening he hosted a short pipe ceremony for all who were interested. Fifty people crowded into the tipi, with as many more gathered around outside. He prayed in Cree as a colleague translated his words into English; Lightning offered thanks for the instruments of prayer, for the opportunity to gather, and for the strength to overcome "all the oppressions and suppressions we suffered from our white skin brothers." The men in the tipi were allowed to draw on the pipe, and then it was over. Afterward some Conference delegates from the north led a brief drum dance outside the tipi. This musical coda came to an abrupt end, however, when they were interrupted by several intoxicated youth from the West Coast who were agitated about the death of Fred Quilt. The militant slogans and foul language eventually faded into the night, but the next morning thunderclouds moved in from the west and poured heavy rain for an hour. The coming of the storm was "a solemn spectacle," one camper reported, and it foreshadowed other rumblings on the horizon.[25]

The Indian Ecumenical Conference began later on Thursday when several Creek and Cherokee leaders laid a sacred fire, some Navajo elders blessed the grounds, and others present added prayers from various tribal and Christian traditions. The Stoneys had built an arbor over the meeting area and set up a public-address system. Anticipating a "huge turnout," they had also enlarged the cookshack, installed a second barbeque pit, and stockpiled deer, elk, and moose meat. The number of delegates participating in the Conference was up about ten percent from the year before, but for the first time young people outnumbered older adults. Estimates of overall attendance ranged from six hundred to more than fifteen hundred, depending on when and how one counted the numerous casual participants wandering in and out of the encampment. There were also more non-native observers this year, some of whom had arrived hoping to get in on the action and others who just happened to be camping elsewhere in the park, which was becoming a popular destination for summer tourists. The presence of so many who were not schooled in native etiquette or the protocol of tribal ceremonies was cause for concern among Conference delegates.[26]

They were also somewhat concerned about the growing number of journalists asking questions and taking pictures of the proceedings. *The Native People*, Canada's premier intertribal periodical, had announced the Conference in June and plugged it again in early August, and afterward the weekly paper ran a two-page story illustrated with a dozen photos. Staff reporter Cecil Nepoose began his account by making ample use of exclamation points, highlighting the interactions between tribal elders and the native youth who had come looking for guidance. "The young people are gaining while they are rebelling against the white society and their parents," Ojibway ex-seminarian Jim Dumont said to Nepoose. "Now they've started to get more impatient and are starting to demand." Edward Fiske, religion editor for the *New York Times*, covered the Conference with a more measured style and just five photos. His syndicated feature—which also appeared in *Akwesasne Notes* and other newspapers in Canada and the U.S.—focused on the religious dimensions of this ecumenical gathering. But he too noted the unsettling presence of the younger generation: "For some urban youths the conference represents their first exposure to medicine men, pipe ceremonies and other Indian customs. One young man, for instance, upon observing an eagle painted on the side of a tepee, asked, 'What's that pigeon doing there?'" Bob Thomas told Fiske that "these people are grasping for some kind of structure and identity. It may end up creating a new Indian religion." The Canadian government's *Indian News* also carried an illustrated story on the event, its Department of Indian Affairs having contributed a "cultural grant" of five thousand dollars toward Conference expenses. The movement was proving to be nothing if not photogenic.[27]

Morning and afternoon sessions under the arbor were conducted in the familiar format, but Conference regulars noticed that the atmosphere had changed. Gone was the comfortable intimacy of their previous gatherings, displaced by amplified sound and restive crowds and a few nosy journalists. Some elders still stood up to express concern about religious conflict in native communities, but many began avoiding the meeting grounds in favor of ecumenical discussions away from the sacred fire. More and more young people waited in line for the open mike, taking advantage of the opportunity to voice their grievances. "I am full of anger, and of bitterness, and of hatred," admitted one native youth. "I know, I should not hate, but I cannot help it." Conference organizers noted "a shift from spiritual concerns to political considerations," from personal testimony to ideological discourse, and those delegates who stayed at the arbor geared their comments to an audience that was growing younger by the day. "When, on rare occasions, one or another of the old wise men spoke, his talk was invariably of his own personal experiences and of his own community. Like a cool breeze blowing amongst the people," the elders spoke "in the idiom of nature," and any who took the time to listen found neither "bitterness nor hatred in their words but rather the realization that many had not forgotten who they are." Middle-aged participants, on the other hand, mostly lectured the youth about their behavior, and "a generation gap became obvious."[28]

This turn from religious camaraderie to secular controversy was also evident in the resolutions debated during the Conference. Delegates had reached a consensus on eleven resolutions in 1970 and eighteen in 1971, but this year they considered only seven and could agree on just two; a third was passed with opposition, another was tabled, one was referred to the Steering Committee, and two more were acknowledged but not acted on. Even more telling was the fact that these seven submissions addressed social and political issues and the internal dynamics of the movement—none of the 1972 resolutions focused specifically on ecumenical concerns. Stewart Etsitty sponsored a resolution on the Navajo-Hopi land dispute, committing the Conference to "support the Hopi traditionalists" and their Navajo allies. John Mitchell authored a resolution backing his own Prairie Band Potawatomies in their land-claims case against the U.S. government. Elwood Modeste and Ernie Willie submitted a resolution passed at the Vancouver regional meeting opposing "the practice of teaching non-Indians the sacred carving traditions of Indians" and urging "all teachers of carving, whether they be Indian or white, to stop this practice." Delegates also discussed resolutions calling for the development of education and social welfare programs tailored to the needs of native people.[29]

As in previous years, the Conference proceedings were controlled by an all-male Steering Committee. A couple of men who spoke under the arbor went so far as to expound on the health benefits of breast-feeding and other duties of motherhood. Some women kept busy tending camp or helping out in the kitchen, but others were not content to take a backseat in the movement. Bea Medicine, a Standing Rock Sioux anthropologist from the University of Washington, and her future sister-in-law Anne Marr, an Oneida-Seneca academic counselor at the University of Illinois in Chicago, tried to remedy the situation with a resolution: "Whereas there have been consistent statements made concerning the role of Native women in the socialization of children in the continuity of Native heritages, and whereas Native women have continued as religious leaders and spiritual and physical healers besides participating effectively in the dominant society, therefore be it resolved that the inclusion of women past childbearing age on the Steering Committee be considered by that Committee." It was one of the two resolutions approved unanimously by delegates, though the only person added to the Committee at the 1972 Conference was John Snow, representing the gathering's Stoney hosts. Aside from the Steering Committee, nearly half of the "official" and "unofficial" delegates were women, but it would be years before any of them would be allowed to serve in a leadership capacity. More than thirty male delegates received financial assistance to get to Morley, but the only female delegates afforded this courtesy were spouses of these men.[30]

One other resolution was sponsored by a female participant. Renee Tree was a student at Little Big Horn High School, a new magnet school for native youth run by the American Indian Center in Chicago. She had traveled to Stoney Indian Park with a sizeable group from the Chicago area, and she enjoyed hanging out with so many young people from other parts of Canada and the U.S.; at one point members of a rock band even set up their equipment and played an impromptu concert. Some of the youth also volunteered to help out with various camp chores. But Tree and many of her urban peers were disappointed by their limited interaction with the spiritual leaders at the Conference. The younger generation had arrived anxious to learn the tribal traditions they missed while growing up in the city, and now it felt like the elders were avoiding them. "Whereas there seems to be dissatisfaction evidenced by some Native American youth regarding the format of the Indian Ecumenical Conference," Tree proposed, "and whereas many youths have requested a seminar-type forum or small groups led by a Native traditionalist to ensure a more concentrated examination of various tribal beliefs and religious systems, therefore be it resolved that the Steering Committee consider this suggested change for further conferences." This resolution met with a cool reception from delegates and was tabled, though it reflected a demographic transformation already under way. Young people had no official role in the Conference but commanded the numerical strength to shape its future, and at the 1972 gathering they began insisting the movement address their concerns. This venture in interreligious dialogue was giving way to an intergenerational monologue.[31]

Tree's resolution was cosponsored by another youthful participant whose presence reflected a different kind of demographic pressure. Adolf Gutöhrlein was a German-American hippie from southern California, a former Boy Scout and Indian hobbyist who had come under the influence of the Hopi traditionalists during the mid-sixties. In the fall of 1971 his meandering path brought him to the Blackfeet Reservation "in the midst of an emotional crisis," he later admitted. Some amiable elders took him in and called him "Hungry Wolf"; the Blackfoot-language expression is a double entendre with sexual connotations. Within weeks he had divorced his American wife, sold their short-lived homestead in the Canadian Rockies, and taken up residence with Beverly Little Bear, a young woman from the Blood Reserve in southern Alberta. Undaunted by the ribald humor that lay behind Gutöhrlein's new "Indian name," both husband and wife began using it as their surname. A few months later they drove north to Morley, where Beverly's eager mate registered for the 1972 Conference as Adolf Hungry Wolf, an unofficial delegate representing the Bloods.[32]

Gutöhrlein knew this ecumenical gathering had been organized "to help reawaken spiritual feelings in all Indians, no matter from what tribe or religion," but his sympathies lay with the young people who had arrived "hoping to learn ancestral ways" so they could set out "on the path of a traditionally-inspired Holy life." During the Conference he agitated among his peers and even resorted to spying on the Steering Committee, eavesdropping outside a closed session where secret ceremonies were being conducted. Gutöhrlein provoked the resolution he cosponsored with Renee Tree, and toward the end of the proceedings he circulated a more emphatic statement challenging Conference leaders to reorient the movement: "Can you older people not leave behind your microphones and formal meetings for a small part of each conference day and call us young people to be with you—on some nearby hill top or around some campfires—to hear of your Holy Ways—to have them explained when we don't understand them or the words used to describe them—to be told by *You* how *We* may begin to use these Holy Ways to give *our* lives Power," he asked. "And we call on you older people to understand that many of our young Brothers and Sisters do not even *know* of the Power and Holy Ways that you have to give us—much less do they know that you are willing to share these with them." Many native youth "have never been taught respect and understanding for our old Holy Ways," but "it will be *your* fault if *you* do not spend a part of your final years on this earth teaching them that which *you* know they should be taught."[33]

Gutöhrlein's screed was a remarkable display of adolescent impertinence. He had lived near a tribal community for less than a year, but already he was passing himself off as a native person—and passing judgment on tribal elders who did not live up to his self-serving expectations. Other non-native participants were more cautious; anthropologist Richard Pope observed that individuals like Gutöhrlein "had been 'brainwashed' by the white man's schools into thinking that elders could provide him with a kind of 'crash course' in Indian religion, rather than the establishment of personal relationships with knowledgeable people in an environment where they could experience things together."[34]

Conference leaders found it difficult to sustain an ecumenical conversation in this climate, but they did manage to provide ample opportunities for ritual participation. Delegates and observers alike could take part in daily sunrise ceremonies, evening powwows, an all-night peyote meeting, and various tribal observances. On Friday evening John Hascall celebrated a Catholic mass in Albert Lightning's tipi, and on Sunday morning more than a hundred people turned out for an interdenominational service led by several Christian clergy. These were all memorable religious experiences, though they were scarcely enough to satisfy the yearnings of the many urban youth seeking their own tribal conversion narratives. It is hard to make up for years of distance in a few days of summer vacation.[35]

The cross-cultural collaboration between Renee Tree and Adolf Gutöhrlein illustrated the rise of generational politics among those who were products of the postwar baby boom. Many of the Conference's youthful participants, native and non-native alike, were searching for a spiritual inheritance. "Baby boomers have found that they have to discover for themselves what gives their lives meaning, what values to live by," writes Wade Clark Roof in *A Generation of Seekers.* "Not since the cataclysm of World War II have most of us been able simply to adopt the meanings and values handed down by our parents' religion, our ethnic heritage, our nationality. Rather, what really matters became a question of personal choice and experience." Roof's sociological study of *The Spiritual Journeys of the Baby Boom Generation* surveys the lives of a large and diverse cohort. The sixties were "a time when mountains were moving," and those who experienced these seismic shifts as adolescents responded in a variety of ways. "Nowhere were the jolts felt more than within institutional religion, in the churches and synagogues across the country." Most baby boomers "dropped out in their late teenage years or early twenties," and "the youthful protest against organized religion appears to have been far more broadly based than is often thought."[36]

Some of these religious dropouts eventually returned to an institutional fold, but many did not. Roof charts "the great spiritual divide" within this generation, which encompasses both the neoconservatism of evangelical Christianity and the post-Christian eclecticism of the New Age, "two vastly different symbolic worlds." Yet for all their variability over space and time, baby-boom pilgrimages converge in "a discourse that has been greatly shaped by the emotional and psychological dimensions of human experience." If nothing else, Roof argues, baby boomers share a commitment to personal growth and self-fulfillment. "Both ends of the religious spectrum appeal to a popular, do-it-yourself mentality," and "both give expression to a turning inward, an introspection that empowers individuals to take responsibility for their own spiritual lives." Like Tree and Gutöhrlein, many in this generation have been more concerned with their own spiritual destinies than with the integrity of the religious communities they claim.[37]

Still, if native boomers and their non-native peers have lived through similar historical experiences, their adaptive responses have not always been comparable. Renee Tree was willing to endorse a tempered resolution suggesting modifications to the Conference format, but Adolf Gutöhrlein had to go it alone when issuing a more confrontational manifesto; most tribal youth, even those in the urban diaspora, appreciate the value of respecting their elders. Countercultural rebellion is, after all, a function of social location. It plays out differently among those for whom the dominant culture is not an inherited condition but one being imposed through public policies and market forces. Majority privilege is a more significant factor than many mainstream interpreters acknowledge; Roof regards class, ethnicity, gender, race, and region as mere "social niches and categories" that are less determinative than the "psychological and deeply experiential themes" induced by citizenship in the American nation-state. He exacerbates this uncomplicated nationalism with an analogous simplification of religion, organized around a "generic idea of God" that terminates in the rhetoric of Christendom. The intersections of politics, religion, and generational affinity are more difficult to negotiate in Indian country. As Conference leaders discovered at the 1972 gathering, this youthful problematic had become an integral concern within their ecumenical movement.[38]

BATTLE ROYAL

People started leaving on the afternoon of Sunday, August 21. The Steering Committee met one last time to discuss plans for the future; John Snow invited his colleagues to make Stoney Indian Park the permanent home of the Indian Ecumenical Conference, a possibility they agreed to consider. By Monday morning the encampment was nearly deserted, though a few handpicked leaders had stuck around for a private meeting that would begin after lunch. The Conference had been conceived as an opportunity to address interreligious strife in an intertribal context; it was founded in the midst of spiritual and cultural antagonisms, and three years later it was also grappling with tensions generated by native women, urban youth, hippies, journalists, and even the churches that were funding the annual gatherings. The Committee had managed to contain these manifold pressures so far, but the movement was about to erupt in open conflict among Conference organizers.[39]

Bob Thomas and Ian MacKenzie wanted to "create a place where traditional Indian leaders can find common continuing ground to achieve a variety of ends." At the 1971 Conference they had pushed through a resolution authorizing them to establish a "North American Indian Cultural and Religious Centre," and in March 1972 they floated the idea among a few denominational representatives who were attending the Steering Committee's joint meeting with the Canadian Council of Churches. Afterward they asked Anglican executives for seed money, and Thomas discussed the project with friends in Detroit and Chicago while MacKenzie described it to contacts at the Vancouver School of Theology. In May the two of them met in Vancouver to draft a funding proposal. They also formed a "pre-incorporation committee," enlisting the support of fourteen influential professionals—academics and Christian clergy, most of whom were non-native. In June they began contacting Anglican and United Church leaders, inviting them to attend the 1972 Conference and then stay over for a meeting to discuss the proposed center. During the annual gathering Thomas and

MacKenzie spoke privately with a few people, though they were careful to reveal their plans only to certain individuals.[40]

Stoney Indian Park had grown quiet again when the clandestine summit began on Monday afternoon. Just seven members of the Steering Committee were present, along with four other Conference delegates and a half-dozen non-native "advisors." Bob Thomas and Ian MacKenzie presented their proposal and a lengthy discussion ensued, stretching into the evening hours and spilling over to Tuesday morning. At one point Ernie Willie objected to the way this matter was being handled; he pointed out that "if they were acting on behalf of the Steering Committee, then the meeting should have been held when all the members were present," and he asked why there had not been even "a brief mention of this proposed Centre" at either of the Committee meetings held during the Conference. Thomas equivocated, Willie walked out in protest, and the discussion proceeded as planned. Those who were still present at the end of the meeting selected three men to join Thomas and MacKenzie in forming a corporate board, and they "hired" MacKenzie to begin raising money and filing legal papers.[41]

A few days later Bob Thomas and Ian MacKenzie mailed a form letter to each member of the Steering Committee. It was an uncharacteristically formal missive, detailing what had transpired and justifying their actions in a defensive manner. They enclosed the revised funding proposal, and this was the first chance most Committee members had to review what was already a fairly elaborate document. Ernie Willie received his copy of the mailing shortly after he returned to Anglican church headquarters; he was already upset with the "irregularities in procedure and betrayal of trust" evident at the private meeting, and now he was incensed by this "show of contempt for the elders of the Steering Committee." He had come to believe that "Bob Thomas and Ian MacKenzie want control not only of the proposed centre but eventually of the I.E.C. An ill informed Steering Committee fits well as a rubber stamp for whatever ideas they may have for the future of the I.E. movement." In a September 18 letter to MacKenzie, Willie raised a number of questions about recent developments: "Are you and Bob finding it expedient to adopt the methods of 'Indian experts'?" he asked. "I personally feel that there is a battle royal forthcoming in our next Steering Committee meeting, which I firmly believe can be avoided if a halt can be called on this proposed Centre." The fundamental issue at stake was whether Conference organizers should attempt to institutionalize the movement.[42]

Bob Thomas was concerned that the Conference had lost sight of its original mission; he wanted to ground the movement in an organization that could continue to unify grassroots leadership around ecumenical concerns. Ian

MacKenzie supported this vision, and he was a seasoned organizer who had been looking for work since leaving his position with the Anglican church a year earlier. Their proposal would establish a residential facility on a fifty-acre farm in the Vancouver area, available to native people and others on a year-round basis. It would serve as "a clearing house and co-ordinating centre for native cultural leaders," an intertribal "think tank" where elders could come together and "discuss common problems, write material, tape it, share ceremonies and plan and develop training for younger native leaders in their areas." It would also house administrative offices for the Conference, allowing organizers to expand their fundraising efforts, assist local and regional ventures in ecumenical cooperation, and disseminate information through newsletters and other media. "There needs to be a centre for intellectual and religious continuity between conferences, a place where the business of the conference can be carried on," they argued, "a permanent base from which the ideas and resolutions brought up through the movement can be implemented." Hoping to attract financial support from Christian churches and other mainstream institutions, they also pitched the proposed facility as a place to hold "specialized training programs" for professionals serving native communities. Thomas recognized the "danger of over-institutionalization," of giving birth to a self-perpetuating bureaucracy, but he and MacKenzie were convinced that "it is important for the Indian Ecumenical movement to start to institutionalize at this point or it will dissipate."[43]

Ernie Willie was still settling into his new office at Church House, where he was now the most influential native voice within the Anglican church. He did not consider the proposal to be "a true outgrowth of what our elders have deemed necessary," and he called for "thorough consultation" with all members of the Steering Committee before proceeding any further. "My main objection to the idea of such a Centre is that the real leadership amongst our people have not as yet completely surfaced." Those already involved in the Conference "are a movement," he believed, and they did not want to institutionalize "in any way."[44]

Willie had at least one powerful ally in this dispute: Wilf Pelletier, who was still the ostensible leader of the movement as chairman of the Committee. Pelletier had been disillusioned for some time and even tried to resign shortly before the 1972 gathering, but the Committee gave him a vote of confidence and he agreed to continue. When he later learned of the private meeting and proposed center, the news left him "feeling very disturbed" over the "turmoil and conflict" among his colleagues. He found a temporary solution through an impromptu vision quest in which he witnessed a dramatic revelation about the organization of the Conference. "I see that I am Chairman of a Committee which is trying to lead instead of serve," he concluded. "My vision showed me that the Steering Committee should be renamed—it should be called a Service Committee, because that is all it can do. If it attempts to lead—to seek goals— as Ian MacKenzie and Bob Thomas have prompted it to do, the result can only be that energy, resources and people will be drawn out of the circle." This philosophical controversy was exacerbated by a recent falling-out between Pelletier and MacKenzie; their relationship had soured over some personal disagreements, and Willie chastised MacKenzie for having failed to "resolve your differences *for the sake of the movement.*"[45]

The situation was further complicated by other financial and logistical difficulties facing Conference organizers. Bob Thomas and Ian MacKenzie were circulating their proposal among some of the movement's established supporters, competing for money in a small native-friendly donor pool, and Anglican executives were already trying to wean the Conference off their size-able grants. Other Christian sources were drying up as well. The Anglican church eventually donated eleven thousand dollars and the Canadian Catholic missions office added two thousand dollars more, but the 1973 gathering might not have happened without major funding from two agencies of the Canadian government: the Secretary of State contributed eighteen thousand dollars, and the Department of Indian Affairs came up with ten thousand dollars. This transition from church support to government money paralleled a shift in administrative responsibility from the Nishnawbe Institute to the Stoney Band. Wilf Pelletier and his dwindling staff continued to handle the movement's finances, but by February 1973 the Conference had been sched-uled to return to Stoney Indian Park once again, and John Snow's people were coordinating the event. Some welcomed the opportunity to host this inter-tribal gathering; Stoney Band member Lawrence Ear praised Snow's leader-ship in an editorial letter to *Stoney Country*, the reserve newsletter, noting that "he has put Morley on the map by hosting the annual ecumenical confer-ences." Snow had used band funds to cover a budget deficit arising from the 1972 gathering, and in 1973 he would oversee all of the on-site expenses. The ongoing challenge of Conference fundraising was being overshadowed by the increasing complexity of organizing a large rural encampment that was grow-ing bigger every year.[46]

The Steering Committee met in Chicago in the middle of April. Albert Lightning and Stewart Etsitty arrived several days early to officiate at opening ceremonies for the new Center for the History of the American Indian at the Newberry Library. Lightning and Ben Bearskin, a local community leader originally from the Winnebago Reservation, offered a prayer over the grounds, and Etsitty blessed the building's interior. Flathead anthropologist

D'Arcy McNickle, founding director of the Center, described their "nascent ecumenical movement" as "the first organized expression" of spiritual solidarity among native people, telling a reporter from *Newsweek* that the Conference "will eventually provide an ideological basis for Indian resistance and unity."[47]

About half of the Steering Committee members showed up for their three-day meeting. It was a freewheeling conversation, ranging over old and new business while hitting a few rough spots along the way. Huron Miller gave a lengthy presentation on the Wounded Knee occupation—already in its seventh week—and the response from Iroquois leaders, who were especially concerned about the young people involved in this militarized confrontation. Bob Thomas mentioned receiving a telephone call from someone arrested at Wounded Knee, a young man who wanted Conference leaders to get involved in the occupation; Thomas told him to "get a real Sioux chief here to talk with the committee" and they would consider the request. The discussion also turned to the disturbing popularity of Carlos Castaneda. Stewart Etsitty reported that his attorney could not find grounds for legal action, and Wilf Pelletier cautioned against any response that might generate publicity and "help him sell his books." Still, Etsitty wondered how to handle the fact that "whites in California have tried to take over the Native American Church. They have everything, including nice places to talk to God. What's wrong with them now?" Six months earlier Maliseet leader Aubrey Perley, on behalf of the Committee, had circulated a letter pledging solidarity with the Vietnamese, Laotian, and Cambodian peoples who were suffering from the war in Southeast Asia.[48]

The Steering Committee had little difficulty reaching consensus on these and other external concerns, but internal matters often provoked more contentious debates. The first item on the agenda involved money: Wilf Pelletier reported on fundraising efforts, and John Snow explained the financial arrangements for the upcoming Conference. Bob Thomas was willing to accept this setup, but he wanted the Stoneys to host the gathering with a more formal protocol, to start "acting like a tribe, like a nation," and not just open their park to what they viewed as a crowd of "oddball-looking Indians from all over the place." Committee members also discussed ways of making the 1973 gathering a meaningful experience for as many participants as possible. Hoping to balance the needs of spiritual leaders with those of urban youth, they considered suggestions regarding daily activities, food service, communication, and campground security. Most agreed on the need for a printed list of rules to help the uninformed avoid desecrating the sacred fire or the various ceremonies being conducted during the Conference. Those present assented to Pelletier's vision of calling themselves a Service Committee. He also questioned using the term "ecumenical" because it "is so difficult to explain to the

Indian people," but Adam Cuthand, the Cree Anglican priest, urged his colleagues to stick with their original name for the time being.[49]

The last day of the meeting began with a pipe ceremony conducted in a tipi at a home in suburban Chicago. Afterward Andrew Ahenakew expressed appreciation for this prayerful devotion; earlier he had commented on how much he enjoyed being part of this group, which was playing an important role in his own spiritual development. He was a mature and calming presence throughout the three-day meeting, but others on the Committee were wrestling with mundane anxieties, and things unraveled toward the end. Bob Thomas and Wilf Pelletier argued about the presence of non-native people at their annual gatherings; Thomas wanted to monitor their participation and limit them to observer status, but Pelletier wanted the Conference and all of its activities left open to "any human being" who showed up at Stoney Indian Park. Pelletier went on to explain that he was "married to a white woman" and did not want his wife to have to "justify her presence at the conference." Then he resigned from the Committee. Thomas responded by mentioning that Ian MacKenzie had phoned from Vancouver and tendered his resignation as well. The session was adjourned without further discussion.[50]

A few days later Conference organizers announced the dates for the 1973 gathering. It would begin on July 30 and last an entire week, allowing more time for participants to "visit each other informally and seek out the old wise men for lectures to youth groups or to individuals." There might even be opportunities for conferring "Indian names" on those who were so inclined. Conference announcements in previous years had favored native spiritual leaders, but this one extended "an open invitation to all Native people" regardless of their religious stature.[51]

The 1973 announcement also offered a revisionist account of the young movement's history. "As you know," it alleged, "this gathering grew out of a concern about the pollution of the Americas." Fundraising materials aimed at church leaders continued to portray the Conference as a venture in ecumenical organizing, "a totally issue-centred project" rather than a service provider, but this press release described it as "a gathering of Native people which arose out of the concern for our Indian way of life and the ecology of the Americas." Conference leaders realized that "the technological age has polluted our waters and our air, has raped the land, has destroyed our brothers the animals, and it appears now that all life is in danger." The fundamental issue was not interreligious solidarity but environmental stewardship: "When our old wise men chose to come together it was hoped that maybe once again we will have to make a contribution for the preservation of all life on this Island. The Great Spirit placed the Native people here to be the keepers of this island and we are failing in carrying out our mission." The Conference announcement appeared in native, church, and government periodicals on both sides of the Canada-U.S. border. Word of the intertribal encampment reached some people through the moccasin telegraph, including many urban youth who happened to be looking for a mission to carry out.[52]

LIBERATION PROCESS

The fourth annual Indian Ecumenical Conference began on a Monday morning with workmanlike familiarity: a fire was laid, the grounds were blessed, pipe tobacco was smoked. The usual morning and afternoon sessions convened under the arbor, but no resolutions were entertained, by order of the Service Committee. Those responsible for food service had trouble getting supplies delivered from Calgary the first couple of days, but the meal lines eventually ran more smoothly, and a large canvas canopy was erected just in time for the rain. Albert Lightning was back this year with a new tipi "of monumental proportions," thirty feet from hearth to smoke hole, a "prairie cathedral" that could hold a hundred people for daily sunrise ceremonies. Another new development was the week's "first official service," a ceremony mourning delegates who had passed away since the previous gathering. Its own short history now a point of contention among Conference leaders, the movement increasingly turned to self-commemorative observances as an outlet for its many internal tensions.[53]

The number of official delegates was unchanged from the year before and fewer middle-aged participants had shown up, but another surge in the youth presence produced a net increase in overall attendance. The Canadian Indian Youth Workshop, for example, had bussed in two dozen young people, who helped out during the week by hauling firewood, serving meals, policing the campground, "and assisting in whatever chores happened to come along." Every evening, participants gathered at the powwow circle—now an established spot amid the tipis—for tribal singing and dancing. The Stoneys had circumscribed the area with a low fence and installed floodlights and a public-address system. "The result of these well-intentioned 'improvements' was the replacement of an important and valuable social experience with a spectacle," Conference organizers noted. "Just two years ago the pow-wow had been nothing more than a spontaneous party where everyone danced around an open fire," but the burning of wood had been rendered obsolete by modern technology. "Night after night in the white glare of the floodlights hundreds of people gathered around the outside of the fence to watch the dancers performing inside. Rising above the voices of the singers the strident voice of the master of ceremonies was seldom silent. Except for a paid admission, the pow-wow now had all the features of a folk festival."[54]

The *Calgary Herald* dispatched a staff writer and a photographer to cover the 1973 Conference; in a series of three illustrated articles they documented the transformation of the movement. John Snow welcomed this attention from the metropolitan daily, commenting that "there is a growing awareness by non-Indians of the Indian religion. They are starting to come around to a way of thinking about ecology and nature that we have been practising for a long time." He shared Wilf Pelletier's views on Conference participation and extended "an open invitation to any non-Indians who may be interested in attending." Another who wanted to broaden the Conference's audience was Ernest Tootoosis, who had distinguished himself as the most outspoken and energetic member of the Service Committee. "God will soon punish the white man," he told reporter Gillian Lindgren, "because he is beginning to think that he is God. He flies people to the moon, destroys the earth and pollutes the air and water. That cannot continue for too long without repercussions." Tootoosis railed against fossil fuels and flush toilets and other modern dependencies, arguing that "you just can't expect to keep taking and taking from Mother Earth—because every time you destroy something you are destroying part of the spirit of the Creator." It was an apocalyptic warning delivered with prophetic confidence, a performance reminiscent of tribal visionaries in generations past. "Many of us are now getting important messages—God is telling the Indian people what they should be doing and how they should be conducting their lives—and many Indian elders are listening carefully and relating the advice to the young." Snow and Tootoosis were not the only Conference leaders who felt called to preach the gospel of environmental stewardship.[55]

Ernest Tootoosis had already joined and left several different Christian churches. Now he denominated himself a die-hard Cree traditionalist, and many were taken with his charismatic personality. "God sent Christ into the world to give white people another chance," he preached, "because Adam and Eve did not live in harmony with nature when they were first put on this earth. As far as we are concerned, we were still living in the Garden of Eden when the white man first came to this country." Native people "consider everything on earth—trees, plants, animals, rocks—to be our brothers because they were created by the same one who created us," and "for an Indian, the only sin is an act against nature—and for those acts we know we will be punished." John Snow was more deliberate and soft-spoken, but he also had doubts about the Christian faith. "We as native people have given Christianity every opportunity to flourish, and although it is sound theoretically, it just doesn't seem to work." As elected chief of the Wesley Band, he was still on leave from his duties as a United Church minister. "Maybe more than ever men need the re-ligion of the Indian with its emphasis on harmony with nature, for if we are going to survive we must learn to live with nature and not try to control and pollute the whole earth."[56]

Others agreed with these sentiments but took a more synthetic approach to the problem of religious commitment. "I grew up in the Indian way and the white way," said John Hascall, the Ojibwa Catholic priest. "I follow the tradi-tional way as well as the Christian way." He played an active role in the sunrise ceremonies held each morning and also conducted a hybrid baptismal service for Bob Thomas's Papago Catholic grandson. "I come here with the powers of the Christian way and the powers given me by the elders," he explained. "In my heart there are many questions, but also peace because I cannot change what God has made me."[57]

Native youth attending the Conference had a lot of questions as well. Many had come "with the expectation of participating in a number of religious observances with their elders. There was a rumour abroad that a number of old men would be going into the mountains to fast and taking an unspecified number of young people with them." Spiritual leaders, however, "found it dif-ficult to prepare the young people for purification and fasting in the moun-tains," and these ritual opportunities failed to materialize. "As the days passed," Conference organizers noticed, "the disappointment and frustration of the young people became increasingly apparent." Some were also agitated by "the number of non-Indian peoples present. There seems to have been an element of angry young people," particularly among those affiliated with mili-tant groups such as the American Indian Movement and the Ojibway Warriors Society. If they had not found the peace of heart that Hascall and other elders could claim, many youthful participants did see the lighter side of their own predicament: "The tension was finally relieved" when a visiting anthropologist suggested that Conference leaders establish a school of "Indian Studies" where urban youth could learn tribal spiritual traditions in a structured environment. "The young people seized on this as an outlet for their pent-up feelings and made the most of it. Faster than it takes to tell, all over the campground young people were telling each other jokes about taking Fasting 100 and enrolling in Sweat Baths 101." Academic hypotheses always make good fodder for native humor.[58]

Gillian Lindgren began her first story on the Conference by reporting that "Indians from all over North America have gathered on the Stoney Re-serve this week to reaffirm their faith in 'the old ways' as an alternative to Christianity." She had unwittingly identified the single most important devel-opment in the movement. Later in the week she noted that this was supposed to be an "ecumenical" gathering, "but the term seems out of place." Like most of her non-native readers, Lindgren associated the concept with cooperative ventures among Christian denominations. "And if anything did not seem welcome at this week's conference, it was Christianity. Young Indians in particular were adamant about its rejection and publicly denounced what they called the 'incessant indoctrination by both Catholic and Protestant churches on the reserves.'" The Conference was still ecumenical, though only in an intertribal sense, embracing a variety of religious traditions but not those that were conspicuously Christian. "Although there were several Protestant and Catholic ministers and priests on hand, they kept a very low profile and some were obviously uncomfortable during many of the discussions and meetings." The movement was heading down the path of parochial intolerance, a trail blazed by dominant religionists at the dawn of the colonial era.[59]

Only the most optimistic of Christian participants could envision a favorable outcome from this turn of events. Bill Smith, a non-native observer representing the Canadian Catholic missions office, recognized what was happening—and he appreciated the historical circumstances that made the transformation necessary. Native people "are an oppressed people," he reminded his superiors, and "an awareness of that is critical for the Church. Many Indians still believe in the myth of the helplessness of the oppressed. The dominated mind looks inward" and "concludes that it is impotent." Smith saw the Indian Ecumenical Conference as part of "the liberation process of our Native brothers and sisters. This is sufficient justification for its being," notwithstanding "the pain that new birth implies." Behind the angry outbursts and the generic nationalism and the adolescent posturing, he detected the rise of "the critical mind," a postcolonial consciousness able to look outward and perceive that "beyond this situation there is the future, what we must do, the things we must create, the historical futurity we have to bring into being." Conference organizers still had moments of optimism as well; after the 1973 gathering they considered it likely that "in the next few years we will see more meetings between young people and their elders taking place all over the country." If the fire was not burning in the direction they had anticipated, it was still generating considerable heat and light.[60]

Ideology, as unstated assumptions and perspectives, is at work in the myriad choices made in the process of production, choices of subject and narrative, scriptwriting, casting, shooting, and editing. Every feature of a film is consciously selected to produce a film that says, as precisely as possible, what its producer and director want it to say.

Margaret R. Miles, *Seeing and Believing*

There was a certain amount of opposition to the media being present. It rained daily and heavily and many saw this as a sign of the Great Spirit's displeasure in having this sacred event interrupted by cameras, lights and microphones.

Roy Bonisteel, Canadian Broadcasting Corporation

CHAPTER EIGHT

"THIS SACRED
EVENT INTERRUPTED"

IN SEPTEMBER 1973 BOB THOMAS finally had a chance to collect his thoughts on the movement. The Indian Ecumenical Conference was nearly four years old; organizers had convened the annual gathering four times, the last three at Stoney Indian Park. Thomas and his colleagues had found a way to get people talking across tribal and religious boundaries, but now their conversation was veering from its original course. The Cherokee traditionalist was dismayed by the proliferation of anti-Christian rhetoric—and by his realization that the Conference was in danger of going the way of the traditional movement. He was also tired of being caught in the middle of intertribal ceremonial tensions caused by the growing presence of urban youth and non-native spectators.[1]

Thomas was back in Detroit, caught up in another year of teaching at Wayne State University. He pondered the situation from the relative comfort of his Monteith College office. It was a Saturday; he was used to working seven days a week, and a few quiet moments could be hard to find for the patriarch of a large family. He fiddled with his pipe, then picked up a lined tablet and began writing in longhand. The lone remaining Conference coordinator was composing a letter to members of the Service Committee; later he would find a secretary to type it up for him. "My brothers," he began. "If I sensed the mood of our last Conference right, it seemed that most people there felt that the Conference itself was too disorganized and unstructured. Further, many people felt that our whole movement was just drifting and not getting anywhere." He accepted a share of the blame for this sad state of affairs, then told his colleagues "we have to 'pull up our socks' and get to work to remedy the situation."[2]

Thomas opened his lengthy epistle with a preamble on the history of the movement. "When we first started out our main goal at the Conference was to bring all the elders of different tribes and different religious backgrounds together so they could work for spiritual unity" and "talk together about how to deal with various community problems. A secondary goal was to encourage young people to attend the Conference so they could learn from these elders. It seems to me that this second goal, of providing a way for young people to learn, has almost snuffed out our first goal." The movement needed to maintain "more of a balance between these goals. But at our last conference we spent nearly all our time talking to young city people and very little time talking to each other. Even our daytime sessions were taken up talking to young people or hearing from them." Thomas appreciated the need for spiritual training, but he believed native youth would "learn a lot more if, at least in our formal sessions, they could listen to elders talk to each other about common concerns. We can't teach them very much directly in four or seven days." Those young people who insisted on speaking publicly "should be encouraged to speak as equals, as men; not little children asking for religious instruction nor scolding us because we don't focus everything on their needs."[3]

Having identified the central problem facing Conference leaders, Thomas turned to some specific recommendations for their annual gathering, enumerating a dozen points regarding its format, schedule, and coordination. He wanted the next Conference to be only four days in length, because "seven days is just too much for everyone and people drift off." He hoped delegates could once again endorse official resolutions, since "the Conference is getting more well known and our resolutions might have some influence now." He still thought John Snow and other "Stoney religious leaders, both Christian leaders and traditional leaders, should have the main responsibility for ceremonies at our Conference; at least the opening and closing ceremonies." Thomas's most detailed recommendations addressed the growing presence of non-native observers and recording technology. "Last time a lot of people felt overwhelmed by the number of white visitors there. Some of the whites were there on legitimate business and others were just looking around. But many of them received hostile looks or remarks whether they were on legitimate business or not." He proposed that "only those whites be admitted who come for legitimate reasons" and that those admitted be formally introduced to Conference participants. Furthermore, "we should have some sessions that are closed to outsiders. Some people just do not feel that they can speak openly and honestly to their fellow Indians with outsiders present. I, myself, feel that way; not because I dislike whites, but because I am afraid I will hurt someone's feelings." He also noted that "some people got upset by all the cameras and tape recorders" at the 1973 gathering. "A few didn't speak because of this. Perhaps we should think about having one official tape recorder only at the meetings; then everyone else who wants to, could send for copies of that one. We should ask people with cameras to ask permission before taking pictures."[4]

Thomas also listed nine recommendations of a more general nature, outlining what they needed to do to "get us back on course and start things moving again." These points focused on communicating their message to tribal communities, church officials, and urban youth. He had several suggestions for how Conference organizers might involve more native spiritual leaders in the movement and support ecumenical activism on the regional and local levels. They should "do some publicity to make the Conference more known in Indian circles. If local leaders are going to follow up at home with what they leave the Conference with, then the Conference has to back them up at home by having a name as a well-known and influential outfit." Encouraging "the celebration of the Indian Day of Prayer in Indian communities" was one way to unify native people across tribal, religious, political, and geographic distances; the Ojibway reserve at Garden River, for example, "now has a feast on that day."[5]

Thomas realized that the success of grassroots ecumenism would be affected by church mission policy as well. He hoped more denominational bureaucrats could be persuaded to "foster religious brotherhood in Indian communities," recommending that "we try to get the national offices of churches to strongly encourage their Indian clergy and local lay Indian church officers to attend the I.E.C. Right now at our Conference about ten traditional leaders attend for every one Indian Christian leader." The most worrisome variable in this postcolonial formula was the militant bloc, whose clumsy protest tactics often caught native Christians in the crossfire. Thomas urged the Service Committee to "make a public statement on the evils of spiritual disunity and circulate this statement to *all* young Indian activist organizations and to as many individual young Indian activists as possible. We should send these groups speakers if they request them," and "encourage summer workshops for the traditional education of city young people, to be held in rural areas and taught by Indian elders."[6]

Organizational confusion, logistical difficulties, non-native intrusions, inadequate publicity, opposition from reactionaries and radicals alike—these and other problems pointed to one solution, in Thomas's mind. "I think we need a central office with one or two full-time staff members," he concluded, summing up his long brief with another argument in favor of establishing a "permanent year-round" center to carry out the work of the Conference. This proposal was nearly identical to the one he and Ian MacKenzie had circulated a year earlier, though now Thomas wanted to locate the facility near Sault Ste. Marie, on a six-hundred-acre parcel owned by an acquaintance with philanthropic leanings. Centrally located on the Canada-U.S. border, the new center would be "a meeting ground and Indian 'think tank'" open to "*all* Indian elders." It would also be close to the Keewatinung Institute—an educational organization similar to the Nishnawbe Institute—and its Potowatomi director, Rolland Nadjiwon, who had helped organize the last several Conferences. Thomas already traveled to Sault Ste. Marie on a regular basis, lecturing in classes and assisting with other Keewatinung Institute projects.[7]

He closed the letter on a folksy note. "Well, my brothers, these are all the thoughts I want to pass along about where we are in our movement and about how to push our movement further along in the direction the Indians seem to want to go," he wrote. "I hope to shake hands soon. Peace, Bob Thomas." He and his colleagues on the Service Committee favored this kind of personable demeanor among themselves, though they were less clear on how to communicate with the movement's varied constituencies. The Conference had never sought out the mass-market patronage other native activist groups relied on during the early seventies, but as attendance at the annual gathering had grown, so had the need for publicity that was both accurate and effective. Unable to escape the media glare, Conference leaders would struggle to convey the right messages to the right audiences.[8]

IDEOLOGICAL INVESTMENT

In January 1974 the Service Committee convened in Winnipeg, where their inaugural meeting had taken place just over four years earlier. Committee members were given only a few weeks to make travel arrangements; responsibility for organizing the group had fallen to Ernie Willie, and he was finding the "ambiguity" of the situation "very difficult to handle." John Snow had agreed to serve as acting chairman of the Committee but was deferring to Willie on most decisions, and Bob Thomas was preoccupied with other commitments as well. Willie thought the meeting would help resolve these organizational uncertainties while allowing them to "sharpen our minds in accordance with our original aims and objectives towards the spiritual oneness of our people." He also wanted to address the issues raised by Thomas in his earlier letter, in hopes that the Indian Ecumenical Conference might continue "providing, to as many as possible, the spiritual strength they need to carry on working out their own self-determination."[9]

Bob Thomas responded to Ernie Willie's invitation with a letter explaining that he could not attend a three-day meeting on such short notice. He then offered a detailed rationale for why "we should *not* have an annual conference this summer." Another late start in the planning process meant they would "end up again with a patchwork conference" thrown together at the last minute. "I, for one, am just not up to going through that again," Thomas grumbled. "I would like to see the next conference financed and planned well enough in advance so I wouldn't end up running around like a crazy man for a week at Morley. I have never really attended one of our conferences because I am too busy handling 'foul-ups' that we should have taken care of weeks before." More important, the Committee needed time to reorient the movement. "The word is getting around that our conference is a combination 'camp meeting and outing for Indian hippies and whites.' That is going to turn off a lot of Indian elders," whose involvement was crucial for promoting ecumenical solidarity in grassroots communities. "We have held our conferences for four years straight now. That is the holy number." He suggested they take a year off to "think about where we are at and which way we want to go."[10]

Those who showed up for the Winnipeg meeting spent the weekend discussing the past, present, and future of the Conference. Hoping to "continue the momentum" of the movement, they decided to go ahead with plans for their annual gathering at Stoney Indian Park. It would be a four-day event, as Bob Thomas had originally proposed, and other logistical recommendations he had made would be implemented as well. But the Service Committee parted company with Thomas on the more fundamental questions driving their goals and strategies. "The movement has grown out of the Indian's concern over the failure of Western and Eastern religions to achieve a harmonious world," they claimed in a press release announcing the upcoming Conference. Native spiritual leaders "feel the pending destruction of the world can only be averted if everyone heeds the basic beliefs of the North American Indians." Intergenerational and environmental concerns had supplanted Thomas's ecumenical mission: "At the conference, religious leaders will devote most of their time to reviewing ancient truths and instructing young people. Members of the movement are united in the belief that destruction of their native religion will mean their own disappearance," and "at the core of their religion is the firm conviction that Indians were placed in North America by the Great Spirit and charged with the responsibility of the land and the environment. They are the real keepers of the land and it is their reason for being." Native people "know how to live in harmony with nature and have never indulged in religious persecution and religious warfare," an assertion Thomas found particularly ironic, having established the Conference in order to resolve the religious conflicts within contemporary tribal communities. The Committee also wanted to take on "the heavy burden of instructing non-Indians on how to live harmoniously with both nature and their fellow man."[11]

The Service Committee confirmed John Snow as its chairman and empowered Ernie Willie to coordinate fundraising in Canada and to assemble his own advisory panel. Fundraising in the U.S. would be left to Bob Thomas and his American colleagues. Willie had convinced Wilf Pelletier to remain involved with the Conference, and the Winnipeg meeting coincided with the release of Pelletier's collaborative autobiography. Published on both sides of the Canada-U.S. border by one of the leading commercial presses in North America, *No Foreign Land* surveyed forty-five years of cross-cultural turmoil and personal growth. Pelletier narrated the story in a gregarious voice, using his life experiences to mount a critique of the dominant culture and to outline an alternative to the existential anxiety generated by industrial civilization. He was especially concerned with social roles and relationships in an institutionalized world. "It takes a long time not to feel like an alien, a long time to feel at home, a long time to search out and discover who you are," he told his coauthor. "But if you go all the way with that exploration it takes you beyond race, beyond color, beyond class, beyond every kind of category, and you find that you belong to humanity. And *that's* who you are." This arduous path can also "take you beyond property," beyond the folly of a utilitarian subsistence, "to where you find you belong to the land. And *that's* who you are. And when you are *that*, there is no foreign land. Wherever you are is home. And the earth is paradise and wherever you set your feet is holy land." Pelletier filled the book with engaging anecdotes and persuasive observations, though he had little to say about his recent organizational involvements; he included only a few sentences on the Conference and did not mention the Nishnawbe Institute at all. By the time the book was released he had moved to southern British Columbia, where he basked in his own rising celebrity.[12]

Ernie Willie struggled to keep up with the demands of Conference organizing while fulfilling his many other responsibilities as consultant in human rights for the Anglican Church of Canada. In 1973 General Synod had authorized the formation of the Sub-Committee on Native Affairs, which held its initial meeting in Winnipeg during the last weekend of November. The first two items on a very busy agenda were the Indian Ecumenical Conference and the Indian Day of Prayer; committee members approved plans for producing a pew leaflet to guide congregations in "special observances" on the Sunday before June 21. They met again in February 1974, and several months later Willie traveled to Vancouver to meet with a regional committee interested in discussing the Anglican church's progress in implementing the recommendations of the Hendry report. The Sub-Committee affirmed all nine recommendations and agreed that "top priority must be directed to changes in basic attitudes, especially attitudes toward Native peoples," suggesting that church leaders devote more attention to public relations. In April Willie tried to explain native spiritual traditions to an Anglican women's group in Calgary. "Jesus Christ was probably the best Indian that ever lived," he told them. "Christ lived our way of life." It was a provocative reversal—and a conclusion many tribal people had reached.[13]

In May Service Committee member Stewart Etsitty and some Papago spiritual leaders held a regional ecumenical gathering in Tucson, Bob Thomas's old stomping ground. A month later Thomas circulated yet another long letter detailing his apprehensions about the movement. "I now feel that my usefulness is at an end," he wrote. "Funding sources are drying up in the U.S. and I don't see any hope of raising money for the Conference on this side." Furthermore, "our Conference is going in a direction that I am not too interested in or approve of." He had detected a rift in the movement's transnational bedrock. Native communities in the U.S. were struggling most with the social dysfunction caused by chronic religious conflict, he believed, while those in Canada were more concerned about the rapid loss of tribal traditions in the context of post-war urbanization. Thomas was "pleased that my northern brothers want to revive the Law that was given to them by the Creator," but this revival "cannot be at the expense of more bitterness between different religions in our tribes." He was also convinced that most of the urban youth attending their annual gatherings "are just 'playing Indian' because it is a big fad nowadays to be interested in the Indian religion." Native young people "have parents, relatives, home communities, and tribes. We should encourage them to go to their older relatives and tribesmen to learn," not launch a "new cult" by teaching them "some kind of general, 'hodgepodge' Indian religion." He ended his letter by resigning from the Service Committee, urging those who remained to avoid going the way of the traditional movement. "Watch that our present Conference doesn't fall into the same trap. I would hate to see it become just another pow-wow and a 'kick' for city kids, as a place to play with the old Indian religion."[14]

Hoping to correct some of the problems Thomas and others had identified, Stoney officials prepared several flyers to guide Conference participants. An invitation letter welcomed all to Stoney Indian Park, reminding them to bring dance regalia for the evening powwows but to leave behind skimpy clothes and alcoholic beverages. A map of the area oriented first-time visitors to the Conference grounds. A four-page brochure provided details on registration, camping, meals, supplies, showers, and the local swimming hole. It also addressed the use of recording technology. "Before you take pictures or tape recordings of people or events please obtain the permission of those individuals involved," the Stoneys asked. "There are some tribes who do not believe that it is proper to take pictures or tape recordings of religious ceremonies or discussions. Honor the feelings of your brothers and obtain permission before you do something which may cause embarrassment to you or your brother." The Service Committee had, however, decided "to allow and to invite various representatives of the Press and Radio to cover the conference." A press committee would try to monitor their behavior. "We recognize that some individuals and groups may not want to be interviewed or even observed by the Press. We respect these feelings but we also respect the feelings of those who feel that the Press and Radio should be involved."[15]

"We know that you have come to this conference in order to share your personal religious experiences with your brothers," the brochure continued, "and in turn to learn from others so that your spiritual life will become fuller. This conference will be a rewarding experience for those who do want to learn and who are willing to respect the feelings and beliefs of others." Stoney leaders were primarily concerned about personal and tribal differences, making no mention of the Christian presence that had been so prominent in the early days of the movement. The Stoney newsletter pitched the Conference to band members with an angle even further removed from the movement's original trajectory, emphasizing native responsibility for educating non-native people in a postcolonial world. "Unless Indian philosophy is listened to, we are going to destroy ourselves on this earth," John Snow predicted. "Unless we try to protect the environment, unless we respect the creation of God, unless we respect people as well as animals, we are doomed—the very hell that Christianity talks about will become a reality."[16]

The 1974 Conference began on the morning of July 30 when spiritual leaders blessed the grounds and laid a sacred fire. More than seven hundred participants—including indigenous guests from Australia and the Pacific Islands—took the time to fill out a registration form; observers estimated that nearly eighteen hundred were on hand for the transnational gathering. Attendance swelled even higher in the evenings, when native people from nearby reserves arrived at Stoney Indian Park to join in nightly powwows. Most of the elders who spoke during daytime sessions under the arbor directed their comments at the youth, and some were willing to meet with young people in small groups as well. This year also brought more opportunities for ritual participation: along with the customary sunrise ceremonies each morning, many urban youth were introduced to the therapeutic rites conducted in a sweat lodge, and a few committed themselves to fast during the Conference. "The personal contacts many of the young people had anticipated making with the elders at the conference of 1973 now began to occur quite spontaneously," Conference organizers noted. "Visions were experienced by several participants." Other ritual highlights included a naming ceremony and a wedding performed in accordance with tribal tradition.[17]

Reporters from native, religious, and government periodicals in Canada covered the proceedings; the articles they produced were distinct representations of the Conference, each reflecting the ideological investment of its publisher. *The Native People* ran the story on page one under a three-column headline, "Native Revival Plotted." The article focused on the effort to help urban youth by teaching them tribal traditions at "North America's largest annual gathering of Native spiritual leaders." Like many Conference participants, this reporter had fallen under the spell of Ernest Tootoosis, who reiterated a revisionist version of the movement's history. "The whole movement is to revive the Indian culture and spiritual life," he said in an interview. "Young Indian people won't get to know the way of life from the white society. There's an exterior darkness in the way of life between the two societies and that's why the younger people are behaving the way they are. They have lost their sense of identity." By the mid-seventies many had reached a similar diagnosis and had joined the call for a nativist remedy. Micmac leader Noel Knockwood praised the Conference for providing "spiritual education" to those who "wish to know the religious beliefs of our ancestors." The movement "has perpetuated and rekindled the flame of Indian conditions prior to European involvement," motivating tribal communities throughout Canada and the U.S. to maintain a "traditional identity" in various ways. "In other words, it has given the Indians a philosophy."[18]

The *Canadian Churchman* relegated the story to page twenty-six of its September issue, next to a large snapshot of Primate Ted Scott draped in a Nishga blanket and accepting a pipe on the last night of the gathering. Earlier in the week Scott had declined an opportunity to address Conference participants, saying "I am not here to speak to you—I am here to listen," but he remained a photogenic totem for an Anglican readership. Titled "Oneness with Nature Describes Aim of Conference," this article highlighted native teachings on environmental relations; the contrast with Christian dogma was obvious. The reporter also emphasized the "pain and bitterness" in the voices of those who criticized the dominant culture. "Most white observers left with conflicting emotions. You knew what it felt like to be a minority for a change and not treated as a person but labelled because of the color of your skin." She endorsed Ernie Willie's conciliatory approach by quoting him at length: "Part of the mental block as native peoples is that we must overcome our past and present feelings of frustration" over "the fragmented denominationalism of Christianity and the seeming insensitivity of the 'white man.' If we see ourselves as being negative in our expressed encounter with these two groups, which are so often held to be one and the same, then the true nature of our various spiritual expressions will not mature as quickly." Like their reporter, other Anglicans present characterized the Conference as an exercise in cross-cultural anxiety.[19]

The Canadian government's *Indian News* carried the most balanced account of the Conference, calling it "an international religious gathering." The article detailed the tribal and religious diversity represented at the Conference, describing it as "the only official convocation of Indian people designed for the promotion and expression of Indian religion." This reporter used the phrase "Indian religion" in an ecumenical sense, encompassing the spiritual traditions maintained by contemporary native people, including those of the Christian persuasion. The Conference was "one of the most important native gatherings in North America" and "an annual coming together of the people unsurpassed in native religious significance." Yet this flattering portrayal could also be read as an insidious form of ideological subversion. Métis scholar Howard Adams considered the movement to be an example of state-sponsored cultural nationalism serving reactionary interests; it reinforced colonialism by promoting activities that "obscure political awareness and action." Given the fact that the Canadian government was now the Conference's most generous benefactor, his assessment was not without merit.[20]

DIVINE DISAPPROVAL

The Indian Ecumenical Conference was finally solvent. Organizers had entered the 1973–74 planning cycle with a small nest egg and then raised nearly fifty-five thousand dollars for the 1974 gathering: ten thousand each from the Anglican and United churches, five thousand from the American Board of Catholic Missions, twenty-five hundred from the Canadian Catholic missions office, and more than twenty-seven thousand dollars from several different agencies of the Canadian government. Bureaucratic delays kept some of the money from arriving in a timely fashion, but when the sacred fire was extinguished on August 2, the movement's financial condition was as good as it had ever been.[21]

Money was, nevertheless, still a source of contention among Conference leaders. Nine months earlier Ernie Willie had been elated when John Snow took charge of the Service Committee, offering to "do everything in my power to be of support to you," but now he questioned Snow's fiscal integrity. Willie was dismayed to learn that certain individuals expected to be compensated for their spiritual leadership; he found "traditionalism for a price rather hard to take." He accused Snow and others of "wanting to get as much money as they can from the I.E.C." and felt that "the spirit of the conference will die if we are only interested in the amount of money which can be rooked from the funding sources." Willie had forwarded nearly fifteen thousand dollars to cover expenses at Stoney Indian Park but was still waiting for an accounting of how these funds had been disbursed. "I am sure that with the amount of money we sent you, you did not spend all of that," he wrote to Snow in September. Willie wanted to use their budgetary surplus to sponsor regional ecumenical meetings, not to line the pockets of Committee members.[22]

Of course, Willie enjoyed the benefits of an Anglican church salary, a professional surety few native people had ever known. And his protest was, at least in part, a defensive gesture. He had arrived at the Conference on the heels of a successful fundraising effort only to encounter "a fair amount of abuse" from colleagues who insinuated that "people from the East" were trying to control the movement. John Snow solidified his authority in the midst of these intramural jealousies, persuading the Service Committee to make Stoney Indian Park the "permanent site" of their annual gathering.[23]

Ernie Willie was still committed to the cause, however, and organized another Committee meeting to be held in March 1975. "From the many comments I have received since the conference," he told his colleagues, "there was a strong opinion that we have become repetitive and that the repetition is expressed in our anti-white and anti–Christian Church feelings. I am a firm believer, in our teaching methods, that we remain positive in our approach." He felt that "negativism" correlates with the loss of personal creativity. "Any criticisms levelled during the conference should be levelled at our own people, i.e., our politicians, friendship centre operators," and other native leaders. "If we are to emerge as a people, we must seek ways and means of corporately rebuilding and remoulding our future."[24]

The Service Committee returned to Winnipeg during the first weekend in March. Among other business, Committee members passed a "special resolution" affirming the Nishnawbe Institute as the movement's administrative headquarters and encouraging all native organizations to send at least one leader to participate in religious ceremonies at the Conference. They also discussed the composition of their Committee, which had evolved considerably since being formed five years earlier. Gone were coordinators Bob Thomas, Ian MacKenzie, and Wilf Pelletier, though most other founding members still appeared on the official roster. The Committee had grown to twenty-four men and now leaned toward the north and away from Christianity; the roster listed sixteen from Canada but only eight from the U.S., and a breakdown distinguishing those who practiced tribal traditions from those who maintained a denominational affiliation showed a comparable imbalance. Having changed even its name, the

Service Committee's one enduring continuity was that it remained an absolutely gendered body. These two dozen male leaders still had not seen fit to include any female elders among their number, though Ernie Willie had tried to get a couple of native women included on a fundraising subcommittee.[25]

As one of the youngest members of the Service Committee, Willie did not claim to be a spiritual authority, but he had become the movement's most indispensable leader. He could relate to tribal elders and he understood the worldview of professional bureaucrats as well, allowing him to broker relations between the Conference and non-native institutions such as the Anglican church. He was also able to mediate between old and young within the movement, a useful skill because a generation gap frequently reared its modernist head in the age of Red Power activism. Willie may have understood better than anyone else what the Conference meant for the religious history of North America. "We, as Native People, are slowly moving towards our own exodus," he told readers of the *Canadian Churchman*, "and whether the Church remains a valid, supportive part of this movement will depend on how willing it is to accept our contribution as a people" whose spiritual values are comparable to "the best in other cultures." In May the Anglican monthly featured a series of articles on native issues, acknowledging that "the re-awakening of Indian culture and religion across North America" was raising some difficult questions. At their biennial assembly a month later, General Synod delegates heard their first report from the Sub-Committee on Native Affairs and approved several resolutions facilitating its work. Willie considered this a "moral victory" and followed up by challenging members of the committee with some questions of his own: "What contribution are we going to make? How are we going to make it and when? To what extent are we prepared to commit ourselves wholly to making the voice of our people heard, understood and heeded?"[26]

With John Snow at the helm, the Service Committee agreed to hold a weeklong gathering in 1975, as it had two years earlier. The Conference was now "one of North America's major annual Indian events," a flyer announced, and was scheduled to precede Banff Indian Days, a tourist-oriented festival held in a nearby resort town and "one of Canada's biggest pow-wows," according to the Stoneys. Various church and government agencies were once again providing major funding for the Conference. The annual budget was still not growing as quickly as attendance, however, so prospective participants were reminded to raise their own travel expenses. Those who made it to Morley could expect "a learning experience," the invitation flyer promised, an open-ended encounter focusing on intergenerational and environmental relations.[27]

The Conference began on July 28, a Monday. Several newspaper reporters dropped by during the week, interviewing the usual suspects—Ernest

Tootoosis, John Snow, Ernie Willie, Albert Lightning—along with a few others including Creek traditionalist Phillip Deere, a spiritual advisor to the American Indian Movement. Also making a brief appearance in the *Calgary Herald* was Snow's wife, Alva, one of the few women ever quoted in media coverage of the Conference. "A hundred years ago," she said, "we'd have been shaking our tomahawks at one another and waving our bows and arrows," though the source for this comic observation on the gathering's intertribal significance was identified only as "Mrs. Snow."[28]

Coincidentally, some youthful participants were once again brandishing weapons, if only as a symbolic gesture; Phillip Deere and other AIM leaders had been invited to speak at the Conference and their followers turned out in force, meeting in drum circles and marching through the encampment to the beat of the AIM anthem. Estimates of overall attendance ranged from fifteen hundred to two thousand people. John Snow hoped some Hollywood celebrities would join the crowd for a buffalo feed and powwow on Friday evening. Location scouts had discovered Stoney country six years earlier, when portions of *Little Big Man* were filmed on the reserve, and now the movie industry was back shooting Robert Altman's *Buffalo Bill and the Indians*, another satiric deconstruction of the Wild West. In more ways than one, the Stoney homeland seemed to be fertile ground for the efflorescence of historical irony.[29]

Altman's entourage was not the only film crew in the area. Many people arriving for the 1975 Conference eager to spend a few days secluded from the dominant culture were dismayed to find several cameras filming the proceedings. Two different crews were shooting documentary footage for broadcast on national television. One was led by Sig Gerber, a producer for the Canadian Broadcasting Corporation's weekly religious affairs series *Man Alive*. The other was headed up by Terry Sanders and Freida Lee Mock, independent filmmakers under contract with the National Geographic Society for its second season of public television specials. In the past this annual encampment had been blessed with nice weather, various outdoor activities only occasionally interrupted by a brief shower, but this year the heavens clouded over and poured rain most of the week. Conference participants sought refuge in waterlogged tents and tipis and nursed campfires that sputtered and smoked, growing more discouraged by the hour. "Maybe there was a reason for it to rain these past two or three days," Wilf Pelletier told a sparse group huddled under the arbor. "Maybe there's a reason that that weather is testing us." Some viewed these unpleasant conditions not as a test but as a sign of divine disapproval, "an expression of displeasure by the Creator because the sacred things were being filmed," as one newspaper reporter described it. More than a few native people left before the sacred fire had been extinguished, blaming non-native filmmakers for their early departure.[30]

ELABORATE REPRESENTATIONS

Both television crews had permission to document the Indian Ecumenical Conference, though neither knew of the other's plans before arriving at Stoney Indian Park. CBC producer Sig Gerber had known Ernie Willie since profiling him in the 1970 program *Kah-Sah-Las*, and several years later they began discussing the possibility of filming an episode of *Man Alive* at the Conference. In May 1974 Gerber flew to Tucson, where Stewart Etsitty was chairing a regional ecumenical gathering, and appeared before a group of Conference leaders. They gave him ten minutes to present his proposal, then spent several hours grilling him on the problem of cross-cultural representation. Most of these elders had serious doubts about the propriety of filming native spiritual traditions for broadcast on national television. They believed that tribal ceremonies should be protected from the secularizing power of mechanical reproduction, and they wondered how the movement itself would be affected by high-profile publicity among non-native Canadians. Gerber returned to Toronto disheartened by the experience.[31]

Several months passed before he was notified that the Service Committee had decided to allow CBC cameras at the 1975 Conference. In the meantime, Ernest Tootoosis agreed to appear on *Man Alive* during the 1974–75 season, narrating Plains Cree spiritual traditions for host Roy Bonisteel and his faithful viewers. *The Great Spirit* was filmed on the Poundmaker Reserve in western Saskatchewan and aired Monday, March 3. Tootoosis offered a rationale for discussing sacred things in such a public manner by explaining that "we was much better people before the white man came here—spiritually. Maybe we didn't have cars or anything but we was rich, very rich people in spiritual life and living with the land." Tribal ancestors "believed in God and his creations and lived in harmony with those creations, and unless we take that back then we're not Indians anymore. We have to restore that back to our young people." Bonisteel acknowledged this point but signed off by framing the social critique for a non-native audience: "Our native people have always seen the world and all its parts as one. Within the whole, each part has its place depending on and giving life to all the others. Western man, blinded by his ideas of progress, has forgotten this fundamental truth." Sig Gerber made a special effort to honor Tootoosis's intentions when the program was rebroadcast a year later, writing to community leaders and distributing posters in hopes that "the native audience, especially the young people," might be persuaded to tune in.[32]

Independent filmmakers Terry Sanders and Freida Lee Mock arrived at the Conference by a shorter and more serendipitous route. They first met each other in 1972 while collaborating on *Of Cowboys and Indians*, a television documentary bankrolled by the Ford Motor Company. In 1974 they had just completed a travelogue on the British Isles for the National Geographic Society and were looking for their next project when Sanders stumbled across *The World of the American Indian*, a lavishly illustrated volume published by the Society earlier that year. He soon proposed a second National Geographic television special, this one focusing on "the spiritual and historical tapestry of the American Indian experience." It would be "a film of beauty and power which celebrates the American Indian as he is today," an intertribal narrative "told with the insight of the Indian, from his own point of view and in the beauty, poetry and clarity of his own words," culminating in a "colorful, emotional and meaningful climax." The project was approved and Sanders and Mock began developing a treatment, touring Indian country in search of telegenic characters and settings.[33]

Aiming to produce an overview of the contemporary situation, they quickly realized the importance of including a segment on the urban diaspora, and during a visit to Chicago in the spring of 1975 they ran into Dorene Porter. She served as media specialist for the Native American Committee, a local community organization, and was herself a budding filmmaker who had just finished a bachelor's degree in mass communication at Northeastern Illinois University. Porter had attended the Conference in 1973 and 1974 and suggested that Sanders and Mock feature the annual gathering in their documentary. They agreed to cover travel expenses for a group of urban youth in exchange for the opportunity to film the journey from Chicago to Morley. Sanders flew to Alberta several times in June and July to meet with John Snow, Albert Lightning, and other Conference leaders, but he was unable to present his proposal to the Service Committee on such short notice. In early July Sanders and Mock wrote to Ernie Willie informing him of their plans to film the upcoming Conference for broadcast "on nationwide Educational Television stations in the United States and Canada, and eventually, around the world. Thereafter, this film on American Indians will be shown in schools throughout North America." They were bringing as many as seven crew members, "some of whom will be Indian," but promised "not to interfere with the normal flow of events, making ourselves very inconspicuous." They intended to "show the Conference in a very positive light, capturing the interest of young people in the knowledge of the elders."[34]

Sig Gerber was surprised to see the National Geographic caravan roll into camp on July 27, and Terry Sanders and Freida Lee Mock were just as surprised to find CBC personnel already on hand; each group had made the trip thinking it would be the first to film the Conference. Both crews covered the opening ceremonies under the arbor, then went their separate ways in search of interesting angles on the event. Sanders and Mock shadowed the Chicago group as they participated in Conference activities and helped with chores, occasionally soliciting their views on the significance of these experiences. The young urbanites proved to be a cooperative cast, flattered by the invitation to fleeting celebrity, and the National Geographic crew had little difficulty getting enough footage. Sig Gerber, on the other hand, sought out elders and spiritual leaders who could explain the movement and its various goals. He had anticipated a rather leisurely shooting schedule, but once the rain began falling he had trouble finding anyone willing to be interviewed. After several frustrating days he finally requested a meeting with members of the Service Committee, persuading a few of them to appear on camera before the Conference ended. "There was a certain amount of opposition to the media being present," Roy Bonisteel later recalled. "It rained daily and heavily and many saw this as a sign of the Great Spirit's displeasure in having this sacred event interrupted by cameras, lights and microphones. Indeed, on the final day, as the equipment was being packed, the rain stopped and the sun burst through the clouds as if to bless the crew's departure."[35]

Returning to network headquarters in Toronto, Sig Gerber ran across a newspaper story on the "religious pow-wow" he had just witnessed. The feature article began with an account of one of the many ceremonies he had been prohibited from filming, and it also included some critical comments about the presence of television crews at the Conference. It was written by Hugh McCullum, former editor of the *Canadian Churchman*, and Gerber asked him to script the narration for the CBC program. Within weeks they had recorded Roy Bonisteel's voice-over transitions and filmed his opening and closing monologues at a local park. Gerber then took his meager footage into the cutting room. He had shot the program on reversal film, an inexpensive stock commonly used for newsreels and other ephemeral cinematography, leaving little room for error in the editing process. His working title, "People of the Centre," was borrowed from a recent book by Jesuit missiologist Carl Starkloff, but Gerber eventually settled on a spatial metaphor used by one of the leaders he interviewed at the Conference. *People of the Sacred Circle* was telecast on the first Monday in November 1975, opening the ninth season of *Man Alive*. A CBC press release emphasized that "Indians from all over North America," particularly "young Indians who are casting about for their own identity," had "gathered to reflect and learn again from their elders about their traditional religion, their language and their culture." Network publicists also acknowledged the controversy involved in making this film.[36]

Terry Sanders and Freida Lee Mock were on a production schedule that was longer and more complicated. After leaving Stoney Indian Park they spent the next year filming additional segments on contemporary Kwakiutls, Navajos, and Miccosukees, completing their work during the summer of 1976. Movie star Robert Redford agreed to read the voice-over narration that Mock and Sanders had written. *The New Indians* finally appeared on the Public Broadcasting Service, though not before PBS executives tried to censor it on behalf of their corporate sponsor; Gulf Oil representatives had been allowed to preview the film, and they objected to a segment critical of strip-mining on Navajo land. The National Geographic Society promoted the February 1977 telecast with slick publicity materials targeting diverse media outlets. Its first season on public television had been "such a smashing success that I was afraid we never could match it," gushed Gilbert Grosvenor, editor of the Society's trademark magazine. "I need not have worried. The four new documentaries for 1976–77 more than live up to the award-winning standards set last season." Other promotional copy promised "a fresh look at Indians in the United States and Canada" showing "how they are coping with the white man's world" while "rediscovering their roots, their pride, and their voice."[37]

    People of the Sacred Circle and *The New Indians* were the most elaborate representations of the movement ever made. Like any text depicting human experience, each was also a highly selective portrayal of the 1975 Conference, telescoping a weeklong event involving thousands of people down to a two-dimensional slot in prime time. *People of the Sacred Circle* is twenty-eight minutes long. The film begins with the lighting of the sacred fire; we hear sounds of friction and combustion as the series and program titles are superimposed on the screen. Then Roy Bonisteel appears, explaining the purpose of this ceremony and offering a brief account of the history of the movement. The rest of the film is composed of five major segments interlaced with four transitional sequences; the segments consist of on-camera interviews with Conference participants addressing key issues, while the transitions expand on these points by showing daily activities accompanied by voice-over narration. The first segment shows American Indian Movement leader Edward Benton wearing a denim jacket and a large beaded medallion necklace. He is standing at ease behind a wooden fence, leaning on a crossbar and talking about the vitality of the native spiritual heritage. This is followed by informal shots of Albert Lightning outside his legendary tipi, which Bonisteel identifies as the site of ceremonies that could not be filmed. The second segment features three men—Wilf Pelletier, an anonymous Sioux youth, and Benton again—expounding on the importance of tribal elders in the revival of spiritual traditions. The lengthy transition that follows reveals that the gathering also had "undercurrents of tension," not only between participants and non-native observers but between Conference leaders and young militants as well. Themes of violence, tribal tradition, and the logistics of a large encampment then converge in graphic footage of the slaughter of two buffalo from the Stoney herd, to be served at the evening meal.[38]

The third segment is the narrative heart of the film, exploring the continuing debate over the role of Christianity within this ecumenical movement: John Snow criticizes the narrow-minded and judgmental proclivities of European religion; Ernie Willie describes his struggle to see tribal and Christian traditions as complementary realities engaged in a constructive dialogue; Edward Benton advances a universalist interpretation of Jesus Christ, suggesting that "the Christian sacred circle is not complete because they are still at the Trinity stage." Another transitional piece shows a daytime session under the arbor, Wilf Pelletier and then an anonymous young man commenting on tribal beliefs and rituals. The fourth segment returns to Snow, who gently explains that native people have a message the world needs to hear; his proposal is seconded by Ruth Blaser, a non-native seminarian who has come to appreciate the value of cross-cultural learning. The final transition is a swirl of motion and color and rhythm and song—scenes from an evening powwow foreshadow the end of the Conference, and of the film. The fifth segment offers some observations on the larger significance of this gathering, Willie and Benton pointing to the importance of intertribal ecumenism and spiritual revival. Roy Bonisteel appears on camera and concludes by drawing implications for his non-native viewers, and then the credits are superimposed over long shots of the encampment.[39]

With a running time of fifty-seven minutes, *The New Indians* is twice the length of its Canadian rival. It is also a more technically sophisticated and narratively complex film, weaving together four distinct story lines in support of an argument set forth in the opening segment. The film begins with a long teaser. We see some teenagers riding in the back of a pickup truck, then scraping a hide under the direction of a native man. "In times of stress, people make pilgrimages," the narrator tells us, and for the modern tribal person this journey has led to "the half-forgotten traditions out of which he came." Native cultural revival is illustrated by several more contemporary scenes: a Kwakiutl potlatch, an open-air rock concert, a tribal elder speaking into a microphone. This is followed by the *National Geographic Specials* theme music, a richly orchestrated number that plays over the series and program titles and the name of narrator Robert Redford. Then the voice-over resumes with another aphorism, this one framing the film's thesis. "Out of hope come prophecies," Redford says, and he cites Oglala Sioux holy man Black Elk as having prophesied that "the fifth generation" would recover their tribal traditions. "It is now the era of the fifth generation," Redford continues, introducing four individuals who will stand for these "new Indians": Creek counselor Susan Supernaw, Kwakiutl chief James Sewid, Navajo lawyer Claudeen Arthur, and Miccosukee musician Stephen Tiger. "Four American Indians, four journeys," though we soon see that Supernaw's pilgrimage from Chicago to Morley is the film's structuring narrative as well. Of the seven segments that follow, four focus on Supernaw at the Conference for a total of twenty-one minutes; Sewid, Arthur, and Tiger are profiled in a single segment each, none over twelve minutes long.[40]

The first segment shows Susan Supernaw and her eight companions arriving at Stoney Indian Park, where they set up tents and tipis, ride horses through the encampment, help build the powwow circle and arbor, observe the lighting of the sacred fire, and listen to several speakers comment on spiritual revival. Moving west, the second segment profiles James Sewid and his efforts to reinvigorate Kwakiutl potlatching and carving traditions after a century of Canadian suppression. The third segment returns to the Chicago group as they contend with daily rain, help dress out a buffalo, participate in an American Indian Movement rally, and listen to AIM leader Phillip Deere discuss treaty rights. Moving south, the fourth segment profiles Claudeen Arthur and her efforts to protect Navajo lands and lifestyles from the ravages of corporate energy development. The fifth segment trails Supernaw and friends while they sit in on a ceremony, dance at an evening powwow, and talk about tribal beliefs with a Conference leader. Moving east, the sixth segment profiles Stephen Tiger and his efforts to bolster Miccosukee self-determination through cross-cultural entertainment. The final segment takes us back to the north, where the Conference is drawing to a close. "There is a day when an Indian leadership will rise," a speaker predicts; we see people shaking hands and saying goodbye, "but for Susan it is more like a beginning," Redford says. The film ends with a musical coda—Tiger performing over a montage sequence—and then the closing credits roll.[41]

NUMINOUS ENCOUNTERS

Like the paired images of a nineteenth-century stereoscope, *People of the Sacred Circle* and *The New Indians* offer complementary views of a single reality; together they render a fairly balanced portrayal of the Indian Ecumenical Conference. Yet few people have seen both films, fewer still in proximate screenings. Considered separately, each film presents a two-dimensional likeness of the movement, and the differences between them sharpen in analytical relief. This representational divergence is a product of technical limitations and stylistic conventions, which affect the outcome of any filmmaking venture. The distinguishing features of *People* and *Indians* also reflect the conceptual biases of their makers. "Ideology, as unstated assumptions and perspectives, is at work in the myriad choices made in the process of production, choices of subject and narrative, scriptwriting, casting, shooting, and editing," observes Margaret R. Miles in *Seeing and Believing*. "Every feature of a film is consciously selected to produce a film that says, as precisely as possible, what its producer and director want it to say."[42]

Miles measures popular film as a barometer of public sentiment in her study, subtitled *Religion and Values in the Movies*. Employing a cultural studies approach, she recognizes that "there may be considerable dissonance between a director's intent and the messages viewers with diverse perspectives and interests receive. While a producer and director are focused on telling one story, other stories can often appear in the interstices." The peculiar status of religion in American life, the inordinate social power of Hollywood movies, the challenges involved in portraying transcendent realities through a visual medium—these and other considerations make the intersection of spirituality and cinema a particularly illuminating spot on the cultural landscape.[43]

Miles grounds her analysis in the history of the religious use of images among European Christians, who have long argued over the practice. "Why do many Americans continue to believe the myth of 'pure entertainment,' that is, that screen images are innocent of social effect?" she asks. "The long answer to this question must take into account American culture's origins in iconoclastic branches of Protestantism for which the word was the bearer of both religious and rational discourse." Protestant hegemony in the U.S. has given way to "religious pluralism and uneasy secularism without altering the assumption that while language is serious, images are irrelevant." Fundamentally concerned with the representation of difference in a pluralistic world, Miles affirms that filmmakers who "attempt to deal honestly and fairly with issues and images of marginalization and oppression should be acknowledged for their courage as well as criticized for their shortcomings." But "to the extent that Hollywood film conventions reiterate a narrow range of desires and repetitiously designate what is desirable, they constrain the collective imagination and impoverish the public symbolic repertoire," hindering our ability to address "the perennial religious question, 'How should we live?'"[44]

Like other scholars who have worked the field of religion and film, Miles focuses on the feature-length movies seen in commercial theaters. Such films are nearly always narrative in form. Most are explicitly fictitious as well, even as they strive for realistic portrayals of human experience; some go so far as to identify the actual events on which their stories are based. Fictional narratives projected on a big screen may be useful for gauging public opinion, but the complex interplay of ideology, perception, and meaning is even more striking in films that operate in a nonfiction mode.[45]

Documentaries typically conform to the conventions of realism while claiming to be factual depictions as well, a discursive rubric that compounds the difficulty of assessing their social function. The "voluntary suspension of disbelief" required by realist cinema can seem involuntary when the action in front of the camera is ostensibly true. Many viewers credit the documentary genre with more expository authority than it deserves, a fallacy we might call—after Miles—the myth of pure information. Simply put, documentary filmmakers contend with technical and stylistic constraints comparable to those limiting their Hollywood counterparts, and like fiction films, documentaries are "cultural products, deeply informed by the perspectives, values, and aspirations of their makers." Miles does analyze one commercially successful documentary, *Paris Is Burning*, though she approaches it as a case study in the representation of disempowered minorities. As important as this issue is, filmmakers who aspire to documenting spiritual experiences in a nonfictional idiom face epistemological dilemmas that are considerably more daunting. Aside from the ethical quandary of whether such things should be recorded in the first place, to what extent can religious realities be faithfully portrayed in a documentary film?[46]

People of the Sacred Circle and *The New Indians* overlap in subject matter but convey very different impressions of the Conference. Not surprisingly, both films address a non-native audience. Roy Bonisteel appears on-screen at the beginning of *People;* his careful use of first- and third-person pronouns signals his position as an outsider, and he admits that "to the white visitor, it is at once a disturbing and exciting experience to be in a minority." Bonisteel serves as both narrator and protagonist, and the viewer is invited to identify with him as he explores an event where "the dominant society was native." *Indians* provokes a more complex spectatorship. The teenagers in the opening scene are non-native pilgrims, and voice-over commentary encourages the viewer to identify with their quest for native wisdom, which "we once tried to erase." Robert Redford is heard and named but never seen, his role limited to that of the omniscient, disembodied narrator. He hovers briefly over four native communities long enough to introduce Susan Supernaw and three other activists, but the structure of the narrative directs viewers to shift their sympathies to Supernaw as the film's protagonist. The stories of the other three individuals—and of Supernaw's companions in the Chicago group—are subsumed under her pilgrimage "across time," which Redford characterizes as "a journey measured not in miles alone; it will be a journey to beginnings, trying to retrace an echo."[47]

Susan Supernaw was not the original choice to play the heroine of this primitivist saga. Terry Sanders and Freida Lee Mock had planned to focus on Dorene Porter, their initial contact in Chicago; the eighteen-page treatment they submitted to National Geographic shortly before the 1975 Conference included scenes that would show her walking in Chicago's Uptown neighborhood, traveling to Morley, watching a buffalo kill, experiencing a ceremony inside a sweat lodge, and reveling in a sun dance at the climax of the intertribal gathering. "With its volatile mixture of thousands of unrestrained young people and hundreds of spiritually important elders," it would be "more of a happening than a conference," an "Indian Woodstock Nation." Sanders and Mock did list Porter in the film's closing credits as a production consultant, but they found her to be too reserved and soft-spoken for the lead in *The New Indians*. Supernaw, on the other hand, had represented the state of Oklahoma in the 1972 Miss America Pageant, where the "petite and ever-smiling" beauty queen won a special award in the talent competition for performing an "ecological drama." She was a natural for the part of an educated urban youth rediscovering her tribal heritage, and Sanders and Mock were happy to find a charismatic player who was comfortable in front of the camera and willing to bare her soul in voice-over commentary.[48]

Sig Gerber tackled the assignment from a very different angle, arriving at the Conference with a single camera, a skeleton crew, and a handful of interview questions jotted in his reporter's notebook. His open-ended approach was partly a consequence of CBC budgetary constraints; as the producer of a weekly series broadcast on a public network, he had less than twelve thousand dollars to cover the direct costs incurred while filming *People of the Sacred Circle*. Sanders and Mock, independent filmmakers enjoying the largesse of a private foundation and a corporate sponsor, were working with a total production budget of around three hundred thousand dollars. Indeed, Sanders budgeted ten thousand dollars for gratuities alone, almost as much money as Gerber had for the entire project. This financial disparity is evident in the production values of the two films, though the qualitative differences between *People* and *Indians* are not as pronounced as their budgetary discrepancy might suggest. The background music in *People*, for example, is limited to a few short interludes played on solo woodwind, while *Indians* has an affluent score performed by a studio orchestra. None of the scored music in either film is recognizably tribal except for the flute solos heard during the Navajo segment of *Indians*.[49]

More important, the two films are differentiated by cinematic techniques that reflect the stylistic preferences of their makers. *People of the Sacred Circle* relies on expository interviews with movement leaders supplemented by shorter statements from several young people; the five major interviewees are identified both by the narrator and by insert titles that include name and organizational affiliation. *The New Indians* incorporates only two brief interviews near the beginning of the film and neither speaker is identified, even though one of them is Conference cofounder Wilf Pelletier; Ernest Tootoosis and

John Snow also make substantive but anonymous appearances in the film. Only four of the twelve individuals seen speaking in the Conference segments of *Indians* are identified by name, an ethnographic tradition of anonymity often used when photographing indigenous people—and endemic to National Geographic publications such as *The World of the American Indian*, the illustrated book that led Terry Sanders into this project. *Indians* relies on dramatic action and voice-over explanation to advance the narrative, techniques *People* employs only in its introductory and transitional sequences. Roy Bonisteel's narration constitutes less than half of the words in *People*, but Robert Redford has nearly sixty percent of the lines in *Indians*, notwithstanding Sanders's original proposal that this be "a story told with the insight of the Indian, from his own point of view and in the beauty, poetry and clarity of his own words." He and Freida Lee Mock likewise failed to honor their promise that their film crew would include some native technicians.[50]

The two films can also be distinguished by how they negotiate the conventions of cinematic realism. None of the action shots in *People of the Sacred Circle* appear to have been staged; most are short fragments conveying atmosphere and supplying a backdrop for the story line implied in Roy Bonisteel's exploration of the Conference. These transitions provide visual counterpoint for the film's main segments, long-take interviews that are clearly staged, a journalistic practice Sig Gerber made no attempt to conceal. As an overtly narrative film, *The New Indians* is composed almost entirely of candid shots, some of which were obviously contrived: an American Indian Movement march that culminates in front of a stationary camera, for example, or the Chicago group alone with an elder in a sun-drenched meadow at a gathering where it rained all week. Other scenes were arranged by the filmmakers in ways that are impossible to detect just by viewing the film. Sanders and Mock initiated and financed the Chicago group's visit to the local riding stables, and they prodded group members to tag along on the buffalo kill, to help raise a tipi, and to dance at an evening powwow, providing their cameramen with stereotypical fodder straight out of a Hollywood Western. A short sequence that the viewer is encouraged to believe depicts a tribal ceremony was, in fact, an informal discussion conducted for the cameras inside Albert Lightning's tipi. Like many ethnographers, the filmmakers from National Geographic were not averse to invoking artistic license in creating an ostensibly factual portrayal of their native subjects, or to employing representational techniques that exploit the naivete of twentieth-century spectators.[51]

In the cutting room this footage was carefully manipulated to highlight the naivete of those in the Chicago group. Arriving at Stoney Indian Park to "take their first step back in time," they struggle to set up two large canvas tents—borrowed equipment they had never used before. At the riding stables,

Louis Amiotte fumbles with a saddle as the narrator suggests that "few of the city-bred Indians have seen a horse outside a movie"—Amiotte grew up riding horseback on the Pine Ridge Reservation. Under the arbor, a speaker talks about native youth who "weren't on the right road" as Colin Wesaw appears in a brief shot that seems to have caught him smoking a joint—it was a hand-rolled tobacco cigarette. Outside their tent, Susan Supernaw and Lynn Nell Begay quibble over a smoldering campfire while Amiotte swings an ax in the background, managing only a glancing blow to the log he is trying to split—there is ample evidence of his proficiency already piled on the fire. Fidgeting at a distance as others butcher a buffalo, Supernaw comments in voice-over that "just seeing an animal killed, and the blood, you want to really get sick is your first impulse," and a close-up of Wesaw shows him grimace and turn away—but a moment later he is the individual, face obscured, who lifts the severed head from the carcass. The final scene finds Begay alone at the sacred fire, where she makes an offering in a "private" gesture; "for a little while she has walked in the moccasins of her ancestors," the narrator concludes, "and they feel like new." No one in the Chicago group would have claimed to be a tribal traditionalist, but *The New Indians* was edited to dramatize the distance between them and their native forebears.[52]

Both films grapple with the problem of cultural adaptation and the interplay of past, present, and future, though they do so using very different interpretive methods. *People of the Sacred Circle* situates the 1975 Conference in historical context, explaining the origin and development of the movement and suggesting how it relates to contemporary political developments among native people. As an investigative journalist, Sig Gerber produced a nonnarrative film reminiscent of the peacetime newsreel, an exercise in reportage meant to inform and, perhaps, to persuade. The intertribal gathering portrayed in *The New Indians* has no history; it is a singular event unfolding in the ethnographic present, a generic milestone on a young tribal woman's token pilgrimage. Independent filmmakers Terry Sanders and Freida Lee Mock produced a narrative film crossing hobbyist anthropology with the road movie, an entertaining feature with no specific historical reference point aside from an apocryphal reference to a pop culture icon; the nineteenth-century prophecy of spiritual revival "in the fifth generation" does not appear in the Black Elk corpus. Both films acknowledge the cultural disruptions of colonization and the challenges facing any nativist undertaking, though the optimism they share is differentiated by subtle distinctions in mood: *People* speaks with a sober and progressive voice, while *Indians* is loaded with cross-cultural nostalgia.[53]

Turning the camera on Conference leaders, *People of the Sacred Circle* affirms the legitimacy of their administrative authority by allowing them to explain the movement in their own words. The end reflects the means: Gerber had worked through official channels and exercised diplomatic restraint in gaining permission to make his film. Of course, like any loose-knit organization, the Conference was fraught with domestic imperfections; the exclusion of women from formal leadership in the movement remained a particularly stubborn inequity. *The New Indians* features a protagonist who is neither authoritative nor male, a debatable subversion consistent with the making of the film: having little patience for the complications of ethnographic etiquette, Sanders and Mock had bought their way into Stoney Indian Park. These divergent angles on the movement circa 1975 also illustrate the competing agendas Bob Thomas had identified two years earlier. *People* foregrounds the ecumenical problematic embraced in the founding vision of the Conference while acknowledging the unanticipated tensions interposed by a large contingent of urban youth. *Indians* documents only the intergenerational dynamic, glossing the Conference as a traditionalist encampment with no discernable Christian presence, an animated "mosaic" where "the past is coming to life."[54]

Perhaps the most consequential distinction between these two films is evident in how they handle the problem of ideological difference. *People of the Sacred Circle* presents the gathering as a human endeavor, replete with internal disagreements and debates. "All was not peace and harmony," Roy Bonisteel concedes, as some youthful participants "did not listen to the council of the elders. They wanted change at a faster pace." Even Conference leaders are depicted expressing contradictory attitudes toward the place of Christianity in this ecumenical movement. More significantly, Sig Gerber's film exhibits a reflexive sensibility that discourages the viewer from being seduced into the subjectivity of the camera. In between his on-screen appearances at the beginning and end of the film, Bonisteel mentions the CBC crew no fewer than three times, finally admitting that their presence had a measurable impact on the event being recorded: "Daily the skies poured rain; this caused discomfort and depression; it was taken as a bad omen. The presence of *Man Alive* and an American film crew drew dark glances," he says over shots of both National Geographic cameras, "and for some was a total invasion by the white man of a purely native event. Some people left early, pointing to the clouds hanging over the mountains as a sign of the Creator's displeasure at having the sacred fire filmed."[55]

The New Indians offers little evidence of dissent within the movement. "I mainly wanted to know deep inside if everybody felt the same way I did," Susan Supernaw reflects in her closing voice-over. "I have yet to meet an Indian who would not agree with me that we are all one." The film itself is a seamless narrative as well, concealing the filmmaking process and confronting viewers with an overdetermined argument. Terry Sanders and Freida Lee Mock managed to portray the antagonism between their subjects and the dominant culture, but only by characterizing native people with a false homogeneity and by employing cinematic techniques that are misleadingly transparent.[56]

A healthy respect for mystery lay at the ideological foundation of the Conference. Prohibitions against documenting tribal ceremonies are not uncommon in Indian country, but the anxieties many interpreters have theorized as anticolonial resistance, intellectual property rights, or the vagaries of identity politics sometimes have more to do with insight acquired through personal experience and prayerful reflection. Albert Lightning humored Sanders and Mock in filming a conversation about religion inside his tipi, but he did not allow anyone to record the many ceremonies held there during the week. "Nothing must interfere with the Great Spirit," he told Sig Gerber, and he also knew that no technological simulation could reproduce the complex sensory intelligence present in ritual expression. Many of the spiritual leaders and elders at the Conference shared these views, having acquired a tribal wisdom as pragmatic as it is moral. Unlike many of their iconoclastic colonizers, they were happy to acknowledge the limitations of a mortal creature whose consciousness is finite, imperfect, and often downright foolish. Descriptive or analytical accounts of religious phenomena can enlighten and challenge, but such representations are never more than pale reflections of the numinous encounters on which they are based.[57]

People of the Sacred Circle was transmitted over Canadian airwaves on November 3, 1975. The Service Committee had just met in Kenora, Ontario, and on November 4 a dozen Conference leaders mailed complimentary letters to CBC headquarters, offering thanks for this accurate report on the movement and for the network's help in disseminating their message. Other native and non-native viewers across the country wrote expressing similar sentiments. "If only white people would listen more to what the Native people have to offer," suggested Carol Kenny from the Ojibway reserve at Lac Seul, "I truly believe the world wouldn't be in such a mess." *The New Indians* finally aired on February 15, 1977, but not before it was previewed in Chicago and other U.S. cities. Several Los Angeles dailies plugged the program, more than one reviewer comparing it to the acclaimed miniseries *Roots* that had appeared just three weeks earlier. "Sometimes it's wry, sometimes it's amusing, but for the most part it's sad," moaned one television critic, and his professional rivals also picked up on the tragic subtext of the narrative. Susan Supernaw and friends had mixed feelings about the film; some enjoyed their momentary fame, but most members of the Chicago group were disappointed to see themselves portrayed in such an unflattering light. National Geographic headquarters got written responses from only six viewers, all of them negative.[58]

John Snow received a copy of each film—one of his conditions for shooting on the Stoney Reserve—and occasionally used them for public relations, cross-cultural education, or fundraising. In 1977 the National Geographic Society issued *The New Indians* on both film and videotape, and in April of that year its Educational Films Division released a twenty-five-minute edition under the title *North American Indians Today*, also available on either film or videotape. The educational version was rereleased in 1987, the same year that the original program began airing as one of the *Best of the National Geographic Specials*, with new opening and closing segments featuring *M*A*S*H* actor Mike Farrell. *People of the Sacred Circle* was rebroadcast only once, in April 1976, and then summarily retired to CBC vaults in Toronto. It has never been seen in the U.S., though the National Geographic film has appeared in Canada and other English-speaking markets. Quality is no match for distribution in the world of mass media.[59]

These cinematic representations determined what many outsiders knew about the Conference, and they even influenced the movement itself, both during the production process and through the mass-media feedback loop. Yet whatever the relative merits of any particular film, viewers are still more or less free to assign their own meanings. The shots and sounds of these two documentaries evoke powerful memories for those who were there; the Conference was a real experience, and participating in it was real in a way that viewing a film—or reading a book—can never be. Like thousands of others who found their way to Stoney Indian Park, everyone in the Chicago group would remember the intertribal gathering as a mecca for people concerned about the revival of native spiritual life. It was a mountaintop encounter that left an indelible impression on many who made the pilgrimage.[60]

Ojibwe activist Dorene Porter, for example, abandoned her interest in filmmaking and eventually became a community college administrator, helping hundreds of native students in Chicago negotiate the pitfalls of higher education. Years later she completed a doctorate in educational leadership and policy, devoting her dissertation to a study of urban elders and the importance of intergenerational relationships in the transmission of tribal knowledge. The Indian Ecumenical Conference was "the place and time where my mind began to open," she recalled. It was "a classroom for many of us. We were surrounded by life: the mountains, lakes, forests, animals. And we were surrounded by elders who knew their traditions and languages, their ways, their sacred songs." Porter credited the movement with providing a wealth of social and ceremonial opportunities, many of which she encountered for the first time. "The things which I learned at Morley have greatly enriched my life and opened my mind over the past 20 years. How did I learn them?" Simply by "being there and experiencing the people and place of Morley, Alberta. I had learned by observing, by listening, and by doing." It was a pedagogy that thousands more would experience in the years to come.[61]

New Agers universally suppose that it is crucial to "work" on what it is to be a person. A new consciousness, *and all that it brings with it, is essential. This alone opens the way to experiencing the spirituality of other people or the natural order; this alone provides the resources for fulfilling the potential of the planet.*

Paul Heelas, *The New Age Movement*

It is the Native woman both by tradition and circumstance who is the single most important variable in the Native people's struggle for self-esteem. It is she who through her children must generate the cultural awareness and pride necessary to implement meaningful change in the Native communities.

Angie Todd-Dennis, The Women's Project

CHAPTER NINE

"TO IMPLEMENT MEANINGFUL CHANGE"

HUNDREDS OF MOURNERS STOOD IN SOLEMN REPOSE as the blanketed coffin was lowered into the ground. Pallbearers lined both sides of the grave; all were leaders of the American Indian Movement, and each wore a four-color armband matching the stripes of the white trade blanket. As soon as the coffin had settled into place, they offered a raised-fist salute to their fallen comrade, then cut off their armbands and threw half into the tomb. Journalists tracked the committal service, photographers and cameramen elbowing their way through the crowd in search of the elusive angle. When it was over Nelson and Florence Small Legs said goodbye to their eldest son one last time, then turned and walked away, embracing as they wept.[1]

The date was May 21, 1976. Nelson Small Legs, Jr., had died five days earlier in his home on the Peigan Reserve. Many knew him as AIM's southern Alberta director, a role he had filled for over a year. Unlike most AIM-related deaths during the mid-seventies, there seemed to be little question as to the identity of his killer. An uncle found the body: dressed in Blackfoot regalia, covered with a Peigan band flag, stilled by a single bullet wound to the heart. Nearby were three handwritten letters addressed to his family, his AIM colleagues, and his people. "You know life is hard for Indians," one note began. "I give my life in protest to the Canadian government for its treatment of Indian people for the past 100 years," and "in the hopes of a full scale investigation into the dept. of Indian Affairs corruption" and their "divide and conquer tactics" on the reserves. "My suicide should open up the eyes of non-Indians into

how much we've suffered." Small Legs was twenty-three years old; he left behind a wife and two young daughters.[2]

The self-inflicted martyrdom of this activist leader was a shocking turn
of events in the native conflict with modern Canada. Family and friends,
media correspondents, government officials, and the Canadian public all
struggled to understand his dramatic act of self-destruction. How could
someone so devoted to redressing material inequities forsake his own physical
existence? Small Legs had been born and raised on the Peigan Reserve. He
attended a Catholic mission school until the age of thirteen, then moved to
Lethbridge to continue his education. Living in a series of foster homes, he
excelled on the athletic field and received a football scholarship at the city's
community college.[3]

Many Canadians were only mildly interested in the 1973 occupation at
Wounded Knee, proud to be living on the peaceful side of the international
border, but during the summer of 1974 they were forced to reckon with the
rise of AIM-inspired militancy among native people in Canada. Armed protesters occupied a city park in Kenora, blockaded a highway at Cache Creek,
and led a cross-country caravan from Vancouver to Parliament Hill, where
hundreds of government troops engaged them by provoking a riot. Other
groups tried to air their grievances through more peaceful forms of civil disobedience. In November the Calgary Urban Treaty Indian Alliance organized
a nonviolent demonstration over social services funding; Nelson Small Legs,
Jr., drove up from Lethbridge to join several dozen men, women, and children
in occupying the local Indian Affairs office. No weapons were brought in,
nothing was removed from the premises, and the only casualties of the two-
day occupation were three wooden chairs, but government officials responded
by calling the protesters "terrorists" and laying charges of "public mischief"
against AIM leaders Ed Burnstick and Roy Little Chief. The Royal Canadian
Mounted Police also singled out Small Legs for retribution; less than a month
later, at the behest of the Department of Indian Affairs, he was expelled from
Lethbridge Community College.[4]

A brief period of alcohol and drug abuse ensued, but then Small Legs
went home to the Peigan Reserve and apprenticed with tribal elder Charlie
Crow Eagle, an authority on Blackfoot spiritual traditions. In February 1975
AIM celebrity Dennis Banks visited southern Alberta to help raise money for
the Burnstick–Little Chief legal defense fund. "No one should have to resort
to arms" to dramatize their suffering, he told a crowd at the University of Calgary. But on both sides of the Canada-U.S. border, he warned, native people
had "reached a point where they would rather die than put up with continued
abuse and mistreatment." Intent on cultivating a nonviolent reputation, AIM

leaders in Canada worked to distinguish their organization from its American counterpart, especially after the controversial deaths of two FBI agents on the Pine Ridge Reservation in June. They spent much of the year trying to keep a lid on the "simmering discontent" among their followers while allaying public fears of an armed uprising. "For so long now they have pitted one reserve against another, band councils against the people, and urban Indians against reserve Indians. But in AIM we are all in this together," Small Legs told a newspaper reporter. "You've got to get your head together. Dignity comes first and materialism last. You can't do dope or drink if you're going to stand up for your people." He and other AIM leaders also had to contend with constant surveillance by RCMP operatives, including wiretaps of dubious legality.[5]

In May 1976 native leaders throughout southern Alberta converged on Calgary for public hearings of the Mackenzie Valley Pipeline Inquiry. Canadian officials wanted to build a twenty-four-hundred-mile pipeline connecting Arctic oil fields with the nation's existing distribution system, but Dene and Métis communities in the North were protesting the plan, forcing Prime Minister Pierre Trudeau to commission an official inquiry. John Snow was one of the tribal leaders who addressed the panel on Thursday, May 13. He reserved his strongest criticisms for the minister of Indian Affairs, a right-wing ideologue who had publicly dismissed the Dene Declaration as "a useless document which a Grade 10 student could have written in a few minutes," a treatise in "gobbledygook," surely an ironic statement coming from the head of the Canadian government's last bastion of colonial bureaucracy.[6]

AIM leaders Ed Burnstick and Nelson Small Legs, Jr., were among those who testified on Friday. "We do not condone violence," Small Legs said, holding a sacred pipe over the heads of the oil industry representatives in attendance. "But the Canadian Indian is unpredictable. We will take anything up to defend ourselves, our children, our wives, our culture, our spiritualism." Small Legs and others present also heard the mayor of Calgary openly condemn the inquiry as "a disastrous and costly mistake," claiming to be "amazed that Canadians have tolerated so far—and even financed—the talk about land claims and compensation claims by people who would, in many cases, rather talk than work." After months of nonstop controversy, AIM leaders were fatigued, and when the hearings concluded on Friday evening some talked about taking a holiday.[7]

Two days later Small Legs was dead. Even his closest friends were stunned to learn that he had taken his own life. "Never again would we feel the joy of his wit and the gentleness of his manner," wrote Calgary anthropologist Joan Ryan, cofounder of an activist support group. "If Nelson who had survived so much had decided that his final protest would be suicide, what remained for us to give?" Burial preparations began on Wednesday, May 19, when the body was dressed in white buckskin and adorned head to toe with the emblems of a Blackfoot hero: face paint, bone breastplate, sacred pipe, red ceremonial blanket, beaded finery. "He was a warrior," explained Devalon Small Legs. "The greatest thing for a warrior is to die in battle. My brother died fighting the system." On Thursday Nelson and Florence Small Legs held the wake in their home; relatives and friends placed some of their son's personal belongings on his sweat lodge and then burned the pyre, burying the ashes on a nearby hill. AIM leaders also assembled on the Peigan Reserve that evening and screened *The Longest War*, a documentary about the Wounded Knee occupation.[8]

On Friday the funeral procession began with a death wail from the steps of the family home. The hearse was accompanied by a riderless horse, led by Nelson and Devalon Small Legs on horseback. People from all over the country packed a local school gymnasium, where a Catholic mass was celebrated by two non-native priests and two Blood lay leaders. Charlie Crow Eagle offered a prayer in Blackfoot, the brown casket was opened so mourners could pay their respects, and then the cortege proceeded to the grave. "Bury me in these hills back of the house so I can look over the land I fought for," one of the suicide notes read, but Florence Small Legs was a devout Catholic and insisted on a churchyard burial. A drum group sang during the committal service, keeping a steady beat in the background. The officiating priest made a few graveside remarks; then Ed Burnstick stepped forward to deliver the final eulogy. "Indian Affairs is, has been, and always will be our biggest enemy," he said, his voice choked with emotion. "They deny us our self-determination. Indians have never been violent people. It is time to think about our children, our families and our future." The death of Nelson Small Legs, Jr., "has brought Indian people together. He has shown us the first step." Then the blanketed coffin was lowered into the ground.[9]

It was a scene rife with contradiction, as any violent drama must be. If protest suicide is the first step, where does the trail lead? Can suffering and humiliation be redeemed through an act of self-destruction? Is personal sacrifice a form of symbolic moral discourse intelligible to an imperialist nation-state? Where does patriarchal heroism leave the wife and kids? After mourners had left the cemetery, AIM leaders rounded up the reporters on hand and held an angry press conference at graveside. Ed Burnstick announced plans for a fundraising rally in Calgary as well as a conference where they would discuss the issues Small Legs had raised in his suicide notes. "Somebody will have to pay for the death of Nelson Small Legs," Roy Little Chief declared. The deceased activist had been "a profile of the new Indian today," and now he was "a martyr and a father to the whole North American Indian nation. We will make sure his wishes are granted." Others also voiced militant threats, making it clear that this was not the last time Canadians would hear from the American Indian Movement.[10]

PERSONAL TRANSFORMATIONS

The Indian Ecumenical Conference returned to Stoney Indian Park during the last week of July. It was sunny and warm as people set up camp on Monday, but then clouds rolled in and rain fell through the night. On Tuesday afternoon the weather cleared long enough to lay the sacred fire and to convene a damp opening session under the arbor, but the powwow that evening was cut short by more rain. "There seemed to be a lack of organization this year," Lutheran observer Ruth Blaser noted, though the rain did not douse her enthusiasm for the opportunity, "as a non-native person, to experience the growing strength in native pride and spirituality." Conference organizers were also inundated with young people; around seventy percent of the thousands who took time to register were between the ages of sixteen and twenty-five. "We did not anticipate drawing so many so quickly," they admitted. "From the second day onwards we fell short as we could not adequately deal with feeding nearly six thousand people," and "the line up for one meal led into the next." The Conference "has become one of the major summer gathering points for North American Indians," wrote *The Native People* reporter Gary George, though this year's edition was hampered by "rain, rain and more rain."[11]

Morley means "different things to different people," he observed, and the 1976 gathering was not without its share of controversy. Many of the native youth in attendance were still talking about Nelson Small Legs, Jr., and early in the week AIM leaders called on the Service Committee to set aside one day of the Conference in commemoration of his death. This request posed quite a dilemma for Conference leaders. They had been reaching out to urban activists for some time, hoping to inject their political aspirations with a healthy dose of tribal spiritual values, but the idea of endorsing suicide as a protest strategy was a hard pill to swallow. The militant groups "have something to say, but they are working against the oppressor and not for themselves as a people," Ernie Willie had remarked over a year earlier. "Their attitude is, 'Our people are dying; we might as well die fighting.'" Even U.S. AIM leader Edward Benton, in an interview filmed at the 1975 Conference, acknowledged the positive effects of native cultural revival: "People are going back to wearing braids, they are trying to find something, they are searching," and "it's those people you do not see drunk on the street, it's those people you do not see hanging from their jail cells or jumping off cliffs."[12]

The Service Committee discussed the issue in private, then announced their decision: they would not grant the AIM request. Committee members believed suicide "wasn't the Indian way" and did not want to "encourage that kind of thing" among native people. "Traditionally the North American Indian did not condone suicide," they explained, advising the young militants to "leave those who had died in that way to their rest, for there was much that needed to be done in our time amongst the living." Many of the youthful participants were upset by a decision they had "great difficulty" understanding. Some felt conflicted as well, torn between their respect for grassroots tribal elders and their desire to venerate a seemingly heroic sacrifice. Small Legs had become a "symbol of resistance" in the midst of colonial domination.[13]

Conference organizers addressed this controversy in their report on the annual gathering. "In the life of the Indian Ecumenical Conference there has begun to emerge the rebirth of the spiritual legacy of the North American Indian," requiring thoughtful self-examination by each individual. "In order to continue we must not be seen to compromise the concept of manhood which belongs to our spiritual legacy. We must concentrate on a meaningful process of human relations which includes and involves the whole of mankind." Ernie Willie's hand was evident in this theological formulation of their position. "The spiritual unity of our people is slowly being realized by our young people in cities across the country. Many of them are beginning to touch the earth," raising their awareness of "the oneness of our Creator" and of their own "ground of being as people of the earth." They are "finding something to be proud of, something that is uniquely their own, something that cannot be taken from them, and they no longer feel oppressed." Having been disavowed by Conference leaders, the death of Nelson Small Legs, Jr., was commemorated in other ways: a nonprofit foundation, a memorial powwow, a powwow song, a couple of book dedications, and a pledge—by the prime minister, in the House of Commons—to launch an "earnest" investigation, a political gesture that turned out to be just another empty promise.[14]

The skies poured rain throughout the Conference, prompting more than a few regulars to recall the troublesome presence of movie cameras a year earlier. To their dismay, two more film crews had shown up to shoot footage during the 1976 gathering. David Lavell, whose wife, Jeannette, cofounded the Nishnawbe Institute and now served as its president, was planning to produce a thirty-minute documentary on the movement. He envisioned this educational film as a fundraising tool for the Conference and other Institute ventures. Conference leaders had already discussed the possibility of producing

their own mass-market publication, a book of photographs depicting their annual gatherings, and Lavell's project garnered the support of several key people on the Service Committee. His crew, led by Japanese-Canadian filmmaker
Jesse Nishihata, would use eight-millimeter handheld cameras in order to be
as unobtrusive as possible. But Wilf Pelletier still held a lot of sway over both
the Conference and the Institute and managed to scuttle the project at the last
minute, concerned about the financial risk to Institute coffers, which still provided him with a healthy stipend.[15]

John Snow was responsible for blocking the other crew from filming on
the Stoney Reserve. Abenaki filmmaker Alanis Obomsawin arrived planning
to work on a segment of her hour-long documentary *Mother of Many Children*.
Obomsawin had come a long way from her 1969 performance at Anglican
General Synod; she was now a producer for the National Film Board of
Canada. Her first film, *Christmas at Moose Factory*, profiled a northern residential school through the eyes of the native children living there, and her current
project explored the importance of women in native communities.[16]

Obomsawin brought her crew to Stoney Indian Park hoping to interview
Jeannette Lavell, plaintiff in a landmark legal case against the Canadian government. Lavell had married her non-native husband in 1970, and under the
provisions of the Indian Act had thereby lost her legal status as a native person;
she could never regain her status, even if she were later divorced or widowed,
and any children she had would inherit her bureaucratic banishment. This
policy applied only to native women, and Lavell filed suit on the grounds that
the Canadian Bill of Rights prohibits such patriarchal discrimination, the Indian Act notwithstanding. Many native leaders lobbied against her case, some
because they were concerned about the erosion of sovereign rights stipulated
elsewhere in the Indian Act, others because they feared the economic impact
of reinstating thousands to band membership when most reserve governments
were already struggling to provide for their existing constituencies. The activist organization Indian Rights for Indian Women was born in the midst of
the political battle provoked by Lavell's case. She won a unanimous decision in
the federal court of appeal, but her victory was reversed by the Supreme Court
of Canada in 1973. John Snow was among those who had opposed Lavell's position, and he refused to let Obomsawin film on his reserve. "I get very upset
at the greediness of people," Obomsawin had said a year earlier. "It is difficult
to admit that some of these people are our own people. To have power can be
very useful and meaningful but if abused it can be very corrupting."[17]

Conference leaders and their militant counterparts might have disagreed
about protest tactics, but they held compatible views on the place of female
personnel within their organizations. Native women affiliated with AIM

addressed this problem in 1974 by founding a sister organization called Women of All Red Nations; the acronym WARN complemented the aggressive connotation of AIM. In 1976 Nishnawbe Institute staff proposed an analogous response to the gender inequities that continued to plague the Conference. Angie Todd-Dennis, a Carrier activist from northern British Columbia, spearheaded their plan for a "Women's Project" based on the Conference. Like many in her generation, Todd-Dennis had spent most of her childhood at residential school, separated from her family and their time-honored domestic traditions. In 1975 she chaperoned a group of Vancouver youth to Morley. She and others readily perceived the need for "sessions specifically oriented towards women" where tribal matriarchs could address issues such as breast-feeding and birth control. "From the Conference," Jeannette Lavell said, "we've found out that our native women have so much to offer and this had not been recognized before." Female elders "have a lot of knowledge and wisdom which we have neglected to use and which has almost been forgotten. They know of medicines, nutrition, care of children, and a way of living which would be more relevant to us as a native people."[18]

In the spring of 1976 Angie Todd-Dennis outlined the rationale behind a separate conference for native women: "The Native woman is in a unique position in Canada. She bears the precious remnants of an ancient matriarchal society while maintaining the dominant social position in modern communities desolated by cultural destruction and economic and political chaos." The controversy surrounding the Lavell case had demonstrated the potential for cross-cultural confusion over gender roles, and for gendered conflict among native people as well. "It is the Native woman both by tradition and circumstance who is the single most important variable in the Native people's struggle for self-esteem," Todd-Dennis argued. "It is she who through her children must generate the cultural awareness and pride necessary to implement meaningful change in the Native communities." An intertribal gathering led by older women "would be able to reach some consensus as to what the Indian women's role has been and what they feel it should be. They would thus be able to communicate their views to the younger women who are now shouldering the responsibility of their own and their communities' future." The Women's Project was never funded, but that summer Todd-Dennis and other native women continued making their presence felt around the Conference.[19]

The 1976 gathering was mired in days of rain until Stoney officials opened the skating rink in Morley, allowing Conference leaders to convene a few indoor sessions before breaking camp. The weather did not seem to be cooperating but the movement was still growing, at least numerically. Attendance had increased dramatically from the year before, and the financial condition of the Conference remained relatively stable. During the 1975–76 fundraising cycle organizers had been able to secure more than fifty-five thousand dollars: forty-three thousand from the Canadian government, ten thousand from the Anglican Church of Canada, and twenty-one hundred from a Canadian program of the World Council of Churches.[20]

John Snow took great pride in the Conference and in his role as host of the annual gatherings; his 1977 tribal history, *These Mountains Are Our Sacred Places*, culminates in a chapter on "The Indian Religious Movement" centered at Stoney Indian Park. "A man must seek to emulate the mountains," he wrote, "strong in body and will and resolve, unchanging in his faith, yet flexible in his relations with his fellow men, compassionate with those who suffer, relentless with those who would stupidly abuse their authority, warm with his brothers and sisters." It was a compelling—if notably gendered—vision of the postcolonial movement flourishing in the foothills of the Rockies. The Conference "has the potential to become a mecca for Native peoples of North America, possibly native peoples of the Americas," university student Emma LaRoque wrote in a term paper, "especially if it expresses more openness to women." Religious leaders as far away as Africa were now taking note of the Conference as a model for ecumenical organizing among colonized peoples, many of whom are "sustained neither by a living primal faith nor by a Christianity they have made their own."[21]

On November 16, 1976, Service Committee member Andrew Ahenakew died of natural causes at the age of seventy-two. He had been involved in the Conference since the founding meeting in Winnipeg, and that is where his earthly life ended four days after the movement's seventh anniversary. He was the first member of the original Committee to go. Like his uncle Edward Ahenakew, he had been known for his loyalty to the Anglican church and his lifelong service to native people. His passing was mourned by many throughout Canada and the U.S., though he had been an unassuming presence at the annual gatherings; most participants were more likely to remember conversations about protest suicide, filmmaking, gender relations, or other controversial issues. And yet the last years of Andrew Ahenakew's life witnessed one of the most dramatic personal transformations to emerge from the ecumenical movement.[22]

Ahenakew did not want to attend the Winnipeg meeting. He had been raised to venerate the pioneering missionaries who brought Anglican teachings to his people, and he and his brothers were not allowed to participate in the Cree ceremonial traditions still practiced on the reserve. A farmer by trade, he served as lay reader for nearly thirty years before being ordained deacon in 1958 and priest two years later. By 1969 he was one of the most prominent native figures in the Anglican church, but he was also "brain-washed," as he would later describe his mind-set at the time. The interreligious conversation in Winnipeg was a strange and difficult experience for the devout Cree priest. Ernest Tootoosis "spoke with a harsh tongue, and he said, 'No more of these white-collared clergy in our circle, they destroyed us so much with all that condemnation.'" Ahenakew sat through two days of discussion confronting him with frank commentary about the spiritual condition of native communities. "I was hurt right to the core of my heart," he recalled. "There was one moment there when I thought I would just get up and go home. But then something compelled me to stay." He attended the first Conference at Crow Agency and the gatherings that followed at Stoney Indian Park, where he "saw great men at work, really praying, really working the spiritual word," and he "learned a little more" each year.[23]

In the spring of 1974 Ahenakew was sent to the remote northern community of Moose Lake to interview a native candidate for ordination. It was a long drive from southern Manitoba, and he had to spend the night in a roadside motel at The Pas. Preparing for bed, he "prayed that night alone, a stranger in a strange town, and very lonely." Several hours later he had a vision. The walls of the motel room disappeared and he saw something coming from the north, across the Saskatchewan River: it was "a beautiful creature, a creature of God," and it smiled and spoke to the lonesome cleric. This friendly apparition explained that it had been sent to teach him how to make medicine using the creature's southern relatives, the bears of the forest. Ahenakew silently scoffed at the message, but the creature knew his thoughts and assured him that he would come to believe; a layer of gold on the surface of the medicine would confirm the integrity of this vision. Then the creature turned and flew back to the north. Ahenakew woke up, switched on the bedside lamp, and stared at his clerical collar on the nightstand. He had known out-of-body experiences in the past, but he always returned with narratives that were amenable to Christian interpretation, not one that promised to lead him into the mysteries of tribal spirituality. He thought to himself, "Andrew, are you going crazy? You're crazy! How are you going to do it—to be a priest in the Anglican church and to be a medicine man?" He went back to bed and tried to put the experience out of his mind.[24]

When he returned home his wife, Alice, took one look at him and said, "There's something wrong with you. What happened?" Andrew told her the whole story, not believing it himself. "It's the most wonderful story that I have ever heard," she declared, and she encouraged him to follow through on the vision. Andrew tried to gather the necessary ingredients but it was not the right season, and eventually he lost interest. Alice kept after him, however; she had been raised by tribal elders who lived off the land and practiced Cree spiritual traditions, and she carried vivid memories of the time when her people were forced to throw their medicine bundles on a bonfire. Several months after Andrew's vision, a bear turned up that provided everything he and Alice needed. Late one night they mixed the formula and cooked it in an enamel pot, then bottled the oily liquid. The next morning Alice got up and brought the bottle to Andrew, and together they marveled at the layer of gold on the surface of the medicine. Both sampled it and were amazed at the effect. "We hardly used to go up them steps," Alice later said. "We soared all over after we had taken the medicine ourselves. We thought, 'My goodness, this medicine is really good.'" Andrew's younger brother was hospitalized at the time, suffering from both cancer and blood poisoning, and when he heard about the medicine he asked Andrew to share it with him. Andrew risked criminal prosecution by bringing the natural remedy into the hospital; two days later his brother was back on his feet. The same brother was later diagnosed with kidney stones, a condition also cured using the Cree medicine.[25]

Word of these healings spread quickly, and soon other native people were looking for Andrew Ahenakew. A man showed up with a large open sore on his leg, saying that Western physicians had been unable to help him for thirty years. Ahenakew prayed and applied some medicine, then sent him home with a short supply and instructions on how to use it. Three weeks later the wound was gone. One family brought a two-month-old baby tormented by terminal cancer, and after Ahenakew treated her she was finally able to sleep peacefully; the little girl went on to make a complete recovery. Patients began arriving at the Ahenakew home at all hours of the day and night. They came from all over Canada and the U.S., and no one was ever turned away. Alice accommodated visitors in the living room and Andrew conducted healing ceremonies in a tipi next to the house. He would begin by praying in Cree while smudging each person with sweetgrass. His prayers intensified until he entered a divine trance. Following this agony of supplication, he used the medicine to anoint those in the circle. Making one last clockwise circuit, he laid hands on each person's head and prayed they might "be healed in the name of Jesus." Every patient went away with a small bottle of medicine to reinforce the treatment.[26]

Ahenakew's reputation grew and he continued to hold healing ceremonies, but he was troubled by the unresolved tensions between his Cree calling and his Anglican vocation. As archdeacon of the diocese, he worked closely with the bishop, though he had not yet revealed his newfound abilities in the presence of church authorities. After a year and a half of covert ministry, he finally went to his bishop and told him about the vision, the medicine, and the miraculous healings. "I have a guilty conscience because of this gift,"

Ahenakew said. "I don't know what you will call it." Concerned that he might be "smearing the white collar of my brother clergy," he offered to resign his ordination. The bishop listened carefully. Then he responded by pointing out that such things were commonplace in biblical times. "This is a spiritual experience which was put aside by a lot of denominations," he said, but he was also humble enough to recognize that unorthodoxy is the hallmark of revelation. The bishop endorsed Ahenakew's gift and encouraged him to continue in his healing ministry. Hundreds more were helped during the final year of Ahenakew's life, including a few non-native people who found their way to the tipi at Sandy Lake. The Ahenakews also conducted healing ceremonies at the Indian Ecumenical Conference on several occasions.[27]

Shortly before his death Ahenakew offered his testimony to a group of Anglicans meeting in Winnipeg. "My friends, you're going to hear the most peculiar story of an Indian clergyman in North America," he began, recounting his visionary experience and the spiritual powers it had brought to him. "People come there with trembling hearts, heart diseases, mental diseases, half-crazy. Withered hands have been made whole. Legs are walking again." It was a postcolonial drama Edward Ahenakew could hardly dream of when he expressed his own spiritual longings through the literary alter ego Old Keyam. Fifty years later his nephew was able to be considerably bolder among Anglican colleagues. "So my friends," he concluded, "this is the story of Andrew Ahenakew, who was angry when the Indian culture men told him that the Indian way of worship is real. It *is* real." He had come to appreciate the full measure of his own religious heritage. "I'm a great respecter of all my Cree elderly people, they were true, those people long ago, but there were also some great Christians that believed in God and the Anglican church." He now knew that "the spiritual world is so great. Sometimes we burn, sometimes we tremble, sometimes we are so weak. But give us time to help other people. We're telling them, we're giving wisdom, and we will speak." Ahenakew may have been the movement's greatest ecumenist, and his passing coincided with a turning point in the history of the Conference.[28]

IMPENDING OBSOLESCENCE

In February 1977 the *Canadian Churchman* ran an illustrated feature on Ahenakew's life, turning to Ernie Willie for the narrative. The two native Anglican priests had been friends since the 1969 meeting in Winnipeg, and Ahenakew's death left "those who had come to know and love him with a deep feeling of loss but a greater understanding of the power of service." Privately,

Willie was contemplating his own departure from church leadership. Several months later he drafted a position paper challenging the Anglican Church of Canada to "face itself, admit its failures, trust in the Lord of History," and "have the courage to change what ought to be changed." Written "after five years as Consultant on Native Affairs," it was a mature and forceful statement on how the denomination might facilitate a greater degree of native religious self-determination. Willie offered a frank assessment of the spiritual condition of native communities, mentioning the Indian Ecumenical Conference as a place "where many of the old tribal elements have surfaced," where the "deep religious instinct" of tribal life "can be strongly experienced." He called for cross-cultural, reflexive training of clergy working among native people, and he also proposed a new administrative structure organized around native "fieldworkers" operating at the regional level. A "transferral of power" would help native people regain "personal control over individual and corporate destiny."[29]

In July Willie sent a letter to the Service Committee, updating everyone on the status of the 1977 Conference and reminding them to arrive early so they could help with final preparations. He also announced his resignation from the Church House bureaucracy. He had accepted a position as chief administrative officer for the Union of British Columbia Indian Chiefs, which was embroiled in conflict with Canadian authorities over land claims, fishing rights, and other critical issues. Willie was looking forward to being closer to home, but he was also concerned about the ongoing work of the Conference. He sensed that the movement was at a crossroads. "The person who will replace me in my office will not necessarily have the same commitment to the Indian Ecumenical Conference that I have," he warned. He proposed an organizational restructuring that would supplant the Service Committee with a "council of elders" concentrating on "the aims and objectives of our religious movement" assisted by a smaller administrative committee responsible for fundraising and logistics. Functionally, this proposal offered little more than a return to the early days of the Conference, when Wilf Pelletier, Bob Thomas, and Ian MacKenzie coordinated day-to-day business on behalf of the original Committee. Yet times had changed and so had the movement, a reality increasingly apparent to participants and observers alike.[30]

The eighth annual gathering began on the last day of July when Stewart Etsitty and his Navajo colleague Tommy Nez laid the sacred fire and blessed the arbor grounds. This year the Stoneys had promised only to serve "some meals," asking that "as many as possible" bring their own food; for the first time, Conference organizers were hoping that attendance would not increase from the year before. They also tried to implement a more structured daily schedule, holding open sessions under the arbor each morning and youth-oriented workshops in the afternoon. Various tribal ceremonies were conducted throughout the week, and nightly powwows "gave all a chance to enjoy themselves." The Conference was becoming a popular destination for native social service agencies as well; programs working with alcoholics, juvenile delinquents, and the mentally ill brought clients to Stoney Indian Park in 1977. These groups were welcome, though their presence did further complicate the ecumenical conversation. "Dialogue across the generation gap was often difficult," noted a Mennonite observer, and some young people were still not getting the message. Service Committee members received "many complaints" of alcohol and drug use in the encampment, explicit prohibitions notwithstanding, and later discussed the possibility of recruiting native constables in the RCMP to provide security at the next Conference.[31]

This year the crowd was estimated at around fifteen hundred people, comparable to the overall numbers seen before the huge turnout in 1976. Attendance had fallen as quickly as it had risen, for a variety of reasons. Inclement weather at the last two gatherings dampened enthusiasm for this rustic outdoor experience. The logistical problems of 1976 also affected word-of-mouth publicity. Hard feelings over the Small Legs incident prompted some of the more militant youth to look elsewhere for spiritual guidance. Discord within the Service Committee was taking its toll as well; some were disappointed that Wilf Pelletier had scuttled David Lavell's film project, others were upset that John Snow had blocked Alanis Obomsawin from interviewing Jeannette Lavell at the Conference, and a few were still concerned about the ethics of mechanical reproduction in general. Yet points of contention such as these were usually just surrogate conflicts, symptomatic of more fundamental problems with the movement's organizational structure. The Nishnawbe Institute was all but defunct—unable to raise enough money for even a small office—and it no longer appeared in Conference publicity; Snow had taken charge of the annual gatherings, with Ernie Willie coordinating communication and fundraising from his office at Anglican church headquarters. Worst of all, the Conference was no closer to being financially self-sufficient than it had been in 1970. The Anglican Church of Canada was the movement's last remaining private donor, and Willie's departure left this commitment more vulnerable to the shifting fortunes of institutional politics. Although most people paid their own way to Morley, the Conference was now heavily dependent on funding from the Canadian government to cover the cost of food service, park maintenance, Service Committee meetings, and travel for selected spiritual leaders.[32]

Apart from these difficulties, there were other reasons for the decline in Conference attendance that could be regarded as cause for celebration. The small group that met in Winnipeg during November 1969 had plotted "a general movement for ecumenicity among American Indians," envisioning "a series of local and regional Indian ecumenical meetings" unified by an annual transnational gathering. Conference delegates had ratified this course of action at Crow Agency in 1970, and although financial limitations had prevented centralized coordination of local initiatives, there were many who began organizing as soon as they returned home. By 1977 regional ecumenical gatherings modeled on the Conference had been held as far east as Shubenacadie, Nova Scotia, as far south as Tucson, Arizona, as far west as Vancouver, British Columbia, and as far north as Yellowknife, Northwest Territories. Two such events were held within weeks of the 1977 Conference, one in northern Ontario and the other in southern Manitoba. Native people in Canada and the U.S. now had other opportunities for ecumenical conversation; many who would have made the long pilgrimage to Stoney Indian Park six years earlier could now find spiritual sustenance closer to home. By demonstrating the power of interreligious organizing at the grassroots level, the Conference had effected its own impending obsolescence.[33]

In December 1977 Anglican executives appointed Cree priest Adam Cuthand to be their new consultant on native affairs. As chair of the Sub-Committee on Native Affairs, he was already one of the most prominent native leaders in the Anglican church, and he had distinguished himself in other arenas as war veteran, educator, and founding president of the Manitoba Metis Federation. His selection augured well for the Conference; he had been part of the Service Committee since 1971, and membership on the Committee was even listed in his new job description. Conference leaders could rely on Anglican funding in the foreseeable future, though the support of the Canadian government was beginning to waver. The Department of Indian and Northern Affairs had been underwriting the Conference since 1973, most recently to the tune of fifteen thousand dollars. In March 1978 a midlevel bureaucrat notified Cuthand that "this department recognizes the significant contribution of the Indian Ecumenical Conference over the past several years in assisting Indian persons and particularly young persons to better understand their spiritual and cultural roots. We wish you continued success with your conferences," but he and his colleagues had unaccountably decided these gatherings were "outside of the range of activities that should be financed by the Program." They were reducing their annual grant to ten thousand dollars in 1978 and five thousand in 1979, and beginning in 1980 "no further contributions from this department should be expected." The Secretary of State's Native Citizens' Program remained considerably more generous, renewing its support in the amount of thirty thousand dollars.[34]

The Service Committee met on the Stoney Reserve during the last week-end in April. Their conversation revolved around mundane problems such as security and sanitation. John Snow wanted money to help build a permanent shelter that could be used as a dining area, and more money to pay for a pub-lic-address system. Southern Ute spiritual leader Eddie Box, the only person on hand from south of the Canada-U.S. border, invited the Committee to meet in his homeland sometime soon as a way of boosting Conference atten-dance from the Four Corners area. Committee members agreed on the need for a work crew, perhaps a "cultural awareness group," to arrive at Stoney In-dian Park a week early so they could help set up camp. Adam Cuthand later arranged for a group of seven young men from the Indian Friendship Centre in Smithers, British Columbia, to take on this responsibility.[35]

The 1978 Conference began on July 30. A new addition to the grounds was a circus big top where meals would be served, and where meetings could be held when it rained. Conference old-timers were reminded of the makeshift accommodations at Crow Agency eight years earlier, though they could not help noticing other changes as well: attendance was down again, and the spiritual integrity of those present seemed to be waning. Service Commit-tee members noted a number of problems during the week. Speakers repre-senting Pentecostal churches and Alcoholics Anonymous groups "took too much valuable time" during Conference sessions, causing "tension with the majority of the participants" because they "were not concerned with tradi-tional Indian values." The proportion of non-native observers seemed to be on the rise, and some were accused of freeloading, taking notes, or making unau-thorized photographs. Alcohol and drugs were still being brought into the en-campment, and "drunken drivers" had become a "menace to safety." More and more participants were showing up with things to sell or trade: jewelry, bead-work, dance regalia, recorded music, medicinal herbs. Barter is an age-old form of intertribal exchange, though commerce is another matter altogether; at any rate, this was a religious gathering, not a rendezvous. Zealots, tourists, partyers, merchants—the Conference was now drawing people who came to feed on the movement, not those who wanted to participate in an ecumenical conversation.[36]

Those who did arrive looking for a spiritual experience often had little in common with the movement's founders. "For many," Adam Cuthand re-ported, "the main reason for attending the Conference is to seek help from the elders with personal problems" such as illness, addiction, loneliness, and mari-tal conflict. "The elders were available in specially designed tipis for individual and group counselling" throughout the week. "As more and more people of all ages leave the reserves for urban centres in search of employment, the importance of maintaining a cultural identity is being recognized," and many were suffering under the "stresses of urban living." Service Committee members recognized that "urban Indians need our helping hands." As the Conference fell into decline, its founding vision of an inclusive solidarity benefiting tribal communities had been eclipsed by an ascendant therapeutic egocentrism. To put it bluntly, the seventies—recently dubbed "the Me Decade"—had come to Stoney Indian Park. Already transformed from an interreligious conversation to an intergenerational monologue, the movement was now diverting its fading energy from collective concerns to psychological issues. Like many in the dominant culture, native people in the urban diaspora were more familiar with the parasitic compulsions of modern individualism than they were with the personal security generated by a communal worldview.[37]

As a social phenomenon, the Conference was manifesting some of the broader cultural displacements Paul Heelas documents in his study of *The New Age Movement*. Scanning the eclectic teachings and practices commonly glossed as New Age, Heelas detects an underlying "*lingua franca*" he dubs "Self-spirituality. New Agers make the monistic assumption that the Self itself is sacred." He characterizes the New Age movement as "a highly optimistic, celebratory, utopian and spiritual form of humanism" in which "the inner realm, and the inner realm alone, is held to serve as the source of authentic vitality, creativity, love, tranquility, wisdom, power, authority and all those other qualities which are held to comprise the perfect life." This kaleidoscopic movement is transnational in scope, but "New Agers universally suppose that it is crucial to 'work' on what it is to be a person. A new *consciousness*, and all that it brings with it, is essential. This alone opens the way to experiencing the spirituality of other people or the natural order; this alone provides the resources for fulfilling the potential of the planet." Heelas focuses on the New Age scene in Britain and the U.S., though he downplays the influence of tribal religious traditions in deference to a conventional Orientalist binary. He also lapses into the familiar Eurocentric practice of labeling "Native American teachings" as a form of paganism.[38]

Heelas's book is subtitled *The Celebration of the Self and the Sacralization of Modernity*. "Why has the self become a spiritual resource?" he asks. "What is it about modernity that has facilitated Self-sacralization?" His primary theoretical concern here is "to provide connections between the New Age and the very considerable body of theories which have been developed in connection with modernity/postmodernity." Heelas argues that "many of those attracted" to the New Age "are unsure of their identities. By virtue of various *uncertainties* of modernity, their sense of 'being' a person is somehow not in order; or they experience difficulties identifying with particular forms of life." At the same time, "those attracted also tend to be those who have faith in various *certainties* of modernity." The New Age "is embedded in, whilst exemplifying, long-standing cultural trajectories." The "paradoxical" relationship between modernity and the New Age movement is a product of "the fall of the traditional self." If "tradition-informed ways of life are those in which the person thinks in terms of external loci of authority, control and destiny," then "detraditionalized selves" are those who "have adopted cultural values and assumptions which articulate what it is to stand 'alone'—as *individuals*—in the world." Heelas concludes that "the New Age shows what 'religion' looks like when it is organized in terms of what is taken to be the authority of the Self." By the late seventies, the Indian Ecumenical Conference was showing what native religious traditions look like when they are organized in terms of the personal problems of urbanized individuals.[39]

The summer of 1978 also witnessed a separate "elders and youth conference" sponsored by the American Indian Movement. Upset over the Small Legs controversy, these young militants had broken with the Conference and developed their own spiritual gathering. Creek traditionalist Phillip Deere led the event on his family's allotment near Okemah, Oklahoma, not far from where Clifton Hill had held a unity convention ten years earlier. The AIM gathering featured ritual furnishings—a sacred fire, sweat lodges, ceremonial pipes—along with an ample supply of intertribal teachings and anti-Christian rhetoric. "By 1978 the interest in traditional religions was so intense," observed Vine Deloria, Jr., "that many experienced older Indians characterized the former activists as the Indian version of 'Jesus freaks.' Indeed the late 1970s saw many Americans, Indian and non-Indian, blindly accept various kinds of religious doctrines without the slightest bit of critical appraisal." It was a time for returning to roots, though the seeds of spiritual revival were being sown so haphazardly that it was often hard to know what would come up.[40]

TARNISHED REPUTATION

On the last weekend of September, the Steering Committee—whose members had reverted to using its original name—gathered in Ignatio, Colorado. Host Eddie Box provided memorable hospitality, though it turned out to be an expensive meeting; travel costs were unusually high because nineteen of the Committee's twenty-four members lived north of the Canada-U.S. border.

They began with a pipe ceremony conducted by Albert Lightning, but in the absence of chair John Snow their deliberations were difficult at times. Mohawk traditionalist Mike Mitchell noted "a certain hostility" within the Committee; Cree academic Joe Couture responded by pointing out that the Indian Ecumenical Conference "is not a simple thing—there will always be tensions" due to tribal, religious, and personal differences. There was some discussion of how the Conference had "moved away from the original intention, which was the gathering of elders from different tribes and including Native clergy for the purpose of pooling human and spiritual wisdom." But little could be resolved on these points, Committee members able to agree only that "future directions of the I.E.C. have to be carefully considered at a future meeting."[41]

Two months later Mike Mitchell mailed an open letter to the Committee expressing concern over "certain board members sitting on the fence on issues that need to be decided one way or the other." He used the example of Stewart Etsitty, a leader among Navajo peyotists who also attended denominational church services every Sunday "so as not to offend his family and neighbors." Mitchell favored an exclusivist notion of religious activity, wondering whether other Conference leaders had "come to grips with the type of conference it should be" and "in what manner it is to be a spiritual meeting." He urged his colleagues to join him in renouncing the Christian option once and for all.[42]

In December Ernie Willie sent a letter to Adam Cuthand, reminding his Anglican successor that the 1979 Conference would be their tenth annual gathering. He hoped members of the Steering Committee could "put aside our petty jealousies" and "put our minds together" in revitalizing the movement. "For too many years we have not made full use of our time together at Morley. We have not fully utilized the beautiful setting of the Tipi Village and we have not taught well." Willie's intervention was remarkably similar to the letter Bob Thomas had composed five years earlier, on the eve of his withdrawal from the movement. Like Thomas, Willie listed a number of philosophical and logistical problems needing "special attention" before the Conference could realize its full potential. Above all, Willie echoed Thomas in championing an inclusive approach to ecumenical solidarity. "As leaders, each of us is vital to the conference, for each has a gift to offer. We should concern ourselves solely with being examples to our people and where necessary help each other to fulfill our giving. There is work at the conference site and recognition for all of us." He closed with a folksy turn that would have made Thomas proud: "This letter, my brothers, has been years in the making" and "it is my sincerest hope that we will, in fact, put our minds together to show our people 'THE VISION OF OUR TOMORROW.'"[43]

Ernest Tootoosis toured northern Europe during the fall of 1978, soliciting financial support for the Conference from sympathetic groups in Sweden, Germany, and the Netherlands. Adam Cuthand, meanwhile, worked to shore up funding from the Canadian government and the Anglican church. In March 1979 Cuthand mailed an upbeat note to Steering Committee members, inviting them to a planning meeting over the first weekend in May. "This is the year of rejoicing and thanksgiving," he wrote, "as we have reached the tenth anniversary of the Indian Ecumenical Conference. Out of the Conference have come many good things." He and his Church House assistant Elizabeth Boyd identified a series of positive developments illustrating the resurgence of "pride in cultural heritage and awareness of spiritual values, both of which have been denigrated since the arrival of the first Europeans." They pointed to the regional ecumenical gatherings springing up all over Canada and the U.S., and to the "elders and youth" workshops—like Phillip Deere's AIM event—that were especially popular on the Canadian prairies. They noted the work of medicine men such as Andrew Ahenakew and his Steering Committee colleagues Albert Lightning, Sam Osawamick, and Dan Pine, whose abilities were "slowly being acknowledged by non-Indian professionals. One hospital in northwestern Ontario is even now considering enlisting a Native healer to work closely with the medical staff." Many social agencies and educational programs serving native people, including native studies centers at several Canadian universities, "can also trace their growing effectiveness" to the movement. Boyd concluded that "it is impossible to estimate how great the effect of the Indian Ecumenical Conference has been and will continue to be on Canada's Native population."[44]

Adam Cuthand and Elizabeth Boyd also appreciated the Conference's effect on the Anglican church as it struggled through the process of institutional reform. Anglican leaders had participated in national and regional "listening conferences" with native political organizations, they reported, and had sponsored a national gathering for native clergy within the denomination. Some Anglicans were still not very open-minded, however, forcing Cuthand to spend part of his time defending the movement from its conservative critics. In April two missionary priests in the Diocese of Calgary submitted "letters of protest" over the "startling and disturbing" news that the Anglican church was supporting the Conference. "Our studied and serious opinion is that this conference is anti-Christian, divisive to community relations, contrary to the teaching we are trying to do in our parishes, and anti-Church." Conference organizers were using the event "to promote a non-Christian form of what they call 'Indian religion.' In summary, the Indian Ecumenical Conference is counter productive to the Church's goals and the Church should not be supporting it." Adam Cuthand drafted the official response, which was signed by Primate Ted Scott. "I can understand your concern but do not share the same views," he explained. "All across the world today, there is growing a need to dialogue or discuss with people who hold different religious views, with the same kind of love with which Jesus loved and with the same kind of openness as He displayed." Scott encouraged his subordinates to approach the situation as an opportunity for honing their Christian humility, enclosing a copy of the Hendry report, an article on Andrew Ahenakew, and a report from the 1978 gathering.[45]

The 1979 Conference began on Sunday, July 29, with the lighting of the sacred fire. On Monday, after ten years as an all-male body, the Steering Committee finally invited a woman to join its ranks: Dolly Seeds, a Cree and Saulteaux activist living in the Vancouver area. Conference organizers also announced that Wednesday would be dedicated to special activities for children and youth in recognition of the United Nations' International Year of the Child. These gestures were largely symbolic, however, and did little to reverse the ongoing dissipation of the movement. "Religious Conference Fizzles in the Drizzle," declared a feature article in *The Native People* two weeks later. "Funded by church organizations and organized by the Nishnawbe Institute in Toronto, the Indian Ecumenical Conference had been touted in 'Indian Country' as *the* place to go during the summer." But "since 1976, the Indian Ecumenical Conference has been on a continual decline in organization and status amongst Indian travellers," and "seems to have lost its appeal after a short-lived trendy reign as Canada's national Indian gathering." The anonymous reporter attributed the low attendance to dissension among Conference leaders. "In the past there were meetings under the arbor near the sacred fire. This year the arbor was empty most of the time. If people met it was in their tents or teepees. Of course, the rain didn't help the organizers' plans."[46]

And yet the Conference, despite its tarnished reputation, still provided the opportunity for meaningful cultural encounters, especially among urban youth searching for their native roots. The Red Sky Cultural Awareness Group in Thompson, Manitoba, for example, sent a busload of thirty-five people to the 1979 gathering. Several chronicled their experiences at the "Morley Ecumenical Conference" with daily journal entries and oral transcriptions that were later compiled in a sixty-page report. "I really didn't know what to expect here," group leader Louise Campbell wrote on the first day. "But the feeling of warmth and friendship is everywhere. No one is a stranger. Since we arrived our camp has been visited by many different people." This "will be an experience I will never forget." Her sister Rita was impressed when "the elders became very emotional about their topics and stories. They would set the mood for everyone who was listening to them under the Arbor." Later in the week she felt "so glad to be here, so far I've learned a tremendous amount about my native culture, and I feel so proud, especially when I am dancing." Russell Keam ended his contribution with a word of thanks for "the opportunity to go to the gathering in Morley. There were so many things that I learned from the elders, that I wasn't aware of. I wasn't forced to learn these things, I was just seeking to find my culture. I hope to see you, the readers next year in Morley." Rita Campbell, a student in Winnipeg, later donated fifteen dollars toward the next Conference.[47]

In October the Steering Committee gathered in Williams Lake, British Columbia. Ten members were present; that none of them had been at the founding meeting in Winnipeg a decade earlier was a reflection of the turnover in Conference leadership. Several arrived early to speak at a native youth workshop and to address the local tribal council, but their own discussions revolved around financial and organizational problems. The Committee met again in May 1980 at the Akwesasne Mohawk community on Cornwall Island. Host Mike Mitchell once more challenged his colleagues to adopt an exclusivist vision of the Conference: "Is it a spiritual movement? A Christian movement? A traditional movement? A drug-and-alcohol movement or what?" His greatest concern seemed to be the growing proportion of non-native people attending their annual gatherings; some New Age entrepreneurs had even been setting up shop in the encampment. Mitchell pushed for stringent rules that would limit non-native participation, and many Committee members agreed with him that "traditional ceremonies belong to Indian people." They also discussed the possibility of changing the name of their organization because "the word 'Ecumenical' is hard to understand." At a brainstorming session one evening someone suggested a theme for the 1980 Conference: "The Coming Together of Natural Peoples for Native Spiritual Fulfillment."[48]

The most controversial issue at this meeting was raised by Adam Cuthand when he reported that John Snow "would like the Committee to consider moving the Conference out of Morley in 1981." Organizing the annual gathering took a great deal of time and energy, and in recent years the Stoneys had been subsidizing on-site expenses out of band coffers. A month later Snow circulated a letter among Committee members clarifying his position: "Over the past couple of years there has been talk of moving the conference to the East or some place else more central," and he was merely responding to this sentiment. "If Morley has fulfilled its purpose in hosting the conference, and if the time has come to move the conference, then I do not want to stand in the way for other arrangements to be made." But "after long hard hours of preparation and a successful conference, of which people leave Morley with renewed strengths, it is not with eagerness or with a light heart that I receive talk of the conference being hosted elsewhere on this Great Island." He considered it "the will of the Great Spirit" that they had been brought together "to plan, to teach, to help each other, and for us as Native people to find ourselves, our history, our language, our heritage, and our belief in the Great Creator. I have fully enjoyed, and I take pride to be part of this Indian Spiritual Movement."[49]

The Anglican Church of Canada convened its twenty-ninth General Synod in June 1980. The Sub-Committee on Native Affairs was now an established and energetic presence within the denomination, and its written submission recalled the Hendry report in evaluating institutional progress over the past decade. Activist priests Ian MacKenzie, Ernie Willie, and Adam Cuthand had led the way in raising money for the Conference, but Anglican support for the ecumenical movement was coming to an end; in 1980 church executives began reducing their contribution toward the annual gathering. The Department of Indian and Northern Affairs had already pulled out, and the Canadian Secretary of State would soon dry up as well. The 1980 Conference attracted less money and fewer people to Stoney country.[50]

By 1981 responsibility for coordinating the annual gathering had fallen to John Snow, who began calling it the "Morley Conference for Indian Spiritual Life." The movement had come to be closely identified with the Stoney people and their homeland, and Stoney Indian Park—not just the sacred fire—had taken on an aura of holiness. "The camping area, the dance pavillion, the tipi and arbour areas—all are SACRED GROUNDS," explained an advertisement for the 1981 Conference. "Natives and other people gather there from across the North American continent and from the four corners of the world to become more aware of their cultural and spiritual heritage. They gather there to purify their bodies, minds, heart and spirits naturally, in balance with nature." The Conference had become a predominantly Canadian movement as well; kitchen duties were allocated by province, with only one day of the weeklong gathering assigned to participants from the U.S.[51]

In December 1981 a few Conference leaders met on the Stoney Reserve to take stock of the movement. They discussed restructuring the Steering Committee along the lines Ernie Willie had suggested four years earlier, and they considered the possibility of incorporating the Conference as a nonprofit organization complete with its own board of directors, corporate officers, administrator, office space, and letterhead. Hoping these changes would make it easier to raise money, they even came up with a marketable name for the new corporation: "North American Red Nation's Spiritual Gathering." The idea of formalizing an organizational bureaucracy was nothing new, though this proposal was more crassly pecuniary than the one Bob Thomas and Ian MacKenzie had put forward in 1972, when they suggested establishing a year-round Conference center. This incorporation attempt failed as well, however, and the 1982 gathering returned to Stoney Indian Park as the "Thirteenth Annual Morley Ecumenical Conference for Indian Spiritual Life."[52]

Adam Cuthand stepped down from his Church House post in August 1982. He had served as an indispensable link between the Anglican church and the Conference, and like Ernie Willie before him he timed his departure to follow the annual gathering. Church officials praised Cuthand's work as consultant on native affairs, but by the early eighties Anglican support for the ecumenical movement had withered. Native commitment to the Conference had been in steady decline as well; spiritual revival remained a dominant theme in Indian country, but many now had other opportunities for connecting with tribal traditions. The 1983 Conference went ahead as scheduled, opening with the lighting of the sacred fire. Only a few hundred people turned out, however, and the fire had to be extinguished two days early for lack of interest.[53]

LINGERING EMBERS

The Indian Ecumenical Conference had never sought legitimation from scholarly authorities, and it does not appear in even the most comprehensive histories of interreligious organizing. Still, by the mid-seventies some of academia's more alert observers had taken note of the movement, and a few even ventured to interpret its cultural and historical significance. Sam Stanley, the Smithsonian Institution anthropologist invited to the initial gathering at Crow Agency, framed the Conference as a case study in "power and powerlessness." In 1972 Conference leaders had asked him to be their "official historian," a role he filled for several years; as a participant-observer engaged in "an atypical anthropological investigation," Stanley had ample opportunity to watch and listen, resulting in what he called "an ethnography of ecumenical communication." He was struck by the "basic ideas and beliefs" that unified this intertribal movement. "In the first place, they are firm in their notion that Indians were put on this continent by the Creator and charged with the responsibility for its care. Similarly, they believe that each tribe has its own special rules for carrying out this divine task. In the eyes of the elders, this is a heavy task, but one that they cannot forsake." Stanley went on to explore the forms of power associated with native prophecy, medicine, and ceremony. "Older Indians at the Ecumenical Conference are looking for Indian solutions to their problems," he concluded. "They must start from an Indian base, and this is provided by their own view of themselves as a chosen people doing the Creator's work. They are continually referring to this task, and this is what the dialogue at the Ecumenical Conference is all about."[54]

York University professor John Price produced a more typical anthropological interpretation of the Conference, calling it "a conscious attempt at pan-Indian religious integration" and "the major institution of religious revitalization among Native Canadians." Devising a chronology illustrating "the evolution of religion," he positioned this ecumenical movement as "the most recent development in pan-Indian religious activity." The Conference—like the Ghost Dance and the Native American Church in times past—"is a new religious revitalization movement, although it is occurring in a very modern form." In keeping with his evolutionary bent, Price theorized that Conference participation was a function of social organization, arguing that native people from "aboriginally band-organized societies" had shown greater interest in the annual gatherings. "Voluntary associations were absent in band societies," and "people with a band heritage tended not to form voluntary associations at all in the historic period, but in the 1970s became the most enthusiastic of all: attending the Ecumenical Conference in Alberta," for example. Unfortunately, Price could offer no explanation for this dramatic cultural mutation. Worse yet, the observation was illusory; he had culled his data from attendance records that were fragmentary at best, analyzing statistics for the 1972 gathering without regard to the various factors that determined delegate selection during the early years of the movement.[55]

Sam Stanley and John Price wrote about the Conference at the height of its popularity. Soon other non-native scholars were citing the ecumenical movement in their studies of contemporary native life. Åke Hultkrantz, a professor of comparative religion in Sweden, mentioned the Conference as a leading effort at strengthening "the common religious heritage from the past." Native spiritual traditions "continue to flourish, sometimes in traditional forms, and sometimes in new appearances. Christianity is often part of the picture, constituting a segment of the Indian religious fabric, but characteristically clothed in an Indian cloak." Church historian John Webster Grant, in his survey of Canadian missions, characterized denominational support for the Conference as "a notable example of readiness to welcome native initiative" in the postcolonial context. "Preachers of the major churches, evangelists from newer Christian groups, and medicine men in the native tradition all have their place. The Anglican Church in particular has shown courage in subsidizing these gatherings, for they obviously involve some risk to historic allegiances." British missiologist Harold Turner, American ethnohistorian Calvin Martin, and Jesuit priest Paul Steinmetz joined

Price in describing the Conference as a "pan-Indian" phenomenon, though none of them applied the extraneous label with any social-scientific precision. Educator Penny Petrone, anthropologist Peter Nabokov, and sociologist Joane Nagel also made passing reference to the Conference in books on native people in Canada and the U.S.[56]

Stoney Indian Park was uncharacteristically quiet during the mid-eighties. In the summer of 1986, three years after the last Conference took place, a freak event caught the attention of many locals. At the time when the annual gathering would have been held—and a buffalo slaughtered to feed Conference participants—three bison in the Stoney herd were killed by lightning during an intense thunderstorm. "We see it as a sign from the Creator that the conference is needed again," John Snow explained. "It is a seed of strength for us." He announced a four-day gathering in 1987, issuing an open invitation to anyone interested "regardless of colour or creed." The Conference was now a Stoney event focusing on tribal traditions, but Snow still displayed some ecumenical intuitions: "Native people are just like Jewish people—they live within a settled form of discrimination and have their own religion from which they gain strength." Tribal communities "have as strong a covenant with the Creator as the Jewish do, but it has been almost snuffed out by overbearing non-Native systems."[57]

The 1987 Conference was held at the end of July. A few old-timers showed up, including Adam Cuthand and Albert Lightning, and there were some first-time participants as well. Lightning prayed with his pipe after the sacred fire had been laid. "Don't put off preparing for tomorrow, do it now," he said under the arbor. "The next century will be spiritual or it will not be at all." The following day he presided over the marriage of Joe Naytowhow and Mary Morin inside his legendary tipi. Other ceremonies and discussions took place during the four-day gathering, though few people were on hand to take advantage of these religious opportunities. John Snow hoped the Conference could be revived to the point where "we have people coming from all over the continent and other lands," but the movement had run its course. After another small gathering in 1988, the Indian Ecumenical Conference once again faded into memory, like the lingering embers of a campfire.[58]

Elder and four children posing for a group portrait at the 1974 Conference. Photograph by Karen Ibbitson, courtesy of General Synod Archives, Anglican Church of Canada.

American Indian Movement rally staged for the National Geographic Society film crew during the 1975 Conference. In this publicity still, AIM spiritual advisor Phillip Deere is the older man at the center of the group, wearing a hat and facing the camera. Photograph by Susanne Page.

Conference leader Ernest Tootoosis talking with Susan Supernaw and her Chicago friends just after the 1975 gathering, in a publicity still shot for The New Indians. *Tootoosis is sporting an I.E.C. button; the other button on his hat reads "Take Me To Your TeePee!" Photograph by Susanne Page.*

Alanis Obomsawin, from musical educator to documentary filmmaker. The top photograph shows her performing at the 1969 Anglican General Synod in Sudbury, Ontario. The bottom photograph was taken at the 1976 Conference as she and cameraman Buckley Petawabano were preparing to interview Jeannette Lavell for Mother of Many Children. *Top photograph courtesy of General Synod Archives, Anglican Church of Canada; bottom photograph by David Mills Lavell.*

Andrew and Alice Ahenakew adjusting the tipi outside their home at Sandy Lake, Saskatchewan, where Andrew conducted healing ceremonies until his death in November 1976. Photograph courtesy of General Synod Archives, Anglican Church of Canada.

Albert Lightning posing for a portrait made at a Service Committee meeting held at Trent University, Peterborough, Ontario, in January 1977. Photograph by Jim Steele.

Conference elder Stewart Etsitty watching the sacred fire, just after opening ceremonies for the 1992 gathering. Still image from video courtesy of National Museum of the American Indian, Smithsonian Institution.

In autobiographies by both Native Americans and African Americans for more than 150 years, in writers with vastly differing religious beliefs and political agendas, the fundamental question addressed to white readers is whether they understand—in practice, in the effect on the lives of people of color in the United States—the full implications of the difference between Christianity and the white man's religion.

John D. Barbour, *Versions of Deconversion*

There are a lot of teachings from this fire. . . . It's like the fire is our mother, because she cooks for us, keeps us warm, gives us light wherever we want to go. . . . Try and take care of the fire.

Tommy Nez, Indian Ecumenical Conference

"TEACHINGS FROM THIS FIRE"

IN THE SUMMER OF 1988 I WAS BROWSING the used books section at Moe's, less than two blocks from the rooming house where I stayed, when I discovered a perfect hardbound copy of John Snow's *These Mountains Are Our Sacred Places*. I had seen references to the book—and to the Indian Ecumenical Conference—in my research on native religious traditions, an interest that was intensifying after a year of exploring various subjects through course work at the Graduate Theological Union. How this obscure Canadian publication had made its way to a Telegraph Avenue bookstore in Berkeley was a mystery to me, but I did recognize the out-of-print book as a bargain at seventeen dollars and quickly added it to my meager library. A year later Snow's insights on creation, natural law, revelation, biculturalism, and "the Indian Religious Movement" figured into my master's thesis, titled "Native Americans, Theology, and Liberation." The research conducted for that project eventually led to the publication of two edited volumes, each of which contains brief mention of the Conference.[1]

I entered the doctoral program on Holy Hill in the fall of 1989, when I also started working as a teaching assistant for the Native American Studies department at the University of California. I still had doubts about pursuing an academic vocation, but I was enjoying the intellectual life, and I appreciated the opportunity to help teach courses in native history, contemporary issues, literature, and composition. Thanks to friends involved with the Bay Area Native American Ministry, an ecumenical agency based in inner-city Oakland, I also began to see how my scholarly work might speak to some of the problems still facing native communities—and many non-native people as well. My first disciplined research into the Conference was conducted during the fall semester of 1990 for a graduate seminar called "American Indian Social Movements." I presented the Conference as an example of "intertribal revitalization through interreligious cooperation," and the following year I submitted an expanded version of this term paper as one of my comprehensive examinations, a comparative and methodological study titled "Cross-Cultural Religious Phenomena: Revitalization Movements."[2]

By the end of 1991 I was considering several possible dissertation topics: I remained interested in native Christian theology; I had done some preliminary research on independent tribal churches; with the Columbus Quincentenary looming on the horizon, I had also gotten involved in analyzing—and confronting—the triumphalist hoopla being promoted by the dominant culture. I eventually settled on writing about the Conference, hoping to address the growing body of literature on interreligious dialogue while documenting an overlooked aspect of the postwar native experience. I already knew that this important movement deserved a historical treatment, but the dissertation had to be framed as a theoretical project to satisfy the rubrics of my academic program, so I proposed using the Conference as a case study for exploring "contemporary native religious identity."[3]

A week after my prospectus was approved, televisual humorist Andy Rooney syndicated a pathetic diatribe scolding native activists for protesting racist sports mascots. "While American Indians have a grand past, the impact of their culture on the world has been slight," he opined. "The time for the way Indians lived is gone and it's doubly sad because they refuse to accept it. They hang onto remnants of their religion and superstition that may have been useful to savages 500 years ago but which are meaningless in 1992." It was a timely provocation, to say the least. In the course of my research I learned that the Conference was being revived that summer, and in July I flew from San Francisco to Calgary, where I rented a small car and drove to Morley.[4]

I had arrived a couple of days early so I could explore the archives at the Nakoda Institute, a Stoney research center located on the reserve. My first night in Stoney Indian Park was very quiet, but the next morning work crews began setting up camp, and Conference participants rolled in throughout the day. One of the first people I met that afternoon was Tommy Nez, a Navajo roadman from Gallup, who invited me into his tipi while he visited with old friends about the legal status of peyote. Stewart and Clara Etsitty arrived a little later, along with several grandchildren, and I mostly watched while Nez and another man put up a tipi for them to stay in. By nightfall the place was alive with the sounds of an intertribal gathering, people visiting from camp to

camp and sharing provisions for the evening meal. John Snow and other Conference organizers were anticipating a crowd of fifteen hundred; there might
have been a hundred people on hand by the time I turned in.[5]

The 1992 Conference began with opening ceremonies on the morning of
Monday, July 27. Tommy Nez used a flint to light some wood shavings, stoked
the flames with his eagle feather fan, and burned some cedar incense in the
fire. Navajo medicine man Joe Bia blessed the grounds with water and the
arbor with corn pollen, acknowledging the four directions. Stewart Etsitty recalled the founding of the Conference in English and then offered a long
prayer in Navajo. Assiniboine elder Jerome Fourstar took the lead for a pipe
ceremony, smudging with a braid of sweetgrass before lighting the tobacco.
John Snow concluded the morning agenda by welcoming everyone to the
Stoney Reserve and explaining the purpose of this event: as pre-Conference
publicity had indicated, this was an "Indian Cultural and Spiritual Gathering"
reinforcing native traditions and introducing them to those who were too
young to have participated in previous Conferences. It was also being held in
response to the Columbus Quincentenary and in recognition of the "International Year for the World's Indigenous People" proclaimed by the United Nations General Assembly. Conference sessions were being filmed by a crew
from the Smithsonian Institution's new National Museum of the American Indian. Canada's minister of Indian and Northern Affairs and five local commercial interests had donated money toward Conference expenses, allowing the
Stoneys to serve three meals a day.[6]

After a spartan lunch of sandwiches and fruit, a few dozen people returned
to the arbor and settled in for the afternoon session. Adam Cuthand chaired
the proceedings, commenting on the history and significance of this ecumenical movement and then inviting the native participants on hand to share from
their own experiences. "This is a sacred ground," he said. "It has been made
sacred since that time" in 1971 when the Conference was first held at Stoney
Indian Park. "This is the platform on which our native people talk." Several
individuals found the courage to stand up and speak: a Catholic deacon and
Anishinabe pipe carrier told about his ministry to prison inmates in northern
Minnesota; a young Mohawk woman born at Kahnawake lamented the cultural conflict and language loss she experienced growing up in an urban environment; a Stoney tribal council member recounted her journey through the
residential school system, various Christian denominations, and ten years of
alcohol abuse on the way back to the spiritual traditions of her grandmother, a
medicine woman; an Assiniboine man, retired from the military and "pushing
sixty," voiced humble words of encouragement to those of us resting in the
shade of the arbor.

Others related their own insights over the next three days. Each speaker stood on a short rostrum directly behind the sacred fire; with a slight breeze blowing in from the back of the arbor, those who spoke were often veiled in smoke and sprinkled by flecks of ash. Wind, water, and other earthly elements were occasionally invoked as religious metaphors, but the central and unifying motif of this intertribal gathering was natural combustion. One person after another extemporized on the sacred fire and its symbolic meaning in the context of native spiritual revival. Conference old-timers were especially taken with this situational tradition, which was now over two decades old. "There are a lot of teachings from this fire," said Tommy Nez before drawing sparks from his flint. "It's like the fire is our mother, because she cooks for us, keeps us warm, gives us light wherever we want to go" when things are dark. "Try and take care of the fire." After the opening ceremonies John Snow read his poem "The Sacred Fire," and he recited it again on the last morning, just before closing ceremonies. He prefaced the first reading with an imperative: "This is a sacred fire. You respect the fire—you come here to pray, you come here to meditate, you come here to share religious experiences with others. Many people have come here, they used to gather here in the evenings and share stories, spiritual teachings," and other personal narratives. The sacred fire is "a very special place, and many have expressed that they found something here."

One of the oldest individuals to speak was Stewart Etsitty, the most senior Conference leader in attendance. On Monday morning he reminisced about the 1971 gathering at Stoney Indian Park, where Bob Thomas had laid their first sacred fire. "I know around this fireplace there's a lot of prayers been said, a lot of teaching. The word of wisdom been said around this fireplace here." Etsitty mourned the passing of Thomas and other Steering Committee colleagues who were gone—Albert Lightning, Andrew Ahenakew, Ernest Tootoosis, Clifton Hill—and called for a moment of silent prayer to remember them. He also appreciated the many intertribal and transnational relationships he had formed through his work on behalf of the ecumenical movement. Toward the end of the Conference, Etsitty returned to the microphone: "There's already been a lot of things said about the fire. I don't think anybody knows the power of fire. The scientists all over the world measure different things," but "the power of that fire no one knows. If they do find out, something's going to happen if they don't be careful with it. You know, we all know, just a tiny little spark will move a big automobile, trucks, train, things like that. A little tiny spark will send a man to the moon." Tribal medicine people also know a few things about fire, but "I don't know if there's any limit to the power of fire."

An omnipotent flame may have been at the center of this spiritual gathering, but it was not a hegemonic force. The fire was sacred yet open to interpretation, a dynamic focal point that looked different from every angle. Those who gathered under the arbor in 1992 embodied the four directions, their homes scattered from the Northwest Territories to the American Southwest, from the East Coast to the Pacific Rim; indigenous visitors representing the Mapuches of Chile and the Maoris of New Zealand had joined the circle as well. Conference sessions were chaired by an Assiniboine traditionalist and an Anglican priest and a peyote roadman, and various participants spoke on the basis of their familiarity with tribal creeds or denominational customs or some combination of native and Christian traditions. During the four-day event we heard from octogenarians and teenagers and those somewhere in-between. Three speakers needed translators to convey their verbal messages. This casual program of testimony, prayer, storytelling, and gentle exhortation was interspersed with the occasional joke and a few tears. Despite the passage of time, the ecumenical movement still sustained a multifaceted conversation transcending political and ethnic and linguistic boundaries, closing the geographic and religious and generational distances separating native people. The Conference had preserved its egalitarian ethos, even if the 1992 gathering was a pale reflection of the movement's mid-seventies glory days.

On Tuesday afternoon I met Darin Keewatin, who would become my good friend. I enjoyed visiting with him and sharing a buffalo steak dinner while standing under the eaves of the cookhouse, and his rambunctious son, Russell, turned out to be a reliable source of comic relief. Later that evening I stopped by Tommy Nez's tipi, where he and some Navajo friends were singing peyote songs to the beat of a water drum; Colleen Seymour, a Shuswap teacher from Kamloops, served homemade herbal tea to those of us listening. There were other evening activities as well: a twelve-step meeting, a talking circle for women, and two teaching sessions with the youth. The powwow on Wednesday night was a small, subdued affair but featured some impressive music by the Nakoda Nation Singers, a local drum group.

Closing ceremonies began late Thursday morning, and the sacred fire was extinguished a couple of hours later. There were less than a hundred people on hand; many paused to collect ashes from the fire before breaking camp. John Snow announced that the Steering Committee had reached a consensus on gathering again in 1993, and other Conference leaders voiced support for the idea, though it seemed a tentative gesture. The Committee had met twice to discuss plans for coming years, but those who spoke during morning and afternoon sessions spent more time recalling past pilgrimages to Morley than they did envisioning the future of the movement. The 1992 Conference felt more like a reunion than a revival, and overall attendance—less than three hundred people, mostly from southern Alberta—did not suggest a groundswell of interest in the transnational spiritual gathering. Indian country was a different place than it had been in 1969. A good share of the credit for this remarkable transformation could be assigned to the ecumenical movement.

Writing in 1992, Vine Deloria, Jr., praised Conference leaders for having "succeeded in reaching people of all ages far beyond their most optimistic expectations." He recognized that the ecumenical movement had played a crucial role in the rise of "modern traditionalism" in many native communities. During the seventies and eighties "an impressive number of young people abandoned their careers in Indian organizational work and returned to their reservations determined to learn the tribal ways and become carriers of the traditions. Since the conditions under which the old ways were practiced no longer exist, the most satisfactory solution for these young people was to derive principles of action and understanding from the traditions and apply them to modern circumstances in which they found themselves." The Conference helped define modern traditionalism by seeking to "transform old ways of behaving into standards of action with definable limits set by the conception of Indian identity itself. Indians therefore find themselves at a unique point in their history," Deloria inferred, and the future of native communities in Canada and the U.S. will hinge on the contest between modern traditionalism and its polar alternatives, assimilative progressivism and obstinate conservatism.[7]

I returned to Berkeley on the last day of July and dived back into my dissertation, finishing a draft six weeks later. The Columbus Quincentenary came and went, accompanied by dubious fanfare on both sides of the colonial divide. Looking for an appropriate way to conclude my interdisciplinary study of the Indian Ecumenical Conference, I was drawn to a compelling narrative by another kind of Indian. Born and raised in Bombay, Jayant Kothare learned to revere the Hindu traditions of his devout Brahmin family. His parents and grandparents also encouraged him to explore other religious communities in the city, and among his earliest memories were the "huge Victorian Gothic church buildings looming over poor housing areas. There, surrounded by war memorials and monuments of imperial Britain, brown Anglicans worshipped in strict adherence to the 1662 version of the *Book of Common Prayer*, in blissful ignorance of the rich indigenous spirituality of India." Kothare later migrated to Germany and then Canada, converting to Christianity along the way and seeking ordination as a Christian minister. "I was twice stripped of my ordinand status in two mainline churches of Canada because of my concern to incorporate my Hindu spiritual tradition into my Christian faith," he recalled. "As a convert from an ancient spiritual tradition, I have watched over the years the monochrome European church painting itself into a lonely corner, slowly but surely alienating itself from Christians hailing from different religious and different racial backgrounds."[8]

Kothare eventually found a home in the Anglican Church of Canada, working with several native parishes while completing his seminary education. He "had little difficulty in making a connection" between what he had witnessed at the Bombay cathedral and "the cultural and spiritual alienation of native Christians in Regina, Saskatchewan, or Kenora, Ontario." He attended the Indian Ecumenical Conference four times during the mid-seventies; his sensitive reflection on what he discovered there was the antithesis of Andy Rooney's shallow invective. "Each visit was a blessing and an enrichment of my spiritual life," Kothare wrote. "I would spend most of my time walking around, meeting and talking to people. These were ordinary native folk with extraordinary insights into the dilemma of modern civilization and the possible ways of healing Mother Earth and her children." He was struck by the "sensual, earthy, incarnational quality to their experiences, so unlike the earth-negating pseudo-spirituality prevalent among the bohemian white people disenchanted with materialism." Every native person he met seemed to understand that "mystical insight was not the prerogative of a chosen few but the birthright of every individual who was willing to live in harmony with creation. It was a democratic mysticism."[9]

"When I listened to the elders holding forth in the sacred arbour," Kothare continued, "this theme of democratic mysticism was repeated again and again. Spirituality and justice issues were mentioned in the same breath with no contradiction as you would find in the traditional teaching of the church." The "bottom line" was this: "Everything spiritual had to be earthed, made incarnate, and shared through a sacramental relationship with everybody around. The feeling of sacredness that permeated the entire proceedings of the Conference was infectious." He had never been around such large crowds while experiencing "so little tension, stress, panic. People looked each other in the eyes. There were long silences and lively banterings. No formalities, no unctuous courtesies." Kothare was a perceptive critic, though many had made similar observations about the annual gatherings. What distinguished this particular narrative was Kothare's reflexive candor: "The time spent at the four Conferences was probably the most enriching time of my life as a Christian minister," he confessed, which is a remarkable admission for a non-native cleric to make. "I had experiences which one normally would not have in the white man's straight and cerebral world." Attending the Conference "opened my whole being—body, mind, and soul—to the Numinous and the Holy as no experience in the church setting has ever done for me either before or since."[10]

I defended my dissertation in December 1992. A few weeks later I moved to Santa Cruz, where I soon found myself engrossed in teaching undergraduates about native people. Over the next decade I published several analytical articles on the Conference[11] while immersing myself in recent scholarship on narrative strategies in historiography, ethnography, and literary criticism; I was particularly inspired by native writers such as Leslie Marmon Silko, N. Scott Momaday, Charles Alexander Eastman, and Joy Harjo, whose work helped me think about the importance of orality, experience, commitment, and perception in any attempt at textual representation.[12] Continuing my research into the history of the Conference, I also tried to keep track of ongoing developments related to the ecumenical movement.

After twelve consecutive terms of office, John Snow met defeat in the biennial band elections held at the end of 1992. He was an influential voice among political leaders on the regional and national levels, but he had become one of the more controversial figures in Stoney affairs. The factionalism that accompanied his twenty-four-year reign also made him a convenient target for the frontier journalism that flares up wherever native people assert their rights. Snow's successor focused on wellness programs addressing the Stoneys' many social problems; he had no particular interest in hosting an intertribal religious gathering, so the 1993 Conference envisioned by Steering Committee members a year earlier did not take place.[13] Snow managed to get reelected in 1996 and served as chief of the Wesley band for four more years. It was an unusually contentious period in Stoney history—complete with court-ordered investigations, grassroots civil disobedience, and federal control of band finances—and Snow was turned out of office again in 2000. Stoney Indian Park remained a scenic destination, perhaps even a sacred site, but its tenure as home of the Indian Ecumenical Conference had come to an end.[14]

The Anglican Church of Canada stopped funding the annual gatherings in the early eighties, around the time Adam Cuthand resigned his Church House position, but native issues continued to play a prominent role in the life of the denomination. Throughout the seventies and eighties Anglican leaders took an active interest in northern development and its effect on native people, advocating on their behalf and publishing materials critical of government policies and corporate practices.[15] The Sub-Committee on Native Affairs was elevated in status in 1980 and renamed the Council for Native Ministries in 1988. In October of that year the denomination sponsored its first National Native Convocation, a weeklong gathering of nearly two hundred native Anglicans, and three months later the first native Anglican bishop was consecrated. In 1991 Anglican executives established the Residential Schools Working Group to coordinate their response amid the growing controversy over historic abuses in the residential school system; at a second National Native Convocation in 1993, the Anglican primate read a formal statement apologizing for the suffering caused by these colonial institutions. In 1994 native Anglican leaders drafted and signed a covenant pledging to "call our people into unity in a new, self-determining community within the Anglican Church of Canada." They also reorganized their administrative body as the Anglican Council of Indigenous Peoples.[16] By the turn of the millennium, when residential schools litigation threatened to bankrupt Canada's mainline denominations, the Anglican church had documented its support for native concerns in numerous books[17] and videos,[18] including a 1998 reprint of the Hendry report.

The Anglican and United churches played a critical role in another important legacy of the ecumenical movement. In 1971, after the Steering Committee declared June 21 as a National Indian Day of Prayer, both denominations passed resolutions endorsing this action and encouraging their parishes and congregations to participate. Conference leaders promoted the observance as long as Bob Thomas was involved in the movement, and many Christian bodies continued to support the annual commemoration throughout the seventies. In 1982 the newly formed Assembly of First Nations—led by David Ahenakew, a nephew of Andrew Ahenakew—launched a campaign to get June 21 designated as National Aboriginal Solidarity Day in Canada. The first official response came in 1990, when the Quebec legislature acknowledged June 21 as a day to celebrate native cultural traditions. Delegates to the 1995 Sacred Assembly, an ecumenical gathering of native and non-native religious leaders organized by Ojibwa-Cree politician Elijah Harper, renewed the call for a national commemoration. In 1996 the Canadian government finally responded by proclaiming June 21 to be National Aboriginal Day, which is now celebrated annually at hundreds of events across the country. Few Canadians realize that this holiday began as a holy day conceived at the Indian Ecumenical Conference, fewer still that the idea was first suggested by Browning Pipestem, an Otoe-Missouria lawyer from the U.S.[19]

Bob Thomas and Ian MacKenzie had both withdrawn from the movement by the summer of 1974. Unable to persuade the Steering Committee to institutionalize the Conference by adopting a corporate structure and establishing an administrative headquarters, they set up their own organization. The first board meeting of the Centre for Indian Scholars was held in August 1975 at Masset in the Queen Charlotte Islands, a Haida settlement where

MacKenzie served as Anglican priest. The Centre sponsored a number of small ecumenical gatherings over the years, organizing native spiritual leaders at the regional level, but never obtained the funding necessary for a large-scale effort. In the mid-eighties the Centre developed a close relationship with the Native Ministries Consortium based at the Vancouver School of Theology, an interdenominational seminary affiliated with the University of British Columbia. Thomas chaired the Centre for Indian Scholars until his death in August 1991, after which the organization increasingly focused on commemorating his life and work.[20]

Over the course of his forty-year career, Bob Thomas had come to know a multitude of academics, activists, and just plain folks. He was a Cherokee traditionalist from the U.S. whose personal experiences convinced him of the importance of working in intertribal, ecumenical, and transnational contexts. His many friends and colleagues remembered him smoking a pipe, and wearing a variety of hats: social scientist, grassroots organizer, college teacher, postcolonial theorist, spiritual leader. A lengthy collection of essays published in his honor credited him with numerous professional accomplishments, not the least of which was founding the Indian Ecumenical Conference. "The fact that it held together at all is a miracle," Thomas admitted in a lecture at the Vancouver School of Theology during the summer of 1986. "Considering the difficulties, I think it was a smashing success," since "a lot of positive things" came out of the movement. "I think I would be game for starting it again, and may yet."[21]

He would not live long enough to achieve that goal, though he did fulfill a "lifelong dream" just before his untimely death. During the 1957–58 academic year, while conducting field research among the Eastern Cherokees, Thomas had noted some interest in "reviving the old Cherokee religion. Many of them talked about this in informal groups all through the winter and spring." When he finished his work in June, one of the local leaders told him that "sometime next winter we may want you to ask some of those Oklahoma chiefs to come down here and teach us all about the fire." Thomas kept in touch with the North Carolina Cherokees and other tribal communities in the eastern U.S., and thirty years later the time was finally right for "lighting the Cherokee fire" on the Qualla Boundary Reservation. In September 1989 a delegation of Oklahoma Cherokees laid a fire at the Raven Rock Ceremonial Grounds, then joined their eastern relatives for an all-night stomp dance, the first such event there in over sixty years. The following summer Thomas and his colleagues helped the Eastern Cherokees revive their green corn ceremony, a four-day undertaking. "There are few things I have wanted more in my life than to see a Fire again in North Carolina," he told those who had made financial contributions to the effort. "I thank you from the bottom of my heart, my friends. God bless you!"[22]

Stoney Indian Park, the Anglican Council of Indigenous Peoples, National Aboriginal Day, the Centre for Indian Scholars, Raven Rock Ceremonial Grounds—these are some of the more conspicuous sites where the impact of the Indian Ecumenical Conference can be documented. Organizational developments involving government institutions, Christian denominations, and modern tribal communities leave paper trails that are relatively easy to follow. It is considerably more difficult to map the boundaries of a social phenomenon as expansive as the ecumenical movement, particularly when this indeterminate domain overlaps the territory claimed for other cultural nationalisms. The resolutions approved at the first three Conferences, for example, expressed concerns that were also voiced through various community associations, tribal governments, advocacy groups, and militant organizations during the early seventies.

One of the most far-reaching effects of the Conference was a product of its unanticipated transformation from interreligious conversation to intergenerational encounter. Phillip Deere and his AIM advisees were not the only people to borrow the Conference model in planning their own spiritual event; as Adam Cuthand and Elizabeth Boyd noted in the late seventies, "elders and youth" gatherings were becoming a popular communal practice throughout Indian country. During the three decades since the Conference began catering to urban youth, local encampments bringing together tribal elders and young people have become a familiar feature of native life, especially during the summer months. Formalizing the pedagogical relationships that once characterized daily existence—before the proliferation of modern communication and transportation technologies—these annual events typically focus on demonstrating the contemporary relevance of tribal cultural traditions. Some elders-and-youth gatherings are offspring of the Conference, having been founded by people who witnessed the model firsthand at Stoney Indian Park. Other such gatherings followed, organized as part of a more general movement of cultural revitalization. Like the competition powwow circuit that developed in the postwar period, this casual network of intergenerational encampments is an emergent intertribal expression.[23]

The grassroots popularity of elders-and-youth gatherings, competition powwows, and other modern cultural institutions highlights a deficiency in the historiography of contemporary intertribal activism. Conventional accounts of recent native history foreground the militant groups that attracted media attention during the early seventies. Embracing the sensationalist biases of their journalistic precursors, most scholars portray the Red Power era as a pageantry of confrontational protest, an interpretive approach that fails to account for much of what has transpired in tribal communities since that time. Privileging the more flamboyant expressions of native activism also oversimplifies the politics of Indian country; many tribal people were critical of the militant groups, and many remain so today. Writing in the mid-seventies under the Cherokee pseudonym of Stand Middlestriker, Bob Thomas suggested that "many of the young Indian people who are called militants have learned to think like young city whites." Living in a world of "symbol and image," these "Indian revolutionaries" began "wearing long hair and feathers, not to express their Indianness, but to *be* an Indian, to create themselves an image." Few could see that "the ultimate 'cop out' is to try to create your own self, as do young whites, by hanging symbols on you to project an image." While many native militants are sincere, "they are pretty misguided. They go out and protest for justice. They have a big public tantrum which just shows off how politically powerless we are and how much we have learned to perform for whites. Whites won't pay attention to their own children unless they have a tantrum, so our young people have learned to act like white children."[24]

"And all of that protesting will come to naught, anyhow," Thomas continued. "Powerful whites won't keep their agreements anyway. We just get 'set up' in our war with whites to get it socked to us again. Further, what young Indians don't know when they go out and protest, I think, is that protesting just ties us in more to the system," which manages dissent by co-opting dissenters. "We not only look foolish and we are not only playing a no-win game, but we are becoming more involved with whites. Every time powerful whites in the system meet the demands of a minority it just means that the minority has to work more with whites and to become more involved with them in some way." Both militant rhetoric and the co-optive response it provokes tend to exacerbate tribal factionalism. "Nowadays, since the Indian religion is a big fad among young whites, the fad has rubbed off on some Indians so they go around playing Indian traditionalists, wearing a lot of bead work and going to a lot of ceremonies. At the same time, some of them violate the most important thing in the Indian religion and that is the harmony that has to be among the Indians to make our medicine work."[25] Secular academics have inscribed the militant activists as the leading voices of their generation, and materialist books and articles keep rolling off the presses. Readers can already choose from among nine published volumes recounting the occupation of Alcatraz Island,[26] for example, and there are at least forty graduate theses documenting the heyday of the American Indian Movement.[27] As fascinating as these historic episodes may be, there were many other expressions of native activism that helped make Indian country what it is today. And a lot of native activists during the Red Power era were inspired by motivations more substantive than those driving the angry outbursts viewers occasionally witnessed on the evening news.

Writers who privilege political organizing among native people, like native activists who chase concessions from modern nation-states, usually end up reinforcing the nationalist ideology that is a hallmark of colonial aggression. Less concerned with recognition than autonomy, the Indian Ecumenical Conference developed out of a different tradition of grassroots activism. Founded by native leaders from both sides of the Canada-U.S. border, the ecumenical movement was postnationalist at its inception, and it remained so through an era when tribal sovereignty evolved into the leading euphemism for postmodern vassalage. The movement's transnational orientation corresponded with the inclusivity signaled by the three terms of its official designation: the Indian Ecumenical Conference was an intertribal interreligious interchange. These descriptors suggest constructive contacts between diverse social realities, transcending boundaries to generate reciprocal solidarities among human communities separated by cultural, spiritual, and geographic distances. "Indians get pressured all the time into planning these big programs," Bob Thomas wrote in the mid-seventies. "That's bound to fail" because "it's not the way things are done in our communities. Everything I've seen succeed happened when a small group of Indians sat down and decided what they wanted to do and then went ahead and did it. And whatever organizations that formed simply came out of that getting together and doing it. Organizations among the Indians" emerge out of "what we are doing together and what we have going among each other and what kind of relationships we have to each other."[28]

The Conference emerged out of an interreligious conversation, and although this agenda was eventually overshadowed by the intergenerational encounter, ecumenical solidarity remained a central—if sometimes controversial—goal throughout the life of the movement. Participating in the annual gatherings inspired many to ecumenical activism back home, and helped some gain a broader understanding of the ecumenical strategies being developed by native people. "From talking to most of the spiritual leaders at the Conference," Thomas ascertained that "the majority want to achieve some spiritual unity in their home communities." He identified "seven different paths" various tribal communities were following, illustrating each ecumenical path with specific examples. Some Choctaws "are trying to strengthen their native religion without causing trouble between people who follow Christianity and those who are more traditional." Some Ojibways "want to revive their religion," hoping that tribal traditions such as

Ojibway-language hymn singing "will also bridge the gap between Anglican and Catholic factions on the reserve." Some Dogribs "are trying to integrate their two religions," working to achieve "what some of the Southwestern tribes have had for years." Some Yaquis "integrated Christianity and their old religion years ago" and "simply want to hold that integration, but white church officials are now attacking that integration." Some Cheyennes "have been both devout Christians and devout in their native religion for many years," an accommodation now under attack, "and they want to hold the line." Some Iroquois "simply want to develop some kind of peaceful co-existence and cooperation between the separate religious groups" among their people. Some Navajos "are trying to integrate the Peyote religion and the old native religion together and at the same time make some kind of peace between the Christians on one hand and the native and Peyote people on the other hand."[29]

This typology of tribal ecumenism is just one example of the theoretical insights elaborated through the ecumenical movement. Bob Thomas and many of his friends and colleagues believed the Conference had demonstrated that interreligious organizing can be a powerful mechanism of social change, particularly when it is guided by personalist values. Interpersonal relationships are among the most precarious of vocations, but community-building is also our highest calling. Religious conflict may be an intractable feature of the human condition; embracing our differences, wrestling them to the ground with all the humility we can muster, is a more pragmatic response than the cocksure proselytizing of fundamentalists and materialists alike. Bureaucratic elites—spiritual leaders as well as scholars of religion—can learn a great deal from those who gave life to the Conference: effective interreligious dialogue has less to do with theologies and liturgies and polities than with a shared commitment to meaningful coexistence. In framing each chapter of this book with paired epigraphs from religious scholars and Conference participants, I have pointed to some ways in which the story of the ecumenical movement speaks to recent scholarship on religion in Canada and the U.S.

Of course, dialogue sometimes entails criticism, especially when the relationships involved have been compromised by chronic social inequity. "Native Americans and African Americans have criticized whites' use of Christianity to justify power and privilege over people of color," observes John D. Barbour in *Versions of Deconversion*. "Writers as diverse as Frederick Douglass, Charles Eastman, Malcolm X, and Lame Deer have sought to deconvert white readers from various false understandings of Christianity that sanction such injustices." Barbour's book is a comparative study of *Autobiography and the Loss of Faith*, exploring the flip side of the conversion narrative. "The 'turning from' and 'turning to' are alternative perspectives on the same process of personal metamorphosis, stressing either the rejected past of the old self or the present convictions of the reborn self." The loss of faith has become a modern metaphor for "experiences of change involving radical doubt, moral revulsion from a way of life, emotional upheaval, and rejection of a community." Deconversion "expresses modernity's search for authenticity, which so often takes the form of a flight from authority, from inherited paradigms of thought, and from various forms of pressure to conform." In the hands of minority writers, both the genre of autobiography and the metaphor of deconversion are powerful weapons in the struggle for social justice.[30]

"What is most striking about multicultural autobiography," Barbour writes, "is the commonality of the central goal of seeking the reader's deconversion from the white man's religion," a heresy of racist proportions. "In autobiographies by both Native Americans and African Americans for more than 150 years, in writers with vastly differing religious beliefs and political agendas, the fundamental question addressed to white readers is whether they understand—in practice, in the effect on the lives of people of color in the United States—the full implications of the difference between Christianity and the white man's religion." Recognizing this difference "has not always come easy for white people, since there are deep-rooted and tenacious links between certain Christian attitudes and the belief in white superiority." Encouraging deconversion from the white man's religion "is a central goal of autobiographies of persons of color. This has been so whether the author is a Christian, is committed to some other religious tradition, or is reassessing an ambivalent relationship to Christianity," three categories that also typify those who attended the Indian Ecumenical Conference. "The autobiographer's effort to discriminate between Christianity and the white man's religion represents not only a critique of ideology but an act of religious imagination, of identity formation, and of cultural creativity."[31]

If it is difficult to trace the contours of the ecumenical movement as a social phenomenon, how much more enigmatic is its meaning in the lives of individual participants? Spiritual experience is a mysterious reality, even at firsthand, and hardly something susceptible to objective representation. "The religious dimension of autobiography is not simply located in an author's record of past loyalties but also in the 'autobiographical act,'" Barbour notes, "in the author's process of writing, as the articulation of those central convictions that shape a perspective on the past." How people today recount their memories of the Conference is bound up with where those experiences have led them, just as writing this book is now part of my own pilgrimage, and reading it part of yours. Like religious personalities the world over, "autobiographical writing itself reenacts, continues, and extends in new directions the essentially religious quest for truth and human community."[32]

Fair enough, but literacy is a hallowed dogma of the white man's religion and his irreligion as well, bibliophilia a central sacrament. The printed word has become a formidable tradition; still, writing and reading can never be more than penultimate feats. Verbal artifacts that terminate in psychological revision are less remedy than symptom. The deconversionist tract in your hands closes with two critical questions, a modest confession, and an overture: Is peaceful coexistence possible in a world of divergent truth claims and fierce competition over material resources? I believe it is. Will we survive our own epistemological arrogance and ravenous desire? Perhaps, if enough literates moderate their textual devotions in deference to the priority of interpersonal experience.

ACKNOWLEDGMENTS

I AM GRATEFUL FOR THE MANY FRIENDS AND COLLEAGUES who helped me complete my work on the Indian Ecumenical Conference. Faculty mentors George Cummings, Tim Lull, David Steward, Russell Thornton, and Gerald Vizenor supervised my initial efforts while I was a student at the Graduate Theological Union. John Dizikes and Forrest Robinson perused my dissertation after I joined them on the faculty of the University of California at Santa Cruz. Historians Karin Gedge, Phil Gleason, Gene McCarraher, Linda Przybyszewski, Kathleen Riley, Beth Schweiger, Roberto Treviño, Beth Wenger, and David Yoo critiqued an early draft of chapter one as part of our collaboration through the Young Scholars in American Religion program. Beth Bailey, Trina Carter, Margaret Connell-Szasz, Ruth Salvaggio, and Ferenc Szasz read other portions of this manuscript while I was a faculty member at the University of New Mexico. Vine Deloria, Jr., Jack Forbes, Darin Keewatin, Ian MacKenzie, Jean Molesky, Kerry Riley, Victoria Rue, and Dorene Wiese also responded to draft material at various stages of the project. Scholarly editors Henk Vroom, Lee Irwin, and P. Jegadish Ghandi and George Cheriyan published my articles on the ecumenical movement. At the University of Oklahoma, Steve Gillon, Andy Horton, Clara Sue Kidwell, and Randy Lewis offered helpful readings, Malinda Brown retouched the video stills, Josie Adams prepared the map, and Karen Sheriff LeVan copyedited the entire manuscript. Four anonymous readers reviewed the manuscript while it was under consideration by several academic publishers.

I am indebted to the numerous librarians, archivists, administrators, clerks, technicians, journalists, photographers, and Conference participants throughout Canada and the U.S. who supplied me with invaluable books, articles, manuscripts, audiotapes, photographs, films, and memories relating to the ecumenical movement.

I am thankful for the internal and external funding that sustained my work on the Indian Ecumenical Conference: a Junior Faculty Development Award from the Division of Humanities at the University of California at Santa Cruz; a Summer Stipend Award from the National Endowment for the Humanities; travel expenses from the Center for the Study of Religion and American Culture at Indiana University–Purdue University at Indianapolis; a Faculty Research Grant from the Research Allocations Committee at the University of New Mexico; and an Individual Research Grant from the American Academy of Religion.

Finally, I am fortunate that religion editor Gayatri Patnaik believed in this project, and that I had the opportunity to work with her and the other fine people at Palgrave.

James Treat
treaty@ou.edu

NOTES

ABBREVIATIONS

ACC/AJ	Anglican Church of Canada General Synod Archives (Toronto, Ontario), Anglican Journal / Canadian Churchman
ACC/NMO	Anglican Church of Canada General Synod Archives (Toronto, Ontario), Native Ministries Office
ACC/PC	Anglican Church of Canada General Synod Archives (Toronto, Ontario), Program Committee
ACC/PO	Anglican Church of Canada General Synod Archives (Toronto, Ontario), Primate's Office
ACC/PWRDF	Anglican Church of Canada General Synod Archives (Toronto, Ontario), Primate's World Relief and Development Fund
CCCB	Canadian Conference of Catholic Bishops (Ottawa, Ontario), Archives
DL	David Lavell (Kingston, Ontario), Personal Collection
GTU	Graduate Theological Union Library (Berkeley, California)
JT	James Treat (Norman, Oklahoma), Personal Collection
MHS/AICC	Minnesota Historical Society Library (St. Paul), American Indian Chicago Conference Collection
NAA/AICC	National Anthropological Archives, National Museum of Natural History, Smithsonian Institution (Washington, DC), American Indian Chicago Conference Manuscripts
NAA/CSM	National Anthropological Archives, National Museum of Natural History, Smithsonian Institution (Washington, DC), Center for the Study of Man Collection
NAC	National Archives of Canada (Ottawa, Ontario)
NGS	National Geographic Society (Washington, DC), Archives
NI	Nakoda Institute, Goodstoney Band of the Stoney Tribe (Morley, Alberta)
NIYC	National Indian Youth Council (Albuquerque, NM), Archives
SG	Sig Gerber (Toronto, Ontario), Personal Collection
SU/SS	Stanford University Libraries (Palo Alto, CA), Special Collections, Stan Steiner Papers
TU/KEK	Trent University Archives (Peterborough, Ontario), Kenneth E. Kidd fonds

UA/HTM — University of Arizona Library (Tucson), Special Collections, Hopi Traditional Movement Papers

UCC/BHM — United Church of Canada Archives (Toronto, Ontario), Board of Home Missions fonds 509, series 2

UCC/DMC — United Church of Canada Archives (Toronto, Ontario), Division of Mission in Canada fonds 512, series 3

UCC/EEMJ — United Church of Canada Archives (Toronto, Ontario), Elgie Ellingham Miller Joblin fonds 3148

UNC/NC — University of North Carolina Library (Chapel Hill), North Carolina Collection

UT/RC — University of Toronto (Ontario), Thomas Fisher Rare Book Library, Rochdale College Collection

YULL — York University Law Library (Toronto, Ontario)

PROLOGUE

1. Vine Deloria, Jr., *Custer Died for Your Sins: An Indian Manifesto* (New York, NY: Macmillan, 1969), 31–32, 148; James Treat, "Introduction: An American Critique of Religion," in *For This Land: Writings on Religion in America* by Vine Deloria, Jr., edited by James Treat (New York, NY: Routledge, 1999), 8–11.
2. Deloria, *Custer*, 2, 121, 268.
3. Deloria, *Custer*, 101–124.
4. Deloria, *Custer*, 2, 112, 115, 119, 167, 243, 246, 248, 263.
5. Deloria, *Custer*, 19, 83, 195, 197–224.
6. Deloria, *Custer*, 122; "A Proposal for an Indian Ecumenical Conference Presented by the Institute for Indian Studies," [December? 1969], 4–8, NAA/AICC, collection MS 4806, box 2; "Indian Ecumenical Conference Announced," July 7, 1970, 1, ACC/NMO, collection GS85–6, box 1, file 16; Robert K. Thomas, *The Indian Ecumenical Movement: A Grassroots Religious Movement*, lecture delivered at the Summer Public Lecture Series of the Vancouver School of Theology, July 21, 1986 (Vancouver, British Columbia: Vancouver School of Theology, 1986), audiocassette; Vine Deloria, Jr., e-mail to author, February 29, 2000.
7. *You Are on Indian Land*, produced by George C. Stoney, directed by Mort Ransen (Montreal, Quebec: National Film Board of Canada, 1969), videotape, 37 min.; Ernest Benedict, "Indians and a Treaty," in *The Only Good Indian: Essays by Canadian Indians*, edited by Waubageshig (Toronto, Ontario: New Press, 1970), 137–140; Troy R. Johnson, *The Occupation of Alcatraz Island: Indian Self-Determination and the Rise of Indian Activism* (Urbana, IL: University of Illinois Press, 1996), 49ff.

CHAPTER 1

1. "Plan to Attend!" *Akwesasne Notes* 1, no. 3 (1969): 14; "Indian Unity Convention," *Akwesasne Notes* 1, no. 7 (1969): 48; Mike Power, "1,000 at Parley Light Pipe of Unity," *Akwesasne Notes* 1, no. 8 (1969): 5; "Indians Gather to Form Own Policy, Exchange Views on Minority Plight," *Akwesasne Notes* 1, no. 8 (1969): 1.
2. Power, "1,000 at Parley," 5; Laurence M. Hauptman, *The Iroquois Struggle for Survival: World War II to Red Power* (Syracuse, NY: Syracuse University Press, 1986), 216–217.

3. Power, "1,000 at Parley," 5; "6 Indian Nations Gather in Effort to Save Lands," *Akwesasne Notes* 1, no. 8 (1969): 5; Charles Russo, "Unity Hope of Indians," *Syracuse Herald-Journal*, August 20, 1969.

4. "Mohawk Indian Wants to Fight against Customs with Groceries," *Akwesasne Notes* 1, no. 8 (1969): 5; "Iroquois Will Rule Land Again Indians Told," *Akwesasne Notes* 1, no. 8 (1969): 6; Russo, "Unity."

5. "Iroquois Will Rule Land Again Indians Told," 6; Russo, "Unity."

6. Vine Deloria, Jr., *Custer Died for Your Sins: An Indian Manifesto* (New York, NY: Macmillan, 1969), 18, 113–114, 119, 124, 246, 278.

7. Elizabeth Chidester Duran, "Clinton Rickard: Chief of the Tuscaroras—Grand President, Indian Defense League of America," *Contemporary Indian Affairs* 1, no. 1 (1970): 39–41; "Clinton Rickard, 91, Tuscarora's Chief," *New York Times*, June 17, 1971, 44; Jack Forbes, "The New Indian Resistance?" *Akwesasne Notes* 4, no. 3 (1972): 21; Clinton Rickard, *Fighting Tuscarora: The Autobiography of Chief Clinton Rickard*, edited by Barbara Graymont (Syracuse, NY: Syracuse University Press, 1973), 58–66, 75–77; Barbara Graymont, "Editor's Introduction," in *Fighting Tuscarora: The Autobiography of Chief Clinton Rickard*, edited by Barbara Graymont (Syracuse, NY: Syracuse University Press, 1973), xxvii–xxviii; Laurence M. Hauptman, *The Iroquois and the New Deal* (Syracuse, NY: Syracuse University Press, 1981), 16–17; "Deskaheh: An Iroquois Patriot's Fight for International Recognition," in *Basic Call to Consciousness*, rev. ed., edited by Akwesasne Notes (Summertown, TN: Book Publishing Company, 1991), 18ff.

8. Duran, "Clinton," 41–42; Rickard, *Fighting*, 13, 52–53, 69–89, 125–128; Hauptman, *Iroquois and the New Deal*, 17, 181; Hauptman, *Iroquois Struggle*, 5–6, 205–207.

9. A. M. Rosenthal, "Indian Tribesmen Call at U.N. in Vain," *New York Times*, May 9, 1950, 10; "Iroquois See Vishinsky in Annual U.N. Protest," *New York Times*, October 24, 1950, 9; Rickard, *Fighting*, 70–71, 78, 131–132, 161–162; Joane Nagel, *American Indian Ethnic Renewal: Red Power and the Resurgence of Identity and Culture* (New York, NY: Oxford University Press, 1996), 160–161.

10. "Hopi Claim Religion Is Bar to Service," *Arizona Republic*, May 24, 1941, 10; Frank Waters, *Book of the Hopi* (New York, NY: Ballantine Books, 1969), 388–392; Earl Shorris, *The Death of the Great Spirit: An Elegy for the American Indian* (New York, NY: Simon and Schuster, 1972), 122–126; Richard O. Clemmer, *Continuities of Hopi Culture Change* (Ramona, CA: Acoma Books, 1978), 71; Shuichi Nagata, "Dan Kochhongva's Message: Myth, Ideology and Political Action among the Contemporary Hopi," in *The Yearbook of Symbolic Anthropology*, Vol. I, edited by Erik Schwimmer (London, England: C. Hurst and Company, 1978), 76–77; Shuichi Nagata, "Political Socialization of the Hopi Traditional Faction: A Contribution to the Theory of Culture Change," *Journal of the Steward Anthropological Society* 11, no. 1 (1979): 114ff; Peter M. Whitely, *Deliberate Acts: Changing Hopi Culture through the Oraibi Split* (Tucson, AZ: University of Arizona Press, 1988), 223ff; Armin W. Geertz, *The Invention of Prophecy: Continuity and Meaning in Hopi Indian Religion* (Berkeley, CA: University of California Press, 1994), 139–140; Richard O. Clemmer, *Roads in the Sky: The Hopi Indians in a Century of Change* (Boulder, CO: Westview Press, 1995), 179ff.

11. Hopi Indian Empire, "Letter to President Harry Truman, March 28, 1949," in *The Invention of Prophecy: Continuity and Meaning in Hopi Indian Religion* by Armin W. Geertz (Berkeley, CA: University of California Press, 1994),

441–446; Clemmer, *Continuities*, 70–72; Geertz, *Invention*, 139–143, 261ff; Clemmer, *Roads*, 186–187; Richard O. Clemmer, "'Then Will You Rise and Strike My Head from My Neck': Hopi Prophecy and the Discourse of Empowerment," *American Indian Quarterly* 19, no. 1 (1995): 61–65.

12. Andrew Hermequaftewa, "The Hopi Way of Life Is the Way of Peace," in *Red Power: The American Indians' Fight for Freedom*, edited by Alvin M. Josephy, Jr. (New York, NY: McGraw-Hill, 1971), 41–51; Harry C. James, *Pages from Hopi History* (Tucson, AZ: University of Arizona Press, 1974), 102–105; Clemmer, *Continuities*, 83ff; Geertz, *Invention*, 143; Clemmer, *Roads*, 188–190; John Mohawk, "Hopi-Haudenosaunee: Sharing Prophetic Traditions," *Native Americas* 16, no. 3–4 (1999): 90–92.

13. Geertz, *Invention*, 143; Clemmer, *Roads*, 144ff, 191–192.

14. "The Hopi Stand," [1958?], UA/HTM, manuscript AZ 374; Clemmer, *Continuities*, 72, 83; Geertz, *Invention*, 143–146, 400–403; Clemmer, *Roads*, 192; Thomas E. Mails and Dan Evehema, *Hotevilla: Hopi Shrine of the Covenant—Microcosm of the World* (New York, NY: Marlowe and Company, 1995), 285–290.

15. "Indian League Elects," *New York Times*, June 25, 1956, 14; Edmond Wilson, *Apologies to the Iroquois* (New York, NY: Vintage Books, 1960), 137–168; Forbes, "New," 22; Rickard, *Fighting*, 138–152; Vine Deloria, Jr., *Behind the Trail of Broken Treaties: An Indian Declaration of Independence* (New York, NY: Delta Books, 1974), 20–21; Hauptman, *Iroquois Struggle*, 85ff.

16. "Tribe on Wrong Trail," *New York Times*, November 19, 1958, 39; Dan Katchongva, "Copy of Message Delivered to Albuquerque Indian Meeting," March 21, 1958, UA/HTM, manuscript AZ 374; Wilson, *Apologies*, 270–272; Deloria, *Custer*, 247; Forbes, "New," 22; Clemmer, *Continuities*, 84; Geertz, *Invention*, 147; Clemmer, *Roads*, 192; Jack Forbes, telephone conversation with author, April 1, 1998; Steven Crum, telephone conversation with author, June 2, 1998; Jack Forbes, letter to author, July 20, 1998.

17. "Indians Seize Control of Tribes, Set Up Own Regime in Canada," *New York Times*, March 6, 1959, 8; "One Hundred Indian Raiders Move in on Capital," *New York Times*, March 19, 1959, 35; "Chiefs Back Plan to Unite Indians," *New York Times*, April 2, 1959, 25; Lawrence Fellows, "Grim Omen Sinks in U.N. Channels," *New York Times*, May 6, 1959, 2; "Impasse Persists at U.N. on Friendly Warning of War," *New York Times*, May 8, 1959, 4; Wilson, *Apologies*, 260–264; Roy Bongartz, "Do These Indians Really Own Florida?" *Saturday Evening Post*, February 1, 1964, 62–65; Roy Bongartz, "The New Indian," *Esquire*, August 1970, 107–108; Forbes, "New," 22; Hauptman, *Iroquois Struggle*, 172, 207–208.

18. Sunbird, "Further to Report on Preliminary Eastern Seaboard Conference at Haverford College, Haverford, PA," April 8–11, 1961, NAA/AICC, collection MS 4806, box 2; "Board of Directors of the National Indian Youth Council," *Aborigine* 1, no. 1 (1961): iii; Karen Rickard, "Letter to the Editor," *Indian Voices*, April 1964, 12; Robert C. Day, "The Emergence of Activism as a Social Movement," in *Native Americans Today: Sociological Perspectives*, edited by Howard M. Bahr, Bruce A. Chadwick, and Robert C. Day (New York, NY: Harper and Row, 1972), 514–530; Forbes, "New," 22; Rickard, *Fighting*, xviii; Hauptman, *Iroquois Struggle*, 208–214; Robert K. Thomas, *The Indian Ecumenical Movement: A Grassroots Religious Movement*, lecture delivered at the Summer Public Lecture Series of the Vancouver School of Theology, July 21, 1986 (Vancouver, British

Columbia: Vancouver School of Theology, 1986), audiocassette; Robert Paul Brown, "'The Year One': The American Indian Chicago Conference of 1961 and the Rebirth of Indian Activism" (M.A. thesis, University of Wisconsin, Eau Claire, 1993), 23–24.

19. Thomas Banyacya, letter to M. Muller-Fricken, January 12, 1961, UA/HTM, manuscript AZ 374; "The Meeting at Shungopavy," May 6–7, 1961, UA/HTM, manuscript AZ 374; "Indian Chiefs Meet for Grand Council," *New York Times*, June 23, 1963, 13; Francis Le Quier, "Francis Le Quier (Ojibwa), Chairman, Committee for the Great Council Fire, 1963," in *The Indian in America's Past*, edited by Jack D. Forbes (Englewood Cliffs, NJ: Prentice-Hall, 1964), 72; "The Native American Movement, 1963," in *The Indian in America's Past*, edited by Jack D. Forbes (Englewood Cliffs, NJ: Prentice-Hall, 1964), 72; Clemmer, *Continuities*, 84; Forbes, July 20, 1998.

20. Deloria, *Custer*, 18, 113–114, 182, 246.

21. William Rickard, *Report of Land Grab Attempt on the Tuscarora Indian Reserve by the New York State Power Authority* (Niagara Falls, NY: Indian Defense League of America, 1959); William Rickard, letter to Anita de Frey, April 17, 1961, NAA/AICC, collection MS 4806, box 2; League of Nations Pan-American Indians, "Civil Rights and the Indians," *Indian Voices*, February–March 1966, 23–24; Deloria, *Custer*, 18; Rickard, *Fighting*, 154–156; Hauptman, *Iroquois Struggle*, 161–163, 177, 209–214.

22. Clifton Hill, "Traditional Indians More Active Than Ever," *Indian Voices*, Winter 1968, 3; American Friends Service Committee, *Uncommon Controversy: Fishing Rights of the Muckleshoot, Puyallup, and Nisqually Indians* (Seattle, WA: University of Washington Press, 1970), 108–113; James S. Olson and Raymond Wilson, *Native Americans in the Twentieth Century* (Urbana, IL: University of Illinois Press, 1984), 160; Hauptman, *Iroquois Struggle*, 214.

23. Hill, "Traditional," 3; Clifton Hill, "Creek Leader Issues Invitation to Meeting," *Indian Voices*, Winter 1968, 30–31; *The Great Law of Peace of the Longhouse People* (Mohawk Nation via Rooseveltown, NY: Akwesasne Notes, [1971?]); Harold Courlander, *The Fourth World of the Hopis* (New York, NY: Crown Publishers, 1971); *Traditional Teachings* (Cornwall Island, Ontario: North American Indian Travelling College, 1984), 17ff; John Mohawk, "Prologue," in *The White Roots of Peace* by Paul A. W. Wallace (Saranac Lake, NY: Chauncy Press, 1986), xv–xxiii.

24. Hill, "Traditional," 3; Hill, "Creek Leader Issues," 30–31.

25. "'Mad Bear' Anderson Leads California 'Unity' Trek," *Niagara Falls Gazette*, September 3, 1967, 1-C; Hill, "Traditional," 3; Hill, "Creek Leader Issues," 30–31; "Indian Travelling College No Longer Dream but Reality," *Akwesasne Notes* 1, no. 6 (1969); Deloria, *Custer*, 114, 246; Vine Deloria, Jr., "This Country Was a Lot Better Off When the Indians Were Running It," *New York Times Magazine*, March 8, 1970, 54; Hauptman, *Iroquois Struggle*, 216, 222; Doug Boyd, *Mad Bear: Spirit, Healing, and the Sacred in the Life of a Native American Medicine Man* (New York, NY: Simon and Schuster, 1994), 28, 31, 65.

26. Robert S. Ellwood, *The Sixties Spiritual Awakening: American Religion Moving from Modern to Postmodern* (New Brunswick, NJ: Rutgers University Press, 1994), 7–8.

27. Ellwood, *Sixties*, 331–336.

28. Stan Steiner, *The New Indians* (New York, NY: Dell Publishing Company, 1968), 168.

29. Clifton Hill, "Creek Leader Makes Policy Statement," *Indian Voices,* December 1965, 16–17; Steiner, *New,* 110–115; "Council Candidates," *Muscogee Nation News,* 1989; "Obituaries: Clifton F. Hill," *Muscogee Nation News,* December 1990, 11; Jean Chaudhuri and Richinda Sands, "Letter of Thanks," *Muscogee Nation News,* December 1990, 11.

30. Angie Debo, *And Still the Waters Run: The Betrayal of the Five Civilized Tribes* (Princeton, NJ: Princeton University Press, 1940), 63–65; "Creek Tribe Fights for Elected Tribal Government," *Indian Voices,* June 1965, 3–4; Hill, "Creek Leader Makes," 16–17; Steiner, *New,* 206; Clifton Hill, letter to Tribal Traditionalists, October 28, 1969, ACC/NMO, collection GS85–6, box 1, file 15.

31. "New Indian Language Program on the Air," *Indian Voices,* December 1966–January 1967, 19; Steiner, *New,* 5–6, 84, 92, 110–111; Vine Deloria, Jr., "Religion and Revolution among American Indians," *Worldview* 17, no. 1 (1974): 13.

32. Steiner, *New,* 111–115.

33. "First Cherokee Picket Line Surprises Village Guests," *Indian Voices,* Winter 1968, 13–15; Robert W. Buchanan, "Patterns of Organization and Leadership among Contemporary Oklahoma Cherokees" (Ph.D. dissertation, University of Kansas, 1972), 96; Albert L. Wahrhaftig and Jane Lukens-Wahrhaftig, "New Militants or Resurrected State? The Five County Northeastern Oklahoma Cherokee Organization," in *The Cherokee Indian Nation: A Troubled History,* edited by Duane H. King (Knoxville, TN: University of Tennessee Press, 1979), 238.

34. Hill, "Creek Leader Issues," 30–31; Clifton Hill, "A Petition to the Education for Mankind Conference," in "At the Fork in Our Trail" by Stand Middlestriker [Robert K. Thomas], [1977?], April 1968, 211–212, NIYC; Thomas Banyacya, "A Message to the Education for Mankind Conference," in "At the Fork in Our Trail" by Stand Middlestriker [Robert K. Thomas], [1977?], April 1968, 213–215, NIYC.

35. "Rolling Thunder Speaks," *Akwesasne Notes* 1, no. 6 (1969): 36–38; Deloria, *Custer,* 18, 114.

36. "George A. Thomas Dead at 57, Chief of Iroquois Confederacy," *New York Times,* October 24, 1968, 47; Charles Barney, "Pow-wow Planned by Disturbed Indians," *Syracuse Post-Standard,* January 6, 1969; William N. Fenton, "The Funeral of Tadodaho: Onondaga of Today," *Indian Historian,* Spring 1970, 43–47, 66; Hauptman, *Iroquois Struggle,* 216–217; Leon Shenandoah, "Foreword," in *White Roots of Peace: The Iroquois Book of Life* by Paul A. W. Wallace (Santa Fe, NM: Clear Light Publishers, 1994), 9–15; Doug George-Kanentiio, "Tadodaho," *News from Indian Country,* September 15, 1996, 18A; "Iroquois Gather to Remember Their Spiritual Leader," *Ojibwe News,* October 4, 1996, 2; "In Memoriam Leon Shenandoah: 'A Champion of Indian Rights,'" *Native Americas* 13, no. 2 (1996): 13.

37. Ernest Benedict, "Indians and a Treaty," in *The Only Good Indian: Essays by Canadian Indians,* edited by Waubageshig (Toronto, Ontario: New Press, 1970), 137–140; Hauptman, *Iroquois Struggle,* 148–149, 216.

38. "Conference of Indians Called by Area Band in Sequel to Dispute," *Akwesasne Notes* 1, no. 2 (1969); Barney, "Pow-wow"; "Western Hemisphere Meeting of Indians Called," *Akwesasne Notes* 1, no. 3 (1969): 14; Herbert G. Pelkey, "Iroquois Plan Big Meeting for Summer," *Akwesasne Notes* 3, no. 1 (1969); Hauptman, *Iroquois Struggle,* 216.

39. Barney, "Pow-wow"; "Plan to Attend!" 14.

40. Pelkey, "Iroquois"; Gene Goshorn, "Chief Shenandoah Opposes School Integration Proposal for Indians," *Syracuse Herald-Journal*, June 5, 1969; "Indian Unity Convention," 48; Hauptman, *Iroquois Struggle*, 218–221.

41. Russo, "Unity"; Michael O'Toole, "Indian Unity Weighed," *Syracuse Post-Standard*, August 22, 1969; "46 Indian Tribes Ask Hickel Ouster," *New York Times*, August 24, 1969, 87; Charles Russo, "Indians Find Theme Accord," *Syracuse Herald American*, August 24, 1969; Dick Macdonald, "Enforce Law Fairly–Indians," *Akwesasne Notes* 1, no. 8 (1969): 4.

42. Michael O'Toole, "Indians Issue Protest, End Council on Unity," *Syracuse Post-Standard*, August 25, 1969; Gerald Vizenor, "Thomas White Hawk," in *Crossbloods: Bone Courts, Bingo, and Other Reports* (Minneapolis, MN: University of Minnesota Press, 1990), 101–151.

43. O'Toole, "Indians"; "Indians Gather to Form Own Policy," 2; Leonard H. Prince, "Indians Protest Curb on Travel Freedom between U.S.-Canada," *Akwesasne Notes* 1, no. 8 (1969): 4.

44. "Indians Gather to Form Own Policy," 2; Prince, "Indians," 4; "St. Regis Is Paradise Says Oklahoma Indian," *Akwesasne Notes* 1, no. 8 (1969): 5; "Chiefs Gather in Longhouse: Hope to Improve Indian Life," *Akwesasne Notes* 1, no. 8 (1969): 6.

45. "Glenna Shilling," *Akwesasne Notes* 1, no. 8 (1969): 4.

46. Prince, "Indians," 4; "St. Regis Is Paradise Says Oklahoma Indian," 5; "Indians Plan Unity Ceremony," *Akwesasne Notes* 1, no. 8 (1969): 5.

47. Macdonald, "Enforce," 4; Bongartz, "New," 107–108, 125–126.

48. "Indian Unity Convention Special Issue," *Akwesasne Notes* 1, no. 8 (1969): 1, 4–6.

49. John Lawson, "Iroquois Leader Seeking Better Deal for Indians," *Akwesasne Notes* 1, no. 9 (1969); "White Roots of Peace," *Akwesasne Notes* 1, no. 9 (1969); Indians of All Tribes, "Indians of All Tribes Conference," in *Alcatraz Is Not an Island*, edited by Peter Blue Cloud (Berkeley, CA: Wingbow Press, 1972), 49–50; Troy R. Johnson, *The Occupation of Alcatraz Island: Indian Self-Determination and the Rise of Indian Activism* (Urbana, IL: University of Illinois Press, 1996), 40–41, 51; Dagmar Thorpe, "An Interview with Tommy Porter," in *People of the Seventh Fire*, edited by Dagmar Thorpe (Ithaca, NY: Akwekon Press, 1996), 38; Steve Talbot, "Indian Students and Reminiscences of Alcatraz," in *American Indian Activism: Alcatraz to the Longest Walk*, edited by Troy Johnson, Joane Nagel, and Duane Champagne (Urbana, IL: University of Illinois Press, 1997), 105–106; Luis S. Kemnitzer, "Personal Memories of Alcatraz, 1969," in *American Indian Activism: Alcatraz to the Longest Walk*, edited by Troy Johnson, Joane Nagel, and Duane Champagne (Urbana, IL: University of Illinois Press, 1997), 116–117.

50. "A Proposal for an Indian Ecumenical Conference Presented by the Institute for Indian Studies," [December? 1969], NAA/AICC, collection MS 4806, box 2.

CHAPTER 2

1. Stand Middlestriker [Robert K. Thomas], "At the Fork in Our Trail," [1977?], 79, NIYC; John A. MacKenzie, "A Legend in His Own Time: Some Initial Reflections on the Work of Robert K. Thomas," in *A Good Cherokee, A Good Anthropologist: Papers in Honor of Robert K. Thomas*, edited by Steve Pavlik (Los

Angeles, CA: American Indian Studies Center, University of California at Los Angeles, 1998), 219.

2. "A Proposal for an Indian Ecumenical Conference Presented by the Institute for Indian Studies," [December? 1969], 3–4, NAA/AICC, collection MS 4806, box 2; Robert K. Thomas, *The Indian Ecumenical Movement: A Grassroots Religious Movement*, lecture delivered at the Summer Public Lecture Series of the Vancouver School of Theology, July 21, 1986 (Vancouver, British Columbia: Vancouver School of Theology, 1986), audiocassette; Robert K. Thomas, *Getting to the Heart of the Matter: Collected Letters and Papers*, edited by Daphne J. Anderson (Vancouver, British Columbia: Native Ministries Consortium, Vancouver School of Theology, 1990), 14–15.

3. Middlestriker, "Fork," 78; Thomas, *Indian Ecumenical*; Thomas, *Getting*, 14–15, 105.

4. Middlestriker, "Fork," 65, 79; Thomas, *Indian Ecumenical*.

5. Middlestriker, "Fork," 65, 79, 94; Thomas, *Indian Ecumenical*.

6. Middlestriker, "Fork," 79.

7. Grant Foreman, *The Five Civilized Tribes* (Norman, OK: University of Oklahoma Press, 1934), 281–284, 291ff; Angie Debo, *And Still the Waters Run: The Betrayal of the Five Civilized Tribes* (Princeton, NJ: Princeton University Press, 1940), 379ff; Angie Debo, *The Five Civilized Tribes of Oklahoma: Report on Social and Economic Conditions* (Philadelphia, PA: Indian Rights Association, 1951), 1–3; Robert K. Thomas, "The Origin and Development of the Redbird Smith Movement" (M.A. thesis, University of Arizona, 1954), 71ff; Albert Wahrhaftig and Robert K. Thomas, "Redskins and Rednecks: The Myth of Cherokee Assimilation," in *Indian Education: Hearings before the Special Subcommittee on Indian Education of the U.S. Senate Committee on Labor and Public Welfare*, 90th Congress, 1st and 2nd sessions, part 2, February 19, 1968, Twin Oaks, [OK] (Washington, DC: USGPO, 1968), 894–895; Albert L. Wahrhaftig, "The Tribal Cherokee Population of Eastern Oklahoma," in *The Emergent Native Americans: A Reader in Culture Contact*, edited by Deward E. Walker, Jr. (Boston, MA: Little, Brown and Company, 1972), 220–224; Robert D. Cooter, "Individuals and Relatives," in *A Good Cherokee, A Good Anthropologist: Papers in Honor of Robert K. Thomas*, edited by Steve Pavlik (Los Angeles, CA: American Indian Studies Center, University of California at Los Angeles, 1998), 57–58.

8. Debo, *Five*, 3–4; Robert K. Thomas and Albert L. Wahrhaftig, "Indians, Hillbillies and the 'Education Problem,'" in *Anthropological Perspectives on Education*, edited by Murray L. Wax, Stanley Diamond, and Fred O. Gearing (New York, NY: Basic Books, 1971), 243–245; Anderson Dirthrower [Robert K. Thomas], "The White Man's Rule," in *Who Is the Chairman of This Meeting? A Collection of Essays*, edited by Ralph Osborne (Toronto, Ontario: Neewin Publishing Company, 1972), 26–27; Middlestriker, "Fork," 162; Robert K. Thomas, "Chapter III," 1–8, NIYC; Robert K. Thomas, "Community and Institution among Indian Groups," *Interculture* 17, no. 4 (1984): 9–11; Steve Pavlik, "In Memoriam to Robert Knox Thomas (1925–1991)," *Social Science Journal* 34, no. 4 (1997); Steve Pavlik, "Introduction," in *A Good Cherokee, A Good Anthropologist: Papers in Honor of Robert K. Thomas*, edited by Steve Pavlik (Los Angeles, CA: American Indian Studies Center, University of California at Los Angeles, 1998), xiv; Cooter, "Individuals," 57–79.

9. Robert K. Thomas, letter to Magowan, May 27, 1971, DL; Anderson
    Dirthrower [Robert K. Thomas], "Nationalism," in *Who Is the Chairman of This
    Meeting? A Collection of Essays,* edited by Ralph Osborne (Toronto, Ontario:
    Neewin Publishing Company, 1972), 83; Middlestriker, "Fork," 15–17;
    Thomas, "Chapter III," 3–11; Thomas, "Community," 10; Pavlik, "Memo-
    riam"; Cooter, "Individuals," 64, 70–71.

10. Robert K. Thomas, "The Role of the Church in Indian Adjustment," *Kansas
    Journal of Sociology* 3, no. 1 (1967): 23; Middlestriker, "Fork," 69–74, 152;
    Thomas, "Chapter III," 11; Thomas, "Community," 10; Cooter, "Individuals,"
    63–64, 71–72.

11. Dirthrower, "White," 26–28; Middlestriker, "Fork," 103–106; Thomas, "Chap-
    ter III," 12–13; Thomas, "Community," 10; Cooter, "Individuals," 61, 74.

12. Dirthrower, "White," 28–33.

13. Thomas, "Origin," 4–7; Anderson Dirthrower [Robert K. Thomas], "The
    Prophecy," in *Who Is the Chairman of This Meeting? A Collection of Essays,* edited
    by Ralph Osborne (Toronto, Ontario: Neewin Publishing Company, 1972),
    34–35; Middlestriker, "Fork," 115–116; Thomas, *Getting,* 117.

14. Dirthrower, "Nationalism," 86–90; Middlestriker, "Fork," 62, 71; Thomas,
    "Chapter III," 16–18; Pavlik, "Memoriam"; Pavlik, "Introduction," xv; Cooter,
    "Individuals," 75–79; Jim Griffith, "Another Aspect of an Old Friend: Robert K.
    Thomas as Hillbilly," in *A Good Cherokee, A Good Anthropologist: Papers in Honor
    of Robert K. Thomas,* edited by Steve Pavlik (Los Angeles, CA: American Indian
    Studies Center, University of California at Los Angeles, 1998), 342.

15. Dirthrower, "Nationalism," 86–88; Middlestriker, "Fork," 74; Robert K.
    Thomas, "Afterword," in *The New Peoples: Being and Becoming Metis in North
    America,* edited by Jacqueline Peterson and Jennifer S. H. Brown (Winnipeg,
    Manitoba: University of Manitoba Press, 1985), 243–244.

16. Middlestriker, "Fork," 58; Pavlik, "Memoriam."

17. Thomas, "Role of the Church (1967)," 22–24; Middlestriker, "Fork," 74–75.

18. Robert K. Thomas, "Papago Land Use: West of the Papago Indian Reservation,
    South of the Gila River, and the Problem of Sand Papago Identity," in *Ethnology
    of the Indians of Northwest Mexico,* Spanish Borderlands Sourcebooks, Vol. 6, ed-
    ited by Randall H. McGuire (New York, NY: Garland Publishing, 1992), 1–7,
    41; Middlestriker, "Fork," 74.

19. Middlestriker, "Fork," 57–58; Griffith, "Another," 335–345.

20. Murray L. Wax, "Old Man Coyote: The Anthropologist as Trickster, Buffoon,
    Wise Man," in *A Good Cherokee, A Good Anthropologist: Papers in Honor of Robert
    K. Thomas,* edited by Steve Pavlik (Los Angeles, CA: American Indian Studies
    Center, University of California at Los Angeles, 1998), 17–19; Cooter, "Individ-
    uals," 58–59, 79; Raymond D. Fogelson, "Bringing Home the Fire: Bob
    Thomas and Cherokee Studies," in *A Good Cherokee, A Good Anthropologist: Pa-
    pers in Honor of Robert K. Thomas,* edited by Steve Pavlik (Los Angeles, CA:
    American Indian Studies Center, University of California at Los Angeles, 1998),
    105–106.

21. Dirthrower, "Nationalism," 90; Middlestriker, "Fork," 48, 58; Thomas,
    "Community," 10; Thomas, *Getting,* 13; Pavlik, "Introduction," xv; Albert L.
    Wahrhaftig, "Robert K. Thomas and the Monteith Theory," in *A Good
    Cherokee, A Good Anthropologist: Papers in Honor of Robert K. Thomas,* edited by
    Steve Pavlik (Los Angeles, CA: American Indian Studies Center, University

of California at Los Angeles, 1998), 10; Vine Deloria, Jr., "Bob Thomas as Colleague," in *A Good Cherokee, A Good Anthropologist: Papers in Honor of Robert K. Thomas*, edited by Steve Pavlik (Los Angeles, CA: American Indian Studies Center, University of California at Los Angeles, 1998), 35; Cooter, "Individuals," 64, 77; Fogelson, "Bringing," 108; Kenneth Fink, "Riding Behind with a Pillow Strapped On," in *A Good Cherokee, A Good Anthropologist: Papers in Honor of Robert K. Thomas*, edited by Steve Pavlik (Los Angeles, CA: American Indian Studies Center, University of California at Los Angeles, 1998), 119.

22. Thomas, "Origin," 3–7; Thomas, "Afterword," 244; Pavlik, "Memoriam"; Albert L. Wahrhaftig, "Looking Back to Tahlequah: Robert K. Thomas' Role among the Oklahoma Cherokee, 1963–1967," in *A Good Cherokee, A Good Anthropologist: Papers in Honor of Robert K. Thomas*, edited by Steve Pavlik (Los Angeles, CA: American Indian Studies Center, University of California at Los Angeles, 1998), 100.

23. Thomas, "Origin," 10, 26, 34–39, 59–61, 69–70, 87–90, 113, 118–119, 135–142, 153; Robert K. Thomas, "The Redbird Smith Movement," in *Symposium on Cherokee and Iroquois Culture*, Bureau of American Ethnology Bulletin 180, edited by William N. Fenton and John Gulick (Washington, DC: Smithsonian Institution, 1961), 161–165.

24. Thomas, "Origin," 4–8; Pavlik, "Introduction," xv.

25. Sol Tax, *The North American Indians: 1950 Distribution of Descendants of the Aboriginal Population of Alaska, Canada and the United States*, 4th ed. (Chicago, IL: Department of Anthropology, University of Chicago, 1960); Robert K. Thomas, "Pan-Indianism," *Midcontinent American Studies Journal* 6, no. 2 (1965): 75; Robert K. Thomas, "Howdy Folks!" *Indian Voices*, August 1966, 1; Vine Deloria, Jr., *Custer Died for Your Sins: An Indian Manifesto* (New York, NY: Macmillan, 1969), 82–85; Beatrice Medicine and Robert Thomas, "A Conversation with Bea Medicine and Robert Thomas," in *Educating the Educators: A Report of the Institute on "The American Indian Student in Higher Education,"* edited by Roy H. Sandstrom (Canton, NY: St. Lawrence University, 1971), 64; Middlestriker, "Fork," 77–78; Robert Thomas, "Farewell to a Chief," *Americans Before Columbus* 18, no. 2 (1990): 3; Pavlik, "Memoriam"; Pavlik, "Introduction," xv; Samuel Stanley, "Staying the Course: Action and Reflection in the Career of Robert K. Thomas," in *A Good Cherokee, A Good Anthropologist: Papers in Honor of Robert K. Thomas*, edited by Steve Pavlik (Los Angeles, CA: American Indian Studies Center, University of California at Los Angeles, 1998), 3, 6; Wax, "Old," 22; Fogelson, "Bringing," 107; Peter Iverson, *"We Are Still Here": American Indians in the Twentieth Century* (Wheeling, IL: Harlan Davidson, 1998), 135–136.

26. Rosalie H. Wax and Robert K. Thomas, "American Indians and White People," *Phylon: The Atlanta University Review of Race and Culture* 22, no. 4 (1961): 316; John Gulick, *Cherokees at the Crossroads*, 2nd ed., edited by Sharlotte Neely Williams (Chapel Hill, NC: Institute for Research in Social Science, University of North Carolina, 1973), 197–208; Fogelson, "Bringing," 106–107.

27. Robert K. Thomas, "Report on Cherokee Social and Community Organization," February 1958, UNC/NC, call number Cp970.03 T461r; Robert K. Thomas, "The Present 'Problem' of the Eastern Cherokees," June 1958, UNC/NC, call number Cp970.03 T461p1; Robert K. Thomas, "Eastern

Cherokee Acculturation," October 1958, UNC/NC, call number Cp970.03 T461e; Robert K. Thomas, "Culture History of the Eastern Cherokee," October 1958, UNC/NC, call number Cp970.03 T461c1; Robert K. Thomas, "Cherokee Values and World View," November 1958, UNC/NC, call number Cp970.03 T461c; Wax, "Old," 17.

28. Pavlik, "Introduction," xv; Wahrhaftig, "Robert," 13–15; Wax, "Old," 22–23; Otto Feinstein, "From Experience to Theory, from Theory to Experience: Robert K. Thomas and the Tradition of Book VII of Plato's Republic," in *A Good Cherokee, A Good Anthropologist: Papers in Honor of Robert K. Thomas*, edited by Steve Pavlik (Los Angeles, CA: American Indian Studies Center, University of California at Los Angeles, 1998), 261–273; Rolland H. (Bud) Wright, "Experience as Narrative, Culture, and Person," in *A Good Cherokee, A Good Anthropologist: Papers in Honor of Robert K. Thomas*, edited by Steve Pavlik (Los Angeles, CA: American Indian Studies Center, University of California at Los Angeles, 1998), 327–328.

29. American Indian Chicago Conference, "Declaration of Indian Purpose," in *New Directions in Indian Purpose: Reflections on the American Indian Chicago Conference*, edited by Terry Straus (Chicago, IL: Native American Educational Services, 1988), 7; Robert K. Thomas, "Howdy Folks!" *Indian Voices*, April 1, 1963, 1; Robert K. Thomas, letter to Sol Tax, April 22, 1963, MHS/AICC; Robert K. Thomas, "Howdy Folks!" *Indian Voices*, December 1964, 1; Shirley Hill Witt, "Nationalistic Trends among American Indians," in *The American Indian Today*, edited by Stuart Levine and Nancy Oestreich Lurie (Baltimore, MD: Penguin Books, 1968), 112; Sol Tax and Robert K. Thomas, "An Experiment in Cross-Cultural Education, 1962–1967: Report of the University of Chicago," in *Indian Education: Hearings before the Special Subcommittee on Indian Education of the U.S. Senate Committee on Labor and Public Welfare*, 90th Congress, 1st and 2nd sessions, part 2, February 19, 1968, Twin Oaks, [OK] (Washington, DC: USGPO, 1968), 946; Pavlik, "Introduction," xv–xvi; Wahrhaftig, "Looking," 94.

30. Wax, "Old," 23–24.

31. Thomas, "Howdy Folks! (April 1, 1963)," 1; Thomas, April 22, 1963; Tax and Thomas, "Experiment," 940–943; Thomas, *Getting*, 105; Wax, "Old," 21.

32. Albert Wahrhaftig, "Community and the Caretakers," *New University Thought* 4, no. 4 (1966–67): 66–74; Tax and Thomas, "Experiment," 940–948; Wahrhaftig, "Looking," 95–97.

33. Wahrhaftig, "Community," 66–74; Tax and Thomas, "Experiment," 940–948; Robert W. Buchanan, "Patterns of Organization and Leadership among Contemporary Oklahoma Cherokees" (Ph.D. dissertation, University of Kansas, 1972), 65–70; Wax, "Old," 19; Wahrhaftig, "Looking," 95–97.

34. Robert K. Thomas, "Howdy Folks!" *Indian Voices*, September 1964, 1–2; Albert L. Wahrhaftig, *The Cherokee People Today*, translated by Calvin Nackedhead (Tahlequah, OK: Carnegie Corporation Cross-Cultural Education Project, 1966); Tax and Thomas, "Experiment," 945–949; Wahrhaftig, "Looking," 97–98.

35. Robert K. Thomas, "Howdy Folks!" *Indian Voices*, February 1965, 1; Robert K. Thomas, "Howdy Folks!" *Indian Voices*, August 1965, 1–2; Albert Wahrhaftig, "An Anti-Poverty Exploration Project: A Suggestion for Non-Reservation Indian Communities," *Journal of American Indian Education* 5, no. 1 (1965); Wahrhaftig, "Community," 54–55; Tax and Thomas, "Experiment," 947–948.

36. Dirthrower, "Prophecy," 34–38; Middlestriker, "Fork," 115–117; Thomas, *Getting*, 117.

37. Robert K. Thomas, "Cross-Cultural Cannibalism," *New University Thought* 7, no. 3 (1971): 7–11; Thomas, *Getting*, 13–14, 76–77; Wahrhaftig, "Looking," 101–102.

38. Thomas, "Howdy Folks! (February 1965)," 1; Thomas, "Pan-Indianism," 75, 81–82 ; Tax and Thomas, "Experiment," 946.

39. Thomas and Wahrhaftig, "Indians," 230–233, 249–250.

40. "A Statement of Purpose," *New University Thought* 4, no. 3 (1966): 81; Robert K. Thomas, "Colonialism: Classic and Internal," *New University Thought* 4, no. 4 (1966–67): 37–42; Robert K. Thomas, "Powerless Politics," *New University Thought* 4, no. 4 (1966–67): 45, 51–53; Deloria, "Bob," 30–31.

41. Thomas, "Colonialism," 37–42; Thomas, "Powerless," 45, 51–53.

42. Tax and Thomas, "Experiment," 950; Buchanan, "Patterns," 70–71; Wahrhaftig, "Looking," 99–102.

43. Harry Wilensky, "Cherokee Group on Hunting Laws Warpath over Oklahoma," *Indian Voices*, August 1966, 26–27; "Furor in Eastern Oklahoma," *Indian Voices*, August 1966, 7; Tax and Thomas, "Experiment," 949–950; Stan Steiner, *The New Indians* (New York, NY: Dell Publishing Company, 1968), 1–16; Albert L. Wahrhaftig and Robert K. Thomas, "Renaissance and Repression: The Oklahoma Cherokee," *Trans-action* 6, no. 4 (1969): 46–47; Murray L. Wax, *Indian Americans: Unity and Diversity* (Englewood Cliffs, NJ: Prentice-Hall, 1971), 128–130; Rosalie Wax, H., *Doing Fieldwork: Warnings and Advice* (Chicago, IL: University of Chicago Press, 1971), 301–302, 333–339; Buchanan, "Patterns," 70–78; Peter Collier, *When Shall They Rest? The Cherokees' Long Struggle with America* (New York, NY: Holt, Rinehart and Winston, 1973), 141–144; Albert L. Wahrhaftig and Jane Lukens-Wahrhaftig, "New Militants or Resurrected State? The Five County Northeastern Oklahoma Cherokee Organization," in *The Cherokee Indian Nation: A Troubled History*, edited by Duane H. King (Knoxville, TN: University of Tennessee Press, 1979), 230–237; Wahrhaftig, "Looking," 97–98.

44. Wilensky, "Cherokee," 26–27; "Furor in Eastern Oklahoma," 7; Tax and Thomas, "Experiment," 949–950; Steiner, *New*, 1–16; Wahrhaftig and Thomas, "Renaissance," 46–47; Wax, *Indian*, 128–130; Wax, *Doing*, 301–302, 333–339; Buchanan, "Patterns," 70–78; Collier, *When*, 141–144; Wahrhaftig and Lukens-Wahrhaftig, "New," 230–237.

45. "Cherokee Advocate to Be Revived," *Indian Voices*, December 1966-January 1967, 6; "First Cherokee Picket Line Surprises Village Guests," *Indian Voices*, Winter 1968, 13–15; Tax and Thomas, "Experiment," 949–950; Deloria, *Custer*, 18; Buchanan, "Patterns," 78–97; Wahrhaftig and Lukens-Wahrhaftig, "New," 237–240; Kenneth Fink, "A. Dreadfulwater: In Memoriam," *Interculture* 17, no. 4 (1984): 25.

46. Thomas, "Howdy Folks! (August 1966)," 1; Tax and Thomas, "Experiment," 950.

47. Middlestriker, "Fork," 76–77; Thomas, *Getting*, 14.

48. Middlestriker, "Fork," 76.

49. Thomas, "Origin," 88–93, 153, 206–208; Thomas, "Role of the Church (1967)," 23; Tax and Thomas, "Experiment," 947, 950–951; Andrew Dreadfulwater and Kenneth Fink, "The Dreadfulwater-Cherokee Education Project,"

[1973?], 4–7, NAA/CSM, series 8—American Indians General, box 51; Albert L. Wahrhaftig and Jane Lukens-Wahrhaftig, "The Thrice Powerless: Cherokee Indians in Oklahoma," in *The Anthropology of Power: Ethnographic Studies from Asia, Oceania, and the New World*, edited by Raymond D. Fogelson and Richard N. Adams (New York, NY: Academic Press, 1977), 226; Wahrhaftig and Lukens-Wahrhaftig, "New," 238; Kenneth Fink, telephone conversation with author, April 13, 1992; Tom Holm, "Politics Came First: A Reflection on Robert K. Thomas and Cherokee History," in *A Good Cherokee, A Good Anthropologist: Papers in Honor of Robert K. Thomas*, edited by Steve Pavlik (Los Angeles, CA: American Indian Studies Center, University of California at Los Angeles, 1998), 44.

50. Mary R. Sawyer, *Black Ecumenism: Implementing the Demands of Justice* (Valley Forge, PA: Trinity Press International, 1994), 8, 176.

51. Sawyer, *Black*, 55, 65, 108–109; Ian MacKenzie, telephone conversation with author, June 18, 1992.

52. "Canadian Indian Workshop," *Indian Voices*, April–May 1966, 23; "A Proposal for an Indian Ecumenical Conference Presented by the Institute for Indian Studies," 1; John A. MacKenzie, "Robert K. Thomas's Contributions to the Native People of Canada," paper presented at the annual meeting of the Western Social Science Association, Oakland, CA, April 29, 1995, JT; MacKenzie, "Legend," 217–219; Carol Nadjiwon, "Dr. Robert K. Thomas: A Cherokee War Chief in Modern Times," in *A Good Cherokee, A Good Anthropologist: Papers in Honor of Robert K. Thomas*, edited by Steve Pavlik (Los Angeles, CA: American Indian Studies Center, University of California at Los Angeles, 1998), 227–229.

53. "A Proposal for an Indian Ecumenical Conference Presented by the Institute for Indian Studies," 2–4; Robert K. Thomas, letter to Walter Redsky, November 19, 1970, ACC/NMO, collection GS85–6, box 1, file 16; Thomas, *Indian Ecumenical*; MacKenzie, "Legend," 219–222.

CHAPTER 3

1. *Journal of Proceedings of the 24th Session of the General Synod* (Toronto, Ontario: Anglican Church of Canada, 1969), 34; "Ottawa Paving Way for Violence," *Akwesasne Notes* 1, no. 8 (1969); Bill Portman, "Indian Leader Raps Ottawa's Proposals," *Canadian Churchman* 96, no. 8 (1969): 10; Dave Courchene, "Address to General Synod," in *Bulletin 201: Recent Statements by the Indians of Canada, General Synod Action 1969, Some Government Responses, Suggested Resource*, edited by Robert D. MacRae (Toronto, Ontario: Anglican Church of Canada, 1970), 8, 12; James Burke, *Paper Tomahawks: From Red Tape to Red Power* (Winnipeg, Manitoba: Queenston House Publishing, 1976), 5, 50ff.

2. Courchene, "Address," 8.

3. Courchene, "Address," 9–11.

4. Courchene, "Address," 11–14.

5. Ernest Willie, "Address to General Synod," in *Bulletin 201: Recent Statements by the Indians of Canada, General Synod Action 1969, Some Government Responses, Suggested Resource*, edited by Robert D. MacRae (Toronto, Ontario: Anglican Church of Canada, 1970), 19; *Journal of Proceedings of the 24th Session of the General Synod*, 34; Portman, "Indian Leader"; "Beaten Race Needs Friend in Church," *Canadian Churchman* 96, no. 8 (1969): 10.

6. Charles E. Hendry, *Beyond Traplines: Does the Church Really Care? Towards an Assessment of the Work of the Anglican Church of Canada with Canada's Native Peoples* (Toronto, Ontario: Ryerson Press, 1969), 71ff, 91–92; "The Hendry Report," *Canadian Churchman* 96, no. 5 (1969): 1; Willie, "Address," 19.

7. Alanis Obomsawin, "Commentary," in *Bulletin 201: Recent Statements by the Indians of Canada, General Synod Action 1969, Some Government Responses, Suggested Resource*, edited by Robert D. MacRae (Toronto, Ontario: Anglican Church of Canada, 1970), 16–17; *Journal of Proceedings of the 24th Session of the General Synod*, 34; "Anglicans Back Indian Fight for Better Deal," *Akwesasne Notes* 1, no. 8 (1969); Francie Miller, "'They Listened Today' Singer Says of Synod," *Canadian Churchman* 96, no. 8 (1969): 10.

8. Linda Bohnen, "Fear and Guilty Conscience of the Structured Church," *Akwesasne Notes* 1, no. 8 (1969); Shirley Bruton, "A Time to Care," *Canadian Churchman* 97, no. 3 (1970): 16.

9. Philip Carrington, *The Anglican Church in Canada: A History* (Toronto, Ontario: Collins, 1963), 29–31, 41–44; Hendry, *Beyond Traplines (1969)*, 41; Henry Warner Bowden, *American Indians and Christian Missions: Studies in Cultural Conflict* (Chicago, IL: University of Chicago Press, 1981), 135–136; John Webster Grant, *Moon of Wintertime: Missionaries and the Indians of Canada in Encounter Since 1534* (Toronto, Ontario: University of Toronto Press, 1984), 66, 71; Williston Walker, Richard A. Norris, David W. Lotz, and Robert T. Handy, *A History of the Christian Church*, 4th ed. (New York, NY: Charles Scribner's Sons, 1985), 574.

10. Carrington, *Anglican*, 36ff, 68–69; John Melling, *Right to a Future: The Native Peoples of Canada* ([Toronto, Ontario]: Anglican Church of Canada and United Church of Canada, 1967), 15–16; Hendry, *Beyond Traplines (1969)*, 41; Grant, *Moon*, 3, 66ff, 82; Walker and others, *History*, 578–579, 596ff, 611–614; Janet Hodgson and Jay Kothare, *Vision Quest: Native Spirituality and the Church in Canada* (Toronto, Ontario: Anglican Book Centre, 1990), 44; John Bird, Laverne Jacobs, Terry Thompson, and Doug Tindal, *A Brief Prepared by the Anglican Church of Canada for Submission to the Royal Commission on Aboriginal Peoples at a Special Consultation between the Members of the Commission and Representatives of the Historic Mission Churches, Citadel Hotel, Ottawa, ON, November 8–9, 1993* (Toronto, Ontario: Anglican Church of Canada, 1993), 2.

11. Carrington, *Anglican*, 69–71, 84–85; Melling, *Right*, 16–18; Grant, *Moon*, 97–100; Robert Coutts, "Anglican Missionaries as Agents of Acculturation: The Church Missionary Society at St. Andrew's, Red River, 1830–1870," in *The Anglican Church and the World of Western Canada, 1820–1970*, edited by Barry Ferguson (Regina, Saskatchewan: Canadian Plains Research Center, University of Regina, 1991), 50–54; Bird and others, *Brief*, 2–4, Appendix 1.

12. Coutts, "Anglican," 54; Olive Patricia Dickason, *Canada's First Nations: A History of Founding Peoples from Earliest Times* (Norman, OK: University of Oklahoma Press, 1992), 225–240; Norman Andrew Gull, "The 'Indian Policy' of the Anglican Church of Canada from 1945 to the 1970s" (M.A. thesis, Trent University, 1992), 6–8; Bird and others, *Brief*, 4.

13. Carrington, *Anglican*, 162; Gull, "Indian," 8–9; Bird and others, *Brief*, 3–4, Appendix 1.

14. Carrington, *Anglican*, 199–204, 260; Grant, *Moon*, 191–198; H. R. S. Ryan, "The General Synod of the Anglican Church of Canada: Aspects of Constitu-

tional History," *Journal of the Canadian Church Historical Society* 34, no. 1 (1992): 51–56; Gull, "Indian," 9–20, 126; Bird and others, *Brief*, 4–6, Appendix 1.

15. Carrington, *Anglican*, 70, 74, 97–99, 107, 184, 305; Hendry, *Beyond Traplines (1969)*, 41; Grant, *Moon*, 88, 109, 115, 118, 148, 171, 174; Hodgson and Kothare, *Vision*, 63–67; Bird and others, *Brief*, 2, Appendix 1.

16. Carrington, *Anglican*, 100; Edward Ahenakew, "The Story of the Ahenakews," edited by Ruth Matheson Buck, *Saskatchewan History* 17, no. 1 (1964): 12–20; Ruth Matheson Buck, "Introduction," in *Voices of the Plains Cree* by Edward Ahenakew, edited by Ruth Matheson Buck (Toronto, Ontario: McClelland and Stewart, 1973), 12–14; Maria Campbell, *Halfbreed* (New York, NY: Saturday Review Press, 1973), 32; Stan Cuthand, "Introduction to the 1995 Edition," in *Voices of the Plains Cree* by Edward Ahenakew, rev. ed., edited by Ruth M. Buck (Regina, Saskatchewan: Canadian Plains Research Center, University of Regina, 1995), x.

17. Ahenakew, "Story," 12–14; Edward Ahenakew, "Little Pine: An Indian Day School," edited by Ruth Matheson Buck, *Saskatchewan History* 18, no. 2 (1965): 55ff; Edward Ahenakew, *Voices of the Plains Cree*, edited by Ruth M. Buck (Toronto, Ontario: McClelland and Stewart, 1973), 130–135; Buck, "Introduction," 14, 17–18; Cuthand, "Introduction," x–xi.

18. Ahenakew, "Story," 14; Ahenakew, "Little," 55–62; Ahenakew, *Voices*, 122–124, 186; Buck, "Introduction," 14–15, 17–18; Stan Cuthand, "The Native Peoples of the Prairie Provinces in the 1920s and 1930s," in *One Century Later: Western Canadian Reserve Indians Since Treaty* 7, edited by Ian A. L. Getty and Donald B. Smith (Vancouver, British Columbia: University of British Columbia Press, 1977), 32–33; Peter Kulchyski, "'A Considerable Unrest': F. O. Loft and the League of Indians," *Native Studies Review* 4, no. 1–2 (1988): 100; J. R. Miller, *Skyscrapers Hide the Heavens: A History of Indian-White Relations in Canada*, rev. ed. (Toronto, Ontario: University of Toronto Press, 1991), 217–218; Dickason, *Canada's First*, 328; Cuthand, "Introduction," xi–xii.

19. Ahenakew, "Story," 14, 22–23; Ahenakew, *Voices*, 23–26ff.

20. Edward Ahenakew, "Cree Trickster Tales," *Journal of American Folklore* 42, no. 166 (1929): 309ff; Ahenakew, *Voices*, 72; Buck, "Introduction," 10–16; Cuthand, "Introduction," xii–xiii.

21. Ahenakew, *Voices*, 75–76, 103, 186; Buck, "Introduction," 13–14, 16, 20; Cuthand, "Introduction," xiii–xiv.

22. Carrington, *Anglican*, 255; Ahenakew, "Story," 14; Ahenakew, "Little," 58; Ahenakew, *Voices*, 92–102, 136–145; Buck, "Introduction," 18–19; Cuthand, "Introduction," xi, xv–xvii.

23. "Given Task of Recruiting for Mission Field," *Canadian Churchman* 89, no. 4 (1962): 2; Carrington, *Anglican*, 270; Ahenakew, "Story," 14–15; Buck, "Introduction," 19–20; Cuthand, "Introduction," xvii–xx.

24. Ahenakew, *Voices*, 157, 189.

25. Melling, *Right*, 35, 44–48; Hendry, *Beyond Traplines (1969)*, 41–42; Grant, *Moon*, 232–233; Dickason, *Canada's First*, 273–275, 377–378; Gull, "Indian," 19–20.

26. Gull, "Indian," 20–34, 40–44; Bird and others, *Brief*, 5–6, Appendix 1.

27. Gull, "Indian," 20–34, 40–44.

28. Miller, *Skyscrapers*, 220–222; Dickason, *Canada's First*, 328–329; Gull, "Indian," 32–40, 44–55; Bird and others, *Brief*, 6, Appendix 1.

29. Carrington, *Anglican*, 282–283, 292–293; Gull, "Indian," 56–71; Bird and others, *Brief*, 6, Appendix 1.

30. Carrington, *Anglican*, 282–283, 292–293; Dickason, *Canada's First*, 328–329; Gull, "Indian," 56–71; Bird and others, *Brief*, 6, Appendix 1.

31. Carrington, *Anglican*, 290; Ian MacKenzie, *Native Rights and the Church: An Historical and Political Analysis*, lecture delivered at the Summer Public Lecture Series of the Vancouver School of Theology, July 23, 1986 (Vancouver, British Columbia: Vancouver School of Theology, 1986), audiocassette; Dickason, *Canada's First*, 324, 328–333; Gull, "Indian," 71–82; Bird and others, *Brief*, 6, Appendix 1; Peter Hamel and Catherine Morrison, *Anglican Church of Canada Policy Relating to Aboriginal Peoples, 1959–1998*, 3rd ed. (Toronto, Ontario: Anglican Church of Canada, 1998), 1.

32. Carrington, *Anglican*, 250–251; Melling, *Right*, 80–82, 104–114; R. D. MacRae, "Suggestions Concerning Anglican Church Participation in Community Development among Native Canadians," April 19, 1968, 1, ACC/PC, collection GS76–11, box 2; Edward Pulker, *We Stand on Their Shoulders: The Growth of Social Concern in Canadian Anglicanism* (Toronto, Ontario: Anglican Book Centre, 1986), 172–173, 177; Gull, "Indian," 82–87; Hamel and Morrison, *Anglican*, 1–2.

33. "Unified Plan Proposed for Indian Work in James Bay Watershed," *Canadian Churchman* 90, no. 11 (1963): 1; D. A. Ellis, "Ungava Eskimos Caught in Political Switch," *Canadian Churchman* 91, no. 5 (1964): 1, 9; "Eskimos Have Rights," *Canadian Churchman* 91, no. 5 (1964): 4; Gerald Waring, "Canada's Crisis in Eskimoland," *Canadian Churchman* 91, no. 5 (1964): 9; M. A. Stephens, "Moose Pasture or Integration?" *Canadian Churchman* 91, no. 10 (1964): 19; Maurice Western, "Ungava Eskimos Policy Statement Welcomed," *Canadian Churchman* 92, no. 8 (1965): 5, 18; Maurice Western, "The Indian Situation Studied," *Canadian Churchman* 93, no. 2 (1966): 5; Melling, *Right*, 80–81; MacKenzie, *Native*.

34. Department of Christian Social Service, *The Church in the Modern World: Our Social Responsibility in the Light of Rapidly Changing Patterns of Society* (Toronto, Ontario: Anglican Church of Canada, 1965), 4, 16; Edward W. Scott, "A Position Paper Concerning the Stance of the Anglican Church to Indian Work, Prepared for Discussion Purposes, May 9, 1966," in *Beyond Traplines: Does the Church Really Care? Towards an Assessment of the Work of the Anglican Church of Canada with Canada's Native Peoples* by Charles E. Hendry (Toronto, Ontario: Ryerson Press, 1969), 98–100; Pulker, *We*, 173–176; MacKenzie, *Native*; Gull, "Indian," 63, 91; Hamel and Morrison, *Anglican*, 2.

35. Melling, *Right*, iii, v.

36. Melling, *Right*, ix-x, 3–8, 40, 77, 104ff, 138–140.

37. "Valuable Island Centennial Gift by Caughnawaga," *Indian Voices*, June 1966, 7; Melling, *Right*, ix; "Tepee Presents Uncomfortable Point-of-View," *Canadian Churchman* 94, no. 6 (1967): 9; Jay Walz, "Canadian Indians' Expo Exhibit Indicts White Man," *New York Times*, July 16, 1967, 25; William Bothwell, "Pavilion Impressed Sceptics," *Canadian Churchman* 94, no. 11 (1967): 1; Dickason, *Canada's First*, 358, 383; Peter McFarlane, *Brotherhood to Nationhood: George Manuel and the Making of the Modern Indian Movement* (Toronto, Ontario: Between the Lines, 1993), 89–90; Jeffrey Stanton, *Expo 67—Montreal World's Fair* (July 23, 1997), cited July 14, 1999, available from http://naid.sppsr.ucla.edu/expo67/.

38. Joint Interdepartmental Committee on Indian/Eskimo Affairs, "A Centennial Profile of Indian and Eskimo Canadians," in *Journal of Proceedings of the 23rd*

Session of the General Synod, edited by Anglican Church of Canada (Toronto, Ontario: Anglican Church of Canada, 1967), 327–332; "No Indians on Native Committee," *Canadian Churchman* 94, no. 8 (1967): 2; Grant, *Moon*, 207; Hamel and Morrison, *Anglican*, 3.

39. W. G. Portman, "New Anglican Policy Set," *Canadian Churchman* 94, no. 11 (1967): 13; Gull, "Indian," 86–91; Gordon Beardy, "Foreword," in *Beyond Traplines: Does the Church Really Care? Towards an Assessment of the Work of the Anglican Church of Canada with Canada's Native People* by Charles E. Hendry, rev. ed. (Toronto, Ontario: Anglican Book Centre, 1998), vii–viii.

40. W. G. Portman, "Indian Centennial: What to Celebrate?" *Canadian Churchman* 94, no. 11 (1967): 1, 7; Maurice Western, "Winds of Change in Department Bring Action," *Canadian Churchman* 94, no. 11 (1967): 7; Portman, "New," 13; Hendry, *Beyond Traplines (1969)*, 83.

41. MacRae, "Suggestions," 5–10; R. D. MacRae, memorandum to George Davey, April 29, 1968, ACC/PC, collection GS76–11, box 2; R. D. MacRae, memorandum to T. D. Somerville, May 13, 1968, ACC/PC, collection GS76–11, box 2; Pulker, *We*, 174.

42. "Report First Step in Indian Program," *Canadian Churchman* 96, no. 5 (1969): 3; "Man Who Challenged Church to Change Is United Layman," *Canadian Churchman* 96, no. 5 (1969): 6; Hendry, *Beyond Traplines (1969)*, ix–x, 53–56.

43. Audrey Paterson, "Notes of a Meeting to Discuss the Proposal for a Consultant in Community Development," March 3, 1969, 1–2, ACC/PWRDF, collection GS78–13, box 1; "Report First Step in Indian Program," 3; *Journal of Proceedings of the 24th Session of the General Synod*, 190–191; MacKenzie, *Native*; Gull, "Indian," 92–97.

44. Paterson, "Notes," 1–2; Howard H. Clark, letter to All Clergy, June 13, 1969, ACC/PO, collection GS75–99, box 2; Hugh McCullum, "Does the Church Really Care?" *Canadian Churchman* 96, no. 5 (1969): 1–2; "Get into the World," *Canadian Churchman* 96, no. 5 (1969): 4; Maurice Western, "Church Warned Be Sure of Actions," *Canadian Churchman* 96, no. 5 (1969): 7; "Letterbasket," *Canadian Churchman* 96, no. 7 (1969): 22; Bruton, "Time," 16; Gull, "Indian," 97–101.

45. Hendry, *Beyond Traplines (1969)*, ix–x, 11–12, 25; Hodgson and Kothare, *Vision*, 7–8, 29, 130–133.

46. Melling, *Right*, v; Hendry, *Beyond Traplines (1969)*, 4–5, 7–8, 31ff.

47. Hendry, *Beyond Traplines (1969)*, 59–60, 71–74, 79ff, 91–92.

48. "Report First Step in Indian Program," 3; Carolyn Purden, "Church Exits from Historic Field," *Canadian Churchman* 96, no. 5 (1969): 17; "'Traplines' Approved for Synod," *Canadian Churchman* 96, no. 6 (1969): 6; MacKenzie, *Native*; Gull, "Indian," 87–91.

49. T. E. Jones, letter to Redfern Loutitt, July 2, 1969, ACC/PC, collection GS76–11, box 2; "Indians Take Over Diocesan Executive," *Canadian Churchman* 96, no. 7 (1969): 19; "Anglicans Back Indian Fight for Better Deal"; "Indians Gather to Form Own Policy, Exchange Views on Minority Plight," *Akwesasne Notes* 1, no. 8 (1969): 1; *Journal of Proceedings of the 24th Session of the General Synod*, 34–35; Ahenakew, *Voices*, 169; Bohnen, "Fear"; "Radical Changes in Native Policies," *Canadian Churchman* 96, no. 8 (1969): 10.

50. Carolyn Purden, "A Gutless Pussycat," *Canadian Churchman* 96, no. 7 (1969): 19; "Poverty, Hendry Reports to Be Implemented Jointly," *Canadian Churchman*

96, no. 7 (1969): 19; *Journal of Proceedings of the 24th Session of the General Synod*, 35–36; "Anglicans Back Indian Fight for Better Deal"; Bohnen, "Fear"; "Radical Changes in Native Policies," 10; "Poverty, Hendry Report Fund Approved," *Canadian Churchman* 96, no. 8 (1969): 11; Hugh McCullum and Karmel Mc-Cullum, *This Land Is Not for Sale: Canada's Original People and Their Land; A Saga of Neglect, Exploitation, and Conflict* (Toronto, Ontario: Anglican Book Centre, 1975), 179–182, 185–189; Grant, *Moon*, 207, 210; John Webster Grant, *The Church in the Canadian Era* (Burlington, Ontario: Welch Publishing, 1988), 231–232; Pulker, *We*, 176–177; Bird and others, *Brief*, 7ff; Beardy, "Foreword," vii-viii.

51. Vine Deloria, Jr., "GCSP: The Demons at Work," *Historical Magazine of the Protestant Episcopal Church* 48, no. 1 (1979): 83–92; Owanah Anderson, *Jamestown Commitment: The Episcopal Church and the American Indian* (Cincinnati, OH: Forward Movement Publications, 1988), 129–132; Owanah Anderson, *400 Years: Anglican/Episcopal Mission among American Indians* (Cincinnati, OH: Forward Movement Publications, 1997), 316–321.

52. John A. MacKenzie, letter to Social Economic Program of the Public Service Commission, October 22, 1972, NAA/CSM, series 8—American Indians General, box 57; MacKenzie, *Native*; Michael B. Friedland, *Lift Up Your Voice Like a Trumpet: White Clergy and the Civil Rights and Antiwar Movements, 1954–1973* (Chapel Hill, NC: University of North Carolina Press, 1998), 3–5, 8, 49ff.

53. MacKenzie, October 22, 1972; Pulker, *We*, 179; MacKenzie, *Native*.

54. John A. MacKenzie, "The Indian: The Only True Christians?" in *Religion and the Indian*, edited by Indian-Eskimo Association of Canada (Toronto, Ontario: Indian-Eskimo Association of Canada, 1969), 10–13.

55. MacKenzie, *Native*; Ian MacKenzie, telephone conversation with author, June 18, 1992.

56. Paterson, "Notes," 2–5; "Report First Step in Indian Program," 3; Gull, "Indian," 93–101.

57. John A. MacKenzie, "Consultant Welcomes Report: Analysis Well Documented," *Canadian Churchman* 96, no. 5 (1969): 8, 13, 15.

58. *The Holy Bible*, King James Version (Cambridge, England: Cambridge University Press, 2000), Isaiah 58:51–59a; Friedland, *Lift*, 2.

59. Friedland, *Lift*, 2–9, 47–52ff, 69–75ff, 252.

60. "A Proposal for an Indian Ecumenical Conference Presented by the Institute for Indian Studies," [December? 1969], 4, NAA/AICC, collection MS 4806, box 2; MacKenzie, *Native*; John A. MacKenzie, "A Legend in His Own Time: Some Initial Reflections on the Work of Robert K. Thomas," in *A Good Cherokee, A Good Anthropologist: Papers in Honor of Robert K. Thomas*, edited by Steve Pavlik (Los Angeles, CA: American Indian Studies Center, University of California at Los Angeles, 1998), 219–222.

CHAPTER 4

1. *Rochdale College Catalogue, September 1968* (Toronto, Ontario: Rochdale College, 1968), 12–15; Francie Miller, "Where They're Learning to Live," *Canadian Churchman* 96, no. 1 (1969): 8; Howard Adelman, *The Beds of Academe: A Study of the Relation of Student Residences and the University* (Toronto, Ontario: Praxis Press, 1969), 254–258; Barrie Zwicker, "Rochdale: The Ultimate Freedom,"

Change, November-December 1969, 37–40; David Sharpe, *Rochdale: The Runaway College* (Toronto, Ontario: House of Anansi Press, 1987), 28–34.

2. Harold Cardinal, *The Unjust Society: The Tragedy of Canada's Indians* (Edmonton, Alberta: M. G. Hurtig, 1969), 23; "The Institute for Indian Studies," [1969?], Appendix D, NAA/CSM, series 8—American Indians General, box 53; Sharpe, *Rochdale*, 175, 231; Henry Mietkiewicz and Bob Mackowycz, *Dream Tower: The Life and Legacy of Rochdale College* (Toronto, Ontario: McGraw-Hill Ryerson, 1988), 47, 85, 223; Brian J. Grieveson, *Rochdale: Myth and Reality, a Personal Experience* (Haliburton, Ontario: Charasee Press, 1991), 6, 10, 29.

3. "A Proposal for an Indian Ecumenical Conference Presented by the Institute for Indian Studies," [December? 1969], 1–4, NAA/AICC, collection MS 4806, box 2; Robert K. Thomas, *The Indian Ecumenical Movement: A Grassroots Religious Movement*, lecture delivered at the Summer Public Lecture Series of the Vancouver School of Theology, July 21, 1986 (Vancouver, British Columbia: Vancouver School of Theology, 1986), audiocassette; Ian MacKenzie, *Native Rights and the Church: An Historical and Political Analysis*, lecture delivered at the Summer Public Lecture Series of the Vancouver School of Theology, July 23, 1986 (Vancouver, British Columbia: Vancouver School of Theology, 1986), audiocassette; John A. MacKenzie, "A Legend in His Own Time: Some Initial Reflections on the Work of Robert K. Thomas," in *A Good Cherokee, A Good Anthropologist: Papers in Honor of Robert K. Thomas*, edited by Steve Pavlik (Los Angeles, CA: American Indian Studies Center, University of California at Los Angeles, 1998), 219–222.

4. *Rochdale College Catalogue*, 12–15; "A Proposal for an Indian Ecumenical Conference Presented by the Institute for Indian Studies," 1–4.

5. "A Proposal for an Indian Ecumenical Conference Presented by the Institute for Indian Studies," 4; *Rochdale College Catalogue*, 12–15; Miller, "Where," 8; Zwicker, "Rochdale," 37–40; Wilfred Pelletier, "Interview," in *There Can Be No Light without Shadow*, edited by Peter Turner (Toronto, Ontario: Rochdale College, 1971), 417; Sharpe, *Rochdale*, 175, 231; Mietkiewicz and Mackowycz, *Dream*, 47, 85, 223; Grieveson, *Rochdale*, 6, 10, 29.

6. "Rochdale College," *Rochdale College Bulletin* 1, no. 1 (1966): 6; Adelman, *Beds*, 252–253; Zwicker, "Rochdale," 38; Sharpe, *Rochdale*, 19–20, 24; Mietkiewicz and Mackowycz, *Dream*, 7–10; Grieveson, *Rochdale*, 22–23.

7. Adelman, *Beds*, 189–190, 252–254; Peter Turner, *There Can Be No Light without Shadow* (Toronto, Ontario: Rochdale College, 1971), 32–33; Sharpe, *Rochdale*, 19–20, 24–25; Mietkiewicz and Mackowycz, *Dream*, 10–11; Grieveson, *Rochdale*, 22–24.

8. Rochdale College Education Project, "Proposal for the Rochdale College Education Project," in *There Can Be No Light without Shadow*, edited by Peter Turner (Toronto, Ontario: Rochdale College, 1971), 97–106; Adelman, *Beds*, 189–190; Sharpe, *Rochdale*, 15–20; Mietkiewicz and Mackowycz, *Dream*, 10–12, 16–17; Grieveson, *Rochdale*, 24–25.

9. Rochdale College Education Project, "Proposal," 97–106; "A Start," *Rochdale College Bulletin* 1, no. 1 (1966): 3–6; Adelman, *Beds*, 190–191; Sharpe, *Rochdale*, 20; Mietkiewicz and Mackowycz, *Dream*, 17; Seymour R. Kesten, *Utopian Episodes: Daily Life in Experimental Colonies Dedicated to Changing the World* (Syracuse, NY: Syracuse University Press, 1993), 2.

10. William Dowther, "Our New College Where (Almost) Anything Goes," *Toronto Daily Star*, July 12, 1967, 27; Adelman, *Beds*, 190–191; Sharpe, *Rochdale*, 20, 26;

Mietkiewicz and Mackowycz, *Dream*, 16–19; Howard Adelman, "Rochdale College: Power and Performance," *Canadian Literature*, no. 152–153 (1997): 89n14.

11. Dennis Lee, "Getting to Rochdale," in *This Book Is About Schools*, edited by Satu Repo (New York, NY: Random House, 1970), 354–359; MacKenzie, *Native*.

12. *Rochdale College Calendar, 1967–1968* (Toronto, Ontario: Rochdale College, 1967), 64ff, 75–79; Michael Hamilton, "[Announcements]," *Anything but Son of Rochdale* 1, no. 4 (1967); *Rochdale College Catalogue*, 15–16; Lee, "Getting," 363–370; Sharpe, *Rochdale*, 20–21; Mietkiewicz and Mackowycz, *Dream*, 17–20.

13. *Rochdale College Catalogue*, 2–4; Lee, "Getting," 363–370; Sharpe, *Rochdale*, 20.

14. *Rochdale College Catalogue*, 2–4.

15. Howard Adelman and Dennis Lee, eds., *The University Game* (Toronto, Ontario: House of Anansi Press, 1968), 1–3, 173–174.

16. Adelman, *Beds*, 191; Sharpe, *Rochdale*, 25–29, 35–36; Mietkiewicz and Mackowycz, *Dream*, 20–23, 39–41; Grieveson, *Rochdale*, 25–27; Ron Mann, Len Blum, and Bill Schroeder, *Dream Tower*, produced and directed by Ron Mann (Montreal, Quebec: National Film Board of Canada, 1994), videocassette, 47 min.

17. *Rochdale College Catalogue*, 1–2ff, 16; Turner, *There*, 33–34; Sharpe, *Rochdale*, 35ff; Mietkiewicz and Mackowycz, *Dream*, 42ff.

18. Edward Cowan, "An Experimental Anti-Institution College Flourishing in Toronto," *New York Times*, November 3, 1968, 14; Michael Valpy, "Rochdale's Reality Is Something Else," *Toronto Globe and Mail*, December 16, 1968, 1, 8.

19. "Their Own Thing," *Newsweek*, November 25, 1968, 98–99; Miller, "Where," 8, 10.

20. *Rochdale College Catalogue*, 12; "Their Own Thing," 98–99; Mark Satin, *Manual for Draft-Age Immigrants to Canada* (Toronto, Ontario: House of Anansi, 1968); Turner, *There*, 34.

21. Marc Zwelling, "Rochdale, Seminary-in-a-Dormitory, Is Alive," *Toronto Telegram*, April 22, 1969, 24; Alan Edmonds, "The New Learning: It Starts When the Walls Come Down," *Maclean's* 82, no. 5 (1969): 68–70, 75, 77; Zwicker, "Rochdale," 40–43; Kent Gooderham, "Come Live With Us," in *There Can Be No Light without Shadow*, edited by Peter Turner (Toronto, Ontario: Rochdale College, 1971), 376; Turner, *There*, 34–37, 44–46; Adelman, *Beds*, 188–189, 191; Sharpe, *Rochdale*, 27ff; Mietkiewicz and Mackowycz, *Dream*, 26–41, 86–99.

22. Zwelling, "Rochdale," 24; Adelman, *Beds*, 188; Sharpe, *Rochdale*, 148–160; Mietkiewicz and Mackowycz, *Dream*, 50–67.

23. Sharpe, *Rochdale*, 155; Mietkiewicz and Mackowycz, *Dream*, 66; Kesten, *Utopian*, 2–3, 58–66.

24. Kesten, *Utopian*, 3–8, 32, 37, 42, 81–88, 293.

25. *Rochdale College Catalogue*, 3, 9; Kesten, *Utopian*, 11–12, 36–37, 113ff.

26. Frances Sanderson, "Introducing the 'Meeting Place,'" in *The Meeting Place: Aboriginal Life in Toronto*, edited by Frances Sanderson and Heather Howard-Bobiwash (Toronto, Ontario: Native Canadian Centre of Toronto, 1997), 2; A. Rodney Bobiwash, "The History of Native People in the Toronto Area, An Overview," in *The Meeting Place: Aboriginal Life in Toronto*, edited by Frances Sanderson and Heather Howard-Bobiwash (Toronto, Ontario: Native Canadian Centre of Toronto, 1997), 5ff; John Steckley, *Toronto or Is That Taranteau?* (April 6, 1999), cited November 19, 1999, available from http://www.torontohistory.on.ca/archives/origin.html.

27. Roger Obonsawin and Heather Howard-Bobiwash, "The Native Canadian Centre of Toronto: The Meeting Place for the Aboriginal Community for 35 Years," in *The Meeting Place: Aboriginal Life in Toronto*, edited by Frances Sanderson and Heather Howard-Bobiwash (Toronto, Ontario: Native Canadian Centre of Toronto, 1997), 26–34; Eleanor Hill and Lorraine Le Camp, "My Recollections of the 'Indian Club,'" in *The Meeting Place: Aboriginal Life in Toronto*, edited by Frances Sanderson and Heather Howard-Bobiwash (Toronto, Ontario: Native Canadian Centre of Toronto, 1997), 60–64; Frances Sanderson and Heather Howard-Bobiwash, eds., *The Meeting Place: Aboriginal Life in Toronto* (Toronto, Ontario: Native Canadian Centre of Toronto, 1997), 165.

28. "The Institute for Indian Studies," 8; Wilfred Pelletier, "Growing Up in an Indian Village," *New York Times*, March 3, 1971, 43; Wilf Pelletier, "Time," in *Who Is the Chairman of This Meeting? A Collection of Essays*, edited by Ralph Osborne (Toronto, Ontario: Neewin Publishing Company, 1972), 57–60; Obonsawin and Howard-Bobiwash, "Native," 31–32.

29. Wilfred Pelletier and Ted Poole, *No Foreign Land: The Biography of a North American Indian* (New York, NY: Pantheon Books, 1973), 3ff, 24–30, 39–46, 51, 72–83.

30. "The Institute for Indian Studies," Appendix A; Pelletier and Poole, *No Foreign*, 80–117ff.

31. Pelletier and Poole, *No Foreign*, 134–140ff; Obonsawin and Howard-Bobiwash, "Native," 31.

32. "National Indian Council Centennial Office Reopens in Winnipeg," *Indian Voices*, April 1965, 10; Wilfred Pelletier, "Some Thoughts about Organization and Leadership: From a Paper Presented to the Manitoba Indian Brotherhood 1967," in *Two Articles* (Toronto, Ontario: Neewin Publishing Company, 1969); "The Institute for Indian Studies," Appendix A; Wilf Pelletier, "Dumb Indian," in *Who Is the Chairman of This Meeting? A Collection of Essays*, edited by Ralph Osborne (Toronto, Ontario: Neewin Publishing Company, 1972), 3; Pelletier and Poole, *No Foreign*, 140–155; Obonsawin and Howard-Bobiwash, "Native," 31, 40.

33. Pelletier, "Some"; Pelletier, "Dumb," 3; Pelletier and Poole, *No Foreign*, 140–155.

34. MacKenzie, *Native*; MacKenzie, "Legend," 217–218; Peter McFarlane, *Brotherhood to Nationhood: George Manuel and the Making of the Modern Indian Movement* (Toronto, Ontario: Between the Lines, 1993), 75–78.

35. "The Institute for Indian Studies," 1–3, 8–9, Appendix A, Appendix D.

36. "The Institute for Indian Studies," 3, Appendix B, Appendix D; MacKenzie, *Native*; Ian MacKenzie, telephone conversation with author, June 18, 1992; John A. MacKenzie, "Robert K. Thomas's Contributions to the Native People of Canada," paper presented at the annual meeting of the Western Social Science Association, Oakland, CA, April 29, 1995, JT; MacKenzie, "Legend," 218.

37. *Rochdale College Catalogue*, 2, 4, 6; "Rochdale College Institute for Indian Studies," [1969?], UT/RC, call number T-10/13, box 5; "The Institute for Indian Studies," 3–4, Appendix A, Appendix D; "Statement of Financing of Institute," [1970?], ACC/PWRDF, collection GS93–27, box 7; Sharpe, *Rochdale*, 60–62; Mietkiewicz and Mackowycz, *Dream*, 47–48.

38. Miller, "Where," 10; John A. MacKenzie, "Consultant Welcomes Report: Analysis Well Documented," *Canadian Churchman* 96, no. 5 (1969): 13; Adelman, *Beds*,

188; Zwicker, "Rochdale," 43; "The Institute for Indian Studies," 4–9, Appendix D; Mietkiewicz and Mackowycz, *Dream*, 261–262.

39. "Link," *Canadian Churchman* 96, no. 7 (1969): 10; "Statement of Financing of Institute"; Gooderham, "Come," 376–378; Sharpe, *Rochdale*, 60–62, 89ff, 101; Mietkiewicz and Mackowycz, *Dream*, 47–48, 82–84, 152–155.

40. "The Institute for Indian Studies," Appendix B; Stand Middlestriker [Robert K. Thomas], "At the Fork in Our Trail," [1977?], 79, NIYC; Thomas, *Indian Ecumenical*; MacKenzie, "Legend," 219.

41. Charles E. Hendry, *Beyond Traplines: Does the Church Really Care? Towards an Assessment of the Work of the Anglican Church of Canada with Canada's Native Peoples* (Toronto, Ontario: Ryerson Press, 1969), 61–63, 74, 87; "The Institute for Indian Studies," 2, 7, Proposal, Appendix E; "A Proposal for an Indian Ecumenical Conference Presented by the Institute for Indian Studies," 4; Hugh McCullum, "NEC Moves to Implement Hendry, Coalition Reports," *Canadian Churchman* 96, no. 11 (1969): 8.

42. Robert K. Thomas, "The Role of the Church in Indian Adjustment," *Kansas Journal of Sociology* 3, no. 1 (1967): 20–28; Robert K. Thomas, "The Role of the Church in Indian Adjustment," in *For Every North American Indian Who Begins to Disappear I Also Begin to Disappear: Being a Collection of Essays Concerned with the Quality of Human Relations Between the Red and White Peoples of This Continent*, edited by Nishnawbe Institute (Toronto, Ontario: Neewin Publishing Company, 1971), 87.

43. Thomas, "Role of the Church (1967)," 20–28.

44. "A Proposal for an Indian Ecumenical Conference Presented by the Institute for Indian Studies," 1–2; MacKenzie, "Legend," 219–221.

45. "A Proposal for an Indian Ecumenical Conference Presented by the Institute for Indian Studies," 3–4; MacKenzie, "Legend," 221.

46. Hugh McCullum, "Anglican Stand on Indian Policy Gets Little Response," *Canadian Churchman* 96, no. 10 (1969): 18–19; Howard H. Clark, "Synod 'Deeply Perturbed' by Indians' Discontent," *Canadian Churchman* 96, no. 10 (1969): 19; Jean Chrétien, "Chrétien Promises Talks with Indians Will Continue," *Canadian Churchman* 96, no. 10 (1969): 19; "Canadian Churchman," *Akwesasne Notes* 1, no. 10 (1969): 38.

47. "The Institute for Indian Studies," Appendix B; "Hendry Report Implementation Job Description," [October?] 1969, 3, ACC/PC, collection GS76–11, box 2; McCullum, "NEC Moves," 8; "A Proposal for an Indian Ecumenical Conference Presented by the Institute for Indian Studies," 4–5; "Approximate Expenditures from Community Development Budget," May 1, 1970, ACC/PWRDF, collection GS78–13, box 1; Thomas, *Indian Ecumenical*; MacKenzie, "Legend," 221–222.

48. Cardinal, *Unjust*, 1–2ff, 17, 162; *Canada's Indians*, Ideas series (Toronto, Ontario: CBC Radio, [1970?]), audiocassette, 59 min.; Jon Ruddy, "Uncle Tomahawks Need Not Apply: Canadian Red Power Is on the Rise," *Atlas*, February 1970, 56–58; Indian Chiefs of Alberta, *Citizens Plus* (Edmonton, Alberta: Indian Association of Alberta, 1970), 1–4; "Spokesman for Indians: Harold Cardinal," *New York Times*, July 6, 1970, 13; James Burke, *Paper Tomahawks: From Red Tape to Red Power* (Winnipeg, Manitoba: Queenston House Publishing, 1976), 21ff; Daniel David Moses and Terry Goldie, eds., *An Anthology of Canadian Native Literature in English* (Toronto, Ontario: Oxford University Press, 1992),

371–372; McFarlane, *Brotherhood*, 86–87, 92, 94–95; Harold Cardinal, telephone conversation with author, April 13, 2000.

49. Cardinal, *Unjust*, 1–2, 78–79.

50. Cardinal, *Unjust*, 52–55ff, 80–89, 135; John A. MacKenzie, "A Cree Exposes Indian Tragedy," *Canadian Churchman* 97, no. 1 (1970): 17; Ruddy, "Uncle," 58.

51. Cardinal, *Unjust*, 80, 88–89, 162–171.

52. Cardinal, *Unjust*, 13–14, 20–21, 77, 96ff, 107ff, 164.

53. "A Proposal for an Indian Ecumenical Conference Presented by the Institute for Indian Studies," 4–5; Cardinal, *Unjust*, 74, 82–83.

54. Vine Deloria, Jr., *Custer Died for Your Sins: An Indian Manifesto* (New York, NY: Macmillan, 1969), 54ff, 243ff; Cardinal, *Unjust*, 1, 140ff, 162ff; Ruddy, "Uncle," 58; James Treat, "Introduction: An American Critique of Religion," in *For This Land: Writings on Religion in America* by Vine Deloria, Jr., edited by James Treat (New York, NY: Routledge, 1999), 4–5; Cardinal, April 13, 2000.

55. Cardinal, *Unjust*, 1, 3, 18, 35, 39, 75–76, 78, 91, 95, 107, 108, 111, 133, 170; "The Institute for Indian Studies," Appendix A; Harold Cardinal, *The Rebirth of Canada's Indians* (Edmonton, Alberta: Hurtig Publishers, 1977), 204–206; MacKenzie, *Native*; McFarlane, *Brotherhood*, 96–97.

CHAPTER 5

1. "A Proposal for an Indian Ecumenical Conference Presented by the Institute for Indian Studies," [December? 1969], 4–5, NAA/AICC, collection MS 4806, box 2; Ian MacKenzie, telephone conversation with author, February 18, 2000.

2. "A Proposal for an Indian Ecumenical Conference Presented by the Institute for Indian Studies," 4–5; Sol Sanderson, "The Past—Present—Future," *Saskatchewan Indian* 1, no. 1 (1970); "Indian Ecumenical Conference," [February? 1973], 2, ACC/NMO, collection GS85–6, box 1, file 18; Margaret Tanton, "Indian Ecumenical Movement," [1973?], 1, ACC/NMO, collection GS85–6, box 1, file 18; Andrew Ahenakew, *Sometimes We Burn, Sometimes We Tremble* (Toronto, Ontario: Anglican Church of Canada, [1977?]), videotape, 23 min.; Robert K. Thomas, *The Indian Ecumenical Movement: A Grassroots Religious Movement*, lecture delivered at the Summer Public Lecture Series of the Vancouver School of Theology, July 21, 1986 (Vancouver, British Columbia: Vancouver School of Theology, 1986), audiocassette; Claire R. Farrer, *Thunder Rides a Black Horse: Mescalero Apaches and the Mythic Present*, 2nd ed. (Prospect Heights, IL: Waveland Press, 1996), 9–10; John A. MacKenzie, "A Legend in His Own Time: Some Initial Reflections on the Work of Robert K. Thomas," in *A Good Cherokee, A Good Anthropologist: Papers in Honor of Robert K. Thomas*, edited by Steve Pavlik (Los Angeles, CA: American Indian Studies Center, University of California at Los Angeles, 1998), 222; MacKenzie, February 18, 2000.

3. "A Proposal for an Indian Ecumenical Conference Presented by the Institute for Indian Studies," 4–5; MacKenzie, February 18, 2000.

4. "A Proposal for an Indian Ecumenical Conference Presented by the Institute for Indian Studies," 1–4; Ian MacKenzie, telephone conversation with author, June 18, 1992; MacKenzie, February 18, 2000.

5. "The Institute for Indian Studies," [1969?], Appendix A, NAA/CSM, series 8—American Indians General, box 53; "A Proposal for an Indian Ecumenical

Conference Presented by the Institute for Indian Studies," 5; MacKenzie, February 18, 2000.

6. "A Proposal for an Indian Ecumenical Conference Presented by the Institute for Indian Studies," 5–8; Thomas, *Indian Ecumenical*; MacKenzie, February 18, 2000.

7. "A Proposal for an Indian Ecumenical Conference Presented by the Institute for Indian Studies," 5–7; "Report of the Indian Ecumenical Conferences for Years 1970 through 1973," [1973?], 2–3, ACC/NMO, collection GS85–6, box 1, file 18; Thomas, *Indian Ecumenical*; MacKenzie, "Legend," 222.

8. "Indian Ecumenical Conference Report," [August 13–19], [1970], 4, ACC/PWRDF, collection GS93–27, box 7; James Treat, "Introduction: Native Christian Narrative Discourse," in *Native and Christian: Indigenous Voices on Religious Identity in the United States and Canada*, edited by James Treat (New York, NY: Routledge, 1996), 8–9; MacKenzie, February 18, 2000.

9. "A Proposal for an Indian Ecumenical Conference Presented by the Institute for Indian Studies," 4–9; "Indian Ecumenical Conference Summary Report of the Second Steering Committee Meeting," February 28–March 2, 1970, ACC/NMO, collection GS85–6, box 1, file 16; "Indian Ecumenical Conference Budget," [1970], ACC/NMO, collection GS85–6, box 1, file 15; "Indian Ecumenical Conference 1970 Financial Report," 1970, ACC/NMO, collection GS85–6, box 1, file 15; Thomas, *Indian Ecumenical*.

10. "Indian Ecumenical Conference Summary Report of the Second Steering Committee Meeting"; "Indian Ecumenical Conference Budget"; "Nishnawbe Institute Progress Report of the Board of Directors," January 31, 1973, 2, UCC/DMC, location 83.054C, box 40, file 11; Dianne Meili, *Those Who Know: Profiles of Alberta's Native Elders* (Edmonton, Alberta: NeWest Press, 1991), 79–81; Ian MacKenzie, e-mail to author, March 19, 2000.

11. "Indian Ecumenical Conference Summary Report of the Second Steering Committee Meeting"; "Indian Ecumenical Conference Budget"; MacKenzie, March 19, 2000.

12. "General Synod of the Anglican Church of Canada Position Description," [October?] 1969, ACC/PC, collection GS76–11, box 2; "Indians in Attendance at Ottawa Meeting with Ian MacKenzie and Trevor Jones," October 22, 1969, 1–3, ACC/PWRDF, collection GS78–13, box 1; "Hendry Report Implementation Job Description," [October?] 1969, 1–4, ACC/PC, collection GS76–11, box 2; Hugh McCullum, "NEC Moves to Implement Hendry, Coalition Reports," *Canadian Churchman* 96, no. 11 (1969): 8; "Churches Unite to Support Indians in Federal Talks," *Canadian Churchman* 97, no. 1 (1970): 17; Robert D. MacRae, ed., *Bulletin 201: Recent Statements by the Indians of Canada, General Synod Action 1969, Some Government Responses, Suggested Resource* (Toronto, Ontario: Social Action Unit, Anglican Church of Canada, 1970), 40; Francie Miller, "Guiding the New Approach," *Canadian Churchman* 97, no. 3 (1970): 16; "Beyond Traplines—So What?" 1970, 1–3, ACC/PC, collection GS76–11, box 2; "Hendry Recommendations Making Progress," *Canadian Churchman* 97, no. 6 (1970): 15; T. E. Jones, "The Implementation of the Hendry Report Recommendations," December 3, 1970, 2–3, ACC/PWRDF, collection GS78–13, box 1.

13. McCullum, "NEC Moves," 8; "Denominations Plan Joint Fund Promotion," *Canadian Churchman* 96, no. 11 (1969): 8; Robert D. MacRae, "Introduction," in *Bulletin 201: Recent Statements by the Indians of Canada, General Synod Action*

1969, Some Government Responses, Suggested Resource, edited by Robert D. MacRae (Toronto, Ontario: Social Action Unit, Anglican Church of Canada, 1970), 4; Ronald S. Fellows, "Let's Play Anglicans and Indians," *Canadian Churchman* 97, no. 3 (1970): 13; Shirley Bruton, "A Time to Care," *Canadian Churchman* 97, no. 3 (1970): 16; "Grant Requests Received by Rev. Trevor Jones for P.W.R.D.F. Allocations Committee," April 3, 1970, 1–2, ACC/PWRDF, collection GS78–13, box 1; John A. MacKenzie, "Primate's World Relief and Development Fund Application for Grant," April 27, 1970, ACC/PWRDF, collection GS93–27, box 7; Trevor E. Jones, ed., *Bulletin 202: Extracts from "Native Rights in Canada"* (Toronto, Ontario: Social Action Unit, Anglican Church of Canada, 1970), 7ff; "Beyond Traplines—So What?" 1–3; "Hendry Recommendations Making Progress," 15; "First Canadian Grants Approved," *Canadian Churchman* 97, no. 7 (1970): 9; "Primate's World Relief and Development Fund Grants Relating to the Hendry Report Implementation," May 3, 1977, ACC/PWRDF, collection GS78–13, box 1.

14. Barrie Zwicker, "Rochdale: The Ultimate Freedom," *Change*, November-December 1969, 37–43; "Link," *Canadian Churchman* 96, no. 7 (1969): 10; Wilfred Pelletier, "Childhood in an Indian Village," in *Two Articles* (Toronto, Ontario: Neewin Publishing Company, 1969); William Bartlett, "Grand Jury's Report," in *There Can Be No Light without Shadow*, edited by Peter Turner (Toronto, Ontario: Rochdale College, 1971), 275–281; Kent Gooderham, "Come Live with Us," in *There Can Be No Light without Shadow*, edited by Peter Turner (Toronto, Ontario: Rochdale College, 1971), 29–33; Peter Turner, *There Can Be No Light without Shadow* (Toronto, Ontario: Rochdale College, 1971), 46–48; D. Mills Lavell, "Nishnawbe Institute: 1976 Annual Board Meeting," February 7–8, 1976, DL; David Sharpe, *Rochdale: The Runaway College* (Toronto, Ontario: House of Anansi Press, 1987), 61–62.

15. John A. MacKenzie, letter to Kent Fitzgerald, March 23, 1970, ACC/NMO, collection GS85–6, box 1, file 15; Kent FitzGerald, letter to John A. MacKenzie, April 1, 1970, ACC/NMO, collection GS85–6, box 1, file 16.

16. MacKenzie, March 23, 1970.

17. Kent FitzGerald, "Proposal Summary JSAC Coordinating Committee," March 30, 1970, 1–2, ACC/PWRDF, collection GS93–27, box 7; FitzGerald, April 1, 1970; Wilfred Pelletier, John A. MacKenzie, and Robert K. Thomas, letter to Kent Fitzgerald, April 10, 1970, ACC/NMO, collection GS85–6, box 1, file 15.

18. John A. MacKenzie, letter to F. J. Spence, April 22, 1970, ACC/NMO, collection GS85–6, box 1, file 15; J. E. Y. Levaque, letter to John A. MacKenzie, April 23, 1970, ACC/NMO, collection GS85–6, box 1, file 16.

19. Wilfred Pelletier, letter to J. E. Y. Levaque, May 4, 1970, ACC/NMO, collection GS85–6, box 1, file 16; Wilfred Pelletier, "For Every North American Indian Who Begins to Disappear I Also Begin to Disappear," in *For Every North American Indian Who Begins to Disappear I Also Begin to Disappear: Being a Collection of Essays Concerned with the Quality of Human Relations Between the Red and White Peoples of This Continent*, edited by Nishnawbe Institute (Toronto, Ontario: Neewin Publishing Company, 1971), 18–22.

20. Robert K. Thomas, letter to Bernard Second, June 24, 1970, ACC/NMO, collection GS85–6, box 1, file 16.

21. Kent FitzGerald, letter to John A. MacKenzie, June 8, 1970, ACC/NMO, collection GS85–6, box 1, file 16; R. D. MacRae, letter to W. G. Waugh, June 9,

1970, ACC/PWRDF, collection GS93–27, box 7; R. D. MacRae, letter to Wilfred Pelletier, June 17, 1970, ACC/PWRDF, collection GS93–27, box 7; "First Canadian Grants Approved," 9; "Indian Ecumenical Conference 1970 Financial Report"; Stand Middlestriker [Robert K. Thomas], "At the Fork in Our Trail," [1977?], 143–144, NIYC; MacKenzie, March 19, 2000.

22. "Indian Ecumenical Conference Summary Report of the Second Steering Committee Meeting"; "Indian Ecumenical Conference Budget"; "Indian Ecumenical Conference Summary Report of the Third Steering Committee Meeting," June 18–21, [1970], 1, ACC/NMO, collection GS85–6, box 1, file 16; "Indian Ecumenical Conference Steering Committee Members," [June? 1970], ACC/NMO, collection GS85–6, box 1, file 15.

23. "A Proposal for an Indian Ecumenical Conference Presented by the Institute for Indian Studies," 7; Pelletier, MacKenzie, and Thomas, April 10, 1970.

24. "Minutes of the Meeting Held in Henryetta, Oklahoma," June 18–21, [1970], ACC/NMO, collection GS85–6, box 1, file 16; "Indian Ecumenical Conference Summary Report of the Third Steering Committee Meeting," 2; Thomas, June 24, 1970.

25. "Indian Ecumenical Conference Summary Report of the Third Steering Committee Meeting," 2–3; Wilfred Pelletier, letter to R. D. MacRae, June 25, 1970, ACC/PWRDF, collection GS93–27, box 7; "Nishnawbe Institute Progress Report of the Board of Directors"; Allan Campbell, "Cultural Persistence and Plains Cree Identity" (M.A. thesis, University of Regina, 1975), vi-viii.

26. Robert K. Thomas, letter to Chief Rube, June 29, 1970, ACC/NMO, collection GS85–6, box 1, file 16; Robert K. Thomas, letter to Chief Wesley, June 29, 1970, ACC/NMO, collection GS85–6, box 1, file 16; Robert K. Thomas, letter to Irving Powless, June 29, 1970, ACC/NMO, collection GS85–6, box 1, file 16; Robert K. Thomas, letter to Tom [Banyacya], June 29, 1970, ACC/NMO, collection GS85–6, box 1, file 16; Robert K. Thomas, letter to Harvey Twins, June 30, 1970, ACC/NMO, collection GS85–6, box 1, file 16; Robert K. Thomas, letter to Donald Wanatee, June 30, 1970, ACC/NMO, collection GS85–6, box 1, file 16; MacKenzie, March 19, 2000.

27. T. E. Jones, memorandum to J. C. Bothwell, April 29, 1970, ACC/PWRDF, collection GS93–27, box 7; Pelletier, June 25, 1970; "Conference—The Total Picture of What Has to Be Done and by Whom," [1970], ACC/NMO, collection GS85–6, box 1, file 16; Robert K. Thomas and John A. MacKenzie, "Survey Report to the Anglican Church on the Northwest Territories," in *For Every North American Indian Who Begins to Disappear I Also Begin to Disappear: Being a Collection of Essays Concerned with the Quality of Human Relations between the Red and White Peoples of This Continent*, edited by Nishnawbe Institute (Toronto, Ontario: Neewin Publishing Company, 1971), 109–114, 118, 123–125, 129–131; "Church Seen as 'Progressive' by Indians," *Canadian Churchman* 98, no. 5 (1971): 14.

28. "Misc. Stuff That Has to Be Done," [1970], ACC/NMO, collection GS85–6, box 1, file 16; "Indian Ecumenical Conference Announced," July 7, 1970, 1–3, ACC/NMO, collection GS85–6, box 1, file 16; Letter to Ernest Willie, July 20, 1970, ACC/NMO, collection GS85–6, box 1, file 16.

29. "Indian Ecumenical Conference Announced," 1–3.

30. Ernest Willie, draft letter to delegates, [July? 1970], ACC/NMO, collection GS85–6, box 1, file 16; Ernest Willie, letter to Sam Stanley, July 15, 1970, NAA/CSM, series 8—American Indians General.

31. B. A. Prince, letter to John A. MacKenzie, July 31, 1970, ACC/NMO, collection GS85–6, box 1, file 16; "Delegates of the First Indian Ecumenical Conference," August 13–19, 1970, 1–7, ACC/NMO, collection GS85–6, box 1, file 15; "Indian Ecumenical Conference 1970 Financial Report."

32. Middlestriker, "Fork," 12–14, 138–139, 166–174; Carol Nadjiwon, "Dr. Robert K. Thomas: A Cherokee War Chief in Modern Times," in *A Good Cherokee, A Good Anthropologist: Papers in Honor of Robert K. Thomas*, edited by Steve Pavlik (Los Angeles, CA: American Indian Studies Center, University of California at Los Angeles, 1998), 229.

33. Ernest Willie, letter to Trevor [Jones], November 17, 1970, ACC/PWRDF, collection GS93–27, box 7; "The Indian Ecumenical Conference," [April? 1973], 3, ACC/NMO, collection GS85–6, box 1, file 18; "Report of the Indian Ecumenical Conferences for Years 1970 through 1973," 3–4; MacKenzie, June 18, 1992; MacKenzie, "Legend," 222.

34. "Crow Indian Celebration Starts Today," *Hardin Tribune-Herald*, August 13, 1970, 1; "Indian Ecumenical Conference Announced," 3; "Report of the Indian Ecumenical Conferences for Years 1970 through 1973," 3–4; Omer C. Stewart, *Peyote Religion: A History* (Norman, OK: University of Oklahoma Press, 1987), 299–300, 305; MacKenzie, June 18, 1992; Stewart K. Etsitty, "Memories of Robert K. Thomas," in *A Good Cherokee, A Good Anthropologist: Papers in Honor of Robert K. Thomas*, edited by Steve Pavlik (Los Angeles, CA: American Indian Studies Center, University of California at Los Angeles, 1998), 311.

35. "Indian Ecumenical Conference Report," 2; "Report of the Indian Ecumenical Conferences for Years 1970 through 1973," 4–6; Sam Stanley, "American Indian Power and Powerlessness," in *The Anthropology of Power: Ethnographic Studies from Asia, Oceania, and the New World*, edited by Raymond D. Fogelson and Richard N. Adams (New York, NY: Academic Press, 1977), 237; Meili, *Those*, 81.

36. "Indian Ecumenical Conference Report," 2–3; Beatrice Medicine and Robert Thomas, "A Conversation with Bea Medicine and Robert Thomas," in *Educating the Educators: A Report of the Institute on "The American Indian Student in Higher Education,"* edited by Roy H. Sandstrom (Canton, NY: St. Lawrence University, 1971), 64; "Report of the Indian Ecumenical Conferences for Years 1970 through 1973," 4–5; Thomas, *Indian Ecumenical*; Charles Red Corn, telephone conversation with author, April 18, 2000.

37. Allan Campbell, "Indian Ecumenical Conference Press Release," August 13–19, 1970, ACC/NMO, collection GS85–6, box 1, file 15; "Indian Ecumenical Conference Report," 2–3; "Report of the Indian Ecumenical Conferences for Years 1970 through 1973," 5–6; Stanley, "American," 237; Sam Stanley, telephone conversation with author, May 7, 1992; MacKenzie, June 18, 1992.

38. Campbell, "Indian"; "Indian Ecumenical Conference Report," 3; Robert K. Thomas, "Indian Religious Leaders Gather at Crow," *Americans Before Columbus* 2, no. 4 (1970); "Report of the Indian Ecumenical Conferences for Years 1970 through 1973," 5–6; John Snow, *These Mountains Are Our Sacred Places: The Story of the Stoney Indians* (Toronto, Ontario: Samuel-Stevens, Publishers, 1977), 144.

39. "Crow Fair Draws Record Crowd," *Hardin Tribune-Herald*, August 20, 1970, 1; Campbell, "Indian"; "Indian Ecumenical Conference Report," 3; "Resolutions Made at the First Indian Ecumenical Conference," August 13–19, 1970,

ACC/NMO, collection GS85–6, box 1, file 15; "Report of the Indian Ecumenical Conferences for Years 1970 through 1973," 4; Stanley, "American," 237–238.

40. "Resolutions Made at the First Indian Ecumenical Conference."

41. "Resolutions Made at the First Indian Ecumenical Conference"; Stewart, *Peyote*, 311–312.

42. "Resolutions Made at the First Indian Ecumenical Conference."

43. "Resolutions Made at the First Indian Ecumenical Conference"; John Hascall, telephone conversation with author, April 13, 1992.

44. "Resolutions Made at the First Indian Ecumenical Conference."

45. Campbell, "Indian"; "Resolutions Made at the First Indian Ecumenical Conference"; Stanley, May 7, 1992; Red Corn, April 18, 2000.

46. "Indian Ecumenical Conference Report," 3; "Report of the Indian Ecumenical Conferences for Years 1970 through 1973," 5–7.

47. "Motions Passed at the First Indian Ecumenical Conference," [August 13–19], [1970], ACC/NMO, collection GS85–6, box 1, file 15; Campbell, "Indian"; "Indian Ecumenical Conference Report," 3; "Second Annual Indian Ecumenical Conference," July 18–21, 1971, DL.

48. Gary Woolsey, letter to [Trevor] Jones, December 2, 1970, ACC/PWRDF, collection GS93–27, box 7; "Report of the Indian Ecumenical Conferences for Years 1970 through 1973," 3; "Indian Ecumenical Conference (February 1973)," 2; Snow, *These*, 144.

49. Campbell, "Indian."

50. Campbell, "Indian"; Allan Campbell, "New Hope Discovered by Indian Priests, Medicine Men," *Canadian Churchman* 97, no. 8 (1970).

51. "Indian Ecumenical Conference Report," 1–4; Thomas, "Indian Religious."

52. "Indian Ecumenical Conference Report," 1–4.

53. "Indian Ecumenical Conference Report," 1; "Steering Committee of the First Indian Ecumenical Conference," August 13–19, 1970, ACC/NMO, collection GS85–6, box 1, file 15; "Delegates of the First Indian Ecumenical Conference," 1–7; "Report of the Indian Ecumenical Conferences for Years 1970 through 1973," 4–5; Snow, *These*, 144.

54. Campbell, "Indian"; "Indian Ecumenical Conference Report," 1; Thomas, "Indian Religious"; "The Indian Ecumenical Conference (April 1973)," 3.

55. T. E. Jones, letter to Anglican Participants at the Indian Ecumenical Conference in Montana, November 4, 1970, ACC/PWRDF, collection GS93–27, box 7; [Andrew] Ahenakew, letter to T. E. Jones, [November 1970], ACC/PWRDF, collection GS93–27, box 7; Harry S. Rose, letter to T. E. Jones, [November 1970], ACC/PWRDF, collection GS93–27, box 7; John S. Hascall, letter to Anglican Church of Canada, November 13, 1970, ACC/PWRDF, collection GS93–27, box 7; Willie, November 17, 1970; Woolsey, December 2, 1970.

56. Vine Deloria, Jr., "The Rise of Indian Activism," in *The Red Man in the New World Drama: A Politico-Legal Study with a Pageantry of American Indian History* by Jennings C. Wise, rev. ed., edited by Vine Deloria, Jr. (New York, NY: Macmillan, 1971), ix, 389, 397–398.

57. Deloria, "Rise," 389, 397–398.

58. Charles Carroll Bonney, "Words of Welcome," in *The Dawn of Religious Pluralism: Voices from the World's Parliament of Religions, 1893*, edited by Richard Hughes Seager (La Salle, IL: Open Court Publishing Company, 1993), 17–22;

Richard Hughes Seager, "General Introduction," in *The Dawn of Religious Pluralism: Voices from the World's Parliament of Religions, 1893*, edited by Richard Hughes Seager (La Salle, IL: Open Court Publishing Company, 1993), 3–6; Richard Hughes Seager, *The World's Parliament of Religions: The East/West Encounter, Chicago, 1893* (Bloomington, IN: Indiana University Press, 1995), xv-xxiv, 3–23, 47.

59. Richard Hughes Seager, "Appendix," in *The Dawn of Religious Pluralism: Voices from the World's Parliament of Religions, 1893*, edited by Richard Hughes Seager (La Salle, IL: Open Court Publishing Company, 1993), 477ff; Seager, *World's Parliament*, xv-xvi, xxvi-xxix, 24–27, 43–46, 94–95, 160.

60. Richard Hughes Seager, ed., *The Dawn of Religious Pluralism: Voices from the World's Parliament of Religions, 1893* (La Salle, IL: Open Court Publishing Company, 1993), iii, 8–11; Seager, *World's Parliament*, xvi, 95–97.

61. Bonney, "Words," 17ff; Protap Chunder Majumdar, "The World's Religious Debt to Asia," in *The Dawn of Religious Pluralism: Voices from the World's Parliament of Religions, 1893*, edited by Richard Hughes Seager (La Salle, IL: Open Court Publishing Company, 1993), 448–449; Seager, *World's Parliament*, 47–53, 65–67, 78, 100ff, 114–116.

62. Bonney, "Words," 21; Frederick C. Mish, ed., *Merriam-Webster's Collegiate Dictionary*, 10th ed. (Springfield, MA: Merriam-Webster, 1999), 241, 845.

63. "A Proposal for an Indian Ecumenical Conference Presented by the Institute for Indian Studies," 7–8.

64. "Indian Ecumenical Conference Report," 3–4.

65. Wilfred Pelletier, letter to R. D. MacRae, October 14, 1970, ACC/PWRDF, collection GS93–27, box 7.

66. Pelletier, October 14, 1970.

67. "Minutes of the Indian Ecumenical Steering Committee Meeting," November 19–22, 1970, 1, ACC/NMO, collection GS85–6, box 1, file 15.

68. "Minutes of the Indian Ecumenical Steering Committee Meeting," 1–4; Etsitty, "Memories," 311.

69. "Misc. Stuff That Has to Be Done"; "Delegates of the First Indian Ecumenical Conference," 2; "Minutes of the Indian Ecumenical Steering Committee Meeting," 2; Middlestriker, "Fork," 33–34.

70. Alan Fry, *How a People Die: A Novel* (Toronto, Ontario: Doubleday Canada, 1970); "Resolutions Made at the First Indian Ecumenical Conference"; "Minutes of the Indian Ecumenical Steering Committee Meeting," 1–3; Tom Holm, *Strong Hearts, Wounded Souls: Native American Veterans of the Vietnam War* (Austin, TX: University of Texas Press, 1996), 18–21, 117ff.

71. "Indian Ecumenical Conference 1970 Financial Report"; "Minutes of the Indian Ecumenical Steering Committee Meeting," 3–6; "Nishnawbe Institute Report of the Board of Directors," January 30, 1971, 13, ACC/PWRDF, collection GS93–27, box 7.

72. "Minutes of the Indian Ecumenical Steering Committee Meeting," 3, 6–7.

73. "Indians Ask Churches Stop Dividing People," *Canadian Churchman* 97, no. 8 (1970); Jones, "Implementation," 1–6.

74. Trevor Jones, memorandum to J. Bothwell, July 6, 1970, ACC/PC, collection GS76–11, box 2; "Minutes of the Indian Ecumenical Steering Committee Meeting," 2–4; Andrew Ahenakew, letter to E. S. Light, January 19, 1971, ACC/NMO, collection GS85–6, box 1, file 16; *Journal of Proceedings of the 25th*

Session of the General Synod (Toronto, Ontario: Anglican Church of Canada, 1971), 29–30, 60–62, 200; "Indian Prayer Day June 21," *Canadian Churchman* 98, no. 2 (1971): 40; Jean Goodwill and Norma Sluman, *John Tootoosis* (Winnipeg, Manitoba: Pemmican Publications, 1984), 215, 227; John Webster Grant, *The Church in the Canadian Era* (Burlington, Ontario: Welch Publishing, 1988), 239.

75. John A. MacKenzie, letter to Ernest Long, January 19, 1971, ACC/NMO, collection GS85–6, box 1, file 16; *Journal of Proceedings of the 25th Session of the General Synod*, 59, 178–179, 205–207, 212–213; *Record of Proceedings of the 24th General Council* (Toronto, Ontario: United Church of Canada, 1971), 72, 111–113; "Missions," *Akwesasne Notes* 3, no. 2 (1971): 22; MacKenzie, "Legend," 223.

76. "Indian Prayer Day June 21 (February 1971)," 40; "Native Work Assured Five Years," *Canadian Churchman* 98, no. 2 (1971): 40; "Indian Prayer Day June 21 (June 1971)," 1; Graham Everett, "June 21 Is Joy for Lonely Quebec Hunters," *Canadian Churchman* 98, no. 6 (1971): 3; "Suggested Indian Prayer," *Canadian Churchman* 98, no. 6 (1971): 3.

77. "Minutes of the Indian Ecumenical Steering Committee Meeting," 6; "Nishnawbe Institute Report of the Board of Directors," 1–4, 7–8; "Indian Ecumenical Conference 1971 Proposal," January 1, 1971, 1–4, ACC/NMO, collection GS85–6, box 1, file 16; Wilfred Pelletier, letter to Chairman of the Primate's World Relief and Development Fund, March 9, 1971, ACC/PWRDF, collection GS93–27, box 7; R. D. MacRae, letter to Wilfred Pelletier, March 25, 1971, ACC/PWRDF, collection GS93–27, box 7; "The Algonquian Project: A Proposal for Research and Publication of Indian Music and Legends," [1971?], 1–7, ACC/PWRDF, collection GS78–13, box 1.

78. John A. MacKenzie, letter to Chairman of the JSAC Indian Ministries, February 17, 1971, ACC/NMO, collection GS85–6, box 1, file 16; "Indian Ecumenical Conference 1971 Proposal," 1–4.

79. *Journal of Proceedings of the 25th Session of the General Synod*, 213; J. A. MacKenzie, "Consultant's Report to Program Committee on Implementation of Hendry Report Recommendations," March 19, 1971, 1–4, 19–20, 26–28, ACC/PWRDF, collection GS78–13, box 1; "Extract from National Program Committee Minutes," March 17–19, 1971, ACC/PC, collection GS76–11, box 2.

80. "Extract from National Program Committee Minutes"; Jane Organ, "Indian Report May Die," *Akwesasne Notes* 3, no. 4 (1971): 36; J. A. MacKenzie, "Submission to PWRDF Committee," [April? 1971], 4, ACC/PWRDF, collection GS93–27, box 7; "Program Committee Task Force on the Continuing Implementation of the Hendry Report Recommendations," June 8–11, 1971, 1–2, ACC/PWRDF, collection GS93–27, box 7; "Resolutions Passed at Meeting of Program Committee Task Force," June 8–11, 1971, 1–2, ACC/NMO, collection GS85–6, box 1, file 16.

81. Wilfred Pelletier, letter to [Steering Committee Members], [February? 1971], ACC/NMO, collection GS85–6, box 1, file 16; "Indian Ecumenical Conference 1971 Proposal," 2.

82. "Second Indian Ecumenical Conference Announcement," April 1971, 1–3, DL; "Morley Reserve to Host American Indian Religious Leaders," *Native People* 3, no. 11 (1971): 5; "Ecumenical Conference," *Akwesasne Notes* 3, no. 4 (1971): 38.

83. K. Harriet Christie, letter to John A. MacKenzie, April 7, 1971, UCC/DMC, location 83.054C, box 40, file 11; John Bothwell, memorandum to Trevor Jones, May 26, 1971, ACC/PC, collection GS76–11, box 2; "Indian Ecumenical Conference Financial Report," July 13, 1971, ACC/PWRDF, collection GS93–27, box 7; "Second Indian Ecumenical Conference Report," [July 18–21], 1971, 2–3, ACC/PWRDF, collection GS93–27, box 7.

84. Nishnawbe Institute, ed., *For Every North American Indian Who Begins to Disappear I Also Begin to Disappear: Being a Collection of Essays Concerned with the Quality of Human Relations between the Red and White Peoples of This Continent* (Toronto, Ontario: Neewin Publishing Company, 1971), iv; Pelletier, "Every," 5, 12–13; *Speaking Together: Canada's Native Women* (Ottawa, Ontario: Secretary of State, 1975), 92–93; Aboriginal Art Leasing, *Apikan Aboriginal Art Gallery: Artist Biographies* (December 31, 1999), cited April 5, 2001, available from http://infoweb.magi.com/~apikan/biographies/daphnebio.html.

85. John A. MacKenzie, "On the Demonic Nature of Institutions," in *For Every North American Indian Who Begins to Disappear I Also Begin to Disappear: Being a Collection of Essays Concerned with the Quality of Human Relations between the Red and White Peoples of This Continent*, edited by Nishnawbe Institute (Toronto, Ontario: Neewin Publishing Company, 1971), 144, 147, 149, 153, 157–158.

CHAPTER 6

1. "Second Indian Ecumenical Conference Report," [July 18–21], 1971, 3, ACC/PWRDF, collection GS93–27, box 7; Samuel Stanley, "The Indian Experience in Education," in *Educating the Educators: A Report of the Institute on "The American Indian Student in Higher Education*," edited by Roy H. Sandstrom (Canton, NY: St. Lawrence University, 1971), 38; "Report of the Indian Ecumenical Conferences for Years 1970 through 1973," [1973?], 10, ACC/NMO, collection GS85–6, box 1, file 18; John Snow, *These Mountains Are Our Sacred Places: The Story of the Stoney Indians* (Toronto, Ontario: Samuel-Stevens, Publishers, 1977), 142; Dave Billington, *Spirit of the Hunt*, produced and directed by Deborah Peaker (Boulder, CO: Centre Productions, 1982), videotape, 29 min.; Dianne Meili, *Those Who Know: Profiles of Alberta's Native Elders* (Edmonton, Alberta: NeWest Press, 1991), 78ff; Darin Keewatin, telephone conversation with author, February 24, 2001.

2. "Community Profiles: Morley," *Native People* 2, no. 11 (1970): 18; "Second Indian Ecumenical Conference Report," 3; Snow, *These*, 18, 32ff, 41–42, 140–142.

3. "Morley People in Movie," *Native People* 2, no. 7 (1969): 6; "Community Profiles," 18; "Second Indian Ecumenical Conference Report," 1; Snow, *These*, 2, 42ff; Claudia Notzke, *Indian Reserves in Canada: Development Problems of the Stoney and Peigan Reserves in Alberta* (Marburg/Lahn, Germany: Department of Geography, Marburg University, 1985), 23ff; Jon Whyte, *Indians in the Rockies* (Banff, Alberta: Altitude Publishing, 1985), 120; *Internet Movie Database: Little Big Man*, cited February 21, 2001, available from http://us.imdb.com/Details?0065988.

4. "Community Profiles," 18; "Stoney Indian Park—Unique Experience," *Native People* 3, no. 5 (1970): 11; Snow, *These*, 43ff, 113–124.

5. "Second Indian Ecumenical Conference Report," 3; "Report of the Indian Ecumenical Conferences for Years 1970 through 1973," 10; Hugh McCullum,

People of the Sacred Circle, produced and directed by Sig Gerber (Toronto, Ontario: Canadian Broadcasting Corporation, 1975), 16mm film, 28 min.; Meili, *Those*, 78–87.

6. Snow, *These*, 142; Meili, *Those*, 78ff; Keewatin, February 24, 2001.

7. Grant MacEwan, *Tatanga Mani: Walking Buffalo of the Stonies* (Edmonton, Alberta: M. G. Hurtig, 1969), 22–25; Raoul R. Andersen, "Alberta Stoney (Assiniboin) Origins and Adaptations: A Case for Reappraisal," *Ethnohistory* 17, no. 1–2 (1970): 49–54; Wayne Edwin Allen Getty, "A Case History and Analysis of Stoney Indian-Government Interaction with Regard to the Big Horn Dam: The Effects of Citizen Participation—A Lesson in Government Perfidy and Indian Frustration" (M.S.W. project, University of Calgary, 1975), 20–21; Snow, *These*, 2; Peter M. Jonker, *Stoney History Notes* (Morley, Alberta: Chiniki Band of the Stoney Tribe, 1983); Eleanor G. Luxton, "Stony Indian Medicine," in *The Developing West: Essays on Canadian History in Honor of Lewis H. Thomas*, edited by John E. Foster (Edmonton, Alberta: University of Alberta Press, 1983), 108; Notzke, *Indian Reserves*, 9–10; Treaty 7 Elders and Tribal Council, Walter Hildebrandt, Sarah Carter, and Dorothy First Rider, *The True Spirit and Original Intent of Treaty 7* (Montreal, Ontario: McGill-Queen's University Press, 1996), 89–96.

8. Snow, *These*, 2–3, 11–13; *Our Own Way*, produced by the Stoney Tribal Administration (Morley, Alberta: Nakoda Institute, 1977), 16mm film, 28 min.; Donald K. Spence and Earle Waugh, *The Sacred Circle*, produced and directed by Donald K. Spence (Edmonton, Alberta: University of Alberta Video Production Centre, 1980), videotape, 29 min.; John W. Friesen, *Aboriginal Spirituality and Biblical Theology: Closer Than You Think* (Calgary, Alberta: Detselig Enterprises, 2000), 154ff.

9. Diamond Jenness, *Indians of Canada*, 7th ed. (Ottawa, Ontario: University of Toronto Press, 1977), 308–316; MacEwan, *Tatanga*, 23–25; Snow, *These*, xii-xiv, 2–11; Spence and Waugh, *The Sacred Circle*; Jonker, *Stoney*; Luxton, "Stony," 112–113; Frederick C. Mish, ed., *Merriam-Webster's Collegiate Dictionary*, 10th ed. (Springfield, MA: Merriam-Webster, 1999), 69.

10. MacEwan, *Tatanga*, 25 ; Andersen, "Alberta," 55–56; Wayne Edwin Allen Getty, "Perception as an Agent of Sociocultural Change for the Stoney Indians of Alberta" (M.A. thesis, University of Calgary, 1974), 11–14; Getty, "Case," 21–22; Snow, *These*, 16–18, 32; Jonker, *Stoney*; Notzke, *Indian Reserves*, 9–10; Hugh A. Dempsey, *Indian Tribes of Alberta*, rev. ed. (Calgary, Alberta: Glenbow Museum, 1986), 42–44; Treaty 7 Elders and Tribal Council and others, *True*, 104–107.

11. John McDougall, *In the Days of the Red River Rebellion* (Edmonton, Alberta: University of Alberta Press, 1983), 52–55, 236–240; MacEwan, *Tatanga*, 54–59.

12. Snow, *These*, 16, 18–23; Treaty 7 Elders and Tribal Council and others, *True*, 157–158, 359–360; David Wilson, "Histories Collide at Morley, Alta.," *United Church Observer*, May 1999, available from http://www.ucobserver.org/archives/ma99_chu.htm.

13. MacEwan, *Tatanga*, 60–65; Snow, *These*, 21–23; J. R. Miller, *Skyscrapers Hide the Heavens: A History of Indian-White Relations in Canada*, rev. ed. (Toronto, Ontario: University of Toronto Press, 1991), 160–161; Treaty 7 Elders and Tribal Council and others, *True*, 262–269.

14. Robert J. Surtees, *Canadian Indian Policy: A Critical Bibliography* (Bloomington, IN: Indiana University Press, 1982), 41–51; Notzke, *Indian Reserves*, 10–11;

Miller, *Skyscrapers*, 116ff, 152–169; Olive Patricia Dickason, *Canada's First Nations: A History of Founding Peoples from Earliest Times* (Norman, OK: University of Oklahoma Press, 1992), 257ff; Treaty 7 Elders and Tribal Council and others, *True*, 206–212; *Treaty 7 Tribal Council: A Brief History of Treaty Seven First Nations* (June 19, 2000), cited January 25, 2001, available from http://www.treaty7.org/info/info.htm.

15. Andersen, "Alberta," 55–56; *Our Own Way*; Jonker, *Stoney*; Notzke, *Indian Reserves*, 10–13.

16. Indian Chiefs of Alberta, *Citizens Plus* (Edmonton, Alberta: Indian Association of Alberta, 1970), 24–28; Getty, "Case," 22–23; Snow, *These*, 24–38; John Leonard Taylor, "Two Views on the Meaning of Treaties Six and Seven," in *The Spirit of the Alberta Indian Treaties*, edited by Richard Price (Edmonton, Alberta: Pica Pica Press, 1987), 9ff; Treaty 7 Elders and Tribal Council and others, *True*, 230–239, 262, 268–269.

17. Snow, *These*, 23, 39–53.

18. MacEwan, *Tatanga*, 76ff; Snow, *These*, 23, 39–53; *Our Own Way*; Donald K. Spence and Earle Waugh, *The Sacred Circle: Recovery*, produced and directed by Donald K. Spence (Edmonton, Alberta: University of Alberta Video Production Centre, 1980), videotape, 29 min.; Notzke, *Indian Reserves*, 13–14; Claudia Notzke, *Aboriginal Peoples and Natural Resources in Canada* (North York, Ontario: Captus University Publications, 1994), 180; Treaty 7 Elders and Tribal Council and others, *True*, 146ff, 167–170, 233.

19. MacEwan, *Tatanga*, 76ff; Snow, *These*, 50–63; Miller, *Skyscrapers*, 189ff; Treaty 7 Elders and Tribal Council and others, *True*, 146ff.

20. MacEwan, *Tatanga*, 78; Andersen, "Alberta," 57; Snow, *These*, 63–65, 76, 90–91; Dempsey, *Indian*, 47; Treaty 7 Elders and Tribal Council and others, *True*, 374.

21. Getty, "Case," 23; Snow, *These*, 48, 65–89; Notzke, *Indian Reserves*, 15, 17–18.

22. Snow, *These*, 90–91; Miller, *Skyscrapers*, 220–223; Dickason, *Canada's First*, 328–333.

23. Getty, "Case," 23–25; Snow, *These*, 91–103, 125; Notzke, *Indian Reserves*, 37–38.

24. Getty, "Case," 23–25; Snow, *These*, 91–103; Notzke, *Indian Reserves*, 37–38.

25. Snow, *These*, 106–108, 113–117; Miller, *Skyscrapers*, 222–224.

26. Nancy Millar, "John Snow: 'Who's Heathen Now?'" *United Church Observer*, March 1974, 26; Snow, *These*, 108–109; Treaty 7 Elders and Tribal Council and others, *True*, 372–373.

27. MacEwan, *Tatanga*, 81–88; Okhiambo Okite, "A Talk with Chief John Snow," *International Review of Mission*, April 1974, 182; Snow, *These*, 83, 109–111; Treaty 7 Elders and Tribal Council and others, *True*, 372.

28. MacEwan, *Tatanga*, 178ff; Cecil Nepoose, "Personality Profile: Reverend John Snow, Chief," *Native People* 5, no. 21 (1972): 11; Snow, *These*, 111–112, 134, 146–147.

29. Okite, "Talk," 181–182; Snow, *These*, 111–112; Treaty 7 Elders and Tribal Council and others, *True*, 372–373.

30. MacEwan, *Tatanga*, 203–204; Snow, *These*, 112–113; Ken Thompson, "New Warrior Needed to Fight for Rights," *Native People* 14, no. 5 (1981); *A New Path in the Mountains: A Financial Report to Stoney Members on Major Expenditures 1976–1985* (Morley, Alberta: Stoney Tribal Administration, 1986); Treaty 7 Elders and Tribal Council and others, *True*, 373.

31. Getty, "Perception," 29–30; Getty, "Case," 30–31; Snow, *These*, 113–114, 116.

32. "Former Stony Chief Dies," *Native People* 3, no. 5 (1970): 3; Okite, "Talk," 181; Getty, "Perception," 29–34; Getty, "Case," 31–32; Snow, *These*, 114–118, 122–123.

33. Indian Chiefs of Alberta, *Citizens*, 38; "Community Profiles," 18; Getty, "Perception," 27ff; Getty, "Case," 179–181; Snow, *These*, 118, 123–124, 136, 139, 154–155; *Our Own Way*.

34. Snow, *These*, 123–124, 136, 139, 154–155.

35. "Morley People in Movie," 6; "Community Profiles," 18; "Stoney Indian Park—Unique Experience," 11; Nepoose, "Personality," 11; Snow, *These*, 42, 118, 136, 140–141, 158; Notzke, *Indian Reserves*, 85–86.

36. "Why the Big Horn Dam Should Not Be Built" (1969), in "A Case History and Analysis of Stoney Indian-Government Interaction with Regard to the Big Horn Dam" by Wayne Edwin Allen Getty (M.S.W. project, University of Calgary, 1975), 143–152; Carol Hogg, "Area Near Dam Site Demanded by Stonys," *Akwesasne Notes* 2, no. 4 (1970): 42; Getty, "Perception," 43–45, 119; Getty, "Case," 39–48ff, 76–78; Snow, *These*, 101–102, 128–131, 153; *Our Own Way*; Whyte, *Indians*, 78–79; Claudia Notzke, "Indian Land in Southern Alberta," in *A Cultural Geography of North American Indians*, edited by Thomas E. Ross and Tyrel G. Moore (Boulder, CO: Westview Press, 1987), 112–114; Treaty 7 Elders and Tribal Council and others, *True*, 373.

37. National Indian Brotherhood, "Statement," in *Bulletin 201: Recent Statements by the Indians of Canada, General Synod Action 1969, Some Government Responses, Suggested Resource*, edited by Robert D. MacRae (Toronto, Ontario: Anglican Church of Canada, 1970), 29; Indian Chiefs of Alberta, *Citizens*; Snow, *These*, 114–116, 118–121; Miller, *Skyscrapers*, 223, 230–232; Dickason, *Canada's First*, 384–388; Peter McFarlane, *Brotherhood to Nationhood: George Manuel and the Making of the Modern Indian Movement* (Toronto, Ontario: Between the Lines, 1993), 115–116.

38. "Stoney Indian Park—Unique Experience," 11; Snow, *These*, 136, 142, 144, 158; Notzke, *Indian Reserves*, 87; Dickason, *Canada's First*, 198.

39. "Delegates of the First Indian Ecumenical Conference," August 13–19, 1970, ACC/NMO, collection GS85–6, box 1, file 15; Getty, "Perception," 118; Snow, *These*, 142–144.

40. Snow, *These*, 142–144.

41. *The Holy Bible*, King James Version (Cambridge, England: Cambridge University Press, 2000), Psalm 121:121; Snow, *These*, 13, 143; Edwin Bernbaum, *Sacred Mountains of the World* (Berkeley, CA: University of California Press, 1997), xiii.

42. Bernbaum, *Sacred*, xiii-xxiii, 208ff, 236–238.

43. Bernbaum, *Sacred*, ix, xiii, xxii, 142–144.

44. Snow, *These*, 13; Bernbaum, *Sacred*, xiii, xviii, xxii, 206ff, 256–258; T. C. McLuhan, ed., *The Way of the Earth: Encounters with Nature in Ancient and Contemporary Thought* (New York, NY: Simon and Schuster, 1994), 451–455.

45. "Second Indian Ecumenical Conference Report," 3; "Second Annual Indian Ecumenical Conference," July 18–21, 1971, DL.

46. "Second Indian Ecumenical Conference Announcement," April 1971, 1, DL; "Second Indian Ecumenical Conference Report," 3.

47. Leland C. Wyman, *Blessingway* (Tucson, AZ: University of Arizona Press, 1970), 3–35; "Second Indian Ecumenical Conference Report," 3; "Report of the Indian Ecumenical Conferences for Years 1970 through 1973," 8–9; Sam D. Gill, *Sacred Words: A Study of Navajo Religion and Prayer* (Westport, CT: Greenwood

Press, 1981), 61–85; Peter Iverson, *The Navajos* (New York, NY: Chelsea House Publishers, 1990), 31–34; Peggy V. Beck, Anna Lee Walters, and Nia Francisco, *The Sacred: Ways of Knowledge, Sources of Life*, rev. ed. (Tsaile, AZ: Navajo Community College Press, 1992), 14, 29, 41–42; Sam D. Gill and Irene F. Sullivan, *Dictionary of Native American Mythology* (New York, NY: Oxford University Press, 1992), 32–33, 211–212.

48. Wyman, *Blessingway*, 3–35; Gill, *Sacred*, 61–85; Iverson, *Navajos*, 31–34; Beck, Walters, and Francisco, *Sacred*, 14, 29, 41–42; Gill and Sullivan, *Dictionary*, 32–33, 211–212.

49. "Second Indian Ecumenical Conference Report," 3; Stanley, "Indian Experience," 38; Fine Day, *My Cree People*, edited by Adolf Hungry Wolf (Invermere, British Columbia: Good Medicine Books, 1973), 18–20, 60–63; David G. Mandelbaum, *The Plains Cree: An Ethnographic, Historical, and Comparative Study* (Regina, Saskatchewan: Canadian Plains Research Center, University of Regina, 1979), 157–158, 170–174, 227–228; Katherine Pettipas, *Severing the Ties that Bind: Government Repression of Indigenous Religious Ceremonies on the Prairies* (Winnipeg, Manitoba: University of Manitoba Press, 1994), 51–54, 61.

50. "Second Indian Ecumenical Conference Report," 3; Lester E. Robbins, "The Persistence of Traditional Religious Practices among Creek Indians" (Ph.D. dissertation, Southern Methodist University, 1976), 143–149, 165–166; *Music of the Sacred Fire: The Stomp Dance of the Oklahoma Cherokee*, produced by Charlotte Heth (Los Angeles, CA: Office of Institutional Development, University of California at Los Angeles, 1978), videotape, 57 min.; *Music of the Creek and Cherokee Indians in Religion and Government*, produced by Charlotte Heth (Los Angeles, CA: Office of Institutional Development, University of California at Los Angeles, 1978), videotape, 59 min.; James H. Howard and Willie Lena, *Oklahoma Seminoles: Medicines, Magic, and Religion* (Norman, OK: University of Oklahoma Press, 1984), 123–153; Muscogee (Creek) Nation, *Muscogee Culture and Traditions* (December 1, 2000), cited March 15, 2001, available from http://www.muscogeehealth.org/culture_traditions.htm; Cherokee Nation Cultural Resource Center, *Traditional Beliefs of the Cherokee* (January 26, 2001), cited March 15, 2001, available from http://www.yvwiiusdinvnohii.net/Cherokee/TraditionalBeliiefsofCherokee.htm; Jean Chaudhuri and Joyotpaul Chaudhuri, *A Sacred Path: The Way of the Muscogee Creeks* (Los Angeles, CA: UCLA American Indian Studies Center, 2001), 52–55, 89–90.

51. "Second Annual Indian Ecumenical Conference"; Billy Osceola, *Seminole Indian Oral History Interviews* (September 9, 1998), cited June 12, 2001, available from http://web.history.ufl.edu/oral/bosceola.89a.html.

52. "Second Annual Indian Ecumenical Conference"; Stanley, "Indian Experience," 38.

53. "A Proposal for an Indian Ecumenical Conference Presented by the Institute for Indian Studies," [December? 1969], 8, NAA/AICC, collection MS 4806, box 2; Dwight Powell, letter to Board of Home Missions regarding John Snow, March 23, 1971, UCC/BHM, location 83.050C, box 110, file 20; Powell, March 23, 1971; "Second Indian Ecumenical Conference Report," 4–5; "Second Annual Indian Ecumenical Conference"; *A New Path in the Mountains*; Robert K. Thomas, *The Indian Ecumenical Movement: A Grassroots Religious Movement*, lecture delivered at the Summer Public Lecture Series of the Vancouver School of Theology, July 21, 1986 (Vancouver, British Columbia:

Vancouver School of Theology, 1986), audiocassette; Mary Anne Caibaiosai, telephone conversation with author, April 23, 2001.

54. "Second Indian Ecumenical Conference Report," 3–4; "Resolutions Made at the Second Indian Ecumenical Conference," July 18–21, 1971, ACC/PWRDF, collection GS93–27, box 7; Stanley, "Indian Experience," 37.

55. "Second Annual Indian Ecumenical Conference"; "Steering Committee Elected at the Second Indian Ecumenical Conference," July 18–21, 1971, ACC/NMO, collection GS85–6, box 1, file 16; "Resolutions Made at the Second Indian Ecumenical Conference"; "North American Indian Cultural and Religious Centre," [August 1972], 1–3, ACC/NMO, collection GS85–6, box 1, file 18; "The Case of Chief Robert Smallboy," in *Native Peoples in Struggle: Cases from the Fourth Russell Tribunal and Other International Forums,* edited by Ismaelillo and Robin Wright (Bombay, NY: E.R.I.N. Publications, 1982), 150; Meili, *Those,* 109–115; Dickason, *Canada's First,* 417–418; Martin F. Dunn, *Congress of Aboriginal Peoples: Past Presidents* (April 2, 2001), cited April 22, 2001, available from http://www.abo-peoples.org/background/pastpres.html.

56. "Second Annual Indian Ecumenical Conference."

57. "Second Annual Indian Ecumenical Conference"; "Resolutions Made at the Second Indian Ecumenical Conference."

58. "Second Indian Ecumenical Conference Report," 3; "Second Annual Indian Ecumenical Conference"; Jennie Goodrich, Claudia Lawson, and Vana Parrish Lawson, *Kashaya Pomo Plants* (Los Angeles, CA: American Indian Studies Center, University of California at Los Angeles, 1980), v, 10.

59. "Second Indian Ecumenical Conference Report," 3; Wilfred Pelletier and Ted Poole, *No Foreign Land: The Biography of a North American Indian* (New York, NY: Pantheon Books, 1973), 186–187; *A New Path in the Mountains.*

CHAPTER 7

1. "Second Indian Ecumenical Conference Report," [July 18–21], 1971, 1, ACC/PWRDF, collection GS93–27, box 7; "Delegates of the Second Indian Ecumenical Conference," [July 18–21], [1971], 1–3, ACC/NMO, collection GS85–6, box 1, file 16; Wilfred Pelletier, letter to chairman of the Primate's World Relief and Development Fund, September 28, 1971, ACC/PWRDF, collection GS93–27, box 7.

2. "Delegates of the Second Indian Ecumenical Conference"; Samuel Stanley, "The Indian Experience in Education," in *Educating the Educators: A Report of the Institute on "The American Indian Student in Higher Education,"* edited by Roy H. Sandstrom (Canton, NY: St. Lawrence University, 1971), 37; Harold W. Turner, "Pan-Indian Ecumenical Conferences," May 22, 1972, 1, ACC/NMO, collection GS85–6, box 1, file 17; Sam Stanley, telephone conversation with author, May 9, 2001.

3. "The Institute for Indian Studies," [1969?], Appendix C, NAA/CSM, series 8— American Indians General, box 53; "Nishnawbe Institute Report of the Board of Directors," January 30, 1971, 12–13, ACC/PWRDF, collection GS93–27, box 7; "Second Indian Ecumenical Conference Announcement," April 1971, 2, DL; "Second Indian Ecumenical Conference Report," 1, 4.

4. Nishnawbe Institute, "Canadian Indian Youth Workshop," [1971?], 3, UCC/DMC, location 83.054C, box 39, file 6; "Canadian Indian Youth Workshop

Conference Report," 1971, 1–3, ACC/NMO, collection GS85–6, box 1, file 16; "Canadian Indian Youth Workshop Delegates," 1971, ACC/NMO, collection GS85–6, box 1, file 16; John A. MacKenzie, letter to K. H. Christie, January 26, 1972, UCC/DMC, location 83.054C, box 40, file 11; "Rocky Mountain Bush School," [1972?], 1–3, UCC/DMC, location 83.054C, box 39, file 9.

5. "Second Annual Indian Ecumenical Conference," July 18–21, 1971, DL; Jim White, telephone conversation with author, May 17, 2001.

6. "Resolutions Made at the Second Indian Ecumenical Conference," July 18–21, 1971, ACC/PWRDF, collection GS93–27, box 7; "Second Annual Indian Ecumenical Conference"; Larry Kroker, *Listen to the Elders* (April 20, 1997), cited May 9, 2001, available from http://www.companysj.com/v133/listen.html; Laura Recalma, telephone conversation with author, May 9, 2001.

7. "Second Annual Indian Ecumenical Conference"; "Report of the Indian Ecumenical Conferences for Years 1970 through 1973," [1973?], 8–12, ACC/NMO, collection GS85–6, box 1, file 18; Stand Middlestriker [Robert K. Thomas], "At the Fork in Our Trail," [1977?], 65, 79–81, 90–91, NIYC.

8. "Second Indian Ecumenical Conference Report," 3–4; "Second Annual Indian Ecumenical Conference"; Pelletier, September 28, 1971; Chris Cromarty, telephone conversation with author, May 24, 2001.

9. "Second Indian Ecumenical Conference Report," 4; "Second Annual Indian Ecumenical Conference"; Edward F. LaCroix, "The National Indian Youth Council: A Guide to the Publications," March 12, 1996, NIYC.

10. Stanley, "Indian Experience," 37; Turner, "Pan-Indian," 1–2; Wilfred Pelletier and Ted Poole, *No Foreign Land: The Biography of a North American Indian* (New York, NY: Pantheon Books, 1973), 56; Harold W. Turner, "Introduction to 'Religious Renewal in Native North America,'" *Missiology: An International Review* 13, no. 1 (1985): 81–82.

11. "Second Indian Ecumenical Conference Report," 2, 4–5; Pelletier, September 28, 1971; Wilfred Pelletier, letter to chairman of the Program Committee, September 28, 1971, ACC/NMO, collection GS85–6, box 1, file 16; Wilfred Pelletier, letter to Everett McNeil, January 11, 1972, ACC/NMO, collection GS85–6, box 1, file 17; Pelletier, January 11, 1972; Wilfred Pelletier, letter to H. M. Bailey, February 14, 1972, UCC/DMC, location 83.054C, box 39, file 4; Sam Stanley, "Indian Ecumenical Conference, St. Augustine's Seminary, Toronto, Canada," March 17–20, 1972, 9–12, ACC/NMO, collection GS85–6, box 1, file 17; "Indians, Christians, and Christian Indians," *Akwesasne Notes* 4, no. 2 (1972): 28; Cecil Corbett, telephone conversation with author, May 11, 1992.

12. H. F. Appleyard, letter to chairman of the General Synod Committee on Program, May 22, 1971, ACC/NMO, collection GS85–6, box 1, file 16; Neville R. Clarke, letter to John Bothwell, June 8, 1971, ACC/NMO, collection GS85–6, box 1, file 16; "Excerpts from Minutes of General Synod Program Committee Meeting," October 16, 1971, ACC/NMO, collection GS85–6, box 1, file 16; P. C. Jefferson, "Minutes of the Program Committee's Task Force on the Indian Ecumenical Religious Conference," December 7, 1971, 1–7, ACC/NMO, collection GS85–6, box 1, file 16; P. C. Jefferson, "Report of the Task Force on the Indian Ecumenical Religious Conference," December 7, 1971, 1–4, ACC/NMO, collection GS85–6, box 1, file 16; "Second Meeting of the Task Group Concerned with the Implementation of the Hendry Report in the Diocese of Huron," February 26, 1972, 1–3, ACC/NMO, collection GS85–6, box

1, file 17; "Indian Ecumenical Conference Grant Approved," *Canadian Church-man* 99, no. 5 (1972): 27.

13. "Second Indian Ecumenical Conference Report," 1–4; "Steering Committee Elected at the Second Indian Ecumenical Conference," July 18–21, 1971, ACC/NMO, collection GS85–6, box 1, file 16; Jefferson, "Minutes," 2; Jefferson, "Report," 1; Philip Jefferson, memorandum to Trevor Jones, May 5, 1972, ACC/NMO, collection GS85–6, box 1, file 17.

14. Carlos Castaneda, *The Teachings of Don Juan: A Yaqui Way of Knowledge* (Berkeley, CA: University of California Press, 1968); Maurice P. Wilkinson, letter to chief executive officers and members of the Joint Committee on Indian Work, January 28, 1972, UCC/DMC, location 83.054C, box 39, file 4; Stanley, "Indian Ecumenical Conference," 1–3; "Indian Day of Prayer Announced by Tootoosis," *Native People* 5, no. 6 (1972): 6; Donald A. Jackson, *Algoma University College and the Keewatinung Anishnabek Institute* (February 1, 2001), cited May 9, 2001, available from http://www.shingwauk.auc.ca/shingwauktrust/shingwauktrust9.html; Huron Miller, telephone conversation with author, June 18, 2001.

15. "Indian Steering Committee," [March 18–19], [1972], UCC/DMC, location 83.054C, box 39, file 4; Stanley, "Indian Ecumenical Conference," 4–9; Maurice P. Wilkinson, "Brief Report of the Meeting of the Canadian Council of Churches' Indian Committee with the Steering Committee of the Indian Ecumenical Conference," March 20, 1972, 1, UCC/BHM, location 83.050C, box 62, file 1272; Middlestriker, "Fork," 65; Winona Arriaga, telephone conversation with author, May 20, 2001.

16. Stanley, "Indian Ecumenical Conference," 4–11; Wilkinson, "Brief," 1.

17. Stanley, "Indian Ecumenical Conference," 9–11; Wilkinson, "Brief," 1–2; "Press Release," March 24, 1972, 2, ACC/NMO, collection GS85–6, box 1, file 17; Maurice P. Wilkinson, letter to chief executive officers and members of the Joint Committee on Indian Work, May 29, 1972, UCC/DMC, location 83.054C, box 39, file 4.

18. Stanley, "Indian Ecumenical Conference," 3, 6–7, 9–12; "Press Release," 1–2; "B.C. Indian Death Still Unresolved," *Canadian News Facts* 6, no. 14 (1972): 864; William Borders, "Canada's Mounties, Now under Criticism, Hailed by Queen on 100th Anniversary," *New York Times*, July 5, 1973, 3; Rex Weyler, *Blood of the Land: The Government and Corporate War Against the American Indian Movement* (New York, NY: Everest House Publishers, 1982), 48–49; Peter Matthiessen, *In the Spirit of Crazy Horse* (New York, NY: Viking Press, 1983), 59–60, 274–275; Howard Adams, *Tortured People: The Politics of Colonization*, rev. ed. (Penticton, British Columbia: Theytus Books, 1999), 83–84.

19. "Report of Trevor Jones' Visitation of Indian and Metis National and Provincial Organizations," November 15–24 1971, 3–4, ACC/PWRDF, collection GS93–27, box 7; "Indian Day of Prayer Announced by Tootoosis," 6; "Ecumenical Conferences," *Akwesasne Notes* 4, no. 3 (1972): 9; "Third Indian Ecumenical Conference Announcement," May 1972, 1–2, UCC/DMC, location 83.054C, box 39, file 4; "Indian Religious Leaders to Meet," *Native People* 5, no. 12 (1972): 2, 7; "Indian Ecumenical Conference Newsletter," June 1972, ACC/NMO, collection GS85–6, box 1, file 17; Donald Marshall, Sr., Denny Alexander, and Simon Marshall, "The Covenant Chain," in *Drumbeat: Anger and Renewal in Indian Country*, edited by Boyce Richardson (Toronto, Ontario:

Summerhill Press, 1989), 90–91; Paul Barnsley, *Georges Erasmus: Fighting for His People's Rights Began at an Early Age* (April 4, 2001), cited May 29, 2001, available from http://www.ammsa.com/achieve/aa98-g.erasmus.html.

20. James P. Spradley, ed., *Guests Never Leave Hungry: The Autobiography of James Sewid, A Kwakiutl Indian* (New Haven, CT: Yale University Press, 1969), 10–13; T. E. Jones, memorandum to J. C. Bothwell, April 29, 1970, ACC/PWRDF, collection GS93–27, box 7; *Kah-Sah-Las*, produced and directed by Sig Gerber (Toronto, Ontario: Canadian Broadcasting Corporation, 1970), 16mm film, 28 min.; John A. MacKenzie, "A Report on the Implementation of the Hendry Report," [April? 1971], 2–3, ACC/PC, collection GS76–11, box 2; "Appointment to Parish and Diocesan Services Division," June 26, 1972, ACC/PC, collection GS80–12, box 3; John Bird, *The Seventh Fire: First Peoples and the Anglican Church*, produced by Anglican Video for the Council for Native Ministries (Toronto, Ontario: Anglican Church of Canada, 1995), videotape, 28 min.; Jim White, telephone conversation with author, June 1, 2001; Maureen Willie, telephone conversation with author, June 11, 2001.

21. Margaret Craven, *I Heard the Owl Call My Name* (New York, NY: Dell Publishing Company, 1973), 92, 121; Gerald Di Pego, *I Heard the Owl Call My Name*, produced and directed by Daryl Duke ([Burbank, CA]: Tomorrow Entertainment, 1973), videotape, 79 min.; Charles E. Hendry, letter to Clarke [Raymond?], May 4, 1975, ACC/PC, collection GS81–15, box 1; Margaret Craven, *Again Calls the Owl* (New York, NY: Dell Publishing Company, 1980), 72ff, 113–116; Willie, June 11, 2001.

22. *Kah-Sah-Las*; Roy Bonisteel, *In Search of Man Alive* (Don Mills, Ontario: Collins Publishers, 1980), 17–19; Craven, *Again*, 114–120; Mary Jane Miller, *Rewind and Search: Conversations with the Makers and Decision-Makers of CBC Television Drama* (Montreal, Quebec: McGill-Queen's University Press, 1996), 410, 502; Blaine Allen, *Directory of CBC Television Series* (November 26, 1999), cited October 1, 2001, available from http://www.film.queensu.ca/cbc/; Sig Gerber, telephone conversation with author, May 29, 2001; White, June 1, 2001; Willie, June 11, 2001.

23. *Kah-Sah-Las*; Gerber, May 29, 2001.

24. Spradley, *Guests*, 82–92, 212–214, 236ff; *Kah-Sah-Las*; Craven, *Again*, 80; U'mista Cultural Centre, *History of the Big House in Alert Bay* (September 9, 1998), cited June 2, 2001, available from http://www.schoolnet.ca/aboriginal/umistweb/art10a-e.html; Gerber, May 29, 2001.

25. Cecil Nepoose, "Reunion of Indians and Their Religion Theme of Ecumenical Conference," *Native People* 5, no. 21 (1972): 9; R[ene] Fumoleau and Georges Erasmus, "The Third Indian Ecumenical Conference," *Aux Glaces Polaires*, no. 44 (1972): 37–38; "Report of the Indian Ecumenical Conferences for the Years 1970 through 1973," [1973?], 9, ACC/NMO, collection GS85–6, box 1, file 18.

26. "Steering Committee Elected at the Third Indian Ecumenical Conference," August 17–20, 1972, CCCB; Edward B. Fiske, "Indians Reviving Religious Heritage," *New York Times*, August 23, 1972, 43; Fumoleau and Erasmus, "Third," 37–38; Nepoose, "Reunion," 8; "Report of the Indian Ecumenical Conferences for Years 1970 through 1973," 8–10; "Report of the Indian Ecumenical Conferences for the Years 1970 through 1973," 9–11; Vine Deloria, Jr., *God Is Red* (New York, NY: Grosset and Dunlap Publishers, 1973), 263.

27. "Indian Religious Leaders to Meet," 2, 7; "Huge Turnout Expected for Ecumenical Conference," *Native People* 5, no. 19 (1972): 13; Fiske, "Indians," 43; Nepoose, "Reunion," 8–9; "Third Indian Ecumenical Conference," August 25, 1972, ACC/NMO, collection GS85–6, box 1, file 17; Edward B. Fiske, "Indian/Christian Ecumenical Meet Seeks Ways to Restore True Ways," *Akwesasne Notes* 4, no. 5 (1972): 19; "Interest in Indian Religion Growing," September 21, 1972, UCC/DMC, location 83.054C, box 39, file 1; Diane Longboat, "Conference Held on Stony Reserve Attracts Hundreds of Indian Delegates," *Indian News* 15, no. 5 (1972): 5; Howard L. Meredith, *The Native American Factor* (New York, NY: Executive Council of the Episcopal Church, 1973), 34; *The Dumont Brothers: Paths of the Spirit*, produced by Mardi Tindal (Etobicoke, Ontario: Berkeley Studio, 1992), videotape, 25 min.; Trans Canada Trail, *Native Roots* (October 1, 1999), cited June 8, 2001, available from http://www.tctrail.ca/roots/roots_oct99.htm; Widmeyer Communications, *Our Principals: Ted Fiske* (May 7, 2001), cited June 8, 2001, available from http://www.twbg.com/our_principals/fiske.html.

28. Nepoose, "Reunion," 9; Fumoleau and Erasmus, "Third," 38–39, 41; Longboat, "Conference," 5; "Report of the Indian Ecumenical Conferences for Years 1970 through 1973," 9–10; "Report of the Indian Ecumenical Conferences for the Years 1970 through 1973," 10–11.

29. "Indian Ecumenical Conference 1972 Resolutions," 1972, 1–4, ACC/NMO, collection GS85–6, box 1, file 17; "Steering Committee Elected at the Third Indian Ecumenical Conference"; Middlestriker, "Fork," 48; Gary Mitchell, telephone conversation with author, June 13, 2001.

30. "Indian Ecumenical Conference 1972 Resolutions," 2; "Steering Committee Elected at the Third Indian Ecumenical Conference"; "Third Indian Ecumenical Conference"; Nepoose, "Reunion," 9; Fumoleau and Erasmus, "Third," 39; Anne Medicine, telephone conversation with author, June 12, 2001.

31. "Little Big Horn High School Honors 1st Three Graduates," *Chicago Tribune*, June 4, 1972, 20; "Indian Ecumenical Conference 1972 Resolutions," 2–3; Fumoleau and Erasmus, "Third," 39; "Report of the Indian Ecumenical Conferences for the Years 1970 through 1973," 9–11; "Report of the Indian Ecumenical Conferences for Years 1970 through 1973," 10–12; Adolf Hungry Wolf and Beverly Hungry Wolf, *Shadows of the Buffalo: A Family Odyssey among the Indians* (New York, NY: William Morrow and Company, 1983), 182–184; David Beck, *The Chicago American Indian Community, 1893–1988: Annotated Bibliography and Guide to Sources in Chicago* (Chicago, IL: NAES College Press, 1988), 128–129, 269.

32. "Steering Committee Elected at the Third Indian Ecumenical Conference"; Hungry Wolf and Hungry Wolf, *Shadows*, 8, 17–34, 51–59, 65, 69, 73–75, 164–165, 180–182; Brett Herolt, John W. Ostman, and Vanessa Touset, *Voices from the Gaps: Women Writers of Color: Beverly Hungry Wolf* (March 9, 2001), cited June 3, 2001, available from http://voices.cla.umn.edu/authors/beverlyhungrywolf.html.

33. "Indian Ecumenical Conference 1972 Resolutions," 1–2; Hungry Wolf and Hungry Wolf, *Shadows*, 111, 182–186, 214.

34. Middlestriker, "Fork," 47–51; Richard K. Pope, "North American Indian Nationalism and the Decline of Sacred Authenticity," *Canadian Journal of Native Studies* 5, no. 2 (1985): 257.

35. Fiske, "Indians," 43; Fumoleau and Erasmus, "Third," 41; "Report to Program Committee on 1972 Hendry Implementation," August 31, 1972, 1, ACC/NMO, collection GS85–6, box 1, file 17; Longboat, "Conference," 5; "Report of the Indian Ecumenical Conferences for Years 1970 through 1973," 10.

36. Wade Clark Roof, *A Generation of Seekers: The Spiritual Journeys of the Baby Boom Generation* (New York, NY: HarperCollins Publishers, 1993), 1–8, 32ff, 54–60.

37. Roof, *Generation*, 117ff, 128–135, 151ff.

38. Roof, *Generation*, 1–4, 26–30, 72ff, 149ff.

39. Robert K. Thomas and John A. MacKenzie, letter to all members of the steering committee, August 27, 1972, ACC/NMO, collection GS85–6, box 1, file 17; Walter A. King, letter to Clarke MacDonald, August 28, 1972, UCC/DMC, location 83.054C, box 27, file 9; "Report to Program Committee on 1972 Hendry Implementation," 2; Fumoleau and Erasmus, "Third," 41.

40. John A. MacKenzie, letter to Elizabeth Loweth, June 19, 1972, UCC/DMC, location 83.054C, box 39, file 4; Thomas and MacKenzie, August 27, 1972; "North American Indian Cultural and Religious Centre," [August 1972], 7, ACC/NMO, collection GS85–6, box 1, file 18; "To All Members of the Steering Committee," [August? 1972], ACC/NMO, collection GS85–6, box 1, file 17; Robert K. Thomas, *The Indian Ecumenical Movement: A Grassroots Religious Movement*, lecture delivered at the Summer Public Lecture Series of the Vancouver School of Theology, July 21, 1986 (Vancouver, British Columbia: Vancouver School of Theology, 1986), audiocassette.

41. Thomas and MacKenzie, August 27, 1972; "North American Indian Cultural and Religious Centre," 7; John A. MacKenzie and Robert K. Thomas, letter to Chairman of the Primate's Fund, August 27, 1972, ACC/NMO, collection GS85–6, box 1, file 17; John A. MacKenzie, letter to Marv Lipman, August 27, 1972, ACC/NMO, collection GS85–6, box 1, file 17; "To All Members of the Steering Committee"; "Report to Program Committee on 1972 Hendry Implementation," 2; Ernest P. Willie, letter to Ian MacKenzie, September 18, 1972, ACC/NMO, collection GS85–6, box 1, file 17.

42. Thomas and MacKenzie, August 27, 1972; "North American Indian Cultural and Religious Centre," 1–7; MacKenzie and Thomas, August 27, 1972; "To All Members of the Steering Committee"; "Report to Program Committee on 1972 Hendry Implementation," 2; Willie, September 18, 1972; E. Willie, memorandum to Bob MacRae, October 26, 1972, ACC/NMO, collection GS85–6, box 1, file 17.

43. "Indian Ecumenical Conference Newsletter"; "North American Indian Cultural and Religious Centre," 1–7; MacKenzie and Thomas, August 27, 1972; "Report to Program Committee on 1972 Hendry Implementation," 2; John A. MacKenzie, letter to Sam [Stanley], November 8, 1972, NAA/CSM, series 8—American Indians General, box 57; Middlestriker, "Fork," 64–65, 92–93; Thomas, *Indian Ecumenical*.

44. "To All Members of the Steering Committee"; Willie, October 26, 1972.

45. Wilfred Pelletier, letter to all steering committee members of the Indian Ecumenical Conference, July 27, 1972, UCC/DMC, location 83.054C, box 39, file 4; Willie, September 18, 1972; John A. MacKenzie, letter to Social Economic Program of the Public Service Commission, October 22, 1972, NAA/CSM, series 8—American Indians General, box 57; Wilfred Pelletier, letter to R. D. MacRae, November 8, 1972, ACC/PWRDF, collection

GS93–27, box 7; Wilfred Pelletier, letter to steering committee members, [November? 1972], UCC/DMC, location 83.054C, box 39, file 4.

46. MacKenzie and Thomas, August 27, 1972; Bob MacRae, memorandum to E. Willie, September 5, 1972, ACC/NMO, collection GS85–6, box 1, file 3; Bob MacRae, memorandum to Clarke Raymond, December 29, 1972, ACC/NMO, collection GS85–6, box 1, file 17; Philip Jefferson, memorandum to Clarke Raymond, January 12, 1973, ACC/PWRDF, collection GS93–27, box 7; Richard Lightning, "Community Profile: Morley Reserve," *Native People* 6, no. 5 (1973): 3; Wilfred Pelletier, letter to R. D. MacRae, February 9, 1973, ACC/PWRDF, collection GS93–27, box 7; "Indian Ecumenical Conference," [February? 1973], 3–4, ACC/NMO, collection GS85–6, box 1, file 18; Ernest Willie, memorandum to Bob MacRae, March 15, 1973, ACC/PWRDF, collection GS93–27, box 7; R. D. MacRae, letter to Wilf Pelletier, March 19, 1973, ACC/PWRDF, collection GS93–27, box 7; "Minutes of Steering Committee Meeting, Indian Ecumenical Conference, Chicago, Illinois," April 13–15, 1973, 1–2, ACC/NMO, collection GS85–6, box 1, file 18; Lawrence Ear, "Letter to the Editor," *Stoney Country*, May 1973, 4; C. William Smith, letter to Wilfred Pelletier, May 4, 1973, CCCB; Andrea J. Williams, letter to Ernest Willie, June 1, 1973, ACC/NMO, collection GS85–6, box 1, file 18; "Ecumenical Conference General Information," July 30, 1974, 1, ACC/NMO, collection GS85–6, box 1, file 19.

47. "Indians: The Great Spirit," *Newsweek*, May 14, 1973, 71–72; "Looking Back: Stories Taken from the Pages of *Meeting Ground*," *Meeting Ground*, no. 37 (1997): 6; "McNickle Center Celebrates Its 25th Anniversary," *Meeting Ground*, no. 37 (1997): 1; Michele Linck, "Winnebagos Work to Keep Their Native Language Alive," *Sioux City Journal*, July 3, 1999, available from http://www.trib. com/scjournal/ARC/1999/JUL/Jul_11_99_Sun/LocalNews/Winnebagos.html.

48. Aubrey Perley, letter to International Assembly of Christians in Solidarity with the Vietnamese, Laotian and Cambodian Peoples, October 4, 1972, UCC/DMC, location 83.054C, box 39, file 4; "Steering Committee (Revised) Elected at the Third Indian Ecumenical Conference," April 1973, CCCB; "Minutes of Steering Committee Meeting," 1–4, 6.

49. "Minutes of Steering Committee Meeting," 1–2, 7–12; Thomas, *Indian Ecumenical.*

50. "Minutes of Steering Committee Meeting," 5–7, 11–12; Bob Thomas, letter to [service committee members], June 24, 1974, ACC/NMO, collection GS85–6, box 1, file 19; Ian MacKenzie, telephone conversation with author, June 18, 1992.

51. "Fourth Indian Ecumenical Conference Announcement," April 1973, 1–2, CCCB.

52. "The Indian Ecumenical Conference," [April? 1973], 6, ACC/NMO, collection GS85–6, box 1, file 18; "Morley to Host Religious Meet," *Native People* 6, no. 16 (1973): 1–2; "Alberta's Stoney Reserve to Host Fourth Indian Ecumenical Conference," *Indian News* 16, no. 2 (1973): 11; "4th Native Gathering," *Canadian Churchman* 100, no. 7 (1973): 7; "What's Happening on the Powwow Trail," *Akwesasne Notes* 5, no. 4 (1973): 2; Clarice Kootenay, "Local News," *Stoney Country*, August 1973.

53. Bill Smith, "The Fourth Indian Ecumenical Conference," August 13, 1973, 1, CCCB; Elaine Twoyoungmen, "Flashback Events of 1973," *Stoney Country*, December 1973; "Report of the Indian Ecumenical Conferences for Years 1970 through 1973," 13–14; "Report of the Indian Ecumenical Conferences for the

Years 1970 through 1973," 11–12; "Report of the Indian Ecumenical Conference (1970 through 1974)," [1975?], CCCB.

54. "Report of the Indian Ecumenical Conferences for Years 1970 through 1973," 13–14; "Report of the Indian Ecumenical Conferences for the Years 1970 through 1973," 11–13; Robert Sebastian, "Canadian National Indian Youth Workshop 1973," [1973?], UCC/DMC, location 83.054C, box 39, file 6; "Canadian Indian Youth Workshop Report," [1973], UCC/DMC, location 83.054C, box 39, file 6; Jeannette Corbiere Lavell, letter to K. Harriet Christie, February 27, 1974, UCC/DMC, location 83.054C, box 40, file 11; "Canadian Workshop for Young Indians," [1974?], 2, CCCB; "Report of the Indian Ecumenical Conference (1970 through 1974)."

55. Gillian Lindgren, "Indians Gather at Morley to Celebrate 'Old Ways,'" *Calgary Herald*, August 1, 1973; "God Will Soon Punish the White Man," *Calgary Herald*, August 4, 1973, 12; Gillian Lindgren, "Daybreak Service Honors 'Grandfather,'" *Calgary Herald*, August 4, 1973, 12; Sam Stanley, telephone conversation with author, May 7, 1992.

56. Stanley, "Indian Ecumenical Conference," 8; Fumoleau and Erasmus, "Third," 38; Lindgren, "Indians"; "God Will Soon Punish the White Man," 12; Lindgren, "Daybreak," 12; Smith, "Fourth," 3; Nancy Millar, "John Snow: 'Who's Heathen Now?,'" *United Church Observer*, March 1974, 28; Stanley, May 7, 1992.

57. Brad Steiger, *Indian Medicine Power* (Glouchester, MA: Para Research, 1984), 72–75; Robert K. Thomas, "Letter to Pope John Paul II," in *Getting to the Heart of the Matter: Collected Letters and Papers*, edited by Daphne J. Anderson (Vancouver, British Columbia: Native Ministries Consortium, Vancouver School of Theology, 1990), 100, 105.

58. Lindgren, "Daybreak," 12; "Report of the Indian Ecumenical Conferences for the Years 1970 through 1973," 11–13; "Report of the Indian Ecumenical Conference (1970 through 1974)"; Gillian Lindgren, "A Hot Summer? AIM Leader Spends His Time Keeping the Lid On," *Calgary Herald*, June 30, 1975; Olive Patricia Dickason, *Canada's First Nations: A History of Founding Peoples from Earliest Times* (Norman, OK: University of Oklahoma Press, 1992), 392.

59. Lindgren, "Indians"; Lindgren, "Daybreak," 12.

60. Smith, "Fourth," 4; "Report of the Indian Ecumenical Conference (1970 through 1974)."

CHAPTER 8

1. Bob Thomas, letter to all service committee members, September 15, 1973, ACC/NMO, collection GS85–6, box 1, file 18; Bob Thomas, letter to [service committee members], June 24, 1974, ACC/NMO, collection GS85–6, box 1, file 19; Stand Middlestriker [Robert K. Thomas], "At the Fork in Our Trail," [1977?], 53–54, 65–66, 79–84, 90–91, 122–123, 131, NIYC; Robert K. Thomas, *The Indian Ecumenical Movement: A Grassroots Religious Movement*, lecture delivered at the Summer Public Lecture Series of the Vancouver School of Theology, July 21, 1986 (Vancouver, British Columbia: Vancouver School of Theology, 1986), audiocassette.

2. Thomas, September 15, 1973; Bob Thomas, letter to service committee, [January 1974], ACC/NMO, collection GS85–6, box 1, file 19; Rolland H. (Bud) Wright, "Experience as Narrative, Culture, and Person," in *A Good Cherokee, A*

Good Anthropologist: Papers in Honor of Robert K. Thomas, edited by Steve Pavlik (Los Angeles, CA: American Indian Studies Center, University of California at Los Angeles, 1998), 327.

3. Thomas, September 15, 1973; Middlestriker, "Fork," 79–80; Thomas, *Indian Ecumenical.*

4. Thomas, September 15, 1973.

5. Thomas, September 15, 1973; Ltd. Pictographics, *Exploring Algoma: A Guide to the Region*, cited July 22, 2001, available from http://www.explorenorthernontario.com/algoma/top.lasso; Anishinabek News, *Spirit Journey Celebration of Ron Boissoneau's Life* (May 16, 2001), cited August 2, 2001, available from http://www.anishinabek.ca/news/Past%20issues/2000/June%20issue/Jun00ron%20boissoneau.htm.

6. Thomas, September 15, 1973.

7. Robert K. Thomas, "Sixth Annual Canadian Indian Youth Workshop Evaluation Report," 1972, 1–19, UCC/DMC, location 83.054C, box 39, file 6; Thomas, September 15, 1973; Middlestriker, "Fork," 92–93; Donald A. Jackson, *Algoma University College and the Keewatinung Anishnabek Institute* (February 1, 2001), cited May 9, 2001, available from http://www.shingwauk.auc.ca/shingwauktrust/shingwauktrust9.html; Rolland Nadjiwon, telephone conversation with author, July 27, 2001.

8. Thomas, September 15, 1973; Middlestriker, "Fork," 64–65.

9. Ernie Willie, letter to [service committee members], [January 1974], ACC/NMO, collection GS85–6, box 1, file 19; Ernie Willie, letter to Wilfred Pelletier, January 7, 1974, ACC/NMO, collection GS85–6, box 1, file 19.

10. Thomas, [January 1974]; Vine Deloria, Jr., "Religion and the Modern American Indian," *Current History*, no. 67 (1974): 251–252; Middlestriker, "Fork," 53–55.

11. "Morley to Host American Indian," *Calgary Albertan*, February 2, 1974; "Morley to Host American Indian Religious Conference," *Native People* 7, no. 6 (1974): 1, 3; Ernie Willie, letter to John Snow, February 8, 1974, ACC/NMO, collection GS85–6, box 1, file 19; John Snow, letter to [Bob Thomas], [February? 1974], ACC/NMO, collection GS85–6, box 1, file 19; Thomas, June 24, 1974.

12. Wilfred Pelletier and Ted Poole, *No Foreign Land: The Biography of a North American Indian* (New York, NY: Pantheon Books, 1973), 56, 209, 212; Wilf [Pelletier], letter to Elizabeth [Loweth], [January? 1974], UCC/DMC, location 83.054C, box 40, file 11; Willie, January 7, 1974; Snow, [February? 1974]; "Nishnawbe Institute Annual Report of the Board of Directors," March 31, 1974, CCCB; Jeannette Corbiere-Lavell, letter to E. W. Scott, June 18, 1974, ACC/PWRDF, collection GS93–27, box 7.

13. Pelletier and Poole, *No Foreign*, 61–64; "Minutes of Meeting of Sub-Committee on Native Affairs," November 23–25, 1973, 1, ACC/PWRDF, collection GS78–13, box 1; Ernie Willie, memorandum to all members of Sub Committee on Native Affairs, January 10, 1974, ACC/PWRDF, collection GS78–13, box 1; Kris Blak-Andersen, "Increased Emphasis for Social Ministries," *Canadian Churchman* 101, no. 2 (1974): 14; "Jesus 'Best Indian' Ever," *Native People* 7, no. 15 (1974): 4; "Minutes of the Native Affairs Consultant Advisory Committee," May 22, 1974, 1–3, ACC/PWRDF, collection GS78–13, box 1; John Bird, *The Seventh Fire: First Peoples and the Anglican Church*, produced by Anglican Video for the Council for Native Ministries (Toronto, Ontario: Anglican Church of

Canada, 1995), videotape, 28 min.; Peter Hamel and Catherine Morrison, *Anglican Church of Canada Policy Relating to Aboriginal Peoples, 1959–1998*, 3rd ed. (Toronto, Ontario: Anglican Church of Canada, 1998), 8.

14. Ernest Willie, letter to Albert Lightning, March 26, 1974, ACC/NMO, collection GS85–6, box 1, file 19; Thomas, June 24, 1974; Bob Thomas, letter to Ernest Willie, July 3, 1974, ACC/NMO, collection GS85–6, box 1, file 19; Thomas, July 3, 1974; Middlestriker, "Fork," 122–125, 131; Sam Stanley, telephone conversation with author, May 7, 1992; Sig Gerber, telephone conversation with author, September 24, 2001.

15. John Snow, "1974 Indian Ecumenical Conference," [1974], UCC/DMC, location 83.054C, box 39, file 5; *Stoney Indian Park* (Morley, Alberta: SCEP Map Dept., 1974); "Ecumenical Conference General Information," July 30, 1974, 2–4, ACC/NMO, collection GS85–6, box 1, file 19.

16. "Ecumenical Conference General Information," 1; "The Fifth Indian Ecumenical Conference," *Stoney Country*, Summer 1974.

17. "[Indian Ecumenical Conference 1974—Delegates]," [1974], 1–4, ACC/NMO, collection GS85–6, box 1, file 19; "Indian Ecumenical Conference 1974—Observers," [1974], 1–30, ACC/NMO, collection GS85–6, box 1, file 19; "Names without Addresses," [1974], ACC/NMO, collection GS85–6, box 1, file 19; "Non-Indian Guests," [1974], 1–2, ACC/NMO, collection GS85–6, box 1, file 19; Cecil Nepoose, "Native Revival Plotted," *Native People* 7, no. 32 (1974): 1, 5; "Oneness with Nature Describes Aim of Conference," *Canadian Churchman* 101, no. 8 (1974): 26; Winston Halapua, "A Polynesian Observer at the Indian Ecumenical Conference in Morley Reservation," [1974], 1–4, ACC/NMO, collection GS85–6, box 1, file 19; "The Indian Ecumenical Conference: An International Religious Gathering," *Indian News* 17, no. 1 (1975): 8; "Report of the Indian Ecumenical Conference (1970 through 1974)," [1975?], CCCB; "Indian Ecumenical Conference," July 28–August 3, 1975, NGS.

18. Nepoose, "Native"; Noel Knockwood, "Indian Ecumenical Conference," 1974, ACC/NMO, collection GS85–6, box 1, file 19; Noel Knockwood, "Why I Became an Elder," *MicMac Maliseet Nations News*, February 1998, available from http://archives.ayn.ca/pages/nm-eld.htm.

19. "Oneness with Nature Describes Aim of Conference," 26; "Indian Ecumenical Conference," 1974, 1–2, ACC/NMO, collection GS85–6, box 1, file 19; Karen Ibbitson, "Indian Ecumenical Conference," 1974, ACC/NMO, collection GS85–6, box 1, file 19; Bernice [Hergott?], letter to Ernie [Willie], August 9, 1974, ACC/NMO, collection GS85–6, box 1, file 19; Halapua, "Polynesian," 1–4.

20. "The Indian Ecumenical Conference: An International Religious Gathering," 8; Howard Adams, *Prison of Grass: Canada from a Native Point of View*, rev. ed. (Saskatoon, Saskatchewan: Fifth House Publishers, 1989), 169–171; Howard Adams, *Tortured People: The Politics of Colonization*, rev. ed. (Penticton, British Columbia: Theytus Books, 1999), 115–118.

21. James S. Rausch, letter to Wilfred Pelletier, October 23, 1973, ACC/NMO, collection GS85–6, box 1, file 19; Snow, [February? 1974]; Ernie Willie, memorandum to Clarke Raymond, July 8, 1974, ACC/NMO, collection GS85–6, box 1, file 19; Nepoose, "Native," 5; "Indian Ecumenical Conference (1974)," 1; "My Reflections on the Indian Ecumenical Conference 1974," [1975?], ACC/NMO, collection GS85–6, box 1, file 19; William

Smith, letter to Jeannette Corbiere Lavell, August 15, 1974, CCCB; Ernest Willie, letter to John Snow, September 9, 1974, ACC/NMO, collection GS85–6, box 1, file 19; Ernie Willie, memorandum to members of the Management Unit, October 21, 1974, ACC/NMO, collection GS85–6, box 1, file 19; "Indian Ecumenical Conference—Statement," February 28, 1975, 1–3, ACC/NMO, collection GS85–6, box 1, file 19.

22. Willie, February 8, 1974; "Ecumenical Conference General Information," 1–2; "Indian Ecumenical Conference (1974)"; Willie, September 9, 1974; "Indian Ecumenical Conference—Statement," 2–3.

23. Nepoose, "Native," 1; Willie, September 9, 1974; "My Reflections on the Indian Ecumenical Conference 1974."

24. Ernie Willie, letter to all members of the steering committee, December 6, 1974, ACC/NMO, collection GS85–6, box 1, file 19.

25. Willie, September 9, 1974; "My Reflections on the Indian Ecumenical Conference 1974"; "Service Committee (Revised)," February 1975, ACC/NMO, collection GS85–6, box 1, file 20; "Report of the Indian Ecumenical Conference (1970 through 1974)."

26. "Indian Ecumenical Conference (1974)," 2; "Indian Ecumenical Conference," *Canadian Churchman* 101, no. 10 (1974): 18; "Bishop Calls for Support," *Canadian Churchman* 102, no. 5 (1975): 3; "Give Indians Control," *Canadian Churchman* 102, no. 5 (1975): 3; "Indian Culture and Religion Receive Church Support," *Canadian Churchman* 102, no. 5 (1975): 16; "Native Affairs Sub-Committee Faces Difficult Task," *Canadian Churchman* 102, no. 5 (1975): 17; "Fragmentation, Disunity, among Indian Groups," *Canadian Churchman* 102, no. 5 (1975): 22; *Journal of Proceedings of the 27th Session of the General Synod* (Toronto, Ontario: Anglican Church of Canada, 1975), M26-M27, M37, 152–154; Ernie Willie, letter to all members of the Sub-Committee on Native Affairs, July 8, 1975, ACC/PWRDF, collection GS78–13, box 1.

27. "Indian Ecumenical Conference (1975)"; "Medicine Men and Christians Powwow," *Toronto Star,* July 26, 1975; Jon Whyte, *Indians in the Rockies* (Banff, Alberta: Altitude Publishing, 1985), 79–80.

28. Andrea J. Williams, letter to service committee member, April 22, 1975, ACC/NMO, collection GS85–6, box 1, file 20; Joan Morrison, "Indians Try to Recapture Religion," *Calgary Herald,* July 28, 1975, 26; Gillian Lindgren, "Conference 'Last Chance' to Preserve Native Ways," *Calgary Herald,* July 31, 1975; Hugh McCullum, "Religious Pow-wow Kindles Indian Pride," *Toronto Star,* August 30, 1975; Peter Jonker, *The Song and the Silence: Sitting Wind: The Life of Stoney Indian Chief Frank Kaquitts* (Edmonton, Alberta: Lone Pine Publishing, 1988), 203–212.

29. Hugh McCullum, *People of the Sacred Circle*, produced and directed by Sig Gerber (Toronto, Ontario: Canadian Broadcasting Corporation, 1975), 16mm film, 28 min.; Freida Lee Mock, Terry Sanders, and Arthur Bramble, *The New Indians*, produced by Terry Sanders and Freida Lee Mock, directed by Terry Sanders (Washington, DC: National Geographic Society, 1976), 16mm film, 55 min.; John Snow, *These Mountains Are Our Sacred Places: The Story of the Stoney Indians* (Toronto, Ontario: Samuel-Stevens, Publishers, 1977), 143; Thomas, *Indian Ecumenical*; John William Sayer, *Ghost Dancing the Law: The Wounded Knee Trials* (Cambridge, MA: Harvard University Press, 1997), 77; *Filming Locations for Buffalo Bill and the Indians, or Sitting Bull's History Lesson*, cited February 21, 2001, available from http://us.imdb.com/Locations?0074254.

30. McCullum, "Religious"; McCullum, *People;* Mock, Sanders, and Bramble, *New;* Eric Cohen, "Spanning the Globe: The National Geographic Society's Aggressive Growth Strength," *Philanthropy,* May 2000, available from http://www.philanthropyroundtable.org/magazines/2000–05/.

31. Sig Gerber, interview by author, Toronto, Ontario, September 20, 1999; Terry Sanders, telephone conversation with author, September 21, 2001; Gerber, September 24, 2001.

32. *The Great Spirit,* produced and directed by Sig Gerber (Toronto, Ontario: Canadian Broadcasting Corporation, 1975), 16mm film, 28 min.; Sig Gerber, "The Great Spirit," [1976], SG; Roy Bonisteel, *In Search of Man Alive* (Don Mills, Ontario: Collins Publishers, 1980), 179–183; Gerber, September 20, 1999; "TV Productions by Sig Gerber," [1999], SG; Gerber, September 24, 2001.

33. Jules B. Billard, ed., *The World of the American Indian* (Washington, DC: National Geographic Society, 1974); Terry Sanders, "The World of the American Indian: Proposal for a National Geographic Society Television Special," [1975?], 1–2, 5, NGS; Nicolas Noxon, *This Britain: Heritage of the Sea,* produced and directed by Terry Sanders (Washington, DC: National Geographic Society, 1975), 16mm film, 52 min.; Terry Sanders, letter to Ernie Willie, July 5, 1975, ACC/NMO, collection GS85–6, box 1, file 20; Sanders, September 21, 2001.

34. Sanders, July 5, 1975; David Beck, *The Chicago American Indian Community, 1893–1988: Annotated Bibliography and Guide to Sources in Chicago* (Chicago, IL: NAES College Press, 1988), 97–103, 269; Dorene P. Wiese, "American-Indian Adults and the Construction, Structures, and Meaning of Knowledge" (Ed.D. dissertation, Northern Illinois University, 1996), xii–xv; Sanders, September 21, 2001; Dorene Porter Wiese, telephone conversation with author, September 24, 2001.

35. "July 27–Aug. 3," [1975], SG; "Medicine Men and Christians Powwow"; McCullum, *People;* Mock, Sanders, and Bramble, *New;* Bonisteel, *Search,* 179; Gerber, September 20, 1999; Sanders, September 21, 2001; Wiese, September 24, 2001.

36. Carl F. Starkloff, *The People of the Center: American Indian Religion and Christianity* (New York, NY: Seabury Press, 1974); McCullum, "Religious"; "People of the Centre," [1975], SG; "People of the Sacred Circle," [1975], SG; Gail McIntyre, "Man Alive Begins Its New Season with 'People of the Sacred Circle,'" October 8, 1975, 1–2, SG; McCullum, *People;* Gerber, September 20, 1999; "TV Productions by Sig Gerber."

37. Stan Steiner, *The New Indians* (New York, NY: Dell Publishing Company, 1968); "Bibliography for The New Indians," [1976], 1–5, NGS; "The New Indians Production Credits," [1976], 1–2, NGS; Mock, Sanders, and Bramble, *New;* Gilbert M. Grosvenor, "From the Florida Keys to the Volga: The New Season on Public Television," [1976], NGS; "New Indians Regain Past, Look to Future," [1977], NGS; Donald J. Frederick, "National Geographic TV Show Offers a Fresh Look at 'The New Indians,'" January 25, 1977, 1, NGS; "See 'The New Indians' Tuesday, February 15, on PBS TV," *National Geographic* 151, no. 2 (1977): front cover; C. D. B. Bryan, *The National Geographic Society: 100 Years of Adventure and Discovery* (New York, NY: Harry N. Abrams, 1987), 385–386; Sanders, September 21, 2001.

38. McCullum, *People.*

39. McCullum, *People.*

40. Mock, Sanders, and Bramble, *New.*

41. James P. Spradley, ed., *Guests Never Leave Hungry: The Autobiography of James Sewid, A Kwakiutl Indian* (New Haven, CT: Yale University Press, 1969); Gordon Young, "Will Coal Be Tomorrow's 'Black Gold'?" *National Geographic* 148, no. 2 (1975): 248–249; Mock, Sanders, and Bramble, *New;* Tiger Tiger, *Eye of the Tiger* (Clouds, 1980), sound recording.

42. Margaret R. Miles, *Seeing and Believing: Religion and Values in the Movies* (Boston, MA: Beacon Press, 1996), 81.

43. Miles, *Seeing,* ix-xiii, 3, 14–16, 22–32, 43, 49–50, 69–70, 81, 95–96, 182, 186–193, 195–197.

44. Miles, *Seeing,* ix-xiii, 3, 14–16, 22–32, 43, 49–50, 69–70, 81, 95–96, 182, 186–193, 195–197.

45. Miles, *Seeing,* x, xii-xv, 17–21, 26–29, 53, 70–72, 77, 157–158, 167–181, 193.

46. Miles, *Seeing,* x, xii-xv, 17–21, 26–29, 53, 70–72, 77, 157–158, 167–181, 193.

47. McCullum, *People;* Mock, Sanders, and Bramble, *New.*

48. Freida Lee Mock and Terry Barrett Sanders, "American Indian," [1975], 1–2, 7–9, 11, 14–15, NGS; Mock, Sanders, and Bramble, *New;* Louis Amiotte, interview by author, Alameda, CA, June 29, 1992; Eleanor Lillesand and Thomas Baldwin, *Laurie Lea Schaefer* (October 7, 2000), cited July 9, 2001, available from http://www.pressplus.com/missam/pw_1972.html; Wiese, September 24, 2001.

49. Terry Sanders, "Revised Cost Estimate," May 8, 1975, NGS; "Interview notes—Eddie Benton, John Snow, Wilf Pelletier," [1975], SG; McCullum, *People;* Mock, Sanders, and Bramble, *New;* Sanders, September 21, 2001; Gerber, September 24, 2001.

50. Billard, *World;* Sanders, "World," 1; Sanders, July 5, 1975; McCullum, *People;* Mock, Sanders, and Bramble, *New;* Vine Deloria, Jr., "The Coming of the People," in *The American Land,* edited by Alexix Doster III, Joe Goodwin, and Robert C. Post (Washington, DC: Smithsonian Exposition Books, 1979), 53; Catherine A. Lutz and Jane L. Collins, *Reading National Geographic* (Chicago, IL: University of Chicago Press, 1993), 57–81, 89, 96–98; Linda Steet, *Veils and Daggers: A Century of National Geographic's Representation of the Arab World* (Philadelphia, PA: Temple University Press, 2000), 75–77; Sanders, September 21, 2001.

51. Adam Cuthand, "Service Committee Meeting of Indian Ecumenical Conference held in Kenora, Ontario," October 27–28, 1975, ACC/NMO, collection GS85–6, box 1, file 20; McCullum, *People;* Mock, Sanders, and Bramble, *New;* Louis Amiotte, telephone conversation with author, August 6, 2001; Susan Supernaw Kato, e-mail to author, September 21, 2001; Sanders, September 21, 2001; Wiese, September 24, 2001; Lynn Nell Begay, telephone conversation with author, October 5, 2001; Colin Wesaw, telephone conversation with author, October 22, 2001; Terry Patenoude, telephone conversation with author, October 22, 2001.

52. Mock, Sanders, and Bramble, *New;* Amiotte, August 6, 2001; Kato, September 21, 2001; Begay, October 5, 2001; Wesaw, October 22, 2001.

53. John G. Neihardt, *Black Elk Speaks: Being the Life Story of a Holy Man of the Ogalala Sioux* (New York, NY: W. Morrow and Company, 1932); Joseph Epes Brown, *The Sacred Pipe: Black Elk's Account of the Seven Rites of the Oglala Sioux* (Norman, OK: University of Oklahoma Press, 1953); McCullum, *People;* Mock,

Sanders, and Bramble, *New;* Raymond J. DeMallie, ed., *The Sixth Grandfather: Black Elk's Teachings Given to John G. Neihardt* (Lincoln, NE: University of Nebraska Press, 1984); Gerber, September 20, 1999; Sanders, September 21, 2001.

54. Thomas, September 15, 1973; McCullum, *People;* Mock, Sanders, and Bramble, *New.*

55. McCullum, *People.*

56. Mock, Sanders, and Bramble, *New.*

57. McCullum, *People;* Mock, Sanders, and Bramble, *New;* Dianne Meili, *Those Who Know: Profiles of Alberta's Native Elders* (Edmonton, Alberta: NeWest Press, 1991), 82–83.

58. Cuthand, "Service," 1; C. A. Hooker, letter to *Man Alive,* November 3, 1975, SG; Ernest Tootoosis, letter to CBC, [November 4, 1975], SG; Stewart K. Etsitty, letter to *Man Alive,* [November 4, 1975], SG; Carol Kenny, letter to *Man Alive,* November 4, 1975, SG; Victor Pierre, letter to Roy Bonisteel, November 4, 1975, SG; Menno Wiebe, letter to Sig Gerber, December 29, 1975, SG; Ruth Blaser, letter to Sig Gerber, [January 1976], SG; Frederick, "National," 1; Cecil Smith, "'The New Indians'—Back to Roots," *Los Angeles Times,* February 15, 1977, IV, 11; Morton Moss, "'New Indian' Searches Past," *Los Angeles Herald Examiner,* February 15, 1977; "National Geographic Special 'The New Indians,'" *Daily Variety,* February 15, 1977; Amiotte, June 29, 1992; Cathy Hunter, e-mail to author, September 22, 1999; J. B. Bird, *Roots* (September 28, 2000), cited November 6, 2001, available from http://www.mbcnet.org/etv/r/htmlr/roots/roots.htm; Kato, September 21, 2001; Wiese, September 24, 2001; Begay, October 5, 2001; Wesaw, October 22, 2001; Patenoude, October 22, 2001.

59. McCullum, *People;* Mock, Sanders, and Bramble, *New;* R. G. Corey, memorandum to all departments and divisions, April 8, 1977, NGS; *North American Indians Today* (Washington, DC: National Geographic Society, 1977), 16mm film, 25 min.; Sig Gerber, telephone conversation with author, February 24, 1993; Mary Kiervin, telephone conversation with author, June 1, 1994; Sanders, September 21, 2001.

60. Amiotte, June 29, 1992; Kato, September 21, 2001; Wiese, September 24, 2001; Begay, October 5, 2001; Wesaw, October 22, 2001; Patenoude, October 22, 2001.

61. Wiese, "American-Indian," i, xii-xv, 55, 58–64, 70–72.

CHAPTER 9

1. Wendy Gray and Sam Erasmus, "A.I.M. Leader Stages Protest Suicide," *Native People* 9, no. 1 (1976): 1–2; Barry Nelson, "Mourners Gather for Small Legs' Burial," *Calgary Herald,* May 22, 1976, 1–2; Joan Ryan, *Wall of Words: The Betrayal of the Urban Indian* (Toronto, Ontario: PMA Books, 1978), xv-xvi; Duane Champagne, ed., *The Native North American Almanac: A Reference Work on Native North Americans in the United States and Canada* (Detroit, MI: Gale Research, 1994), 1163.

2. Barry Nelson, "Suicide Was His Final Protest," *Calgary Herald,* May 18, 1976, 1–2; Gray and Erasmus, "A.I.M. Leader," 1–2; Ryan, *Wall,* xvi, 19, 49, 73, 84; Ward Churchill and Jim Vander Wall, *Agents of Repression: The FBI's Secret Wars against the Black Panther Party and the American Indian Movement* (Boston, MA: South End Press, 1988), 175, 184–188, 199ff.

3. Nelson, "Suicide," 2; Barry Nelson, "AIM Leader Chose Own Proud Culture," *Calgary Herald*, May 20, 1976, 1–2; Ryan, *Wall*, xvi, 73, 84–86.

4. Nelson, "AIM Leader," 2; Jeremy Schneider, "From Wounded Knee to Capitol Hill: The History, Achievements and Legacy of the American Indian Movement," *Indian Nation* 3, no. 1 (1976); James Burke, *Paper Tomahawks: From Red Tape to Red Power* (Winnipeg, Manitoba: Queenston House Publishing, 1976), 350ff; Ryan, *Wall*, 30–49; "The American Indian Movement," [1982], 3, GTU, call number E77 A495; Rex Weyler, *Blood of the Land: The Government and Corporate War against the American Indian Movement* (New York, NY: Everest House Publishers, 1982), 237; Peter McFarlane, *Brotherhood to Nationhood: George Manuel and the Making of the Modern Indian Movement* (Toronto, Ontario: Between the Lines, 1993), 190–191.

5. Gillian Lindgren, "AIM Leader Says Indians Ready to Die," *Calgary Herald*, February 11, 1975; "Burnstick-Littlechief Fund Grows," *Calgary Herald*, February 11, 1975; Gillian Lindgren, "A Hot Summer? AIM Leader Spends His Time Keeping the Lid On," *Calgary Herald*, June 30, 1975; "RCMP Sees No Massive Confrontation," *Calgary Herald*, June 30, 1975; Gillian Lindgren, "Indian Leaders Accuse RCMP of 'Spying' Tactics," *Calgary Herald*, February 10, 1976; Bill Boei, "AIM Leaders Claim Harassment by RCMP," *Albertan*, February 10, 1976; Nelson, "AIM Leader," 1–2; Ryan, *Wall*, 49–83; Peter Matthiessen, *In the Spirit of Crazy Horse* (New York, NY: Viking Press, 1983), 154ff; Arthur Solomon, "What Is A.I.M.?" in *Songs for the People: Teachings on the Natural Way* by Arthur Solomon, edited by Michael Posluns (Toronto, Ontario: NC Press, 1990), 60–62.

6. Gary George, "Snow Says Judd Buchanan Is a 'Confused Man,'" *Native People* 9, no. 1 (1976): 1–2; Gary George, "Snow Doubts Settlements Will Be Just," *Native People* 9, no. 2 (1976): 8; "Dene Declaration," in *Dene Nation: The Colony Within*, edited by Mel Watkins (Toronto, Ontario: University of Toronto Press, 1977), 3–4; Thomas R. Berger, *Northern Frontier, Northern Homeland: The Report of the Mackenzie Valley Inquiry* (Ottawa, Ontario: Minister of Supply and Services Canada, 1977); Olive Patricia Dickason, *Canada's First Nations: A History of Founding Peoples from Earliest Times* (Norman, OK: University of Oklahoma Press, 1992), 402, 405–406; Roger L. Nichols, *Indians in the United States and Canada: A Comparative History* (Lincoln, NE: University of Nebraska Press, 1998), 305–306.

7. Nelson, "AIM Leader," 2; Gray and Erasmus, "A.I.M. Leader," 1; Ryan, *Wall*, 83–85.

8. *The Longest War* (Salt Lake City, UT: KUTV Documentary Division, 1973), 16mm film, 27 min.; Gray and Erasmus, "A.I.M. Leader," 1; Ryan, *Wall*, 19–21, 28, 84–86; Joan Ryan, telephone conversation with author, December 13, 2001.

9. Nelson, "Suicide," 1; Gray and Erasmus, "A.I.M. Leader," 1–2; Nelson, "Mourners," 1–2; Ryan, *Wall*, xv–xvi.

10. George, "Snow Says," 2; Nelson, "Mourners," 1–2; Ryan, *Wall*, xvi.

11. Gary George, "Morley . . . Different Things to Different People," *Native People* 9, no. 8 (1976); Ruth Blaser, "Reflection on the Indian Ecumenical Conference 1976," [1976], ACC/AJ; James Kaquitts, "Activity Report for Period: July, August, September, 1976," 1976, 1, NAC, record group 10, volume 12805, file E4735-2221; "Indian Ecumenical Conference 1976," [1977], 1, ACC/NMO, collection GS85-6, box 2; John Snow, *These Mountains Are Our Sacred Places:*

The Story of the Stoney Indians (Toronto, Ontario: Samuel-Stevens, Publishers, 1977), 142.

12. "Fragmentation, Disunity, among Indian Groups," *Canadian Churchman* 102, no. 5 (1975): 22; Hugh McCullum, *People of the Sacred Circle*, produced and directed by Sig Gerber (Toronto, Ontario: Canadian Broadcasting Corporation, 1975), 16mm film, 28 min.; George, "Morley"; "Indian Ecumenical Conference 1976," 2.

13. George, "Morley"; "Indian Ecumenical Conference 1976," 2; Edward W. Scott, letter to Rodney Andrews and Donovan V. Browne, May 30, 1979, ACC/PO, collection GS87–10, box 7; McFarlane, *Brotherhood*, 289.

14. Paul Jackson, "PM Pledges 'Earnest' Probe of Protest Death," *Calgary Herald*, May 20, 1976, 1; Eric Denhoff, "Whites Back Call for Indian Affairs Probe," *Albertan*, May 21, 1976; "Trudeau Promises Probe of Complaints in Letters," *Native People* 9, no. 1 (1976): 2; "Indian Ecumenical Conference 1976," 2; Young Grey Horse Society, *Songs of the Blackfeet* (Phoenix, AZ: Canyon Records, 1977), sound recording, 38 min.; Nelson Small Legs Jr. Foundation, "History of the Foundation," 1977, YULL; Ryan, *Wall*, iii, 85; J. Rick Ponting, Roger Gibbins, and Andrew J. Siggner, *Out of Irrelevance: A Socio-Political Introduction to Indian Affairs in Canada* (Toronto, Ontario: Butterworths, 1980), v, 209; "The American Indian Movement," 4.

15. "Minutes of Steering Committee Meeting, Indian Ecumenical Conference, Chicago, Illinois," April 13–15, 1973, 8, ACC/NMO, collection GS85–6, box 1, file 18; D. Mills Lavell, "Nishnawbe Institute: 1976 Annual Board Meeting," February 7–8, 1976, 2–3, DL; "Budget Estimate for Morley Conference Film Project," [1976], ACC/NMO, collection GS85–6, box 2; Kirsten Emiko McAllister, "Narrating Japanese Canadians in and out of the Canadian Nation: A Critique of Realist Forms of Representation," *Canadian Journal of Communication* 24, no. 1 (1999); David Lavell, telephone conversation with author, October 22, 2001.

16. Alanis Obomsawin, *Christmas at Moose Factory*, produced by Wolf Koenig, directed by Alanis Obomsawin (Montreal, Quebec: National Film Board of Canada, 1971), 16mm film, 13 min.; *Speaking Together: Canada's Native Women* (Ottawa, Ontario: Secretary of State, 1975), 104–105; Alanis Obomsawin, *Mother of Many Children*, produced and directed by Alanis Obomsawin (Montreal, Quebec: National Film Board of Canada, 1977), 16mm film, 58 min.; Zuzana Pick, "Storytelling and Resistance: The Documentary Practice of Alanis Obomsawin," in *Gendering the Nation: Canadian Women's Cinema*, edited by Kay Armatage, Kass Banning, Brenda Longfellow, and Janine Marchessault (Toronto, Ontario: University of Toronto Press, 1999), 76ff; *National Film Board of Canada: Alanis Obomsawin*, cited November 25, 2001, available from http://www.onf.ca/e/highlights/alannis_obomsawin.html.

17. *Speaking Together*, 94–95; Kathleen Jamieson, *Indian Women and the Law in Canada: Citizens Minus* (Ottawa, Ontario: Minister of Supply and Services Canada, 1978), 79–88; "Religious Conference Fizzles in the Drizzle," *Native People* 12, no. 5 (1979); Dickason, *Canada's First*, 331–332; McFarlane, *Brotherhood*, 146–148; *PAR-L: Milestones in Canadian Women's History* (February 23, 2000), cited November 26, 2001, available from http://www.unb.ca/par-l/research21.htm; Lavell, October 22, 2001; Alanis Obomsawin, telephone conversation with author, November 27, 2001.

18. *Speaking Together,* 22–23, 95; Lavell, "Nishnawbe"; "Native Woman's Project," March 1976, 1–2, DL; *Women of All Red Nations* (Porcupine, SD: We Will Remember Group, [1977]); M. Annette Jaimes and Theresa Halsey, "American Indian Women: At the Center of Indigenous Resistance in Contemporary North America," in *The State of Native America: Genocide, Colonization, and Resistance,* edited by M. Annette Jaimes (Boston, MA: South End Press, 1992), 326, 329; Alvin M. Josephy, Jr., Joane Nagel, and Troy Johnson, eds., *Red Power: The American Indians' Fight for Freedom,* 2nd ed. (Lincoln, NE: University of Nebraska Press, 1999), 51–52; Angie Todd-Dennis, telephone conversation with author, November 27, 2001; Jeannette Corbiere-Lavell, telephone conversation with author, November 27, 2001.

19. "Native Woman's Project," 1–2; Todd-Dennis, November 27, 2001; Corbiere-Lavell, November 27, 2001.

20. Ernest Willie, letter to Ed File, October 7, 1975, ACC/NMO, collection GS85–6, box 1, file 20; E. F. File, letter to Ernie Willie, October 22, 1975, ACC/NMO, collection GS85–6, box 1, file 20; "Accounting—Indian Ecumenical Conference," September 1, 1976, ACC/NMO, collection GS85–6, box 1, file 20; Blaser, "Reflection."

21. John Bernard Taylor, *Primal World-Views: Christian Involvement in Dialogue with Traditional Thought Forms* (Ibadan, Nigeria: Daystar Press, 1976), 6; Snow, *These,* 142–149; John Snow, "Treaty Seven Centennial: Celebration or Commemoration?" in *One Century Later: Western Canadian Reserve Indians since Treaty 7,* edited by Ian A. L. Getty and Donald B. Smith (Vancouver, British Columbia: University of British Columbia Press, 1978), 4; Emma LaRoque, "The Anglican Church and Native People," April 1987, 15, ACC/NMO, collection GS85–6, box 1, file 1; Warren Harbeck, telephone conversation with author, October 9, 2001.

22. Margaret Jaspar, "A. Ahenakew to Help at 'Pen,'" *Saskatchewan Anglican,* January 1973, 1, 7; "In Memoriam: Andrew Ahenakew," *Saskatchewan Anglican,* January 1977, 4; "Clerical Obituaries: Ahenakew, Andrew," *Canadian Churchman* 104, no. 1 (1977): 27; Ernie Willie, "Cree Priest Was Healer in Last Years of Ministry," *Canadian Churchman* 104, no. 2 (1977): 18; Andrew Ahenakew, *Sometimes We Burn, Sometimes We Tremble* (Toronto, Ontario: Anglican Church of Canada, [1977?]), videotape, 23 min.

23. "In Memoriam: Andrew Ahenakew," 4; "Clerical Obituaries," 27; Willie, "Cree," 18; Ahenakew, *Sometimes;* Janet Hodgson and Jay Kothare, *Vision Quest: Native Spirituality and the Church in Canada* (Toronto, Ontario: Anglican Book Centre, 1990), 117; H. C. Wolfart and Freda Ahenakew, eds., *They Knew Both Sides of Medicine: Cree Tales of Curing and Cursing Told by Alice Ahenakew* ([Winnipeg, Manitoba]: University of Manitoba Press, 2000), 81.

24. Willie, "Cree," 18; Ahenakew, *Sometimes;* Hodgson and Kothare, *Vision,* 118–122; Wolfart and Ahenakew, eds., *They,* 63–67.

25. Willie, "Cree," 18; Ahenakew, *Sometimes;* Hodgson and Kothare, *Vision,* 42–43, 106, 117, 122–125; Wolfart and Ahenakew, *They,* 33ff, 67–73, 79–81.

26. Willie, "Cree," 18; Ahenakew, *Sometimes;* Hodgson and Kothare, *Vision,* 123–125; Wolfart and Ahenakew, *They,* 73–79.

27. Blaser, "Reflection"; Willie, "Cree," 18; Ahenakew, *Sometimes;* Hodgson and Kothare, *Vision,* 106, 125–126; Wolfart and Ahenakew, *They,* 81.

28. Hugh McCullum, "Religious Pow-wow Kindles Indian Pride," *Toronto Star,* August 30, 1975; Donna Philips, Robert Troff, and Harvey Whitecalf, eds.,

Kataayuk: Saskatchewan Indian Elders ([Saskatoon, Saskatchewan]: Saskatchewan Indian Cultural College, 1976); Willie, "Cree," 18; Ahenakew, *Sometimes;* Stand Middlestriker [Robert K. Thomas], "At the Fork in Our Trail," [1977?], 17, NIYC; Hodgson and Kothare, *Vision,* 126–129.

29. Willie, "Cree," 18; "New Direction," [April? 1977], 1–3, ACC/PC, collection GS80–12, box 3; "Possible New Structure," April 14, 1977, ACC/PC, collection GS80–12, box 3; *Journal of Proceedings of the 28th Session of the General Synod* (Toronto, Ontario: Anglican Church of Canada, 1977), 19, 280–283.

30. Ernie Willie, letter to all members of the steering committee, July 12, 1977, ACC/NMO, collection GS85–6, box 2; "Two National Staff Resign," *Canadian Churchman* 104, no. 8 (1977): 2; McFarlane, *Brotherhood,* 247ff.

31. "Indian Ecumenical Conference 1976," 2; "Indian Ecumenical Conference," *B.C. Ecumenical News,* July-August 1977, 7; "Indian Ecumenical Conference," [1977], ACC/NMO, collection GS85–6, box 1, file 19; "The Indian Ecumenical Conference," [1977], ACC/AJ; "Indian Ecumenical Conference 1977," 1977, ACC/NMO, collection GS85–6, box 2; "Indian Ecumenical Conference," April 28–30, 1978, 1–2, ACC/NMO, collection GS85–6, box 2.

32. "Indian Ecumenical Conference (1977)"; "The Indian Ecumenical Conference (1977)"; Willie, July 12, 1977; D. J. Krease, "Stoney Tribal Administration: Ecumenical Conference," August 1977, ACC/NMO, collection GS85–6, box 2; Elizabeth Boyd, memorandum to the Primate, Clarke Raymond, Tom Anthony and Don Brown, September 9, 1977, ACC/PO, collection GS82–4, box 4; "Indian Ecumenical Conference—1977," September 30, 1977, ACC/PC, collection GS80–12, box 3; "Indian Ecumenical Conference 1977"; "Religious Conference Fizzles in the Drizzle"; Hodgson and Kothare, *Vision,* 104; Lavell, October 22, 2001.

33. "A Proposal for an Indian Ecumenical Conference Presented by the Institute for Indian Studies," [December? 1969], 7–8, NAA/AICC, collection MS 4806, box 2; "Motions Passed at the First Indian Ecumenical Conference," [August 13–19], [1970], ACC/NMO, collection GS85–6, box 1, file 15; "The Indian Ecumenical Conference (1977)"; "Indian Ecumenical Conference 1977"; Elizabeth Boyd, "Report on the Indian Ecumenical Conference," 1979, 2, ACC/NMO, collection GS85–6, box 2; Hodgson and Kothare, *Vision,* 104.

34. "Steering Committee Elected at the Second Indian Ecumenical Conference," July 18–21, 1971, ACC/NMO, collection GS85–6, box 1, file 16; Ernie Willie, letter to Monique Guibert, March 14, 1977, ACC/NMO, collection GS85–6, box 2; *Journal of Proceedings of the 28th Session of the General Synod,* 19, 283; Boyd, September 9, 1977; "New Native Consultant," *Canadian Churchman* 104, no. 11 (1977): 6; R. D. Brown, letter to A. Cuthand, March 20, 1978, ACC/NMO, collection GS85–6, box 2; Adam Cuthand, "Indian Ecumenical Conference—1978," September 1978, ACC/NMO, collection GS85–6, box 2; Adam Cuthand, "General Synod of the Anglican Church of Canada, Position Description," November 15, 1978, 1, ACC/PC, collection GS83–01, box 1; "Native Priest a Founder of Metis Association," *Anglican Journal,* December 1994, 7; "Rev Dr Adam Cuthand," *Saskatchewan Anglican,* January 1995, 6.

35. "Indian Ecumenical Conference (1978)"; Jeff LaFrance, letter to Adam Cuthand, July 7, 1978, ACC/NMO, collection GS85–6, box 2; "Preliminary Report, Indian Ecumenical Conference—1978," 1978, 1, ACC/NMO, collection GS85–6, box 2; Elizabeth Boyd, letter to Wendy WhiteCloud, June 4, 1979, ACC/NMO, collection GS85–6, box 2.

36. "Indian Ecumenical Conference, July 29–August 6, 1978," 1978, TU/KEK, collection 80–030, box 8, file 9; Cuthand, "Indian Ecumenical Conference (1978)"; "Indian Ecumenical Conference Steering Committee Meeting," September 29–30, 1978, 1–2, ACC/NMO, collection GS85–6, box 2; "Preliminary Report," 1; Boyd, "Report," 1; "Meeting of the Indian Ecumenical Conference Steering Committee," May 4, 1979, 1, ACC/NMO, collection GS85–6, box 2; "Religious Conference Fizzles in the Drizzle"; Kenneth Fink, telephone conversation with author, April 13, 1992; Vine Deloria, Jr., telephone conversation with author, May 4, 1992; Sam Stanley, telephone conversation with author, May 7, 1992.

37. Tom Wolfe, "The 'Me' Decade and the Third Great Awakening," *New York* 9, no. 34 (1976): 26ff; Cuthand, "Indian Ecumenical Conference (1978)"; "Indian Ecumenical Conference Steering Committee Meeting," 1–2; "Preliminary Report," 1; Boyd, "Report," 1; "Meeting of the Indian Ecumenical Conference Steering Committee," 1–2.

38. Paul Heelas, *The New Age Movement: The Celebration of the Self and the Sacralization of Modernity* (Oxford, England: Blackwell Publishers, 1996), 1–2, 5, 15–20, 28–29, 54–55, 84–90, 108–113.

39. Heelas, *New*, 8, 135–138, 153–157, 221.

40. Joseph E. Couture, "Next Time, Try an Elder!" 1979, 2–7, 17, NIYC; "The American Indian Movement," 4; Weyler, *Blood*, 265–267, 276–277; Alvin M. Josephy, Jr., *Now That the Buffalo's Gone: A Study of Today's American Indians* (Norman, OK: University of Oklahoma Press, 1984), 87–91; Christopher Vecsey, "American Indian Spiritual Politics: The Roundhouse at the Middle of the Earth," *Commonweal*, April 6, 1984, 203–207; Christopher Vecsey, *Imagine Ourselves Richly: Mythic Narratives of North American Indians* (New York, NY: Crossroad Publishing Company, 1988), 206–208; Jordan Paper, *Offering Smoke: The Sacred Pipe and Native American Religion* (Moscow, ID: University of Idaho Press, 1988), 108–110; Vine Deloria, Jr., *God Is Red: A Native View of Religion*, 2nd ed. (Golden, CO: North American Press, 1992), 54; Arlene Hirschfelder and Paulette Molin, *The Encyclopedia of Native American Religions: An Introduction* (New York, NY: Facts on File, 1992), 65–66; Russell Means and Marvin J. Wolf, *Where White Men Fear to Tread: The Autobiography of Russell Means* (New York, NY: St. Martin's Griffin, 1995), 371; Stanley, May 7, 1992; Eddie Benton, telephone conversation with author, November 27, 2001.

41. "Indian Ecumenical Conference Steering Committee Meeting," 1–2; "Indian Ecumenical Conference Steering Committee," September 1978, ACC/NMO, collection GS85–6, box 2; "Preliminary Report," 2; Joe Couture, letter to Ahab Spence, March 19, 1980, NIYC; Couture, "Next," 17.

42. Michael Mitchell, letter to Indian Ecumenical Steering Committee members, December 4, 1978, ACC/NMO, collection GS85–6, box 2.

43. Ernie Willie, letter to Adam Cuthand, December 11, 1978, ACC/NMO, collection GS85–6, box 2; Adam Cuthand, letter to members of the steering committee, March 2, 1979, ACC/NMO, collection GS85–6, box 2.

44. "Indian Ecumenical Conference 1977"; "Preliminary Report," 1; Cuthand, "Indian Ecumenical Conference (1978)"; "Indian Ecumenical Conference Projected Budget for 1979," [1978?], ACC/NMO, collection GS85–6, box 2; Cuthand, March 2, 1979; Boyd, "Report," 1–2; Elizabeth Boyd, letter to Cam Mackie, April 27, 1979, ACC/NMO, collection GS85–6, box 2.

45. "Position Paper," June 1976, ACC/PC, collection GS80–12, box 3; "Mailing List re Native Clergy Conference," [1976?], ACC/PC, collection GS80–12, box 3; "Natives Urge United Front," *Canadian Churchman* 102, no. 7 (1976): 15; *Journal of Proceedings of the 28th Session of the General Synod*, 282; Cuthand, March 2, 1979; Boyd, "Report," 2; Rodney Andrews and Donovan V. Browne, letter to E. W. Scott, April 23, 1979, ACC/PO, collection GS87–10, box 7; Rodney Andrews and Donovan V. Browne, letter to George Cramm, April 23, 1979, ACC/NMO, collection GS85–6, box 2; memorandum to Adam Cuthand, May 1, 1979, ACC/PO, collection GS87–10, box 7; memorandum to [Edward W. Scott], May 16, 1979, ACC/PO, collection GS87–10, box 7; Scott, May 30, 1979.

46. "Meeting of the Indian Ecumenical Conference Steering Committee," 1; A. Cuthand, "Indian Ecumenical Conference, Minutes of Meetings of Steering Committee," July 29–30, [1979], ACC/NMO, collection GS85–6, box 2; "I.E.C. Steering Committee Members," [1979?], ACC/NMO, collection GS85–6, box 1, file 16; "Religious Conference Fizzles in the Drizzle"; Louise Campbell, "Morley Ecumenical Conference 1979," August 13, 1979, ACC/NMO, collection GS85–6, box 2; *UNICEF: Special Session on Children* (December 12, 2001), cited December 19, 2001, available from http://www.unicef.org/specialsession/rights/path.htm.

47. Campbell, "Morley"; Eric Robinson, letter to Adam Cuthand, January 18, 1980, ACC/NMO, collection GS85–6, box 2; "Indian Ecumenical Steering Committee Meeting," May 8–11, 1980, ACC/NMO, collection GS85–6, box 2.

48. Cuthand, "Indian Ecumenical Conference (1979)"; "Minutes of Steering Committee, Indian Ecumenical Conference," October 5–6, 1979, 1–3, ACC/AJ; "Report on the Meeting of the Sub-Committee," November 27, 1979, ACC/AJ; "Indian Ecumenical Steering Committee Meeting."

49. "Budget Proposal for Stoney Cultural Education Program," [1979], 1, NAC, record group 10, volume 12806, file E4735–2223; "Indian Ecumenical Steering Committee Meeting"; John Snow, letter to Adam Cuthand, June 3, 1980, ACC/NMO, collection GS85–6, box 2; Hodgson and Kothare, *Vision*, 104.

50. Scott, May 30, 1979; *Journal of Proceedings of the 29th Session of the General Synod* (Toronto, Ontario: Anglican Church of Canada, 1980), 307–310; Hodgson and Kothare, *Vision*, 104, 135–136; John W. Friesen, *Aboriginal Spirituality and Biblical Theology: Closer Than You Think* (Calgary, Alberta: Detselig Enterprises, 2000), 148.

51. "Indian Ecumenical Steering Committee Meeting"; "The Twelfth Annual Morley Conference for Indian Spiritual Life," *Stoney Echo* 1, no. 2–3 (1981): 13; "Morley for a Spiritual Life," *Native People* 14 (1981): 15; Adam Cuthand, "A Native Anglican Indian Speaks," *Interculture* 15, no. 1 (1982): 38.

52. "Minutes of the Finance Committee, Morley Ecumenical Conference," December 14, 1981, 1–6, ACC/NMO, collection GS85–6, box 2; "Morley Alberta, Canada," [1981?], ACC/NMO, collection GS85–6, box 2; "Thirteenth Annual Morley Ecumenical Conference for Indian Spiritual Life," *Stoney Echo* 2, no. 1–2 (1982): 10.

53. Adam Cuthand, letter to Clarke Raymond, June 11, 1982, ACC/PC, collection GS83–01, box 1; L. Clarke Raymond, letter to Adam Cuthand, July 5, 1982, ACC/PC, collection GS83–01, box 1; Dianne Meili, "Lightning Kindles Return to Spirituality at Morley," *Windspeaker* 5, no. 18 (1987): 1; "Some Make

Admirable Attempts to Put Spirituality Back in Place," *Windspeaker* 5, no. 18 (1987): 6; Hodgson and Kothare, *Vision*, 104.

54. Sam Stanley, "American Indian Power and Powerlessness," in *The Anthropology of Power: Ethnographic Studies from Asia, Oceania, and the New World*, edited by Raymond D. Fogelson and Richard N. Adams (New York, NY: Academic Press, 1977), 237–242; Elizabeth Colson, "Power at Large: Meditation on 'The Symposium on Power,'" in *The Anthropology of Power: Ethnographic Studies from Asia, Oceania, and the New World*, edited by Raymond D. Fogelson and Richard N. Adams (New York, NY: Academic Press, 1977), 381–382; Richard N. Adams, "Power in Human Societies: A Synthesis," in *The Anthropology of Power: Ethnographic Studies from Asia, Oceania, and the New World*, edited by Raymond D. Fogelson and Richard N. Adams (New York, NY: Academic Press, 1977), 406; Marcus Braybrooke, *Inter-Faith Organizations, 1893–1979: An Historical Directory* (New York, NY: Edwin Mellen Press, 1980); John Berthrong, "Interfaith Dialogue in Canada," *Ecumenical Review*, October 1985, 462–470; Marcus Braybrooke, *Pilgrimage of Hope: One Hundred Years of Global Interfaith Dialogue* (New York, NY: Crossroad Publishing Company, 1992).

55. John A. Price, *Native Studies: American and Canadian Indians* (Toronto, Ontario: McGraw-Hill Ryerson, 1978), 67, 95, 108–111; John A. Price, *Indians of Canada: Cultural Dynamics* (Salem, WI: Sheffield Publishing Company, 1979), 231, 236.

56. Harold W. Turner, ed., *Bibliography of New Religious Movements in Primal Societies*, Vol. 2: North America (Boston, MA: G. K. Hall and Company, 1978), 27, 30, 34, 39, 41, 42, 45–47, 55, 216, 281; Ake Hultkrantz, *The Study of American Indian Religions*, edited by Christopher Vecsey (Chico, CA: Scholars Press, 1983), 109; Penny Petrone, ed., *First People, First Voices* (Toronto, Ontario: University of Toronto Press, 1983), 190–192; John Webster Grant, *Moon of Wintertime: Missionaries and the Indians of Canada in Encounter since 1534* (Toronto, Ontario: University of Toronto Press, 1984), 211–212; Calvin Martin, "The Metaphysics of Writing Indian-White History," in *The American Indian and the Problem of History*, edited by Calvin Martin (New York, NY: Oxford University Press, 1987), 32; Paul B. Steinmetz, *Pipe, Bible, and Peyote among the Oglala Lakota: A Study in Religious Identity* (Knoxville, TN: University of Tennessee Press, 1990), 209; Peter Nabokov, ed., *Native American Testimony: A Chronicle of Indian-White Relations from Prophecy to the Present, 1492–1992* (New York, NY: Viking Penguin, 1991), 383; Joane Nagel, *American Indian Ethnic Renewal: Red Power and the Resurgence of Identity and Culture* (New York, NY: Oxford University Press, 1996), 191–192.

57. "The Fifteenth Morley Ecumenical Conference for Indian Spiritual Life," *Messenger* 2, no. 4 (1987): 5; Meili, "Lightning," 1; "Some Make Admirable Attempts to Put Spirituality Back in Place," 6; Dianne Meili, *Those Who Know: Profiles of Alberta's Native Elders* (Edmonton, Alberta: NeWest Press, 1991), 81–82.

58. "Wedding Song," *Windspeaker* 5, no. 21 (1987): 1; Dianne Meili, "Elders Urge a Return to Nature," *Windspeaker* 5, no. 21 (1987): 9; "The Sixteenth Morley Ecumenical Conference for Indian Spiritual Life," [1988], JT; John Snow, *The Stoney Nation Presents: Nakoda Olympic Pow-Wow '88* ([Morley, Alberta]: Stoney Tribal Administration, 1988); Ken Tully, telephone conversation with author, April 12, 1989; Meili, *Those*, 81–83; Farley Wuth, interview by author, Morley, Alberta, July 25, 1992.

EPILOGUE

1. John Snow, *These Mountains Are Our Sacred Places: The Story of the Stoney Indians* (Toronto, Ontario: Samuel-Stevens, Publishers, 1977); James A. Treat, "Native Americans, Theology, and Liberation: Christianity and Traditionalism in the Struggle for Survival" (M.A. thesis, Pacific School of Religion, 1989), 85, 89, 91, 94, 105–106; James Treat, "Preface," in *Native and Christian: Indigenous Voices on Religious Identity in the United States and Canada*, edited by James Treat (New York, NY: Routledge, 1996), vii-viii; James Treat, "Introduction: Native Christian Narrative Discourse," in *Native and Christian: Indigenous Voices on Religious Identity in the United States and Canada*, edited by James Treat (New York, NY: Routledge, 1996), 14; James Treat, "Introduction: An American Critique of Religion," in *For This Land: Writings on Religion in America* by Vine Deloria, Jr., edited by James Treat (New York, NY: Routledge, 1999), 18; Vine Deloria, Jr., *For This Land: Writings on Religion in America*, edited by James Treat (New York, NY: Routledge, 1999), 125.

2. James Treat, "Ecumenism in Action: The Bay Area Native American Ministry," *Ecu-log* 5, no. 2 (1990): 3; James A. Treat, "The Indian Ecumenical Conference: Intertribal Revitalization through Inter-Religious Cooperation," December 4, 1990, JT; James A. Treat, "Cross-Cultural Religious Phenomena: Revitalization Movements," July 3, 1991, JT; James Treat, "Engaging Students with Native American Community Resources," *American Quarterly* 45, no. 4 (1993): 621–630.

3. James A. Treat, "Contemporary Native Religious Identity: The Indian Ecumenical Conference" (Ph.D. dissertation, Graduate Theological Union, 1992), 3–5, 39–43; James Treat, "The Challenge of the Past: A Native American Perspective," in *The Challenges of the Past, the Challenges of the Future*, edited by John L. Kater (Berkeley, CA: Church Divinity School of the Pacific, 1994), 25–41; James Treat, "The Canaanite Problem," *Daughters of Sarah* 20, no. 2 (1994): 20–24.

4. Andy Rooney, "Indians Seek a Role in Modern U.S.," *Sacramento Union*, March 11, 1992; Ian Getty, telephone conversation with author, March 12, 1992; Treat, "Contemporary Native Religious Identity (1992)," 1–3, 116–118.

5. Martin Thompson, "Nakoda Lodge . . . Majestic Setting," *Native People* 14 (1981): 5; Ian A. L. Getty and Antoine S. Lussier, eds., *As Long as the Sun Shines and Water Flows: A Reader in Canadian Native Studies*, Nakoda Institute Occasional Paper No. 1 (Vancouver, British Columbia: University of British Columbia Press, 1983); Jean Barman, Yvonne M. Hebert, and Don McCaskill, eds., *Indian Education in Canada: The Legacy*, Nakoda Institute Occasional Paper No. 2 (Vancouver, British Columbia: University of British Columbia Press, 1986); Jean Barman, Yvonne M. Hebert, and Don McCaskill, eds., *Indian Education in Canada: The Challenge*, Nakoda Institute Occasional Paper No. 3 (Vancouver, British Columbia: University of British Columbia Press, 1987); "1992 North American Indian Ecumenical Conference," [1992], JT; Farley Wuth, telephone conversation with author, May 21, 1992; Farley Wuth, letter to author, July 8, 1992, JT; Tommy Nez, telephone conversation with author, January 19, 2002.

6. "1992 North American Indian Ecumenical Conference"; Wendy Dudley, "1,500 Expected at Indian Ecumenical Conference," *Ottawa Citizen*, July 4, 1992, F6; Nora Schmidt, "Morley to Host Native Trade Fair," *Cochrane This*

Week, July 14, 1992, 3; Nora Schmidt, interview by author, Morley, Alberta, July 28, 1992; Fred Nahwooksy, "Stoney," in *Native American Dance: Ceremonies and Social Traditions*, edited by Charlotte Heth (Golden, CO: Fulcrum Publishing, 1992), 142–143; Cheryl Wilson, ed., *This Path We Travel: Celebrations of Contemporary Native American Creativity* (Golden, CO: Fulcrum Publishing, 1994); *United Nations: International Year for the World's Indigenous People* (May 17, 2000), cited January 21, 2002, available from http://www.un.org/documents/ga/res/45/a45r164.htm.

7. Vine Deloria, Jr., "American Indians," in *Multiculturalism in the United States: A Comparative Guide to Acculturation and Ethnicity*, edited by John D. Buenker and Lorman A. Ratner (New York, NY: Greenwood Press, 1992), 47–49.

8. Janet Hodgson and Jay Kothare, *Vision Quest: Native Spirituality and the Church in Canada* (Toronto, Ontario: Anglican Book Centre, 1990), 1–2; Treat, "Contemporary Native Religious Identity (1992)," 228–232; John Watson, "A Priest for the Inner City," *Durham Network*, Lent 1997, available from http://www.durham.anglican.org/reference/network/network97-lent/inner.htm; Jay Kothare, telephone conversation with author, January 10, 2002.

9. Hodgson and Kothare, *Vision*, 1–4, 104–105.

10. Hodgson and Kothare, *Vision*, 105–108.

11. James Treat, "Native People and Interreligious Dialogue in North America: The Indian Ecumenical Conference," *Studies in Interreligious Dialogue* 6, no. 1 (1996): 29–45; James Treat, "Contemporary Native Religious Identity: The Indian Ecumenical Conference," in *A Struggle for Identity: Indigenous People in Asia-Pacific, Existence and Expectations*, edited by P. Jegadish Ghandi and George Cheriyan (Chennai, India: Association of Christian Institutes for Social Concern in Asia, 2000), 3–12; James Treat, "Intertribal Traditionalism and the Religious Roots of Red Power," in *Native American Spirituality: A Critical Reader*, edited by Lee Irwin (Lincoln, NE: University of Nebraska Press, 2000), 270–294.

12. Leslie Marmon Silko, *Storyteller* (New York, NY: Seaver Books, 1981), 6–7; N. Scott Momaday, *The Way to Rainy Mountain* (Albuquerque, NM: University of New Mexico Press, 1969), 46; Charles Alexander Eastman (Ohiyesa), *The Soul of the Indian: An Interpretation* (Lincoln, NE: University of Nebraska Press, 1980), xii; Joy Harjo, *The Woman Who Fell from the Sky: Poems* (New York, NY: W. W. Norton and Company, 1994), 18.

13. John Snow, "Identification and Definition of Our Treaty and Aboriginal Rights," in *The Quest for Justice: Aboriginal Peoples and Aboriginal Rights*, edited by Menno Boldt and J. Anthony Long (Toronto, Ontario: University of Toronto Press, 1985), 41–46; John Snow, "A Cultural Perspective on Stoney Finances," *Bear Hills Native Voice*, March 27, 1986, 2–3; Clint Buehler, "Chief Snow Accuses Media of 'Racial Implications,'" *Windspeaker* 4 (1986): 1; Jeff Vircoe, "Chief Snow and the Stoney's," *Cochrane This Week*, October 22, 1991, 4–5; Nora Schmidt, telephone conversation with author, February 19, 1993; Warren Harbeck, telephone conversation with author, October 9, 2001.

14. Les Sillars, "The Tyranny of Tribalism," *Alberta Report*, 1997, available from http://albertareport.com/24arcopy/24a31cpy/2431ar01.htm; Rob McKinley, "Grass Roots Groups Fire Up in Wake of Reserve Protests," *Alberta Sweetgrass*, November 10, 1997, available from http://www.ammsa.com/sweetgrass/nov97.html#anchor749956; "Everything That Can Go Bad, Has for 'Stoneys,'" *Indian*

Country Today, April 6–13, 1998, B2; Sasha Nagy, "Judge Slams Stoneys Again," *Calgary Herald*, September 18, 1999, A1, A3; Joan Black, "Stoney Tribal Administrator Ousted," *Alberta Sweetgrass*, October 11, 1999, available from http://www.ammsa.com/sweetgrass/OCT99.html#anchor81431; Shawn Clifton, *World Indigenous Peoples Conference on Education—2002: Calgary, Alberta, Canada* (February 11, 2002), cited February 11, 2002, available from http://www.fnahec.org/wipce2002/index.html.

15. Hugh McCullum and Karmel McCullum, *This Land Is Not for Sale: Canada's Original People and Their Land; A Saga of Neglect, Exploitation, and Conflict* (Toronto, Ontario: Anglican Book Centre, 1975); Hugo Muller, *Waswanipi: Songs of a Scattered People* (Toronto, Ontario: Anglican Book Centre, 1976); National Executive Council, *A Transforming Influence: Native Peoples and Northern Development, Social Justice and the Church* (Toronto, Ontario: Anglican Church of Canada, 1977); Hugh McCullum, Karmel Taylor McCullum, and John Olthuis, *Moratorium: Justice, Energy, the North, and the Native People* (Toronto, Ontario: Anglican Book Centre, 1977); Winifred Petchey Marsh, *People of the Willow: The Padlimiut Tribe of the Caribou Eskimo* (Toronto, Ontario: Anglican Book Centre, 1983); Peter J. Hamel, *Anglicans and Aboriginal Peoples: The Ecojustice Connection* (Toronto, Ontario: General Synod Communications, Anglican Church of Canada, 1986); Ian MacKenzie, *Native Rights and the Church: An Historical and Political Analysis*, lecture delivered at the Summer Public Lecture Series of the Vancouver School of Theology, July 23, 1986 (Vancouver, British Columbia: Vancouver School of Theology, 1986), audiocassette.

16. *Life in Its Fullness: Council for Native Ministries, Anglican Church of Canada* (Toronto, Ontario: General Synod Communications, Anglican Church of Canada, [1989?]); John Bird, Laverne Jacobs, Terry Thompson, and Doug Tindal, *A Brief Prepared by the Anglican Church of Canada for Submission to the Royal Commission on Aboriginal Peoples at a Special Consultation between the Members of the Commission and Representatives of the Historic Mission Churches, Citadel Hotel, Ottawa, ON, November 8–9, 1993* (Toronto, Ontario: Anglican Church of Canada, 1993), 8–15, Appendix 13; *The Anglican Council of Indigenous Peoples* (Toronto, Ontario: Anglican Church of Canada, 1998); Peter Hamel and Catherine Morrison, *Anglican Church of Canada Policy Relating to Aboriginal Peoples, 1959–1998*, 3rd ed. (Toronto, Ontario: Anglican Church of Canada, 1998), 8–36.

17. John Bird, ed., *Recovering the Feather: The First Anglican Native Convocation* (Toronto, Ontario: Council for Native Ministries, Anglican Church of Canada, 1989); Hodgson and Kothare, *Vision;* Joyce Carlson, ed., *The Journey: Stories and Prayers for the Christian Year from People of the First Nations* (Toronto, Ontario: Anglican Book Centre, 1991); Joyce Carlson, ed., *1992: Aboriginal Reflections on 500 Years* (Toronto, Ontario: First Nations Ecumenical Liturgical Resources, History and Publications Board, [1992?]); Bird and others, *Brief;* Joyce Carlson, ed., *Dancing the Dream: The First Nations and the Church in Partnership* (Toronto, Ontario: Anglican Book Centre, 1995); Joyce Carlson and Alf Dumont, eds., *Bridges in Spirituality: First Nations Christian Women Tell Their Stories* (Toronto, Ontario: Anglican Book Centre and United Church Publishing House, 1997); Freda Rajotte, *First Nations Faith and Ecology* (Toronto, Ontario: Anglican Book Centre and United Church Publishing House, 1998); Charles E. Hendry, *Beyond Traplines: Does the Church Really Care? Towards an Assessment of the Work of*

the Anglican Church of Canada with Canada's Native Peoples, rev. ed. (Toronto, Ontario: Anglican Book Centre, 1998).

18. *Dialogue on Native Spirituality*, produced by the Division of Communications for the Anglican Diocese of Huron and the United Church of Canada London Conference (Toronto, Ontario: Anglican Church of Canada, 1985), videotape, 32 min.; *The Heart of a People: The Anglican Church in the North*, produced by General Synod Communications for the Council of the North (Toronto, Ontario: Anglican Church of Canada, 1986), videotape, 26 min.; *Share the Dream*, produced by Anglican Video for the Council for Native Ministries (Toronto, Ontario: Anglican Church of Canada, 1988), videotape, 53 min.; *The Spirit in the Circle*, produced by General Synod Communications for the Council for Native Ministries (Toronto, Ontario: Anglican Church of Canada, 1991), videotape, 28 min.; *Dare to Dream*, produced by the Division of Communication for the Council for Native Ministries (Toronto, Ontario: Anglican Church of Canada, 1992), videotape, 18 min.; *Search for Healing*, produced by Anglican Video for the Council for Native Ministries and the Residential Schools Working Group (Toronto, Ontario: Anglican Church of Canada, 1992), videotape, 24 min.; *Dancing the Dream*, produced by Anglican Video for the Council for Native Ministries (Toronto, Ontario: Anglican Church of Canada, 1993), videotape, 30 min.; John Bird, *The Seventh Fire: First Peoples and the Anglican Church*, produced by Anglican Video for the Council for Native Ministries (Toronto, Ontario: Anglican Church of Canada, 1995), videotape, 28 min.; *The Healing Circle*, produced by Anglican Video for the Residential Schools Working Group (Toronto, Ontario: Anglican Church of Canada, 1995), videotape, 55 min.; *A Journey Begins . . . With a Dream*, produced by Anglican Video for the Anglican Council of Indigenous Peoples (Toronto, Ontario: Anglican Church of Canada, 1997), videotape, 34 min.

19. "The First Nations Assembly," *Saskatchewan Indian* 12, no. 4 (1982): 26–29; Elijah Harper, "Sacred Assembly '95: Statement of Chair Elijah Harper," *Akwesasne Notes* 2, no. 1 (1996): 14; *Share in the Celebration!* (Ottawa, Ontario: Minister of Indian Affairs and Northern Development, 2000); *Indian and Northern Affairs Canada: National Aboriginal Day* (June 14, 2000), cited February 8, 2002, available from http://www.ainc-inac.gc.ca/nad/; *Anglican Church of Canada: National Aboriginal Day of Prayer* (May 9, 2001), cited February 8, 2002, available from http://www.anglican.ca/acip/dayofprayer.html; *United Church of Canada: Celebrating First Nations Day* (May 22, 2001), cited July 23, 2001, available from http://www.uccan.org/20010621.htm.

20. John A. MacKenzie, letter to Sam Stanley, July 21, 1975, NAA/CSM, series 8—American Indians General, box 57; "Centre for Indian Scholars Mailing List," March 1989, 1–2, JT; Robert K. Thomas, *Getting to the Heart of the Matter: Collected Letters and Papers*, edited by Daphne J. Anderson (Vancouver, British Columbia: Native Ministries Consortium, Vancouver School of Theology, 1990), 119; Ian MacKenzie, telephone conversation with author, June 18, 1992; Steve Pavlik, "Introduction," in *A Good Cherokee, A Good Anthropologist: Papers in Honor of Robert K. Thomas*, edited by Steve Pavlik (Los Angeles, CA: American Indian Studies Center, University of California at Los Angeles, 1998), xvii; Terence R. Anderson, "Attending to the Sacred: A Christian Learns from a Nighthawk," in *A Good Cherokee, A Good Anthropologist: Papers in Honor of Robert K. Thomas*, edited by Steve Pavlik (Los Angeles, CA: American Indian Studies

Center, University of California at Los Angeles, 1998), 203; John A. MacKenzie, "A Legend in His Own Time: Some Initial Reflections on the Work of Robert K. Thomas," in *A Good Cherokee, A Good Anthropologist: Papers in Honor of Robert K. Thomas*, edited by Steve Pavlik (Los Angeles, CA: American Indian Studies Center, University of California at Los Angeles, 1998), 219, 223–224; *Centre for Indian Scholars: A Native Educational and Religious Institution* (Terrace, British Columbia: Centre for Indian Scholars, [1999?]); *Caledonia School of Mutual Ministry: Native Ministries Consortium* (July 26, 2001), cited February 16, 2002, available from http://www.geocities.com/calministry/tc004.htm; *Centre for Indian Scholars: Home Page*, cited February 15, 2002, available from http://member.tripod.com/c4is/home.htm.

21. Robert K. Thomas, *The Indian Ecumenical Movement: A Grassroots Religious Movement*, lecture delivered at the Summer Public Lecture Series of the Vancouver School of Theology, July 21, 1986 (Vancouver, British Columbia: Vancouver School of Theology, 1986), audiocassette; Steve Pavlik, "In Memoriam to Robert Knox Thomas (1925–1991)," *Social Science Journal* 34, no. 4 (1997); Steve Pavlik, ed., *A Good Cherokee, A Good Anthropologist: Papers in Honor of Robert K. Thomas* (Los Angeles, CA: American Indian Studies Center, University of California at Los Angeles, 1998).

22. Robert K. Thomas, "The Redbird Smith Movement," in *Symposium on Cherokee and Iroquois Culture*, Bureau of American Ethnology Bulletin 180, edited by William N. Fenton and John Gulick (Washington, DC: Smithsonian Institution, 1961), 165; Robert K. Thomas, "Eastern American Indian Communities," in *Technical Problems in Indian Education*, Indian Education Confronts the Seventies, Vol. 3, edited by Vine Deloria, Jr. (Tsaile, AZ: Navajo Community College, 1974); Robert K. Thomas, "A Report on Research of Lumbee Origins," [1976?], UNC/NC, call number C970.03 T459r; Robert K. Thomas, "Open Letter from Thomas," *Americans Before Columbus* 10, no. 5 (1982): 3, 6; Thomas, *Getting*, 119; Robert K. Thomas, "Lighting the Cherokee Fire," *Americans Before Columbus* 18, no. 1 (1990): 3, 5; Raymond D. Fogelson, "Bringing Home the Fire: Bob Thomas and Cherokee Studies," in *A Good Cherokee, A Good Anthropologist: Papers in Honor of Robert K. Thomas*, edited by Steve Pavlik (Los Angeles, CA: American Indian Studies Center, University of California at Los Angeles, 1998), 109–115.

23. Dianne Meili, *Those Who Know: Profiles of Alberta's Native Elders* (Edmonton, Alberta: NeWest Press, 1991), 147, 153; D-Q University, "Seventh Annual Youth and Elders Gathering Summer Encampment," 1992, JT; "Youth and Elders Conference Slated," *Muscogee Nation News*, May 1993, 2; Judy Starkey, "Alaskan Native Elder-Youth Conference: 'Our Wisdom from Generation to Generation,'" *News from Indian Country*, July 31, 1996, 12B; *'Celebrating Success, Past, Present, and Future': A Report on the 1996 AFN Youth and Elders Conference* (Anchorage, AK: Alaska Federation of Natives, 1996); *Listening to the Voice of the Elders: An International Indigenous Youth Camp* (Salmon Arm, British Columbia: Turtle Island Earth Stewards, 1996), videotape, 27 min.; "Youth Elder Camp Brings Generations Together," *Cherokee Advocate* 24, no. 2 (2000): 11; Karen Donahoewah, "The 18th Annual Anishinaabe Way Conference: Elders and Youth Share," *Ojibwe Akiing* 4, no. 2 (2000): 12; Trish Brown, "200 Attend Traditional Circle of Indian Elders and Youth Conference," *Tribal Observer*, August 1, 2000, available from http://www.sagchip.org/tribalobserver/article.asp?article=23.

24. Stand Middlestriker [Robert K. Thomas], "At the Fork in Our Trail," [1977?], 122–124, NIYC.

25. Middlestriker, "Fork," 124–125.

26. Peter Blue Cloud, ed., *Alcatraz Is Not an Island* (Berkeley, CA: Wingbow Press, 1972); Adam Fortunate Eagle, *Alcatraz! Alcatraz! The Indian Occupation of 1969–1971* (Berkeley, CA: Heyday Books, 1992); Troy R. Johnson, ed., *Alcatraz, Indian Land Forever* (Los Angeles, CA: American Indian Studies Center, University of California at Los Angeles, 1994); Troy R. Johnson, ed., *You Are on Indian Land: Alcatraz Island, 1969–1971* (Los Angeles, CA: American Indian Studies Center, University of California at Los Angeles, 1995); Troy R. Johnson, *The Occupation of Alcatraz Island: Indian Self-Determination and the Rise of Indian Activism* (Urbana, IL: University of Illinois Press, 1996); Paul Chaat Smith and Robert Allen Warrior, *Like a Hurricane: The Indian Movement from Alcatraz to Wounded Knee* (New York, NY: New Press, 1996); Troy R. Johnson, *We Hold the Rock: The Indian Occupation of Alcatraz, 1969–1971* (San Francisco, CA: Golden Gate National Parks Association, 1997); Troy Johnson, Joane Nagel, and Duane Champagne, eds., *American Indian Activism: Alcatraz to the Longest Walk* (Urbana, IL: University of Illinois Press, 1997); Adam Fortunate Eagle and Tim Findley, *Heart of the Rock: The Indian Invasion of Alcatraz* (Norman, OK: University of Oklahoma Press, 2002).

27. Michele Tucker Butts, "Red Power: Indian Activism, 1960–1973" (M.A. thesis, Austin Peay State University, 1974); Joyce Hocker Frost, "The Implications of Theories of Bargaining for Rhetorical Criticism" (M.A. thesis, University of Texas at Austin, 1974); Rachel Ann Bonney, "Forms of Supratribal Indian Interaction in the United States" (Ph.D. dissertation, University of Arizona, 1975); Robert E. Schmidt, "The American Indian Movement" (M.A. thesis, Wichita State University, 1976); William Arthur Dicus, "Blackfeet Revitalization: An Interpretive Study of the American Indian Movement among Blackfeet College Students" (M.A. thesis, University of Montana, 1976); Jerry Gold, "The Head Start Secession: Network Analysis of a Social Conflict" (M.A. thesis, University of Montana, 1976); Judith Anola Vick, "The Press and Wounded Knee, 1973: An Analysis of the Coverage of the Occupation by Selected Newspapers and News Magazines" (M.A. thesis, University of Minnesota, 1977); Randall Alan Lake, "Red Power: Consummatory Rhetoric and the Functions of Criticism" (M.A. thesis, University of Kansas, 1978); Edward Justin Streb, "The Rhetoric of Wounded Knee II: A Critical Analysis of Confrontational and 'Media Event' Discourse" (Ph.D. dissertation, Northwestern University, 1979); Jay H. Furlong, "The Occupation of Wounded Knee, 1973" (M.A. thesis, University of Oklahoma, 1980); Natalie P. Wells, "Television News Coverage of the American Indian Occupation of Wounded Knee, South Dakota: An Analysis of Network Newscasts, February-May, 1973" (M.A. thesis, San Francisco State University, 1982); Michael LeRoy Indergaard, "Urban Renewal and the American Indian Movement in Minneapolis: A Case Study in Political Economy and the Urban Indian" (M.A. thesis, Michigan State University, 1983); W. Dale Mason, "The Miner's Canary: Review and Analysis of the American Indian Movement" (M.A. thesis, University of Cincinnati, 1983); Claudine Delhomme, "The American Indian Movement, 1968–1984" (M.A. thesis, Southern Illinois University at Carbondale, 1984); Karen Beth Ziegelman, "Generational Politics and American Indian Youth Movements of the 1960s and 1970s" (M.A. thesis,

University of Arizona, 1985); William Keith Akard, "Wocante Tinza: A History of the American Indian Movement" (Ph.D. dissertation, Ball State University, 1987); Timothy John Baylor, "Social Control of an Insurgent Social Movement: A Case Study of the American Indian Movement" (M.A. thesis, University of North Carolina at Chapel Hill, 1989); John William Sayer, "Social Movements in the Courtroom: The Wounded Knee Trials, 1973–1975" (Ph.D. dissertation, University of Minnesota, 1991); John F. Schuttler, "The American Indian Movement as a Revolutionary Organization" (M.A. thesis, University of Montana, 1991); George Preble Pierce, "Leadership in Crisis: The Lakota Religious Response to Wounded Knee, 1973" (Ph.D. dissertation, Fuller Theological Seminary, 1992); Melanie S. Mason, "Russell Means and the Native American Rights Movement: A Rhetorical Analysis of a Social Movement Leader" (M.A. thesis, Mankato State University, 1993); Timothy John Baylor, "Modern Warriors: Mobilization and Decline of the American Indian Movement (AIM), 1968–1979" (Ph.D. dissertation, University of North Carolina at Chapel Hill, 1994); Michele Joan Witzki, "The Politics of Deviance: The Federal Bureau of Investigation's Repression of the American Indian Movement" (M.A. thesis, University of New Mexico, 1994); Michael J. Bryant, "Legal Aspects of Chiapas, Oka and Wounded Knee Conflicts: Intranational Armed Conflicts between Indigenous Peoples and States" (LL.M. thesis, Harvard Law School, 1994); Elsa Christina Muller, "A Cultural Study of the Sioux Novels of Liselotte Welskopf-Henrich" (Ph.D. dissertation, University of Maryland at College Park, 1995); Steven L. Couture, "The American Indian Movement: A Historical Perspective" (Ed.D. thesis, University of St. Thomas, 1996); Michele D. Dishong, "New York Times Coverage of the Occupation of Wounded Knee, South Dakota, in 1973" (M.A. thesis, Washington State University, 1996); Michael Joseph Engle, "Thunder on the Prairie: The Raymond Yellow Thunder Case and the Rise of the American Indian Movement" (M.A. thesis, University of Texas at El Paso, 1997); Shoba Sharad Rajgopal, "A Comparative Study of Media Coverage of American Indian Issues by the Mainstream Press and the Native American Press, with Special Reference to the 'Red Power Movement' of the 1960s and 1970s" (M.S. thesis, Kansas State University, 1997); Lisa Marie Dutt, "Covering the Fists of the Prairie: The Press and the American Indian Movement" (M.A. thesis, George Mason University, 1997); Mavis Ione Richardson, "Wounded Knee: A Study of Newspaper Style and Coverage" (M.A. thesis, North Dakota State University, 1997); John J. Abner, "Voices of the People: Trail of Broken Treaties Caravan—Pan American Native Quest for Justice" (M.A. thesis, Indiana State University, 1998); Melanie Starr Mason, "Listening to Native American Voices from Wounded Knee, the Black Hills International Survival Gathering and the Tlingit Banishment" (Ph.D. dissertation, Wayne State University, 1998); Dana Poole, "The Role of Women in the Native American Civil Rights Movement" (M.A. thesis, Central Connecticut State University, 1998); Ivy Briana Bohnlein, "Wounded Knee in 1891 and 1973: Prophets, Protest, and a Century of Sioux Resistance" (M.A. thesis, University of Arizona, 1998); Akim David Reinhardt, "A Government Not of Their Choosing: Pine Ridge Politics from the Indian Reorganization Act to the Siege of Wounded Knee" (Ph.D. dissertation, University of Nebraska at Lincoln, 2000); Lucie Moya Melchert, "Wounded Knee, 1973: Consummatory and Instrumental Functions of Militant Discourse" (M.A. thesis, University of Nevada at Las Vegas, 2000); Sara C. Sutler-Cohen, "The Indigenous Diaspora in Academics and the Impact of the Red Power Movement on Inclusion in American Indian Scholarship" (M.A. thesis, Humboldt State University, 2000); Bruce D'Arcus, "The Wounded Knee Occupation and the Politics of Scale: Marginal Protest and Central Authority in a Media Age" (Ph.D. dissertation, Syracuse University, 2001).

28. Middlestriker, "Fork," 167–170.
29. Middlestriker, "Fork," 81–82.
30. John D. Barbour, *Versions of Deconversion: Autobiography and the Loss of Faith* (Charlottesville, VA: University Press of Virginia, 1994), 1–4, 9, 35, 85ff, 210.
31. Barbour, *Versions*, 85–86, 102–105.
32. Barbour, *Versions*, 5, 216.

INDEX